America's Wars

The collapse of the Soviet Union ushered in American global hegemony in world affairs. In the post–Cold War period, both Democrat and Republican governments intervened, fought insurgencies, and changed regimes. In *America's Wars*, Thomas Henriksen explores how America tried to remake the world by militarily invading a host of nations beset with civil wars, ethnic cleansing, brutal dictators, and devastating humanitarian conditions. The immediate post–Cold War years saw the United States carrying out interventions in the name of Western-style democracy, humanitarianism, and liberal internationalism in Panama, Somalia, Haiti, Bosnia, and Kosovo. Later, the 9/11 terrorist attacks led America into larger-scale military incursions to defend itself from further assaults by al Qaeda in Afghanistan and from perceived nuclear arms in Iraq, while fighting small-footprint conflicts in Africa, Asia, and Arabia. This era is coming to an end with the resurgence of great power rivalry and rising threats from China and Russia.

Thomas H. Henriksen is Senior Fellow Emeritus at Stanford University's Hoover Institution. His previous publications include *Cycles in U.S. Foreign Policy since the Cold War* (2018), *America and the Rogue States* (2012), and *What Really Happened in Northern Ireland's Counterinsurgency* (2008). Between 1963–1965, he was a US Army infantry officer and served on the President's Commission for White House Fellows, and US Army Science Board.

Cambridge Military Histories

Edited by

HEW STRACHAN, Professor of International Relations, University of St Andrews and Emeritus Fellow of All Souls College, Oxford

GEOFFREY WAWRO, Professor of Military History, and Director of the Military History Center, University of North Texas

The aim of this series is to publish outstanding works of research on warfare throughout the ages and throughout the world. Books in the series take a broad approach to military history, examining war in all its military, strategic, political and economic aspects. The series complements *Studies in the Social and Cultural History of Modern Warfare* by focusing on the 'hard' military history of armies, tactics, strategy and warfare. Books in the series consist mainly of single author works – academically rigorous and groundbreaking – which are accessible to both academics and the interested general reader.

A full list of titles in the series can be found at:

www.cambridge.org/militaryhistories

America's Wars

Interventions, Regime Change, and Insurgencies after the Cold War

Thomas H. Henriksen

Hoover Institution on War, Revolution and Peace

CAMBRIDGE
UNIVERSITY PRESS

CAMBRIDGE
UNIVERSITY PRESS

University Printing House, Cambridge CB2 8BS, United Kingdom

One Liberty Plaza, 20th Floor, New York, NY 10006, USA

477 Williamstown Road, Port Melbourne, VIC 3207, Australia

314–321, 3rd Floor, Plot 3, Splendor Forum, Jasola District Centre,
New Delhi – 110025, India

103 Penang Road, #05-06/07, Visioncrest Commercial, Singapore 238467

Cambridge University Press is part of the University of Cambridge.

It furthers the University's mission by disseminating knowledge in the pursuit of
education, learning, and research at the highest international levels of excellence.

www.cambridge.org
Information on this title: www.cambridge.org/9781316511602
DOI: 10.1017/9781009053242

First published 2022

A catalogue record for this publication is available from the British Library.

ISBN 978-1-316-51160-2 Hardback
ISBN 978-1-009-05508-6 Paperback

To the Robert and Marion Oster National Security
Affairs Fellows Program

Contents

Acknowledgments

A word is necessary about the dedication of this volume to the Robert and Marion Oster National Security Affairs Fellows (NSAF) Program at Stanford University's Hoover Institution. The Osters generously put the five-decade-old program on a firm foundation. Each year, the NSAF Program welcomes mid-career military officers and Department of State professionals to the institution for year-long fellowships. The intellectual interchanges between military and diplomatic officers and resident scholars have been an enduring feature of the program. The present volume could not have been written without this interaction with the author. Over the years, representatives from the US Air Force, Army, Marines, Navy, Coast Guard, and State Department have offered knowledge and insights about defense issues as well as diplomatic affairs that have deepened my understanding of a sometimes-arcane subject. They merit my collective salute in gratitude. The NSAF Program is ably headed by Amy Zegart, and she is assisted by Nga-My Nguyen and Taylor McLamb.

I am deeply thankful for those who read all or part of the manuscript, including retired US Army generals H. R. McMaster and William C. Hix, former Green Beret Will Irwin, and Middle East expert Cole Bunzel. The errors remain my own.

My research assistant Cass Kramer was indispensable in myriad ways. He distinguished himself by being my top assistant among dozens of Stanford University students who have worked with me over the decades.

A sincere expression of gratitude is due to the administrative staffs who sustain an ideal environment for research and writing. This thank you starts at the top with the director of the Hoover Institution, Condoleezza Rice, who is a first-rate scholar herself. It extends to many others, including Jeff Jones, Kelly Doran, Rick Jara, Tem Ysmael, Mike Nunes, and Darrell Birton.

The computer experts – Dan Wilhelmi, James Shinbashi, and Jamie Walter – deserve a special mention, for without their expertise and helpfulness no book-length manuscript would have ever emerged from missing files and the perplexing problems with software and hardware. Members of the personnel and finance staffs – Karen Weiss Mulder, John Blancas, Christina Anselm, Juanita Rodriquez, Lea Limgenco, and Silvia Sandoval – also played a valuable support role.

Finally, but most importantly, I would like to acknowledge the positive role of my family. My wife, Margaret Mary, provided me with immense support throughout the research and writing of this book as well as the others. I could not have completed this book without her love and encouragement. Our family – Heather, Damien, and Lucy – provided welcome breaks from the demanding process of writing a book. And my granddaughter, Liv, was an absolute delight throughout the project.

Abbreviations

AFP	Armed Forces of the Philippines
AFRICOM	United States Africa Command
AMISOM	African Union Mission in Somalia
ANA	Afghan National Army
ANDSF	Afghan National Defense and Security Forces
AQAP	al Qaeda in the Arabian Peninsula
AQIM	al Qaeda in the Islamic Maghreb
ASG	Abu Sayyaf Group
CENTCOM	United States Central Command
CIA	Central Intelligence Agency
CJTF-HOA	Combined Joint Task Force – Horn of Africa
COIN	counterinsurgency
CPA	Coalition Provisional Authority
CT	counterterrorism
FATA	Federally Administered Tribal Areas
FRY	Federal Republic of Yugoslavia
GDP	gross domestic product
GWOT	Global War on Terrorism
ICU	Islamic Courts Union
IED	improvised explosive device
IMF	International Monetary Fund
ISAF	International Security Assistance Force
ISI	Pakistani Inter-Service Intelligence
ISIS	Islamic State of Iraq and Syria
IS-K	Islamic State – Khorasan
JSOC	Joint Special Operations Command
JSOTF	Joint Special Operations Task Force – Philippines
KLA	Kosovo Liberation Army
LDK	Democratic League of Kosovo
MOOTW	military operations other than war
NCO	non-commissioned officer
OIF	Operation Iraqi Freedom

PDF	Panamanian Defense Force
PMF	Iraqi Popular Mobilization Forces
RMA	Revolution in Military Affairs
SDF	Syrian Democratic Forces
SFA	Security Force Assistance policy
SFAB	Security Force Assistance Brigade
SOF	United States Special Operations Forces
SOUTHCOM	Unites States Southern Command
TFG	Transitional Federal Government of Somalia
UNMIH	United Nations Mission in Haiti
WMD	weapons of mass destruction

Introduction

The Cold War's end marked the start of a three-decade era of serial conflict for the United States, often for lofty humanitarian goals. Unlike the superpower standoff of the preceding epoch, the unique period since the Berlin Wall's fall in 1989 witnessed a series of small-scale conflicts, medium-sized wars, and numerous counterterrorism operations during a time of peace among the great powers. The previous four-decade span recorded nothing similar. Rather, the "limited wars" in Korea and Vietnam were fought to contain the spread of communism. The immediate post-Wall years, instead, saw the United States behave as a liberal hegemon carrying out quasi-wars to make the world safe for Western-style democracy, to feed the starving, or to protect imperiled peoples, all in fulfillment of liberal internationalism dating from Woodrow Wilson.

The frequent hostilities after the Wall were unanticipated by Washington or other world capitals. No threat emerged from the dying Union of Soviet Socialist Republics, the West's arch rival after World War II. Thus, Washington politicians promised peace dividends, slashed military budgets, and talked about non-defense spending for civilian purposes. The US Defense Department did undergo substantial reductions among its service branches, although it got little peace.

Political troubles, not genuine military threats, first erupted in the planet's peripheries. To address hostile regimes, political instability, ethnic cleansing, or mass starvation, the White House occupants looked to the Department of Defense for solutions. The Pentagon, in turn, dispatched the US Cavalry to remove adversarial tyrants, succor the destitute, and halt massacres. None of these quasi-military actions came close to the two world wars, which in Hannah Arendt's words "determined the physiognomy of the twentieth century."[1] In a way, they were America's version of a thirty year's war – far from homeland and of light-to-medium intensity.

The altruistic decision to wade militarily into a host of crises lay not with Pentagon, however. It sat with the White House residents, both Democratic and Republican. These Oval Office denizens spoke of moral obligations to save, uplift, and democratize populations in unforgiving landscapes. While they stayed clear of the phrase noblesse oblige, their thinking was from that school. George Herbert Walker Bush, the first post–Cold War president, set the liberal internationalism course for his successors. His establishment upbringing in New England boarding schools and acculturation in Yale's Skull and Bones society "sent [him] off to the world with a sense of noblesse oblige."[2] The elder Bush's successors, from William J. Clinton through George W. Bush, followed in his footsteps. Even their presidential heirs – Barack Obama and Donald Trump – sustained their predecessors' philosophic outlook, even if their humanitarian impulses were less central to their foreign policies.

Coming off victoriously from a four-decade matchup with its Soviet nemesis, the United States felt emboldened and girded to take on other challenges. So, the stewards of American power employed the US military for humanitarian rescue missions. In his acclaimed book, *Promised Land, Crusader State*, history professor Walter McDougall identified what he termed Global Meliorism as one of the American foreign policy traditions. Global Meliorism is the "American mission to make the world a better place." It "assumes that the United States alone possesses the power, prestige, technology, wealth, and altruism to reform whole nations."[3]

The post-Soviet world presented a nonthreatening strategic environment that permitted an interventionist foreign policy in faithful keeping with long-standing American aspirations. For much of the first quarter of a century after the Iron Curtain went into the historical dustbin, the United States attempted to put in place its historically cherished rules-based international order that harkened back to President Wilson in World War I. The former university professor envisioned a new international system apart from the Old World's secret alliances and frequent wars. Woodrow Wilson called for a peaceful planet safe for democracy, free for the self-determination of all nationalities, and devoid of realpolitik diplomacy.

America's burst of democracy promotion came from an abiding belief that governments benefited from legitimacy of free and fair elections. In turn, elected leadership conferred more benefits on their citizens, plus being more peaceful toward neighbors than authoritarian regimes. As such, representative institutions served concrete American interests as well as humanity's.

During the East-West contest, Washington leveraged democracies as allies against communism. Out of necessity, it also turned to authoritarian strongmen in the non-Western world to arrest the spread of communism. In the post-Soviet world, it dispatched US forces to remove strongmen and replaced them with democratic figures. After the USSR's demise, America hoped for the stability and peace based on the conviction that democracies do not go to war against other democracies.[4] US officials recognized that turbulent environments needed to be prepared for elections and political parties. So, military personnel and civilian professionals worked with locals to pave the way for Western constitutional governance. American officials later cited the necessity of nation-building or stabilization as means to halt Salafi terrorist bands from taking root.

Accordingly, US military forces installed a democratically elected government in Panama, restored democracy twice in Haiti, and later labored to set up popularly elected governments in conflict-ridden Iraq and Afghanistan. In southeastern Europe, the US Agency for International Development funded and assisted a youth movement in Serbia to depose its autocrat leader at the polls after the Balkan wars, both of which the United States entered to safeguard minority populations.

Reflecting on America's liberal internationalist pursuits, professor Colin Dueck writes that "the entire post–Cold War period may be viewed as one of excessive Wilsonian idealism."[5] That period of exuberant internationalism has been questioned. America, its allies, and its adversaries have now entered an age of geopolitical competition most recognizable in its great-power rivalry. The immediate past will, no doubt, linger on and influence the new chapter, as America is still fighting Kalashnikov-totting terrorists in distant lands as it searches for ways to minimize its military involvement around the globe.

The armed goodwill enterprises for humanitarian assistance and democracy promotion were a far cry from the bloody battles fought in the major twentieth-century wars. But the soldiers in human rights conflicts, peacekeeping missions, or regime-change actions faced hostile fire and great numbers died from wounds or accidents. All the military-style deployments, fought under the banner of liberal internationalism, required extensive material mobilization, lengthy supply chains, close air support, and combat maneuvers. Like the past global wars, they brought together large alliances for noble purposes. Led by the United States, the North Atlantic Treaty Organization or ad hoc coalitions intervened first to establish peace and then liberal institutions, not to pursue realpolitik interests of territorial aggrandizement or expropriation of vital natural resources.

One of Washington's consistent pursuits entailed regime-change operations. Getting rid of uncooperative, adverse, or outright aggressive regimes was nothing new to Washington decision-makers even in the course of the bipolar competition with the USSR. What was different were the means used throughout the two eras and the purpose of the US-orchestrated ousters. In the Cold War years, the United States turned to the Central Intelligence Agency to pull off under-the-radar takedowns of leaders frustrating America's anti-communist objectives. Employing resident agents within targeted countries, CIA operatives funded and even instructed local insurrectionists, who were disaffected, ambitious, or just opposed to their leaders. These internal dissidents executed the coup while the CIA operatives watched on the sidelines. In sum, the Agency's designs would have been nonstarters without indigenous actors executing the coups.

An often-cited example of this modus operandi took place in the 1953 unseating of Mohamad Mosaddegh, Iran's duly elected prime minster, for his extra-legal pursuit of power, leftward political reforms, and nationalization of the British-built Iranian oil industry. Next, the CIA carried out a covert operation in 1954 by arming and funding a proxy force headed by an army officer to oust the leftist Guatemalan government of President Jacobo Arbenz Guzman. In 1963, the John Kennedy administration backed a Vietnamese army officers' coup d'état that evicted and murdered South Vietnam's President Ngo Dinh Diem. The Agency was likewise involved in the 1973 coup and death of Salvador Allende, Chile's elected leader, for his socialist agenda and bourgeoning ties with the Soviet Union.

Washington's ouster of anti-US leaders did not stop with the Cold War, however. Gone were the covert activities to defenestrate a leftist opponent as in the bygone times. Rather than relatively low-visibility coups, the United States now shifted to thousand-troop invasions with multinational coalitions or, at least, blessings from international organizations whenever diplomatically feasible. It is not that Washington governments gave up on mounting CIA-run coups; they tried but failed in Panama, Haiti, and Iraq. So, they fell back on US hard power to drive adversaries from power and to install democratic governments, not anti-communist strongmen.

The war on terror overturned America's self-appointed Pax Mundi destiny. Now, the United States perceived terrorist threats and even possibly nuclear risks. These revelations set the stage for large-scale military operations and for a clutch of limited-footprint engagements against Salafi-jihadi insurgents in the Global South. Thus, there exists a division between pre- and post-9/11 attacks. The conflicts before this divide originated from human rights impulses of liberal internationalism. The wars coming after 9/11 sprang from the necessity of hitting back at the threats to the United States. But even those combat enterprises genuflected to liberal international principles for self-determination of nationalities, human rights, and democratic governance.

The 9/11 terrorist attack, if anything, affirmed the propensity of the George W. Bush presidency to plant American-style freedom in the arid soil of Afghanistan and Iraq. At the same time, the administration strenuously backed democratic movements as far afield as the Republic of Georgia, Ukraine, and Kyrgyzstan, despite vehement objections from Russia. Moscow resented US interference in its near-abroad. Regime-change missions, either through invasions or strong-arm tactics, were calculated to foster American or allied security and spread democratic institutions, seen as the obvious go-to model for humankind's betterment.

It was a singular time from the Iron Curtain's disappearance to the rise of a resurgent Russia and a surging China by the second decade of the twenty-first century. The extraordinary ascendancy of American power, unchecked by a weak post-Soviet Russia or an economically developing China, left Washington free to act as it saw fit with scant regard for adverse opinions in Moscow or Beijing. The Soviet Union's fragmentation initially left the Russian Federation without adequate financial or military resources as well as with vacillating political leadership to play effectively on the world stage.

Under the authoritarian leadership of Vladimir Putin since 1999, Russian power and influence grew. Although reliant on revenues from the export of oil and natural gas, the Kremlin leader has reformed and modernized its armed forces enough to energize NATO. As for the People's Republic of China, it cleverly built up its economy using mercantile practices, swiping American information-age technology, and pilfering blueprints for advanced weaponry. As for Western Europe, another geopolitical pole, it was aligned politically with the United States through shared NATO membership and common democratic institutions. Hence, it offered no real counterweight to a powerful America, although Paris and Berlin attempted to slow Washington's race to a second war against Iraq.

In their totality, however, the regime-changes, conflicts, insurgencies, and stability campaigns have fatigued sections of the home-front population.[6] Politicians, pundits, and some members of the general public consider the "forever wars" an economic burden. Occasionally, a Washington-based legislator has lashed out at the exploding national debt as a reason to reign in the wars' costs.[7] Others pointed out that out-of-control federal expenditures are really attributable to hemorrhaging domestic entitlement programs.[8]

After all, peanut-sized endless wars are tolerable for America's powerhouse economy and are essential to preventing 9/11-type attacks being hatched from distant havens in the underdeveloped world. These and other points are narrated and analyzed in the book.

Chapter 1 starts off by describing the transformed international landscape after the Berlin Wall's collapse. With the passing away of the USSR, the United States anticipated an age of extended peace. It sharply cut defense spending between 30 and 40 percent and banked on a "peace dividend" to be spent on long under-funded civilian priorities.

Nearly halfway through his first year in office, George H. W. Bush ratcheted up tensions with the Central American country of Panama, whose military dictator, Manuel Noriega, flouted his undemocratic rule, narcotics smuggling, and threat to the vital free passage through the Panamanian Canal that connected the Atlantic and Pacific oceans.

After a spate of failed US diplomatic efforts through the regional Organization of American States and a fumbled CIA plot to have local military officers usurp the dictatorship, the Bush White House decided to take up the Panamanian ruler's declaration of war against the United States at the end of 1989.

Operation Just Cause was not flawless but it went well. Its apparent smooth execution, in fact, contributed to misleading assumptions in the Afghanistan and Iraq campaigns. Because the United States escaped protracted fighting and messy political issues by avoiding a lengthy occupation in Panama as well as in the aftermath of the Persian Gulf War, the same outcome was foreordained in other invasions.

Two noteworthy speedbumps in Panama heralded problems in future interventions, however. First, the Department of Defense (DoD) didn't adequately anticipate the degree of post-conflict looting, unruly crowds, and smash-and-burn street protests. Second, and related to the first, the DoD neglected to foresee the need for more boots on the ground to keep law and order after the Panamanian Defense Force ceased its resistance. As result, the US command had to call for light infantry reinforcements. Both of these shortcomings reoccurred in the Iraq and Afghan wars, with greater consequences.

Chapter 2 chronicles and analyzes the Persian Gulf War. The George H. W. Bush presidency prudently managed the domestic politics and the international diplomacy in the lead-up to the war. Bush forged a multination, UN Security Council–backed coalition, which included most Arab countries, to launch a counterattack against Iraq's ruthless subjugation of Kuwait.

Operation Desert Storm is assessed not only for its successes and shortcomings but also for its substantial impact on the American way of war. The US air attacks resembled scenes taken from Nintendo video games. The information-age weaponry contributed to the concept of a

Revolution in Military Affairs (RMA), which promised easy American victories in future wars. But RMA proved to be no silver bullet to combat Salafi-inspired terrorism and insurgency.

The war deepened Washington's political and defense involvement in the Middle East. And it introduced tactics applied in the looming campaign against terrorism. One critical facet of the immediate post-bellum Iraq policy arose from the Bush administration's imposition of "no-fly-zones" to shield the Shiite population and the Kurds from Hussein's murderous army and police. The allied air strikes on Iraqi forces constituted a de facto war that spanned the years from the end of the Gulf war to the Iraq War. Bush bent UN resolutions, waged war in a time of peace, and set the precedent for subsequent White House residents to carry on drone (unmanned aerial vehicles, or UAVs) attacks against Salafi terrorists in a host of countries not at war with the United States.

Finally, President Bush broached his "new world order" doctrine to international relations, which borrowed from Woodrow Wilson's idealism. He eschewed isolationism and called for "a *Pax Universalis* built on shared responsibilities." His and subsequent US leadership invoked the principles of liberal internationalism that led to hard-power solutions in the service of humankind for democracy, human rights, and minority populations.

Chapter 3 reviews the combat-styled incursions on behalf of humanity in Somalia, Haiti, and twice into the Balkans. These nontraditional engagements, known as "military operations other than war," or MOOTW (pronounced as "*moot*-wah") were regarded skeptically even by the top Pentagon brass as a diversion from real soldiering and by presidential candidate George W. Bush as a task that wore out the US military on nonessential duties.

In the twilight months of his presidency, George H. W. Bush altruistically deployed thousands of US troops into chaotic and lawless Somalia to distribute food to the starving population. Before leaving office, Bush pulled out most of the forces and made plans to turn over responsibility to the United Nations early in the William J. Clinton administration. Instead, the Clinton White House presided over "mission creep" in combat actions against Somali clan lords. One of these pursuit raids ended disastrously in the seaside capital of Mogadishu in October, 1993.

Although it could have been a mere historical footnote, the Battle of Mogadishu had a far-reaching impact. In addition to ordering a troop withdrawal from Somalia, it made President Clinton ever more cautious about entering volatile political environments. The United States, for example, stood aloof from the Rwanda tragedy, when 800,000 people perished in a genocidal civil conflict. The Mogadishu firefight convinced

Osama bin Laden that, when push came to shove, America will cut and run from a fight. As it turned out, the US abandonment of Somalia offered another negative example for what happens when Washington withdraws from strife-filled lands. These vortexes usually drew in Salafi jihadis, who exploit the roiling instability for their own ends. In Somalia's case, the radical Islamists wasted little time in arriving and colluding with local terrorists. Finally, the Mogadishu skirmish woke up the US Army and Marines to the hazards posed by pitched urban warfare amid ostensibly peace-soldiering missions.

Haiti, the island state close to the Florida coast, became the next test for Clinton's America. A democratic election placed Jean-Bertrand Aristide in the presidential office, where his leftist calls for society's reordering and wealth redistribution unnerved the Haitian elite. They made common cause with the nation's top army officers to overthrow the defrocked Catholic priest in 1991. After the coup, asylum-seekers flocked to American shores, compelling the White House to act. But Washington dallied, except for transporting the Haitian boat people to out-of-the-way Panama. After dragging his feet, the former Arkansas governor at last authorized a democracy-restoring intervention in 1994, after sending an eleventh-hour diplomatic team to negotiate the military junta's departure.

Operation Uphold Democracy encountered next to none of the hostility that greeted US troops in Somalia. Yet official Army studies reported that Green Berets (Special Forces) sharpened their hearts-and-minds skills, which stood them in good stead in the interventions around the corner. Uphold Democracy did restore Aristide to presidential office. But it was beyond American power to establish corruption-free democratic governments. The Clinton administration turned over its Haiti operation to a UN taskforce in 1995. During the George W. Bush presidency, the Pentagon fielded Marines to participate in a United Nations stabilization mission in 2004, which presided over the removal and exile of Aristide, whose flawed rule generated acute political turmoil. Post-Aristide Haiti has endured a series of natural disasters and political unsettledness but generally has been off Americans' front pages.

Unfolding simultaneously with turbulence in Somalia and Haiti, the Balkans plunged into the worst bloodshed seen in Europe since World War II. Violence engulfed Yugoslavia when the southeast European country's long-simmering ethno-nationalistic tensions exploded. The catalyst was Slobodan Milošević, the new president of Serbia, one of the six republics that made up Yugoslavia. The former communist functionary fanned extreme Serbian nationalism and sense of victimhood. Serbian militias intimidated, raped, and murdered to "ethnic cleanse" neighboring territories claimed by Serbia. Other nationalities took up arms in defense, but the chief victims were Bosnia's Muslims and Croats.

The outgoing George H. W. Bush government hastily washed its hands of the messy civil war. The incoming Clinton administration also sought to avoid entrapment in a bloody morass, palming off the civil war to the United Nations and its largely ineffective peacekeeping force, mainly composed of British and French soldiers. When the Serbs went too far in their killing sprees, Washington, London, and Paris struck back with air assaults, forged an alliance between the Bosnian Muslims and the Croatians, and urged the Russians to cease their wholehearted support for the Serbs. The US Department of State hired a private military firm to train the Croatian army, which rolled over the Serb battalions in summer 1995. Months later, the United States brokered an arduous peace settlement in Dayton, Ohio, among the contentious parties.

No sooner had peace descended over Bosnia than shooting and killing broke out in Kosovo, the tiny Muslim enclave ruled by Serbia. The Kosovars staged guerrilla attacks on Serb police and soldiers, who shot back, indiscriminately slaying innocents and assailants alike. To drive Serbia to negotiations, the Clinton White House initiated a lengthy bombing campaign against Serb military and civilian targets on behalf of the Kosovar Muslims. NATO bombed for seventy-eight days before Milošević called it quits over fear of an allied ground intervention.

The twin Balkan wars represented a watershed for their emphasis on saving despised peoples from annihilation at the hands of an extreme nationalistic government. This was a double victory for Wilson's Fourteen Points and the principle of self-determination for nationalities. Muslims, Croatians, and other nationalities living in the defunct Yugoslavia gained their own respective homelands. It was a high point for the liberal international order under American leadership.

This militarized humanitarianism formed a separate historical chapter from the robust combat invasions after the 9/11 attacks, which were undertaken for defense against Salafi-jihadi terrorism in Afghanistan and phantom nuclear arms in Iraq. Even these wars embodied Wilsonian principles, such as the protection of minorities, advocacy for self-determination of nationalities, and the imposition of democracy.

As Chapter 4 relates, Osama bin Laden's terrorist strike catapulted the United States into an invasion and occupation of Afghanistan. Likewise, the 9/11 attack on the World Trade Center and the Pentagon energized fears of more terrorist violence that ushered in the Iraq intervention and the Global War on Terrorism (GWOT). The GWOT led to a dozen light-footprint conflicts worldwide against Salafi-motivated insurgents.

This chapter reviews the innovative American-led incursion to topple Afghanistan's Taliban regime that hosted the Bin Laden network. US Special Forces teams and CIA paramilitaries harnessed anti-Taliban militias to serve as a ground force rather than American troops. The Defense Department provided extensive air cover from US Air Force and Navy warplanes. Together they pushed the Taliban from power in a matter of weeks. This unconventional tactic of leveraging local partners against a common foe was repeated in other theaters.

The multinational occupation implanted a democratic system on a polarized citizenry. It strove to build a modern nation in a pre-Enlightenment society. Both endeavors faced a stubborn insurgency undertaken by reconstituted Taliban militias returning from their sanctuary in neighboring Pakistan. The US counterinsurgency suffered from errors and the diversion of resources to the Iraq War. By the time George W. Bush left office, the Afghan battlefront had badly deteriorated.

The Iraq War is the subject of Chapter 5. This second conflict against Saddam Hussein arose out of the fear and distrust from the 9/11 attack along with the mistaken intelligence assessment that Iraq possessed chemical and nuclear weapons. George Walker Bush went to war in 2003 without the endorsement of the United Nation's Security Council. Instead, Bush formed a coalition of the willing that lacked any participation by leading Arab states as in the Gulf war. More crucially, the Iraq War was a mistake, for it eliminated Hussein, who acted to checkmate Iran's expansionist agenda. His ouster meant that the United States directly confronted Tehran's machinations in the Middle East.

The opening offensive closely tracked the steps of a conventional invasion, with massive airpower and a fast-paced armor drive to take Baghdad, which it did in under three weeks. Like Afghanistan, the initial military attack went exceedingly well before the invading armies became ensnared in Iraq's raging sectarian civil war. The multi-sided insurgency at first confounded US efforts to stymie it. The Sunni and Shiite communities killed each other along with American troops and their coalition partners.

What saved the US-led effort from almost certain defeat were three factors. Chief among them was the Awakening movement within the Sunni Arab tribes, which turned against the jihadis for their excesses and joined up with American troops to rout the extremists. The Pentagon also surged nearly 30,000 additional troops into the fight. And thirdly, it implemented a fine-tuned counterinsurgency strategy. The street bombings and gun battles greatly subsided by the end of 2011, when President Barack Obama withdrew all US combat troops from the country. A significant dimension of the Iraq War centered on

Bush America's exertions to foster democracy amid an intensifying insurgency spearheaded by Salafi-jihadi militants and Iran's Special Groups.

Chapter 6 provides a taxonomy of several small counterterrorism wars including those in the Philippines, Somalia, Yemen, and in the Maghreb-Sahel African countries. These light-footprint conflicts are necessary to thwart Salafi jihadis from establishing bases, from which they could launch terrorist attacks against America and other targets. They are fought mainly by Special Forces. Even so, the US Armed Forces have vigorously partnered with locally recruited combatants, whom they train, equip, and mentor. This special warfare minimizes – but does not eliminate – the US toll in dead and wounded. Working "by, with and through" local fighters also softens some of the xenophobia from the hosting populations against the presence of foreign military personnel.

Underpinning this form of counterterrorism warfare are airstrikes from drones, helicopters, piloted warplanes, and missiles. US forces have proven masters at removing Salafi figures from the battlefield. The constant vigilance of US security agencies and the Pentagon have kept at bay another 9/11-magnitude assault from reaching US shores.

Chapter 7 takes up more on the "forever war" theme by returning to Iraq just prior to Barack Obama's troop pullout and to Afghanistan where he inherited a sputtering war. Arriving at the White House with commitments to end George Bush's "dumb war," President Obama was unmoved by his generals to retain a modest-sized garrison of US personnel in a nearly al Qaeda–free Iraq. Meanwhile, the Shiite government veered toward majoritarian rule. Sitting in Baghdad, it reduced the Sunni population to minority status, excluded its members from decision-making, and created fertile ground for extremism to establish a foothold among the disgruntled community. The terrorist boomerang was not long in returning.

Al Qaeda bands traveled to Syria starting in 2011 to take advantage of the gathering chaos in the scorched-earth civil war. There, the Salafi militias recruited widely and expanded into the world's most vicious terrorist movement. With a militia army numbering in the tens of thousands, the Islamic State of Iraq and Syria (ISIS) network smashed back into Iraq, overturning the flaccid Iraqi defense. A fearful Baghdad called upon Washington to rescue the country. Before sending military forces, Obama sensibly required political changes, including a new prime minister, from the Baghdad government to ease the Sunni-Shiite animosity.

American and allied airpower took a heavy toll among extremist invaders while US Special Ops teams carried out raids and instructed Iraqi troops in proper defense tactics. In stabilizing the front lines,

US military units worked closely with elements of the Kurdish population, Arab fighters, and minority peoples to turn the tide. American forces loosely cooperated with the Syrian government, Russia, and even Iran to expel ISIS from its Syrian enclave, which folded during Donald Trump's presidency. The strange-bedfellow coalition collapsed once ISIS lost its territorial caliphate. Then, Moscow, Tehran, and Damascus picked up their battle with Washington and its small combat contingents in Syria and Iraq.

All the while in Afghanistan, the incoming Obama administration fell heir to a stumbling war against the Taliban. Here the new president pushed a surge-and-withdraw strategy. He agreed to a moderate troop infusion, but not as much as his anointed Afghan commander, Stanley McChrystal, sought for his fully resourced counterinsurgency, with all its nation-building components. The commander in chief's authorization for scaled-up troop numbers included a tight timetable with some service members leaving by 2012. The president required substantial force drawdowns by 2014. Then, the Afghans assumed combat missions, and the United States and allies stepped back to training and mentoring functions, except for copious American air support for air strikes and transportation.

President Obama inherited a failing war and he turned over a forever war to his successor. Donald Trump, after assuming the presidency, made a few minor changes in its conduct. Like his predecessor, Trump favored a pull-out of all American forces from the mountainous country. President Trump did give the Pentagon slightly more resources and greater leeway for managing the war than his predecessor. But he oversaw a less-than-satisfactory withdrawal deal, which required the United States and its allied forces to withdraw in May 2021, although Taliban have persisted in attacking Afghan civilians and security forces. After a few months in office, the Joseph R. Biden Jr. government decided to withdraw all US combat troop by September 11, 2021, the twentieth anniversary of the al Qaeda terrorist attack. This decision ran up against the advice of many military officers and civilian experts, including retired General David Petraeus and Marine General Frank McKenzie, the commander of the US Central Command.

Chapter 8 offers a brief conclusion. It sets forth the argument that the past three decades of large-scale human rights incursions, regime-changes, and prolonged stabilization campaigns in post-invasion nations will unlikely be repeated. The emergence of China and Russia as direct rivals of the United States constricts American options to intervene, regime change, and reconstruct societies along democratic lines.

Societal reordering will have to be undertaken modestly with restricted budgets and sparse military troops, if at all. The Pentagon must be mindful of major power threats in a way not seen since the Soviet

Union collapsed. Yet the United States cannot slacken its fight against terrorism while it confronts great power provocations from China and Russia not seen since the Cold War.

The People's Republic of China's (PRC) astounding economic development and rapid militarization represents a sea change in the international balance of power. At an accelerating pace over the last decade, Beijing has brought on line a panoply of state-of-the-art warplanes, warships, and multi-range missiles. The PRC seeks to dominate the South China Sea by excluding foreign naval craft, particularly US warships, from the international waters. The Chinese Communist Party's obsession with ending Taiwan's autonomy and controlling the island state has become a dangerous flashpoint for war between the United States and China. Elsewhere, China exerts political influence due to its economic clout, military wherewithal, and assertive diplomacy.

Likewise, the Russian Federation strives to play the role of a major global power, without China's deep pockets, but with China's thirst for power, international recognition, and status among the world's nations. Moscow's naked power grab of Crimea and eastern Ukraine, brazen assertiveness in the Baltic and Black Sea regions, and its interference in the Mediterranean all point to a nation on the make for great power acclaim. Not in the same league but still worrisome is Iran, which gained greater political influence with George W. Bush's toppling of Saddam Hussein. The ayatollah regime has harbored four decades of animosity, provocations, machinations, and terrorism toward the United States and Israel, America's main ally in the area. Iran's proxy forces, long-range missiles, and reach for nuclear weapons make it difficult for the United States to pull back from the region as Washington searches for ways to diminish its military footprint in the Middle East and elsewhere.

It is important to recognize that terminating the Pentagon's counter-terrorism partnerships in Africa, Asia, and the Middle East, as the Trump White House favored, would likely heighten the risk of terrorists striking the US mainland in a dramatic fashion. The anti-American jihad fueled by the 9/11 attacks is far from dissipated. So as to reduce its human and monetary costs, the Pentagon turned to local partners to beat back the terrorism scourge. US partners depend on our military forces for training, weapons, mentorship, logistics, intelligence, and transport. Without DoD's assistance, the besieged nations face the possibility of being overrun by jihadi militias in the way that Iraq and Syria fell to the Islamic State in 2014. So, exiting totally from the "9/11 wars" could lead to a murderous replay of history.

There is no realistic alternative to addressing the lurking Salafi terrorist danger than the current strategy. The Pentagon rotates in and out small numbers of Special Operations Forces (SOF) for combat raids against jihadi militias or for enabling local fighters to engage violent extremists. The SOF and their indigenous partners rely on drones and piloted aircraft for close air support. Together, their efforts are metaphorically akin to cutting terrorist branches and removing their leaves without eradicating the tree's roots. Societal reengineering needed to eliminate terrorism often calls for democracy in unstable, impoverished, and corrupt nations at a time when representative institutions are under siege by emboldened autocrats, China, and Russia. Minus victory, the United States fights to keep radical Islamists from striking the homeland. The Lilliputian conflicts have not tied down the US Armed Forces' response to the reoccurring provocations from China and Russia so far, but Washington politicians call for abandoning the defensive outposts.

1   An End and a Beginning
From Cold War to the Panama Invasion for Regime Change

> But the biggest thing that has happened in the world in my life, in our lives, is this: By the grace of God, America won the Cold War.   President George H. W. Bush, State of the Union address, January 28, 1992

> As we reduce defense spending, I ask Congress to invest more in the technologies of tomorrow. Defense conversion will keep us strong militarily and create jobs for our people here at home.   President Bill Clinton, State of the Union address, January 25, 1994

Descending by parachute into Panama from their C-141 Starlifter aircraft, American soldiers, as they looked skyward at their unfolding canopies, never imagined that they were inaugurating a policy of small wars and regime changes in a new era. These 82nd Airborne Division paratroopers not only invaded a Central American country but also toppled an authoritarian ruler and installed a democratically elected president. Their airdrop turned out to be on the leading edge of how the United States came to deal with a host of despots as the Cold War era gave way to one of hot wars, dictatorial ousters, and counterterrorism in the search for peace, stability, and democracy. None of this was anticipated in the rosy days following the sunset of America's most powerful adversary.

1.1   America's New Mission

With the Berlin Wall's crumbling in November 1989, and the Soviet Union's disintegration two years later, the Cold War's demise initially promised blue skies for America. In its decades-long duel with Moscow, the United States had fought two "limited wars" in Korea and Vietnam against expansive communist powers and had propped up dozens of states against the proliferating communist scourge. It spent lavishly on defense in a global contest against its Russian nemesis. Thus, many Americans now expected to be free of international duties. The public yearned to take off its battle armor and concentrate on internal problems.

History threw the United States a political curveball after the collapse of the Union of Soviet Socialist Republics (USSR), its four-decade-long foe. Rather than experiencing peace in the post-Soviet world, Americans found themselves in an "era of persistent conflicts," as noted in 2010 by the Department of Defense (DoD).[1] The United States Armed Forces marched into the Middle East, Central America, Africa, Eastern Europe, and bases in the Western Pacific. Instead of a respite, the Pentagon got interventions, regime changes, insurgencies, and protracted anti-terrorism battles. US fortunes differed greatly at this juncture from post–World War II times, which also beheld a take-charge America. After the 1939–1945 war, Washington presided over the creation of international institutions – the United Nations, International Monetary Fund, North Atlantic Treaty Organization, and the World Bank – to ward off Soviet advances, collectively keep the peace, and grow the world's economies.

Another unanticipated phenomenon burst on the international scene in the form of rogue states, most of which had been former USSR client states. Rogue nations, such as North Korea, Iraq, Iran, and Syria, exported terrorism, provoked their neighbors, and coveted nuclear weapons.[2] These maverick regimes confounded normal diplomacy while engaging in threatening behavior. Unpredictable and hostile, rogue powers compounded Washington's regional defense woes. Other states, such as Somalia or Yugoslavia, simply melted down after the fall of the USSR, leaving a set of intractable and violent problems for the international community to resolve, which required American leadership.

Wherever conflict, disorder, or humanitarian tragedy occurred, the world expected the United States to address the crisis. America's victory in the Cold War predisposed its own citizens as well as allied powers to expect that Washington would handle ethnic killings, brutal dictators, or violent Islamist extremists. The political divisions within the United Nation's Security Council sometimes sidelined the world body from action, leaving Washington to respond. Since it enjoyed a "unipolar moment" when no peer power arose to challenge its sway, the United States possessed the military and political wherewithal to settle disputes, oust tyrants, safeguard beleaguered populations, and even transplant democratic governance.[3] In a word, the United States was the leader of the Free World and its security guarantor. Nevertheless, America's military strength alone did not predetermine its course of action.

Its deep-rooted belief in democracy, emblazoned into the national creed by Woodrow Wilson during World War I, virtually assured an American crusade for democratic values. Professor John J. Mearsheimer of the University of Chicago writes that sometimes a liberal state finds "itself so secure that it can embrace liberal hegemony without having to worry about the balance of power."[4] America was such a hegemon, thanks to its values and unconstrained power. Through a series of overseas travails, the United States set about fulfilling Wilson's dream "to make the world safe for democracy." Another political scientist, Samuel Huntington, labeled the United States a "missionary nation," because it was driven by a principle "that non-Western peoples should commit themselves to the Western values of democracy, free markets, limited government, human rights, individualism, the rule of law, and should embody these values in their institutions."[5] Like Silicon Valley engineers, US policy planners believed that American political software could operate in any cultural hardware. While Western democracy and liberty have universal appeal, the political and cultural institutions sustaining these concepts demand long fermentation before they can flourish.

American presidents, as noted in the Introduction, acted with a sense of moral obligation to right wrongs, restore peace, export democracy, feed the hungry, and safeguard minority populations. With the victory of its nearly half-century containment policy backed by a free-market economy that could produce both guns and butter, Washington mandarins felt encouraged to take up a new mantle. An unstable post-Wall planet, indeed, called for leadership. Long-term international expert Richard Haass perceived the United States as a sheriff with a posse of other states to conduct humanitarian interventions that hopefully would resonate with Americans, who "pride themselves on their morality and their exceptionalism."[6] This liberal internationalism espoused military operations to halt genocide, to succor the helpless, or to evict tyrants, who flaunted their human rights abuses. Two internationalist-minded scholars scored the United States in these endeavors as a "superpower more prone to underachievement than to imperial ambition."[7]

Other nations looked to Washington for diplomatic leadership and for military forces to deal with humanitarian tragedies, war-like autocrats, or spreading instability. As a consequence, the United States mostly paid the lion's share in wartime casualties and financial expenses. In time, these costs taxed American resources and led to popular disenchantment among its citizens, who longed for an end to foreign interventions.[8] These impulses played out in both Barack Obama's and Donald Trump's presidencies, which together sought retrenchment from international military commitments.

Before those events, the Pentagon set up a global management system in the course of the standoff with the USSR that, in fact, prepared the United States to assume worldwide military duties. The Defense Department's Unified Combatant Command system evolved from the start of the Cold War. Currently made up of eleven Combatant Commands, the framework received greater coherence from the Goldwater-Nichols Reorganization Act of 1986. Each of these Unified

Combatant Commands is headed by a four-star officer, either an admiral (US Navy) or a general officer (US Army, Air Force, or Marine Corps). These respective commanders report directly to the secretary of defense, who in turn reports to the president. The commanders possess actual warfighting capabilities for specific regions. Other four-star officers, such as those who sit on the Joint Chiefs of Staff, serve as advisers to the commander-in-chief, but they are outside the chain of command for issuing orders for combat operations. Of the eleven unified commands, six preside over geographical regions. In addition to the Middle East's Central Command (CENTCOM), these zones include African Command (AFRICOM), European Command (EUCOM), Northern Command (NORTHCOM), Indo-Pacific Command (INDOPACCOM), and Southern Command (SOUTHCOM).

The combatant system also has five functional commands. These include the US Special Operations Command (SOCOM), headquartered at MacDill Air Force Base in Tampa, Florida; US Transportation Command (TRANSCOM), which is stationed at Scott Air Force Base, Illinois; and US Strategic Command (STRATCOM), which is garrisoned at Offutt Air Force Base in Nebraska. The two newest commands are the US Cyber Command (CYBERCOM) at Fort Meade in Virginia and the US Space Command (USSPACECOM) at Peterson AFB, Colorado. Of all the geographically oriented organizations, the Central Command oversaw the area of responsibility most in political turmoil in the post–Cold War era. SOCOM, for its part, functioned as an umbrella framework over several small, highly trained, and tightly classified sub-units staffed by special operators from the various military branches, such as the Army's Delta Force and the Navy's SEAL teams. This combatant command incurred repeated service in the fight against Islamist militancy.

1.2   George H. W. Bush and New World Order

President George Herbert Walker Bush (the 41st) came into office in January 1989 with a reconciliation message setting a different tone from his more rhetorically hawkish predecessor in the Oval Office. Whereas Ronald Reagan grasped the Cold War sword by labeling the USSR an "evil empire" and calling for "peace through strength," his former vice president preached a more benign message.[9] In his inaugural address, the new Republican president recognized that the "totalitarian era is passing, its old ideas blown away like leaves." The incoming leader openly prayed to "use power to help people." Then, in other Wilsonian phrases, he stated that "America is never wholly herself unless she is engaged in high moral principle." And now, he added that our purpose is "to make kinder the face of the Nation and gentler the face of the world."[10] These themes shaped Bush's foreign policy. In a grand irony, nonetheless, it was Bush, not Reagan, who ordered American troops into battle more frequently, in larger numbers, and in greater consequence.

Domestically, President Bush and lawmakers in both major political parties turned to the expected "peace dividend" to fund infrastructure projects, educational reform, social programs, or cuts in the federal debt attributable, in part, to heavy defense outlays during the Cold War. Washington did trim the defense budget, which had already begun to decline after Ronald Reagan's military buildup peaked in the mid-1980s. Under President Reagan, defense spending surged to 6.8 percent of gross domestic product (GDP) in 1986 from a low of 5.5 percent in 1979. Even the Reagan increases were historically low when compared to wartime outlays in World War II, when military expenditures spiked to 41 percent. The Korean and the Vietnam Wars at their height also witnessed elevated defense expenditures at nearly 15 percent and 10 percent, respectively.

During the 1990s, defense spending declined sharply after the breakup of the Soviet Union, falling from 5.5 percent to 3.5 percent of GDP by 2001, the year of the September 11 terrorist attack. The Defense Department cut the number of troops overseas by more than half. America's victory in the Cold War validated its winning deterrence strategy and its sacrifices, but the country's leaders and citizens reflected a deep ambivalence about continuing US international exertions.[11]

As a share of overall federal spending, actual defense costs fell in line with their downward percentage of GDP trajectory. During the 1980s, the Reagan defense expenditures reached 32 percent of total federal spending, representing a big uptick since the decline following the Vietnam War at 28.5 percent in 1979. In the course of the Bush 1990s, defense costs dropped to 20 percent of the annual federal budget. But the cutbacks in expenditures were not felt outside the DoD. Spending rose on non-defense discretionary accounts (a catchall for many agencies and programs from the FBI, NASA, health research, education, and housing) and on entitlement programs (from Social Security to Medicare to food stamps). In summary, so-called big government did not shrink in this post–Cold War era. A balanced budget in 1997 was due, in part, to massive DoD cuts and a windfall in tax revenues from a surging economy.

As a consequence of the precipitous falloff in defense spending, America's armed forces drastically shrunk in the decade after the Berlin Wall tumbled. The George Herbert Walker Bush (41st) administration responded to calls for extensive cuts to the Joint Forces by introducing a plan calling for a 25 percent decrease in the defense budget, then at $291 billion, over the next five years. The reductions were sizeable for the military forces. The US Army, for instance, went from 18 divisions (approximately 15,000 troops per division) to 10 divisions during the Bush and Clinton administrations. The Navy's combat fleet shrunk from 546 to 357 warships, and it continued to contract to today's fleet of 289 ships. The Air Force underwent a similar contraction; for instance, its tactical fighter wings (72 planes each) went from 24 to 13. Overall, the Pentagon downsized about 40 percent.[12] No similar reductions occurred in civilian programs. The 1990s, in fact, registered nearly a 23 percent increase in spending on discretionary programs in "real" dollars (or inflation-adjusted money).[13]

The American intelligence services went on the chopping block, too. Over the 1990s, the entire intelligence community, not just the Central Intelligence Agency (CIA), "lost billions of dollars in funding" and its "workforce was slashed by almost 25 percent." As George Tenet, the CIA director from 1997 to 2004, later wrote: "There is no good way to cut an organization's staff by that amount."[14] It left the intelligence agency not only understaffed but also without new-thinking professionals to see beyond the Cold War mindset to emerging threats, a glaring omission that became all too apparent when the 9/11 terrorist attacks announced an age of full-blown terrorism.

In spite of the defense and intelligence cutbacks, it is important to recognize that America was still far and away the most powerful nation on earth. The half century since World War II had seen the United States amass formidable military forces on the land, sea, and air, plus an immense nuclear arsenal. Events since 1941 recorded a transformation of American power from a country without any army, navy, or air force to speak of, to a mighty fortress with a global reach to confront the Soviet Union. As with previous victories, the United States once more decided to scale down its armed forces as its archenemy slipped into the historical dustbin.

Running against the rising tide of popular sentiment for disarmament and disengagement from a peaceful world was a last DoD lurch backward toward possible military action to facedown competitors. Authored by DoD civilian appointees in the Bush administration, a draft document known as the Defense Policy Guidance surfaced in the media in 1992, a few months after the Soviet Union's political disintegration. The strategic blueprint set forth the aim of preventing "the reemergence of a new rival" to replicate the role played by the Soviet Union. Besides the objectives of tackling "sources of regional conflict and instability in such a way to promote increasing respect for international law," it spelled out the

possibility of unilateral military action. "The United States should be pos-
tured to act independently when collective action cannot be orchestrated."
Reflecting the nation's values, the draft recommended that the United
States "encourage the spread of democratic forms of government."[15]

Coming in the wake of Soviet Russia's implosion, the timing could not have
been worse for the security manifesto. Its revelation set off a public storm of
revulsion and rancor. Then US senator Joseph R. Biden Jr. (Democrat from
Delaware) termed it a strategy for "literally a Pax Americana."[16]

This über prescription for an American Goliath was out of sync with
immediate post–Cold War thinking. The political uproar moved Bush
officials to bury the draft before completion. Media coverage faded rapidly,
and Americans looked inward to their own concerns. Moribund for a few
years, the Defense Policy Guidance resurfaced in another Bush administration after the turn of the twentieth century. Following the
September 11, 2001, terrorist attacks on the World Trade Centers and
the Pentagon, George W. Bush (the 43rd) put forward a proactive doctrine
of preemptive war against terrorist havens and Iraq. This unilateralism
propounded in Bush junior's National Security Strategy echoed some of
the language found in the earlier Defense Policy Guidance.[17]

Soon enough, the United States encountered sinister new authoritarian regimes in Moscow, Beijing, Pyongyang, Tehran, and other capitals,
for which the Cold War really never ended. But before that return of
great-power rivalry, the United States entered into a string of military
actions in the world's far corners. There, the DoD found itself in wars,
regime change, and forever counterterrorism campaigns.

1.3   Panama: The Inauguration of Regime Change
          in the Post–Cold War Era

The dust had barely settled from the falling Wall before the United States
embarked on a military intervention and regime-change operation in
Panama. Relatively minor in scope, the overthrowing of Manuel
Noriega was hardly seen as a history-shaping precedent in a Latin
America accustomed to military, political, and covert interference from
the Colossus of the North.[18] The Panamanian intrusion served as an
affirming precursor, if not an often-cited prototype, for subsequent muscular interference to change rulers beyond Latin America. Panama preceded the Persian Gulf War. But the latter conflict defined US military
power in the immediate post–Iron Curtain world because of its large
scale and short burst of intense combat. Although smaller in breadth, the
US involvement in Panama established a well-executed procedure to
eliminate adversarial despots that saw routine application after the Wall.

America undertook regime change for the best of reasons – to limit humanitarian tragedies, to lift oppression, or to further democratic governance. Nowhere did the United States seek empire à la nineteenth-century Britain. Under the Panama model, Washington, in fact, invaded, dispatched its targeted autocrat, and then made a quick exit.

Toppling anti-American figures began well before the Berlin Wall's descent. Because of the Cold War standoff, Washington preferred not to overtly carry out its defenestrations. It conducted regime change and other rollback operations "covertly to minimize the danger that American actions could inadvertently spark a war with the Soviet Union," according to the author of one study.[19] Despite tight secrecy, the CIA's handiwork in a host of countries became public knowledge. In 1953, the CIA provided funds and advice to disgruntled army officers in Iran to subvert Mohammad Mosaddegh, the duly elected prime minister, for his leftward political reforms and nationalization of the British-built Iranian oil industry. In 1954, the CIA carried out a covert operation by arming and funding a proxy force headed by a military officer to remove the leftist Guatemalan government of President Jacobo Árbenz Guzmán. In 1963, the John Kennedy administration backed a Vietnamese officers' coup d'état that brought down South Vietnam's President Ngo Dinh Diem, who was murdered afterward. As usual, the CIA denied any role in the 1973 coup and death of Salvador Allende, Chile's elected leader, for his socialist agenda and growing ties with the Soviet Union. The CIA garnered a sinister public reputation for its skulduggery abroad.[20] But it acted in America's perceived interests, although the political effectiveness of covert regime changes is disputed.[21]

These backdoor operations differed from regime-change activities after the Soviet Union's demise. They were hatched with clandestine operators who harnessed local agents to operationalize the actual dethronements. Thus, small, secretive cadres of CIA operatives assisted in the ejections of foreign rulers from behind the scenes. Although it seems like an exception, the US military intervention into Grenada in 1983 was more about eliminating a budding Soviet presence, as in Cuba, than a post–Cold War-style operation to implant democracy.

In the post–Iron Curtain years, the United States executed regime transitions with large-scale military interventions in Panama, Haiti, Afghanistan, Iraq, and Libya. The removal of Serbia's autocrat during the same period was facilitated by the American-led bombing in nearby Kosovo (see Section 3.11). America's unrivaled power after the Soviet Union's implosion made possible militarized regime-change policies with minimal risk from other nations.

The US intervention into the Republic of Panama in 1989 grew out of two long-standing considerations. First, the United States had a lengthy history of interference in the Panamanian isthmus and, indeed, in the Caribbean basin itself. Second, Washington maintained decades-old relations with the shady Panamanian dictator, Manuel Antonio Noriega. When the relationship soured, George H. W. Bush resolved to oust the army general, who had become a headache to his former North American paymaster.

Washington's particular interest in Central America came about soon after the United States acquired California as a consequence of Mexico's defeat in the war with its northern nemesis. With the start of the Californian gold rush in 1849, thousands of North American prospectors sailed to Panama, where they booked passage northward to the new El Dorado rather than trudge across the Great Plains to the California goldfields. Panama's new railway linked the Atlantic and Pacific oceans in 1855 with modern transport. The railway created an appetite for a transoceanic waterway connecting the two countries. The Frenchman, Ferdinand de Lesseps of Suez Canal fame, first tried to construct a canal but failed as the enterprise went bankrupt and his workforce succumbed to the ravages of malaria and yellow fever.

When President Theodore Roosevelt resurrected the canal project under US auspices, he encountered opposition from Colombia, which dominated the Panamanian isthmus. Failing to persuade the Colombian parliament to cede a strip of territory for a channel, Roosevelt turned to underhanded measures. He facilitated a burgeoning Panamanian rebellion with promises of financial and diplomatic backing. Days after the revolt commenced in 1903, the White House granted de jure recognition to the fledgling Republic of Panama of its sovereignty. It dispatched nearby warships to impede Colombian naval vessels from landing soldiers to put down the rebellion. Next, the Roosevelt government paid off the Colombian admiral to sail his flotilla away from the Panamanian coast. The freshly minted Panamanian government quickly showed its chumminess with their North American benefactor by leasing the Canal Zone, a ten-mile strip on either side of the prospective waterway. Construction resumed not long afterwards.

The opening of the Panama Canal in 1914 was accompanied by a rise in prosperity for Panamanians living within the Canal Zone and by the establishment of US military installations to protect the vital seaway. The local political elite directly benefited from North American largess while the larger society resembled other Latin American "banana republics." Poverty, corruption, and authoritarian rule retarded socioeconomic development and conspired to make Panama a Washington dependency.

For three-quarters of the twentieth century, the United States relied on Panamanian strongmen to keep order and to maintain the Pentagon's control over the Canal Zone. But the ground shifted during the 1980s when a particularly unsavory general, Manuel Antonio Noriega, consolidated power in his hands. As a young officer in the Panamanian Defense Force (PDF), he accepted cash from the Central Intelligence Agency. When Ronald Reagan settled into the White House and covertly fought the Marxist-leaning Sandinistas in Nicaragua, his government turned to Noriega. The Panamanian thug proved useful to his *norteamericano* friends by "airlifting military supplies to the Contras after Congress had banned the direct provision of US military aid to them." Washington reciprocated by turning "a blind eye to Noriega's ties" to South American narcotics cartels.[22]

By the time Reagan left office, Noriega was losing his usefulness to Washington. The Soviet threat of subversion below the Rio Grande evaporated with the downfall of the USSR. Running guns to the Contras was no longer necessary. In 1990, the Sandinistas were voted out of power. Moreover, Noriega's widening role in narcotics trafficking had become a migraine to his former employer. A Florida federal court indicted him for facilitating drug transfers to the United States. The outgoing Reagan government tried to induce the Panamanian gangster to leave his country. It engineered an unsuccessful coup, imposed economic sanctions on Panama, and offered to quash the federal indictment if he went into exile, all to no avail. So, the Reagan officials passed the problem to their successors.

George H. W. Bush had even less patience with Noriega than his predecessor. From his first months in the White House, the new Republican president stepped up rhetorical pressure on the Central American dictator. Even as Ronald Reagan's vice president, he had publicly recoiled from making deals with Noriega for his resignation. Once elected to the presidency, he held that "Noriega must go."[23] Eschewing military force at first, President Bush pinned his hopes on $10 million in assistance to the anti-Noriega political campaign for the May 10, 1989, elections, which pitted a Noriega stooge against a democratic opponent. Despite the presence of international observers to oversee the voting procedures, Noriega flouted the outcome by barring Guillermo Endara, the acknowledged winner with 62 percent of the vote, from taking office.

In reaction to the blatant power grab, America's forty-first president initiated a series of measures to step up pressure on the usurper. The US leader recalled Washington's ambassador to Panama, ordered the evacuation of Americans living outside the protected Canal Zone, and deployed an infantry brigade to the 12,000-troop contingent already garrisoned in the US SOUTHCOM, or Southern Command, at that time stationed in Panama. Along with stepping up the number of defense exercises to unnerve Noriega, the Pentagon removed its commanding general, who suffered from a case of "clientitis" toward the Panamanian dictator, and replaced him with the no-nonsense General Maxwell Thurman, as a precursor to military action.

Striving to bolster its campaign against Noriega, Washington took its diplomatic case to a meeting of the Organization of American States (OAS) in May 1989 to no avail. The OAS feared and loathed US interference in the Southern Hemisphere much more than Panama's suppression of democracy and hobnailed authoritarian rule. The regional bloc stubbornly adhered to its principle of noninterference in the internal affairs of member states, despite the humanitarian and democratic grounds for Noriega's removal from power. This decision looked backward, for the inviolability of sovereignty was no longer insurance against humanitarian-cum-military interventions by the West to be witnessed soon in Somalia, Haiti, Bosnia, Kosovo, East Timor, and later in Libya, Iraq, and even Syria. In the immediate time frame, the Bush administration resolved to go it alone. The more the Soviet Union faltered, the more the United States was free to act unilaterally, without concern for Moscow's exploiting Washington's entanglement in Central America.

The Panamanian caudillo was equally blind to how world politics had changed. Oblivious to the recent decline in Soviet power and the looming shadow of the Colossus of the North, Noriega carried on as if no day of reckoning awaited him. From the start of the Bush administration, James Baker, the Texas-born secretary of state, worried about what he called a "bad chili." Like other post–Berlin Wall administrations, the Bush presidency looked to economic sanctions to achieve its foreign policy goals. Economic punishment became the weapon of first choice, more often than not, instead of military options. Sanctions notwithstanding, Noriega persisted in his international drug dealing and harassment of US servicemen stationed in the Isthmus of Panama. His "growing obstinacy" raised doubts in Baker's mind that economic pain alone would bring the dictator around to Washington's persuasion.[24] That Noriega cozied up to Fidel Castro and received weapons from the communist ruler in Cuba added to Washington's grievances. Cuban advisers also trained Panama's "Dignity Battalions," which were little more than the regime's street goons. Havana's military instruction prompted concerns about the Panamanians being used to destabilize neighbors.

There was another strategic factor in Washington's growing impatience with Noriega's antics. The impending turnover of the Panama Canal to indigenous control overhung US worries for preserving the waterway's open access. Earlier, President Jimmy Carter negotiated a transfer of the sea passage to Panamanian jurisdiction with General Omar Torrijos, the country's former strongman. Under terms of the Torrijos-Carter treaties in 1977, the United States surrendered control over the Canal Zone two decades later but hung onto the perpetual use of the canal by retaining the right to defend it militarily. But the unsavory prospect of allowing Noriega to pick the head of the Canal Commission, as called for in the agreements, gave Washington another reason to be rid of Panama's tyrant.

Just months before the United States marched into Panama, Bush's West Wing hoped for an internal coup d'état that might spare it from militarily intervening to push out Noriega. Its hopes were quickened when an amateurish coup sprung by a Panamanian army major actually seized Noriega. But the officer and his accomplices then farcically released him after Noriega pledged to address their grievances. While the abortive power grab was in progress, the major sought aid from the United States. As if to compound the tragicomedy, only President Bush believed the genuineness of the plotters; his advisers nixed any assistance.[25] The military takeover failed. Noriega repaid the humanity of the military officers by having them tortured and executed. The dismal outcome convinced other would-be coup-makers to sit on their hands. It also sealed the decision by the US government to take matters into their own hands. Noriega appeared oblivious to his fate as rumors circulated around Washington of an impending intervention.[26]

Despots such as Noriega, Iraq's Saddam Hussein, and Serbia's Slobodan Milošević failed to grasp the new realities of the post–Cold War landscape with the primacy of American power. Without the Soviet Union to exercise restraint on US military interventions, small states hostile to Washington now stood alone. North Korea, Iraq, Iran, and Libya took up antagonistic postures, sought nuclear weapons, and sponsored terrorism abroad as a means of regime preservation.[27] Noriega's Panama never adopted rogue-state policies but it did defy Washington, which was enough to bring it into US crosshairs. The United States could risk military action because there was no threat of being confronted by another superpower. After the Berlin Wall disappeared, the Soviet Union continued its way to historical oblivion.

1.4   Operation Just Cause: A Playbook for the Future?

In the last weeks of 1989, the Pentagon was months along in planning for a military invasion of the isthmian country, a change in its regime, and a dismantling of the Panamanian Defense Force, which was a debased and criminal Praetorian Guard to prop up Noriega. The spark that ignited the tinderbox came when Noriega's paramilitary Dignity Battalion shot to death a Marine officer riding in a jeep. Top Washington officials huddled to review their options. Anticipating the officer's killing would be just the first of additional American murders, they resolved to act even though an attack would entail US military casualties. But Noriega's puppet National Assembly preempted the Bush administration's decision by declaring war on the United States.

The Bush foreign policy team laid out its justification for an attack on a neighbor. In addition to the shooting death of the US officer, they argued Noriega's thugs were likely to assassinate other Americans in or out of the Canal Zone. They called attention to Noriega's well-established narcotics peddling and his subsequent federal criminal indictment. They accentuated his threat to an orderly transfer of the Panama Canal to a trustworthy local constituency. They pointed to the Panamanian despot's widely acknowledged contempt for democracy.

Washington also enjoyed some legal justification for breaching Panama's sovereignty. The Canal treaties granted the United States authority to confront internal as well as external threats. The Noriega-controlled National Assembly exacerbated the Bush team's apprehensions about the long-term security of the canal. The legislature proclaimed that "the Republic of Panama is in a state of war for the duration of the aggression unleashed against the Panamanian people by the U.S. Government."[28] Noriega's bravado, in a sense, played into the hands of a still-hesitant superpower. Because of adamant OAS opposition to US military intervention, Washington lacked any active regional partners or any coalition sanctification.

After much inner-circle debate, James Baker, the secretary of state, clinched the administration's thinking when he argued: "Let's take them up on their declaration of war."[29] He summed up the president's thinking, but the commander in chief was concerned about casualties, as the Chairman of the Joint Chiefs of Staff Colin Powell had presented only vague figures about deaths among US troops and civilians. George Bush queried General Powell on when the Pentagon would be ready to go into action. The four-star officer replied: "In two and half days," attesting to how advanced military preparations were at this stage. He added: "We want to attack at night," taking advantage of the element of surprise and America's night-fighting capabilities.[30] After lengthy discussions, President Bush decided: "Okay, let's do it."[31]

D-Day took place on December 20, 1989, and H-Hour at 1:00 AM. Initially code-named Blue Spoon for security reasons, the military operation was soon rebranded as Operation Just Cause, as a more inspiring designation. The Pentagon executed Just Cause in clockwork fashion. It achieved tactical surprise in Panama even though CNN broadcast footage of waves of warplanes taking off from Pope Air Force Base in North Carolina, tipping off viewers that the game was afoot somewhere. US troops garrisoned at Fort Amador in the Canal Zone rolled out of their barracks to link up with paratroopers from the 82nd Airborne Division descending over Torrijos International Airport to the east of Panama City, the capital.

Other Army units entered the city of Colón. Army Rangers, known as hard-driving shock troops, parachuted onto a drop zone west of the airport, where they attacked PDF units in their Rio Hato barracks. The Rangers swiftly cleared the drop zone of Panamanian resistance, allowing troops and aircraft to land. The US ground forces poured heavy fire into the Comandancia, nearly demolishing the PDF headquarters. This assault severed the Comandancia's communications with outlying defenders. All in all, the intervention amounted to the largest military operation since the Vietnam War and the biggest parachute drop since World War II. Forty strategic airlift planes ferried 2,000 paratroopers for the five-hour flight. The super-advanced, radar-evading F-117A stealth Nighthawk fighter saw its first combat deployment by dropping bombs just preceding the Ranger airborne assault.

The powerful invasion force reflected the maturing thought of General Colin Powell. Not long after Panama, the chairman of the Joint Chiefs of Staff came to advocate "overwhelming decisive force" in the Persian Gulf War in 1991. This Powell Doctrine, in time, found its way into the National Military Strategy drafted in 1992. That twenty-seven-page document clearly carried Powell's thinking in the application of "decisive force to overwhelm our adversaries."[32] At the Panama stage of development, the four-star general instinctively sought to spare the United States a repetition of another Vietnam War quagmire that saw military force incrementally deployed in an ambiguous conflict.

Yet, despite the impressive troop numbers and meticulous preparations, things went wrong. Even though it was a relatively minor conflict, Panama recalled the German general Helmuth von Moltke's maxim that "no plan of operations extends with any certainty beyond the first contact with the main hostile force."[33] The American invaders met unexpected resistance from the 4,000 PDF troops and especially the poorly trained Dignity Battalions during the first day and half of fighting. The tide of battle turned quickly enough as the 26,000 US troops outgunned and outfought the ragtag resistance.

Largely unforeseen was the intransigence of the defenders and looters, who ransacked shops and businesses for portable household items, such as televisions and furniture. The Pentagon had planned for three days of chaos, but the disorder extended to over a week. So great was the breakdown of law and order that the Pentagon was forced to call for some 2,000 additional infantry soldiers from the United States to police the streets of Panama City and Colón. Just as the military planners stumbled slightly in force projections, the Pentagon also shortchanged planning for other aspects of post-invasion disorder.

The changeover from combat activities to civilian policing turned out to be harder than anticipated. In the words of one study, the melding of civil-military functions constituted "the most conspicuous lapse in the planning of the U.S. military operation in Panama City."[34] The invading army lacked for proper training and psychological disposition to transition from military attacker to peacekeeper. Even though the Panamanian citizenry welcomed Noriega's ouster, stabilization of a traumatized society demands different skills from warriors, however temporary their stay. Restoring civil order and improving the quality of civilian life are normally better suited to indigenous authorities. In the Panama case, the US Army resorted to its traditional preference for "indirect control" over the local government ministries. Its civil affairs teams "served as advisers, not managers," in the words of post-conflict expert Nadia Schadlow.[35]

The Washington-installed government stood up its own police force, the Fuerza Pública. But the incoming government was compelled by necessity to fall back on rank-and-file PDF manpower (after vetting out criminal elements) as well as untrained recruits to restore order. During the first forays of the novice police patrols, US soldiers reluctantly accompanied the Panamanian policemen. The American infantry were unaccustomed to this civilian role. Some, furthermore, resented trudging alongside Panamanians who just a few days before were shooting at them. Additionally, the US warfighters resented doing police work. The need for a well-trained constabulary would dramatically arise on the heels of the Iraq invasion a decade later. Panama was an unheeded red flare to the Pentagon to prepare for stability tasks after the organized fighting ceased.

As Manuel Noriega went into hiding to elude capture by US forces, Washington moved to replace him with Guillermo Endara, the presumed winner of the presidential election the previous May, who Noriega blocked from taking the reins of government. Brought to Fort Clayton within the Canal Zone during the invasion, Endara and two vice presidents were sworn into office by the head of the Panamanian Commission on Human Rights. The new president's speech to his countrymen was broadcast from Costa Rica. Thus, the Bush administration mastered the tricky transfer of power and avoided a lengthy military occupation of Panama. The Bush

White House also quickly lifted the economic sanctions imposed on Panama and unfroze some of the financial assets held in US banks. Whereas the future George W. Bush administration stumbled in the post-invasion phase, despite the Panama model, his father's government deftly handed off civilian rule to local politicians, sparing Bush's America from entanglement in parochial governance issues.

1.5   A Smooth Transition for Panama

Washington's transference of civil authority to Panamanian officials helped calm the outrage directed at it from South American countries, which rebuked the gringos for their continuance of "gunboat diplomacy" below the Rio Grande. The twenty-member Organization of American States passed a resolution in Spanish "deeply deploring" the US invasion into Panama on December 21, 1989. Six members abstained, and the rest voted for the resolution. President Endara vainly voiced opposition. The Panamanian leader argued that humanitarian concerns inside his country justified a temporary breach of sovereignty. The vote represented a stinging rebuke to the United States. Moreover, opposition spread to the United Nations, where Britain and France sided with Washington to veto a Russian and Chinese resolution demanding an immediate withdrawal of US armed forces. The three Western powers, however, could not head off a General Assembly debate and resolution branding the US military action as a "flagrant violation" of international law. The delegates further demanded an end to America's martial presence.[36]

The impact of the resolutions and verbal condemnations proved to be transient in most of the world, because of the short-lived intervention. The political storm subsided as American forces pulled out; but Latin American memories stayed fresh over the Colossus of the North's heavy-handedness. The overall success of the military operations and the return of democracy to the Central American country also helped mitigate the adverse fallout from the attack. Panama's subsequent history also acted to lessen the negative consequences. The restoration of democratic governance was one of the positive results of Washington's actions. Prior to the US assault, Panama's past was pockmarked by corrupt dictatorship, oligarchy, and military rule. The toppling of Noriega gave the country a fresh start, which it sustained. Five years after the combat venture, Panama held the first of many democratic elections.

Washington's financial assistance to Panama was paltry when compared to the costs of American interventions into Afghanistan and Iraq a decade later. The incoming Endara government estimated reconstruction costs at about $1.5 billion. Over the two years following its military intrusion, the United States furnished slightly more than $1 billion in emergency funds, reconstruction aid, and loans. Contemporaneously, the Bush administration faced financial demands from post-conflict Nicaragua and Central Europe, in the throes of casting off communist governments, along with other recipients with longer established claims on America's largesse.

The United States astounded its critics, particularly numerous South American detractors, by upholding its treaty pledge to withdraw from the Panama Canal Zone. Dissident voices initially condemned the exercise of US military power as a means to keep the Stars and Stripes flying over the isthmus and its military bases. Washington defused the opposition by abiding by its international agreements. First, Washington redeployed SOUTHCOM from the Canal Zone to the state of Florida in 1997. Next, it relinquished its territorial hold on the canal on December 31, 1999, as dictated by the terms of the Torrijos-Carter treaties, signed two decades earlier. Pentagon strategists reasoned that modern warfare made exclusive control of the waterway no longer essential to American naval objectives. Good relations with Latin America outweighed the continued possession of the Canal Zone.

All in all, the Panama intervention succeeded in its goals of replacing Manuel Noriega and placing the country on the road to democratic rule. Militarily, the Panama operation stood as a "testament to the joint planning and execution developed between the armed services following the shortcomings" in the 1983 Grenada invasion to save the tiny island from a Marxist takeover.[37] That operation, known as Urgent Fury, became a Pentagon byword for a tactical mess. The invasion was beset with tactical stumbles, coordination blunders, slip-and-fall plans, and their chaotic execution against the badly trained Lilliputian force of the Grenada's People's Revolutionary Army. In the words of one ring-side seat participant: "Problems caused by constantly changing scenarios, superficial planning, security overkill, lack of service interoperability, service parochialism, and routine 'fog of war' screw-ups turned it into a bloody, six-day fight and nine-day operation."[38] The Defense Department took the Grenada lessons to heart and sidestepped many of Urgent Fury's miscalculations six years later.

By contrast, the Panama military operation went almost flawlessly. "The overwhelming success of JUST CAUSE must be attributed to the fact that the PDF (Panamanian Defense Force) did not put up serious or sustained resistance."[39] By and large, the Panamanian defenders deserted their units. Small numbers, nevertheless, joined other die-hard bands, which did put up brief resistance. The outcome of the gun battles was never in doubt. The defenders were no match for US grunts, who were superiorly armed and trained. American casualties numbered 23 dead. The Defense Department put the Panamanian deaths at 516. Other estimates placed the count at a thousand.[40]

The US Armed Forces enjoyed other advantages. They were familiar with the local terrain and with the "Panamanian military and its strengths having virtually created the Panamanian National Guard."[41] Panama had hosted a US command and thousands of troops for nearly ninety years. Another advantage derived from the Panamanian citizenry's widespread dissatisfaction with Noriega. Panama also lacked an aggressive nationalism, xenophobia, or sectarian militancy seen in subsequent US-targeted states, such as Afghanistan and Iraq. Noriega was unpopular for his abuse of power, corruption, and gross mismanagement of the economy. The incoming President Endara represented the democratic tradition that Panamanians aspired to regain with removal the military dictatorship.

One discordant misstep, which should have served as a wake-up call prior to subsequent US combat operations, took place soon after American boots were on Panamanian soil. The US military planners misjudged the number of ground forces needed in the immediate post-invasion phase of operations. Opposition came from not just ragtag military resistance but also rioters and looters, who flocked into the streets to take advantage of the breakdown in law and order. That lesson was lost on future military leaders at the start of the Iraq War, where the invading US and British forces ran into deadly resistance from remnants of regular forces, as well as street protestors. In time, the sporadic attacks on the invaders gave way to a countrywide insurgency (see Chapter 5).

The chief legacy derived from the Panama intervention was how it altered the American public's perceptions of the military after the frustrating war in Vietnam. Baker, the secretary of state, wrote in his memoir: "In breaking the mindset of the American people about the use of force in the post-Vietnam era, Panama established an emotional predicate that permitted us to build the public support so essential for the success of Iraq's Operation Desert Storm some thirteen months later."[42] The ease of Panama helped pave the way for the Iraq War.[43] One intervention elided into another in the post–Cold War period. As one academic critic of the Pentagon's interventions wrote: "Operation Just Cause was a catalyst for Washington's new role not only as worldwide policeman, but as global armed social worker.[44]

2 The Persian Gulf War and Its Aftermath

The purpose of war is to build a better peace.   St. Augustine

What is at stake is more than one small country [Kuwait], it is a big idea – a new world order where diverse nations are drawn together in a common cause to achieve the universal aspirations of mankind: peace and security, freedom and the rule of law.   George H. W. Bush, State of the Union Address, January 29, 1991

It is a proud day for America and by God, we have kicked the Vietnam syndrome once and for all." George H. W. Bush, March 1, 1991.   Quoted in Ann Devroy and Guy Gugliotta, "Bush to 'Move Fast' on Mideast Peace," *Washington Post*, March 2, 1991, page A 13.

The Persian Gulf War blew up like a haboob, the swirling desert dust storm, which howls down on the unsuspecting without warning. The Republic of Iraq's invasion of neighboring Kuwait took the world by surprise. Notwithstanding Iraqi dictator Saddam Hussein's repeated warlike rhetoric about the Kingdom of Kuwait belonging to Iraq as its nineteenth province, US and Western intelligence agencies failed to warn of the approaching military storm. For his part, Hussein wrongly believed that America had feet of clay, and so his conquest was safe from reversal.

Other ironies abound. US and European armored divisions, trained for decades to repel the Red Army in Central Europe, found themselves waging tank battles in the Arabian Desert, not Germany's Fulda Gap. George H. W. Bush fought a war with a minimalist agenda, unlike his son years later, and yet succeeded beyond his offspring's grandiose mission to implant genuine liberal democracy in Iraq's arid soil. Overnight, Washington's rickety dispensation in the Middle East was transformed. Hussein's attack threatened American interests, allies, and even historic borders between states. All these events and more became clear in time.

The immediate cause of the Persian Gulf War can be traced to the hubris and belligerence of Iraq's Saddam Hussein, who resolved to conquer Kuwait by sending his Republican Guards across their common border in mid-1990. But the roots of the invasion lay at least a decade earlier, when Hussein tried to take advantage of the revolutionary chaos

in Iran. Hussein, who came into power in 1979 as head of Iraq's dictatorial Baath Party, thought he could seize with ease the disputed Shatt al-
Arab waterway, which separates the two countries. Unfettered use of the
river would open access to the Persian Gulf, a long-standing desideratum
in Baghdad.

Hussein's Iraq launched what was expected to be a quick war. Instead
of a short, sharp conflict, the Iran-Iraq war dragged on for eight years of
attritional fighting similar to trench warfare in the Great War
(1914–1918). Iran employed wave upon wave of infantry attacks to repel
Iraq's encroachments, which suffered mass casualties. Iraq turned to
poison gas as a defense against the Iranian manpower-intense offensives.
Hussein's use of chemical munitions saved his embattled forces and
perhaps his own hide. Fearing further chemical warfare, the Iranian
ayatollah agreed to United Nations–brokered talks, which led to peace
in 1988, the end of the longest conventional war in the twentieth century.
Both combatants lost hundreds of thousands in casualties and billions of
dollars in defense expenditures.

Saddam Hussein came to believe that only weapons of mass destruction (WMD) could be counted on to prevail over his enemies. Thus, he
began a pursuit of WMD. There is little dispute about Hussein's ultimate
nuclear ambitions. Uncertainty about Iraq's progress along the nuclear
path existed until the United States discovered no atomic arms on the
heels of its invasion, a decade after the start of Hussein's war with Iran.
Another consequence of the Iran-Iraq war pertained directly to its impact
on Washington's ties with Baghdad.

America leaned toward Baghdad as the lesser of two evils during the
Iran-Iraq War. Both the outgoing Reagan administration and the incoming George Bush presidency perceived the Iraqi leader as a secular and
moderating dictator who could serve as a useful counterbalance to Iran's
Ayatollah Khomeini and his fervent followers. The theocracy resolved to
pay the United States back for buttressing Shah Mohammed Reza
Pahlavi until his 1979 ouster from an internal revolution. The White
House embraced a "realist" approach toward Iraq as a useful counter-
poise to the more dangerous post-shah Iran, which hated America. This
strategy was of a piece with the Cold War practice of allying with
dictatorial regimes against more threatening powers.

Members of the US Congress opposed the administration's pro-
Baghdad policy by seeking economic sanctions against the Republic of
Iraq for its appalling human rights record. But the Bush Oval Office held
this effort at bay and extended financial credit guarantees for American
grain exports to Iraq. Washington's olive branch initially seemed to pay
off. Hussein's regime offered to pay compensation to the families of

37 US sailors killed when an Iraqi missile struck the USS *Stark*, a Navy frigate, in 1987. In fact, the tyrant never actually paid the compensation. The post-Hussein government did so in 2011. Beforehand, Iraq plagued the United States.

Iraq reverted to an American adversary as the 1990s dawned, setting the stage for an inevitable showdown. Hussein demanded that the United States withdraw its warships from the Persian Gulf. He realized that the American eclipse of the Soviet Union meant that the US Navy would have no counterweight in Iraq's waters. He also appealed to other Middle East governments to reactivate the 1970s oil embargos to batter the West's economies. The autocrat turned especially provocative toward Israel by delivering inflammatory pro-Palestinian speeches and by financially rewarding the families of Palestinian terrorists killed by Israeli security forces. In one of his fiery speeches, he voiced again his penchant for the use of weapons of mass destruction. Along with announcing the manufacture of chemical arms on April 3, 1990, Hussein threatened "to make the fire eat up half of Israel with chemical agents, if this nation [Israel] becomes involved in an attack against Iraq."[1]

His provocative behavior and passionate rhetoric thrust Saddam Hussein into the limelight as no Arab leader since Gamal Abdel Nasser, the charismatic Egyptian president, who died in 1970. Unlike Egypt's leader, Hussein actively pursued nuclear arms for a time. The United States foiled an illicit purchase of nuclear-triggering devices and blocked the sale of tungsten furnaces for Iraq's secret nuclear weapons program. During the same period, Hussein lashed out at Kuwait, demanding it compensate Iraq for wartime debts incurred in the war against Iran. He reasoned that Kuwait and other Sunni Arab states owed Iraq for defending them against Shiite Iran. He was convinced that Kuwait was ungrateful for Iraq's sacrifices.

The United States grew increasingly wary of Iraq, although its focus was almost entirely on the momentous tectonic shift in geopolitics with the breakup of the Soviet Union. Bush's foreign policy principals were fixed on the reunification of East and West Germany, the expulsion of the Red Army from Central Europe, and the incorporation of a reunited Germany into the North Atlantic Treaty Organization. Although the eyes of mid-level officers saw a war with Iraq and planned for it, they were ahead of James Baker who later penned in his memoirs that Iraq "was not prominent on my radar screen, or the President's" before it invaded Kuwait.[2] Washington peacefully accomplished its European goals as the Soviet Union stumbled toward oblivion. But its preoccupation with the rapidly unfolding events in Europe accounts, in part, for its ultimately being caught flatfooted by Iraq's tank invasion into Kuwait.

Baghdad's grievances did not stop with complaints about ungrateful neighbors. It grumbled about the practice by Kuwait and the United Arab Emirates of flooding the oil market, thereby contributing to lower world prices. Iraq demanded that these and other oil-producing states cut back on the number of exported barrels so it could capture a higher price for its oil. Its gripes were ignored. Saddam Hussein used the occasion of Iraq's Revolutionary Day on July 17th for a speech that, in retrospect, made the case for invading Kuwait by raking up all the old injustices suffered by Iraq at the hands of others. To him, Iraq was a victim pursuing rightful revenge against its perceived enemies.

The Republic of Iraq's next move should not have come as a surprise, but it did. A week after his speech bemoaning Iraq's tribulations, Hussein rolled his Soviet-made T-72 battle tanks up to the Kuwait border where they stopped just short of crossing the boundary. Washington acted tepidly. But knowing what we do now of Saddam Hussein's bare-fanged aggression, only a very powerful show of force would have deterred him. Minimally, the US Defense Department dispatched a UAE-requested tanker and cargo aircraft to the Gulf for a joint naval exercise. A senior administration official stated that the deployment was intended to "bolster a friend and lay down a marker for Saddam Hussein."[3] It was more of a white flag than a battle streamer.

The Department of State also played its hand irresolutely against Hussein's boldness. The Iraqi ruler summoned the US ambassador to sound out American views on his military threat to Kuwait. At the famous encounter, a day after Iraq parked armored tanks on Kuwait's doorstep, the dictator asked April C. Glaspie, the Arabic-speaking envoy, about the American reaction to his territorial claims and other quarrels with Kuwait. To her legion of critics, the ambassador muttered "diplomatic speak," when she replied "as you know we don't take a stand on territorial disputes."[4] Her rebuttal signaled unconcern, even acquiescence, about Iraq's danger to an American friend. Ambassador Glaspie, in a subsequent account of the meeting, argued that she made it clear to Saddam Hussein that the United States would defend its allies and access to Middle East oil. But congressional members assailed her defense as lame.[5]

There was no Hamlet-like indecisiveness about Saddam Hussein's motives in rolling his Republican Guards to the Kuwaiti frontier. The world soon learned of his intentions on August 2, 1990, when Iraq's armored forces lunged into their defenseless neighbor. Graphic television coverage captured Kuwait City's brutal rape by Hussein's soldiers, who indiscriminately shot civilians and looted valuables in a frenzy resembling the fall of a medieval city. The ruling emir, Sheikh Jaber al-Ahmad al-

Sabah fled for safety in Saudi Arabia. His hapless brother, Sheikh Fahad, was not so lucky; he was gunned down along with hundreds of others. The conquering horde ransacked the tiny country for the next seven months, until expelled by the US-led coalition. The Iraqis stripped paintings off museum walls, lifted art objects, and stole 29,000 automobiles, driving them home. Systematically, the invaders also tried to obliterate Kuwait's statehood by seizing and destroying essential state documents, international treaties, and other historical records to strengthen Baghdad's claims to Kuwait as part of Iraq's territory. The occupying army engaged in further wanton destruction by firebombing oil wells, power stations, and palaces. Outside of their pillaged country, the Kuwaitis would establish the Public Authority for Assessment of Damages Resulting from Iraqi Aggression in May 1991. This commission reckoned the damages at $173 billion.[6]

The prostrated sheikdom painfully roused itself. Looking to the future, it appealed internationally for assistance. In an emergency meeting, the Security Council passed Resolution 660, which condemned Hussein's naked aggression and called on Iraq immediately to yank out its army. Even Russia, a onetime arms supplier of Baghdad, assented to the resolution. As anticipated, Hussein ignored the demand and reasserted Iraq's claims to its nineteenth province. The United Nations' resolution, nonetheless, provided Washington political cover to expel the invaders from Kuwaiti soil.

2.1   The Decision to Go to War

Initially, Iraq's border-crossing infestation left the Bush administration in a quandary over the proper course to follow. Two broad courses lay before it. Either it could launch a counterattack to repel the invasion, or it could place economic sanctions on Iraq. Implementing an economic embargo presented less risk, although it relied on a very slow impact on Iraqi society. Even a tight sanction policy was unlikely to hurt Saddam Hussein and his close cronies at the top of society. Average Iraqi citizens would absorb the pain from shortages in food, medicine, and other goods. Besides, economic blockades are notoriously lethargic and uncertain. Lots of countries, such as Cuba, Iran, and the Soviet Union, withstood years of economic punishment.

The alternative approach, a military counter-assault to eject Hussein's army, won over the Bush administration for a couple of reasons. The sheer tentativeness of an economic embargo undercut its appeal. Moreover, the United States feared that Hussein's intervention into Kuwait was but a stepping-stone for his ultimate invasion of Saudi

Arabia. Both Gulf countries held substantial proven oil reserves, with Saudi Arabia's world ranking just behind Russia and Kuwait standing at sixth. Together, Iraq and Kuwait held about 20 percent the world's proven holdings. Should the Baath regime's Republican Guards overrun Saudi Arabia, Baghdad would possess a near stranglehold over much of the world's oil deposits. At the time, the United States was not solely dependent on Mid-East oil; it imported crude from Venezuela, Canada, and Nigeria in addition to its own domestic production. Japan and Western Europe, however, did rely on Middle Eastern oil wells. Hussein's occupation of Kuwait and possible possession of Saudi Arabia left them fearful about the steady flow of energy for their factories and homes.

Hussein's threat rang alarm bells in Washington and other capitals. Yet oil alone would not become the sole tipping point for war. The violation of Kuwait's border was also of deep concern, for it raised the prospect of conflicts over other border disputes in the Middle East. Hussein's brazenness troubled Saudi Arabia, Syria, and Iran, which earlier experienced firsthand Iraq's contempt for their common frontiers in Baghdad's 1980s aggression. His grab for oil and land upset nearby states. Only Yemen, Jordan, and the Palestinian Liberation Organization backed Iraq. Turgut Özal, the president of Turkey, communicated to President Bush that the Iraqi dictator "must go" inasmuch as "Saddam is more dangerous than Qaddafi," the Libyan tyrant.[7] Iraq's annexation promised to open a Pandora's Box for other border feuds.

The Bush West Wing was moved by several considerations to resort to military force, but the danger posed to Saudi Arabia served as the prime mover. Dick Cheney, the secretary of defense, and Brent Scowcroft, the national security adviser, advanced a hawkish option that persuaded the president to go to war. Although the desert kingdom's security stood foremost in the upper levels of the American presidency, Saudi Arabia initially proved to be a reluctant partner.

Saudi Arabian officials feared the deployment of US and Western troops on their country's sacred soil. As the cradle of Islam, Saudi Arabia fretted about how the presence of infidel soldiers would be seen by fervent Islamic elements in its population and throughout the world. As events turned out, Riyadh sensed what, in fact, happened. To jump ahead, the eventual American military deployment stirred up Muslim extremists, led by Osama bin Laden, who seethed with resentment at this defilement of Islam's birthplace. Bin Laden regarded the US military as modern-day Crusaders, who came to capture the Islamic sanctuary. His hatred for the Saudi government made him break with it and plot terrorism against the United States. Basing himself and his co-conspirators in Afghanistan, they hatched the September 11 terrorist attack on the United States (see Chapter 4).

For its part, the Bush administration worried that Riyadh might make a separate peace with Baghdad. As Iraq prepared to send battle tanks and ground troops to the Saudi border, the Pentagon dispatched a high-level delegation to convince Saudi Arabia of the imminent peril it faced and persuade Riyadh of US resolve to defend the Arabian Peninsula kingdom. Like other observers of past American questionable reliability when it sustained casualties, Saudi officialdom formed a low opinion of their American allies after their withdrawal from Lebanon in the aftermath of the infamous truck bombing of the Marine Corps barracks in 1983.

Led by Cheney and Norman Schwarzkopf, the Central Command's top general, the Defense Department's delegation convinced their Saudi counterparts that their country was in danger and their American partners were reliable. Next, the Department of Defense (DoD) rushed in the 82nd Airborne Division and two Air Force tactical fighter squadrons as the vanguard to Operation Desert Shield. The DoD ordered the buildup of naval forces and additional aircraft to protect the desert kingdom from any Iraq attack. Over the following months, Washington pulled together a large international military coalition that served as the offensive spearhead to push out the Iraqi invaders from Kuwait. The formation of an armed coalition, rather than a go-it-alone policy, constituted a quintessential American way of waging war.

2.2   Rounding Up an International Coalition

Mobilizing the participants for the US-led coalition fell to George H. W. Bush, whose masterful performance earned him lasting acclaim as a statesman. The president's penchant for international affairs turned out to be an asset for America's war diplomacy. Building on King Fahd's consent to the stationing of foreign soldiers on Saudi soil, Bush labored to bring Mid-Eastern nations into the international coalition against Iraq. He met with foreign leaders in the White House and at his vacation home in Kennebunkport, Maine. He "worked the phones" by calling overseas capitals and dispatched James Baker, his able secretary of state, on trips abroad. The United States concentrated on an amicable relationship with the Saudis and by extension the Muslim world. The Pentagon split the military command with Prince Khalid Bin Sultan al-Saud presiding over Arab contingents. General Schwarzkopf, the Central Command chief, led American, British, and other Western forces.

CENTCOM's geographic purview covers twenty countries in the greater Middle East; its boundaries stretch from Egypt to Pakistan and from Kazakhstan to Yemen. It is commanded from Tampa (except for temporary forward deployments during active wars) rather than being based in theater to avoid stirring up anti-American sentiments. This combatant command oversaw America's three major conflicts and other smaller operations from the Persian Gulf War to the present. The Pentagon's introduction of an array of military forces represented a widening of Washington's military and political footprint east of the Suez Canal. The first Iraq war, in sum, drew the United States deeper into the Middle East.

Despite its top-ranked army and air force, Israel was not included in the anti-Iraq ranks. At the time, most Arab nations regarded the Jewish State as an avowed enemy for its recovery of lands in Palestinian areas after World War II and its military victories over their forces. For Israelis, their problem was not simply being excluded from the coalition; they were accustomed to exclusion. But the fragility of the Persian Gulf War coalition demanded that Israel not retaliate against Iraqi missile attacks, because Saddam Hussein could then undermine the Arab cohesion by labeling the conflict as an Israeli war against a brother Arab state. The Arabs refused to make common cause with Israel against one of their own. President Bush wrote in his memoir: "The Israelis understood this point intellectually, although it was emotionally difficult for them to stand aside."[8]

For his part, Hussein tried to goad the Israeli Defense Force into striking back at his Scud missile explosions. The Bush administration worked hard to keep Israel from taking the bait. So as to defend Israel from missiles, the Pentagon deployed Patriot batteries as early as September 1990, four months before the United States began its air campaign against Iraq. The Pentagon also sent Special Operations Forces to ferret out missile batteries in western Iraq's deserts. The defensive operations were somewhat effective but Iraq's rockets still hit the Jewish state. Washington had to wield a lot of political leverage with President Yitzhak Shamir to restrain him from a counterattack when Hussein's Scuds fell on Israel, killing two people but otherwise causing scant damage.[9] Israelis seethed but kept their swords sheathed.

Getting America into a war with Iraq at the head of a multinational coalition under the banner of international legitimacy took effort and time. A critical part in the calculation required approval from the United Nations. Here the United States had the law on its side. Article 51 of the United Nations Charter spelled out the "inherent right of individual or collective self-defense if an armed attack occurs against a member of the United Nations." Clearly, Iraq perpetrated an "armed attack" on Kuwait, a UN member state. The White House won approval in the

Security Council. If only one of the five permanent members had vetoed the war resolution, it would have stopped the United States in its tracks. But Britain, China, France, and Soviet Russia, along with the United States, voted in favor of defending the Gulf sheikdom, a sine qua non for an authorized war. At the same time, the resolution tied Bush's hands by limiting his actions to expelling Baghdad's army from Kuwait and not to entering into Iraq.

Among the five permanent members, Russia held prominent standing, because it still cast a shadow, albeit a pallid one, over the Middle East as America's chief foreign rival in the unstable region. It, moreover, was the key benefactor of President Hussein. Moscow placed great store in its relationship with Hussein. It had signed a friendship and cooperation treaty with Baghdad. And in 1971, Iraq "signed a partnership accord with COMECON (the Council for Mutual Economic Assistance), a bloc of exclusively socialist member states," wrote Yevgeny Primakov, the former Russian prime minister.[10] Over the years, Soviet-Iraqi relations fluctuated between warm and cool, but neither welcomed the prospect of an American military intrusion into the Persian Gulf. As a close adviser to Mikhail Gorbachev, the last Soviet leader and chairman of the USSR Supreme Soviet, Primakov made a last stab at retrieving the Kremlin's traditional Middle East policy. The Soviet functionary flew to Baghdad to persuade Hussein to pull out of Kuwait ahead of Washington's orchestrated counterattack against Iraq's army. Overall, he met three times with the Iraqi president with no success. In his memoir, Moscow's envoy recorded that "Saddam's Micawber-like hope that something would turn up also seemed to rule his head."[11]

As a strategy to placate the Kremlin, the Bush-Baker team was outwardly solicitous toward Moscow's desires in the Gulf. The Kremlin initially favored diplomacy over the use of armed force. When five Iraqi oil tankers sailed toward Yemen in late August 1990, the Russians objected to Washington's insistence on blocking their passage by enforcing the sanction provisions in UN Resolution 661. Joined by France, Russia argued that the resolution did not use the word "force" to make the sanctions stick. Thus, the Pentagon lacked the military authority to impose the UN's will. President Bush reluctantly permitted the ships to proceed, while he granted the Soviets additional days to convince the Iraqis to withdraw from Kuwait.

In retrospect, this incident appears a tiny bump on the flywheel speeding to war. But at the time, the transatlantic media blew it and Margaret Thatcher's reaction out of proportion, much to Bush's consternation. When the American president called the British prime minister to inform her about his decision, he got an earful. The Iron Lady shot back:

"Well, all right, George, but this is no time to go wobbly."[12] The "go wobbly" pronouncement ricocheted through the Washington and London echo chambers reinforcing the press' image of America's forty-first president as a "wimp." In reality, George Bush was neither wobbly nor a wimp. In World War II, he had been a decorated pilot and hero. As American diplomacy consoled Soviet officialdom, the DoD raced ahead with war preparations.

An enduring feature of the Cold War's conduct required that the two protagonists abstain from endangering each other's allies. Otherwise, a clash might get out of hand, leading to a nuclear war. Without the Kremlin's acquiescence to an attack on Iraq, Washington might have been loath to militarily intervene against it. As the USSR's political and economic fortunes capsized, Mikhail Gorbachev needed Washington's blessing of the projected West German monetary assistance more than a troublesome client in Hussein. Bush and Baker convinced Gorbachev to drop Iraq for Western aid. So, the Kremlin voted in the Security Council for the US-led coalition to rescue Kuwait from Hussein's clutches. Now, the United States was free from concerns about Moscow's ultimate intentions. Other anxieties remained, however.

At the Security Council in November, Baker shepherded through the approval of Resolution 678, which called for the use of military force against Iraq unless it departed from Kuwait by January 15, 1991. Of the five veto-wielding powers, only China abstained, allowing the resolution to pass with the concurrence of the others. For the first time since the 1950–1953 Korean War, the UN voted for war, if Iraq refused to comply with its resolutions. But the United Nations' role was not finished.

The UN Secretary General, Javier Pérez de Cuéllar, held out for a peaceful resolution in the weeks prior to the start of the air war. At Pérez de Cuéllar's insistence, Washington worked to bridge its differences with Baghdad. President Bush sent his secretary of state to meet with Hussein's confidant and foreign minister Tariq Aziz in Geneva, Switzerland, less than a week before the January 15, 1991, deadline for Iraq to leave Kuwait. The Americans anticipated that Aziz might offer a last-minute concession that could disrupt the multinational coalition's unity and fuel opposition to a war in the US Congress, while Iraq clung to its ill-gotten territorial seizure.

So, as to defuse any possible eleventh-hour stratagem, the president gave a letter to James Baker for Hussein's henchman to deliver to his leader. Bush's correspondence warned that "the United States would not tolerate the use of chemical and biological weapons or the destruction of Kuwait's oil fields or installations." If Hussein crossed these red lines, his American counterpart made a veiled threat of retaliation with nuclear weapons.[13] As it turned out, Baghdad lacked militarily effective chemical and biological weapons, only possessing some antiquated nerve-gas artillery shells that US forces uncovered during the Iraq War invasion a decade later. The Persian Gulf War led to the disclosure and shuttering of Iraq's fledgling nuclear weapons capacity.[14] Although the Iraqi despot did not resort to megadeath weapons, he ignored Washington's warning about the destruction of Kuwait oilfields. He burned about 3 percent of Kuwait's known reserves and caused a local environmental catastrophe before American firefighters quenched the inferno. In any event, the Geneva talks went nowhere, and the suave Iraqi envoy stuck to Hussein's no-pull-out line.

Yet, by far the biggest obstacle to a war was America's own national legislative body, not the Soviet Union nor the United Nations. The Bush administration realized its foremost obstacle. That is why it sequenced its war-building efforts with easier hurdles ahead of proceeding to the US Congress for a vote. With Moscow and the UN on board, Bush officially asked Congress to pass a resolution authorizing military force against the Hussein regime on January 8, 1991. Following three days of spirited debate, both chambers voted to back the presidential call to arms. The House of Representatives passed the resolution with a comfortable margin of 250 to 181 votes. The Senate, on the other hand, approved it by just a 52 to 47 vote, making it the narrowest margin ever on a war question. Had a mere four senators cast their vote against going to war, America's forty-first commander in chief would have had to risk a constitutional crisis by taking the country into a conflict without congressional sanction. He might have had to settle instead for an economic embargo.

When the war went well, the American public came to embrace the campaign. The Democratic opponents, to skip ahead, regretted their nay votes. Chastened by the popularity of the Persian Gulf War victory, they proved much less ready to object to George W. Bush's war appeal in 2002 (see Chapter 5). In brief, the second war became less burdensome for the White House to win legislative approval to enter, thanks to the lopsided US victory in the first war.

The military triumph in the Persian Gulf War, it was hoped by hawks, would dispel the lurking ghost of America's misadventure in Vietnam nearly two decades earlier. With the victorious Gulf War at hand, President Bush wrote that "Vietnam will be behind us."[15] It proved premature to think that the first war against Iraq completely banished the Vietnam War ghost. This public aversion to American military involvement overseas arose during the height of the Vietnam War, fueled by perceptions of its futility and its reliance on conscripted youth to combat an elusive enemy in distant Indochina. Despite the fact that US troops withdrew undefeated from Vietnam in early 1973 after American delegates signed the Paris Peace Accords with Hanoi (two full years before the Southeast Asian country fell to a conventional military invasion from North Vietnam), the unpopular war's outcome haunted the American psyche as a failure.[16]

Years afterward, the war still cast a giant cloud over every US military involvement that could lead to fighting another drawn out, frustrating insurgency. Washington governments feared re-embarking on another Vietnam-era "slippery slope" into an intractable quagmire, generating massive domestic grassroots opposition and dividing the country into pro- and anti-war camps as in the late 1960s. This polarization left a lasting imprint on American politics and culture, even in today's "forever wars," as will be noted (see Chapter 7). President Richard Nixon's jettisoning of conscription for a volunteer military lessened dissent from draft-resistant youths.

Fighting wars with volunteers eased the angst facing many young men who wanted no part of serving in dangerous assignments far from home. A draft-less military force also made it easier for the United States to enter into a multiplicity of small wars on the world's periphery. A professional armed force stands up, salutes, and moves out when commanded to deploy. That is not to suggest that there were no protests about other American wars; there were demonstrations in the United States and abroad. None, however, caused the societal splintering and cultural reordering that engulfed the nation during the opposition to Southeast Asian conflict.

2.3   Operation Desert Storm: Rapid Dominance, Rapid Withdrawal

Military operations against Hussein's Republican Guard divisions started on January 17, 1991, with a punishing air bombardment led by America's formidable armada of missiles and warplanes. Out at sea, US surface warships and submarines fired salvos of Tomahawk Land Attack Missiles – their first wartime use – to take down Baghdad's puny air defense sites, rendering the Persian Gulf country defenseless from the sky. Lifting off from US Navy aircraft carriers in the nearby waters, Persian Gulf airfields, or even Diego Garcia Island thousands of miles away in the Indian Ocean, US Air Force and Navy aircraft first swooped down on Iraq's Scud installations and then on trench-bound soldiers and dug-in armored tanks.

The Boeing B-52 strategic bombers – built during the Eisenhower presidency – flew several hours from Diego Garcia to release 70,000 pounds of bombs over targets 40,000 feet below their hulking aluminum airframes. F-15E strike fighters, F-117 stealth fighters, and Britain's Tornado planes unloaded their deadly armaments on their ill-prepared ground targets, which fell like wheat before the scythe. Nine percent of their payloads were equipped with the latest guidance systems – either laser-directed or satellite-guided – that put the ordinance squarely on their targets. Their onboard cameras filmed the astounding accuracy of the precision weapons, which mostly struck just a few yards from their computer programmed aim points. Hussein's land armies could neither run nor hide from the state-of-the art weaponry.

Visual footage of this information-age warfare was beamed into American living rooms where viewers noted its resemblance to home video games. Bomb flashes and briefly whited-out TV screens signaled kills. To the viewer it appeared remote, antiseptic, and even harmless so that the screen projected an unrealistic picture. Except for a handful of photos of charred corpses, the war images looked bloodless and even painless. The precise targeting, indeed, minimized civilian deaths. For the coalition pilots far above the fray or push-button operators in air-conditioned launch sites, the war lacked the graphic agony associated with previous twentieth-century hostilities.

The US-led air offensive lasted thirty-nine days before ground units barreled into the fray. Hussein's army was bombed into smithereens by the lopsided aerial assaults. Iraq's president promised to unleash the "mother of all battles," but instead his military beheld America's mid-wifing of an entirely new hunt-them-down-and-kill-them approach from warplanes five miles above and safe from their targets. Observers labeled these computerized air strikes "Nintendo warfare" after a popular video-game. The "smart" bombs and missiles unerringly struck their marks. These satellite-guided weapons shattered Iraqi forces, whose decade-old combat experience resembled World War I static trench warfare against an equally out-of-date Iranian army in the 1980s.

As Iraq's armed forces reeled from the intensive coalition air assault, the land-war phase of Operation Desert Storm commenced on February 24 and ended a mere 100 hours later. The high-tech precision air bombardment accomplished its goal. It shredded Iraq's land army. When American and allied armored tanks and troop carriers rumbled into action, they rolled over the remnants of Hussein's military. With few exceptions, the Coalition ground onslaught encountered little deter-mined or effective resistance.

Innovation figured in the land war, too. General Schwarzkopf feinted an amphibious Marine beach assault against Kuwait City while imple-menting his famed "Hail Mary" pass. Commanded by Major General

J. H. Binford Peay, the 101st Airborne Division executed a "left hook" 150 miles behind enemy lines and 50 more inside Iraq to destroy fleeing Iraqi columns and to cut off a supply route from Basra to Hussein's forces. This bold attack relied on 400 helicopters ferrying 2,000 soldiers to their rendezvous, which hastened the end of the conflict.

On the frontlines, American computer-targeted weaponry vanquished, smashed, and even vaporized with high explosives. US firepower drove its foes from the battlefield. So demoralized were Iraqi combatants that they surrendered in droves to any Westerner, even journalists, who were near the front filing stories. Even greater numbers of Hussein's soldiers discarded their weapons and fled pell-mell for safety. To end the carnage, President Bush declared a ceasefire on February 28.

American soldiers, sailors, airmen, and Marines numbered 500,000 personnel. The non-American coalition troops tallied about 160,000 from 35 countries, bringing the total to around 697,000 coalition service members. Among foreign powers, Britain and France deployed the largest combatant contingents. The coalition faced off against 300,000 Iraqi troops. Like the fighting itself, the casualties were lopsided with the coalition suffering under 400 fatalities (not counting 600 Kuwaiti missing) and Iraq between 10,000 and 26,000 military dead. Civilian deaths probably reached 10,000, mostly from bombing. Among coalition casualties, the United States lost the most personnel with 382 deaths (of whom 7 were women and 147 succumbed to hostile actions, not accidents).

The sizeable number of Iraqi troop fatalities played a part in Washington's hasty termination of its murderous offensive. As Iraq's soldiers fled helter-skelter, often dropping their rifles, over open terrain toward their border, they exposed themselves to the onslaught of decimating firepower. Known as the Highway of Death, the Kuwait-Basra road turned out to be a shooting gallery that was littered with abandoned military paraphernalia. When President Bush called off the war, General Powell gave a succinct reason: "We don't want to be seen as killing for the sake of killing."[17] Humane it was but the decision was strategic also. Amassing huge body counts would poison the post-war atmosphere in the entire Middle East, detracting from the decisive victory over a third-rate military power. The "Arab street" would have regarded Americans as senseless killers.

The quick implementation of a cease-fire averted another calamity. The United States was spared the outright subjugation of Iraq, and with it an occupation of the factious country, likely very costly in lives and money. Seizing Baghdad and ousting the Baath regime went well beyond the UN mandate for the coalition to dislodge the Iraqis from Kuwait.

Viewed in the retrospect of the Iraq War twelve years later, George Bush senior's decision not to follow the fleeing Iraqi troops back home looked inspired. To rebut critics of the administration's policy, Dick Cheney, the secretary of defense, presciently uttered a response less than six weeks after the Pentagon stood down on Iraq's border: "Once you've got Baghdad, it's not clear what you do with it. It is not clear what kind of government you would put in place of the one that's currently there now .... How long does the United States military have to stay to protect the people that sign on for that government, and what happens once we leave?"[18] One reason for Washington's circumspection stemmed from the sound advice of its foremost Arab ally in the Persian Gulf. Saudi Arabia cautioned Washington about upsetting the regional status quo, which might remove restraints on its arch-rival Iran. Cheney responded to a suggestion by another Bush official about overthrowing Hussein and instituting democracy in Iraq by replying: "the Saudis won't like it."[19]

Jumping ahead to the Iraq War, the Saud monarchy opposed the US invasion into Iraq in order to push out Hussein and install a democracy.[20] Riyadh's instincts proved to be keen as evidenced by the 2003 intervention and occupation, which was plagued by widespread violence, terrorism, and insurgency. Moreover, Hussein's eviction from power contributed to the Arab Spring in 2011, which ushered in violence, instability, and the toppling of strongmen in Libya, Egypt, Tunisia, and Yemen. Except for the tenuous democracy in Tunisia, the other countries beheld political turbulence or yet another undemocratic regime. In the separate case of Syria, which suffered a multi-sided and very bloody civil war, the ruler, Bashar al-Assad, emerged victorious. So, the United States stayed clear of intruding into Iraq in 1991, thereby sparing itself so much grief visited upon it a decade later. As result, President Bush was generally lauded as a farseeing statesman for not entering Iraq, except by the neo-cons, or neoconservatives, who wanted American forces to push into Baghdad and displace its dictator.[21]

A curtain raiser on America's coming defense-led humanitarianism unfolded at the Gulf War's conclusion. The United States ordered home-bound warships from Persian Gulf waters to detour to Bangladesh in the throes of a cyclone. A flotilla of eight naval craft dropped anchor in the port of Chittagong to distribute food, water, and medicine to victims of the ravishing storm. "We went to Kuwait in the name of liberty and we've come to Bangladesh in the name of humanity," stated Major General Henry Stackpole, the commander of the visiting task force.[22] These sentiments framed subsequent US humanitarian assistance ventures after the Cold War.

2.4   The War's Consequences: Parades and Revolution in Military Affairs

As America's wars go, the losses were minimal, although not for those directly involved or their families. Longer-duration engagements killed many more personnel. The three-year Korean War (1950–1953) cost more than 33,000 American lives and the longer Vietnam War (1965–1973) cut short more than 58,000 young American lives. The comparatively low casualties along with the war's brevity and easy victory contributed to the popularity of the Persian Gulf War among the American public. Even the estimated military expenditures of over $65 billion were significantly offset by contributions of $54 billion from Arab countries, chiefly Saudi Arabia and Kuwait, and non-combatant Germany and Japan. When marshaling the international coalition, President Bush sent Secretary of State Baker around the world, tin cup in hand, to solicit funds for the war from nations unwilling to commit soldiers and sustain casualties.

The United States capped the Gulf War victory with a welcome home military parade in downtown New York City. The ticker tape promenade drew thousands of people who lined Manhattan's thoroughfares. Many thousands more watched on television as the triumphant procession wound its way down streets cleared of cars and buses. Joy and relief marked the occasion.[23] It turned out to be a one-off celebration, despite myriad military actions to follow. None looked so effortlessly executed as the Persian Gulf War. And none ended in forty-two days. The heady uniformed festival also proved to be an inaccurate barometer of the president's political fortunes. The momentary martial pomp, in reality, exemplified the inevitably *sic transit gloria mundi* of presidential triumph. In April 1991, George Bush's poll numbers spiked to an 89 percent approval rating in a Gallup survey. But Bush's America was less impressed eighteen months later when the incumbent lost a bid for reelection due mainly to a slow economy.

A major consequence of the Persian Gulf War arose from what became known as Revolution in Military Affairs (RMA). RMA was predicated on technological breakthroughs, dating from the 1950s, which included transistors, integrated circuitry, microchips, and the Internet. The information technologies were to deliver networked military forces, information dominance, and long-range precision strikes. RMA was so named by the Office of Net Assessment (ONA), located deep within the Pentagon's bowels along the A-ring, the corridor furthest from the choice outside E-ring, where the military brass resides. Under the legendary defense thinker, Andrew Marshall, the ONA referred to RMA as "the interaction between systems that collect, process, fuse, and communicate information and those that apply force."[24] In plainer English, satellites provided surveillance and guidance for bombs and missiles that unerringly struck their targets dead-center. This information-age warfare fired "smart" projectiles that no longer depended on carpet bombing targets to demolish them.

The "transformationauts" extrapolated from the discharge of precision-guided munitions against Hussein's Republican Guards and rapid coordination among air and ground units. They overpromised and underdelivered because the Gulf War midwifed no disruptive change in how militaries fight. Still, this new conception of armed hostilities carried great weight in the remainder of the 1990s in DoD circles and would later define how the George W. Bush administration initially warred against Afghanistan and Iraq. RMA apostles walked the Pentagon hallways proselytizing the transformation of warfare because of robotic devices, sensor-fitted precision weapons, and closer networked military forces on the ground, sea, and in the air. In their telling, RMA made America the equivalent of an Internet Age force decimating a Bronze Age rabble. The Gulf War did unveil astounding Star Trek gadgetry that pointed toward a game-changing manner of waging – and winning – wars.

A throwback adversary surprised RMA cheerleaders, nonetheless. Hijackers with box cutters commandeered commercial jets and weaponized them against the World Trade Center. On the ground, insurgents melted into crowds to evade contact with US armed pursuers. Their "primitiveness" sideswiped the futuristic notion of ultra-tech warfare that ignored the hard truths of ground fighting with a determined and suicidal adversary. Resolving contemporary insurgencies, to one military scholar, seemed improbable "by the use of sophisticated weaponry, since such weaponry requires delivery from the air."[25] Hiding places are ubiquitous for shadowy infiltrators operating in the dead of night. Even during daylight, ambushes, sniping, and roadside bombings tend to be short engagements broken off by militants when they sense the approach of "precision violence" from the air or ground.

A decade after the Gulf War, the United States found itself bogged down in Afghanistan and Iraq fighting low-kinetic insurgencies against militants who bombed and shot before hiding among the civilian population to escape retribution. These grueling battlefields bore a closer resemblance to Vietnam than the high-intensity battles almost completely fought from the air by Star Wars–style platforms at the start of each invasion. At the village level, GPS-guided air strikes were often less useful than skilled special forces operators living among the local combatants and noncombatants, deciding who must be eliminated and who must be protected.

Yet another impression materializing out of the Gulf War would play a part in misjudging the Iraqi population's reaction to the US and Coalition occupation headed by the United States at the start of the Iraq War. Pentagon civilian war planners mistakenly believed that US and allied soldiers would be perceived as liberators by the long-suffering Iraqi people. They misread events at the end of the Persian Gulf War when the Shia and Kurds rebelled against Hussein's rule. Twelve years later, they thought that foreign armies would be welcomed and feted like American GIs marching down the Avenue des Champs-Élysées to the cheers and admiration of the French people for liberating them from Nazi rule toward the end of World War II. But gratitude, the briefest emotion, was in short supply for US soldiers and their partners in post-Hussein Iraq.

A more immediate and catastrophic blunder took place in the waning hours of the ground war. Speaking in Andover, Massachusetts, in late February 1991, George Bush called upon the Iraqi people to "take matters into their own hands and force Saddam Hussein, the dictator, to step aside."[26] At a press conference on March 1, the commander in chief announced cease-fire talks to be held at Safwan, a town just inside the Iraqi border. He repeated his call for an anti-regime insurrection: "In my own view, I've always said it would be – that the Iraqi people should put him [Hussein] aside and that would facilitate the resolution of all these problems that exist."[27] This statement followed up on his recommendation the day before that Iraqis assume their own destiny.[28]

The Central Intelligence Agency had assessed that Hussein would fall if his forces suffered defeat at the coalition's hands. This assessment turned out to be dead wrong. Before the US attack, the Iraqi dictator survived repeated coup and assassination plots. He was well versed in survival instincts. Because militarily trounced strongmen typically fell from power, the CIA assumed Hussein would follow the pattern. When he did not, the Agency turned with renewed vigor to the use of propaganda to foster an Iraq rebellion, to no avail. The minority Sunni community, which amounted to only one-fifth of the population but formed the backbone of Baghdad's army and bureaucracy, stayed loyal to their benefactor. The White House and CIA succeeded only in fostering rebellion among Kurds and Shiites, who suffered mercilessly from Hussein's suppression.[29] The spooks tried again. During Bill Clinton's presidency, the CIA backed away from assisting in a military coup for fear of becoming entangled in a Bay of Pigs–type adventure that carried a distinct possibility of backfiring on the United States.[30]

When General Schwarzkopf negotiated the surrender terms with the Iraqi generals at the tail end of the fighting, he erred in permitting Hussein's forces to retain their helicopters, ostensibly for safe transport above mined roads. Instead, the Iraqi military used helicopters as gunships to suppress rioters in the streets. Together with Hussein's military forces and police death squads, the regime killed an estimated 300,000 people to crush the opposition.[31] Because of its culpability in the crackdown of the anti-Hussein rebels, the White House crept back into Iraq with an air campaign that lasted until the start of the Iraq War in 2003.

2.5 No Real Exit from Iraq

The Bush administration felt it could not walk away from a problem of its own making. Not only were Iraqis being slaughtered by Hussein's military and secret police, but they were fleeing into Turkey in droves. Turkey, as a NATO member in good standing, recoiled from the influx of Kurds onto its soil. Ankara already suffered from a rebellion of its own Kurdish minority in the southeast quadrant of the country. The Iraqi Kurds flocking over the Turkish border were certain to exacerbate that crisis. The Turks called upon the United States for assistance.

Washington handled the humanitarian outflow in two ways. First, along with fellow NATO allies Britain and France, the Bush administration stretched UN Resolution 688 beyond its more limited intent, using it as their legal authority to defend the Kurdish people. They erected a "safe haven" in northeastern Iraq where the Kurds lived. Next, the three allied powers set up a "no-fly zone" above the thirty-sixth parallel, which they designated the northern zone. Patrolled by American, British, and French warplanes, the airspace above the Kurds was rid of Hussein's helicopters and other aircraft.

To firm up its defense of the Kurdish province, the White House deployed lightly armed US soldiers and CIA operatives into Kurdistan in Operation Provide Comfort. Over time, the Kurds eked out a semi-autonomous enclave with a fairly brisk economy. These achievements rarely get the recognition they are due. The United States facilitated the growth of democratic governance and prosperity among a long-suppressed five million people, living in an inhospitable environment. The democracy-fostering in Kurdistan signaled the start of a campaign in the Middle East, where US military incursions preceded American hopes for the spread of democratic rule as a means toward peace and stability in a turbulent region of the world. Outside of Kurdistan, the ambitious project ran into cultural, political, and historical obstacles more often than not as the coming narrative will relate.

Attempts to mimic a Shiite protectorate met with no success. The mountains and physical remoteness of the Kurdish community facilitated its separation from Baghdad in the north. But no similar conditions in the central and southern parts of the country afforded safety to the Shiite community, who made up nearly two-thirds of the population. The United States, Britain, and France did create a "no-fly-zone" below the country's thirty-second parallel in August, 1992. From time to time, the allied warplanes fired air-to-ground missiles at Hussein's military outposts. He maintained that the aerial bombing demolished mosques and murdered innocents.

But Washington, London, and Paris refrained from even trying to carve out a safe haven for the Shia. So, Hussein's police had free rein to hunt down and murder Shia who they targeted as threats to the authoritarian regime. To hold the Baath regime in check, American, British, and French warplanes policed the two no-fly zones almost daily to exclude Iraqi aircraft. They fired on and chased out intruding aircraft. In the north, the trio applied interdiction operations against the movement of Baghdad's armored vehicles and soldiers into the Kurdish enclave. In short, the allied countries kept Baghdad's army out of Kurdistan, securing its protection.

As George H. W. Bush packed up to leave the White House in late January 1993, after losing reelection in November, he ran into a roadblock to United Nations arms inspections in Iraq. In response, he ordered a large-scale air bombardment. Saddam Hussein provoked his American counterpart into military action by disrupting UN weapons inspections. Apprehensions about a secretive nuclear program had earlier led the Defense Department to bomb Tuwaitha, a suspected facility a dozen miles northeast of the capital. At war's conclusion, it was revealed that the site contained conclusive evidence of a covert nuclear arms facility. The discovery came as a black eye for the International Atomic Energy Agency (IAEA), because the UN body failed to uncover Hussein's hidden nuclear program. This failure cast doubt for years over the IAEA's capacity to detect underground nuclear activities not only in Iraq but also in Iran and North Korea.

The IAEA's failure prompted the Bush administration to lobby for creation of a rival agency to the Vienna-based IAEA. In the Security Council deliberations, the White House achieved its goal. UN Resolution 687 (the cease-fire resolution), in addition to demanding that Iraq pay war reparations to Kuwait for damages, established the UN Special Commission (UNSCOM) to ferret out and dismantle weapons of mass destruction. Still, the fear that Iraq was evading UNSCOM inspectors bred a deep-seated malady of "Iraqnaphobia" that infected subsequent presidential administrations, particularly the George W. Bush government.

Hussein detested the UN weapons searches for their intrusions on Iraq's sovereignty and for their requirement that Iraq must be cleared of any clandestine WMD facilities before the Security Council lifted economic sanctions. He decided to impede the international inspectors. Bush countered this challenge by getting the British and French to join with the Americans to assault Iraqi air defense systems. The 100-warplane strike force punished Iraq for three days before the Baath regime requested a cease-fire and permitted the WMD inspections to resume.

Another intense bombing campaign followed in the course of the Clinton administration but without French participation. In the lead up to the four-day heavy bombing offensive, known as Operation Desert Fox, Paris pulled its aircraft from participation in the southern air-exclusionary zone in mid-December, 1998. American war planes and Britain's Royal Air Force carried on without the French. Under the Desert Fox moniker, the two allied air forces struck out at Baghdad for its thwarting the UN arms inspectors. Thereafter, Anglo-American jets alone policed the two zones until the start of the Iraq War. By that time, approximately 350,000 US sorties had been flown over the northern and southern zones at an estimated cost of $30 billion.

The ongoing air strikes on Iraq constituted a de facto war in the time of peace. They were used as a form of militarized diplomacy that was unprecedented in twentieth-century American history. US and Allied air forces cleared Iraqi planes from wide swathes of Baghdad's own airspace. Pilots rained down bombs and missiles on Iraqi targets with little international outcry. They struck Iraqi missile batteries and radars when they "locked on" American or British planes. United Nations' resolutions were reinterpreted to justify a conflict largely out of sight from the media. This shooting-war statecraft never received the sort of attention it deserved for its departure from the norms of international relations. It set a precedent for subsequent warfare by pilotless drones (also known as unmanned aerial vehicles or UAVs) or piloted warplanes against terrorists in such lands as Somalia, Yemen, Syria, and Pakistan in the next century.

Thus, George Bush's "hot containment" policy served as precursor to waging small-scale conflicts against countries and terrorist groups, which never actually struck targets in America. He acted without first getting a congressional declaration of war. Under the American Constitution, the legislative body holds that power. The Defense Department's below-the-radar military operations, fought from improvised airstrips, with armed drones, and sparse numbers of Special Operation warriors cooperating with CIA field officers, became the norm in Washington's campaign against Salafi-jihadis after the 9/11 terrorist attack.

As a direct consequence of the war with Saddam Hussein, the United States augmented its military presence in the Persian Gulf region. The Pentagon prepositioned tanks, artillery, and ammunition in the Arabian sheikdoms. It constructed the large Al Udeid airbase in Qatar, which later served as Central Command's forward headquarters (the main headquarters remained at MacDill Air Force Base in Tampa, Florida) during the Iraq War. In 1995, the US Navy reactivated the Fifth Fleet and based it on the island of Bahrain, off Saudi Arabia's northeaster coast. From this harbor, it patrolled the Arabian and the Red seas, along with the Persian Gulf. This defensive strategy replicated America's approach to confront an expansive Soviet Union after World War II, when the Defense Department constructed bases, deployed warships, dispatched bombers, and stationed army divisions in Asia and Western Europe. These defensive measure aimed to keep the Soviet threat at arm's length as well as defend allies. Now, the Pentagon applied the strategy to ensure US interests in the greater Middle East.

2.6   Entering a New World Order

Still, another legacy of the victorious conflict was the notion that the United States stood at the head of an emerging new world order, where community interests, collective actions, rule of law, and peaceful partnerships replaced the disintegrating old order of superpower rivalries. This constituted an almost Wilsonian dispensation that prevailed in the years after the Berlin Wall and the Persian Gulf War. Military actions against Iraq were taken up by a wide collection of nations that included the acquiescence of the Soviet Union (without actual military participation) along with the United States, Western states, and non-Western nations.

George Bush first gave voice to his conception of the changed international reality in the run-up to the Persian Gulf War. In a speech to a joint session of Congress on September 11, 1990, the president built on growing cooperation with Soviet leader Mikhail Gorbachev when he set forth his understanding of a "new world order," which would arise "free from the threat of terror, stronger in the pursuit of justice, and more secure in the quest for peace." He defined this emerging planetary order as "a world in which nations recognize the shared responsibility for freedom and justice." He pointed to the American soldiers journeying to the Gulf to beat back Iraq's invasion and serving with "Arabs,

Europeans, Asians, and Africans in defense of principle and the dream of a new world order."[32]

At the height of his popularity after the Gulf War, the American leader returned to the theme of a new international dispensation in an address before the UN General Assembly. George Bush spoke idealistically about unfolding opportunities afforded by the demise of communism, which "held history captive for years." Along with human progress, prosperity with "free-market development," and flourishing democracy, he envisioned international cooperation under the aegis of the United Nations. The United States "has no intention of striving for a Pax America," he made clear. Rather, "we seek a *Pax Universalis* build upon shared responsibilities and aspirations." To him, the "brave men and women" of past conflicts "inaugurated a new world order." Bush's soaring rhetoric, his "offer of friendship and leadership" to the new world order enterprise, and pledge not to "pull back into isolationism" left his detractors uneasy.[33] But Woodrow Wilson must have stirred approvingly in his grave.

Skeptics worried that Bush's global call for action surrendered to a form of world government, collective security, and multinational cooperation, which would bankrupt the country and place the direction of American defense policy in the hands of the United Nations. They feared a new world order policed, patrolled, and pacified by US GIs. This goal teed up the United States for endless do-gooder ventures, peacekeeping missions, and humanitarian causes around the world. Realists argued that national interests must be defended, not some fuzzy social welfare concept paid for by US casualties and American taxpayers. Patrick Buchanan, a prominent author and onetime Republican presidential candidate, dubbed Bush's glittering declaration "the language of empire."[34]

The critics' concerns were justified given America's subsequent history of interventionism and war. But they were wrong to see imperial aspirations as the motivating factor. While not always eager to double-time into a conflict, the United States, once committed to war, resolved to press its democratic values on friends and foes in its battlegrounds.

3   Wars Other Than War
Wars in Somalia, Haiti, Bosnia, and Kosovo[*]

> All shall know that America puts human rights above all other
> rights, and that her flag is the flag not only of America but
> of humanity.   Woodrow Wilson

> Sometimes we must interfere. When human lives are endangered, when
> human dignity is in jeopardy, national borders and sensitivities
> become irrelevant.   Elie Wiesel, Nobel Prize Acceptance Speech, December
> 1986

Between the Persian Gulf War and the Iraq War, a twelve-year span, the
United States executed a host of overseas military operations that ran the
gamut from minor to major commitments in manpower and hardware.
This period overlapped with the second half of George H. W. Bush's
term, all of William Jefferson Clinton's tenure in office, and the initial
months of George Walker Bush's presidency. The United States fought
for humanitarian reasons or to protect allies from spreading instability
rather than exclusively for narrow national interests. Critics characterized
them as America playing global policeman to usher in or to defend
democracy and human rights.[1]

These quasi-wars took place in Asia, Africa, and Europe, and they kept
elements of the American military on a nearly permanent combat
footing. None of these deployments came close to the size, lethality, or
expense in blood and treasure of the two wars in Iraq and Afghanistan
after the 9/11 attacks. But all the hostilities added to America's
expanding national debt, although entitlement spending remained the
largest expenditure. The federal government debt stood at $2.857 trillion
in 1989, the year the Berlin Wall fell, and exceeded $28 trillion in 2021.[2]

The Pentagon characterized these nontraditional engagements as
MOOTW (pronounced as *moot*-wah), "military operations other than
war." These missions were disparaged by some military officers, notably
the chairman of the Joint Chiefs of Staff, Army General John
Shalikashvili, who uttered: "Real men don't do moot-wah" on more than
one occasion.[3] Typified by stability operations, peacekeeping, economic

reconstruction, and even governance restoration, these tasks differed greatly from the regular combat assignments. Traditionalists perceived MOOTW as a distraction from their real mission – to close with and destroy the enemy on the battlefield. US armed forces, nevertheless, gained firsthand military experience from interventions, civic conflicts, or manhunts for clan chiefs or war criminals when they encountered hostile fire from inhabitants opposed to their presence in Somalia and Bosnia. Air Force and Navy pilots ran into surface-to-air missiles or hostile warplanes in the skies over Yugoslavia.

Along with small-bore wars, the period also beheld the rise of rogue states – dictatorial nations that actively pursued WMD, especially nuclear arms, and exported terrorism. But none of these pariah countries were frontally attacked until the Iraq War. However controversial the war against Iraq became, it succeeded in removing the Persian Gulf country from the roster of rogue nations. The US Department of Defense mounted no regime-change invasions against Iran, North Korea, Syria, or Sudan. Iraq proved to be the exception and will be taken up in Chapter 5. The case of Libya is more complicated, as Muammar al-Qaddafi fell from power in 2011 to a Western-backed rebellion undertaken by the dictator's fellow countrymen during Barack Obama's presidency. The United States "led from behind" the international coalition that lent air cover to the Qaddafi rebels.

The United States and allied nations fell back on economic sanctions and diplomatic censure to deter or contain the dangers presented by most rogue regimes. Going to war against North Korea or Iran surfaced as an option from time to time in Washington power circles or the punditocracy. Cooler heads won out after weighing the costs and benefits of a conflict.

The first military action ordered by incoming President William J. Clinton was simply a continuation of his predecessor's missile attacks on Iraq. The new commander in chief retaliated against Saddam Hussein for an attempted assassination of George Bush, when he visited Kuwait just months after leaving the presidency. Former President Bush traveled to the Kuwaiti capital to celebrate the city's liberation from Iraq's occupation two years earlier. The assassination plot was uncovered on April 13, 1993, the day before Bush's scheduled arrival. Evidence found on the plotters pointed to the Iraqi intelligence, or the Mukhabarat.

To throw down a marker, Clinton struck back with little effect by firing twenty-three Tomahawk missiles into Baghdad's intelligence headquarters in the dead of night. When retired from office, Clinton wrote in his memoir that this after-dark strike was a "proportionate response and an effective deterrent."[4] Hussein was neither deterred nor chastened, nevertheless. Wags quipped that the only targets were cleaning ladies working after dark.

The late June missile launch was quickly forgotten; it should be recalled as a sign of America's growing use of missiles and other air strike options as its weapon of choice. Missiles, drones, and aircraft bombardments spared the United States from risky, intractable ground fighting as a means to respond against foreign threats.

The Clinton administration turned to clandestine operations to rid itself of Hussein for his not infrequent provocations. The Iraqi autocrat faced would-be challengers from time to time, which encouraged the CIA to act, despite the fact that all the perpetrators went to the wall. Replacing him with an American-friendly general, even if not a Jeffersonian democrat, was seen as a viable option to pursue. Capitol Hill appropriated $40 million to fund a CIA-instigated coup.[5] On the one occasion the CIA operatives came upon an internal rebellion with a chance of succeeding, the Clinton White House pulled the plug on backing it. The Oval Office feared a reprise of the disastrous Bay of Pigs fiasco that embarrassed President John Kennedy, when Fidel Castro quashed a CIA-run beach invasion of Cuban exiles in 1961.[6] Five months after the Tomahawk firing, the Clinton White House didn't get off so easily in another military operation.

3.1   Somalia: A Small-Scale Raid Goes Wrong

In a seaside capital city nearly 8,000 miles distant from Washington, DC, a sharp sanguinary clash haunted American foreign policy throughout Bill Clinton's presidency. The young, former Arkansas governor came to the presidency with little international experience. Yet his speeches advertised a commitment to democratic values. During the political campaign, for instance, Clinton faulted the pragmatic George Bush, the incumbent, for "coddling the old communist guard in China" after Beijing crushed the pro-democracy protestors in Tiananmen Square in June, 1989.

In his Inaugural Address, Clinton voiced an internationalist agenda not just by restating the commonplace phrase that Washington would resort to military force if America's "vital interests are challenged." But he went further by pledging that if the "will and conscience of the international community is defied, we will act, with peaceful diplomacy whenever possible, with force when necessary."[7] The ill-fated US military raid that rocked Mogadishu, the seat of government, on a bloody Sunday afternoon in October 1993, soon cast into doubt the youthful commander in chief's willingness to use military force there or elsewhere.

Such an outcome ran counter to the initial aspirations of what his predecessor largely intended to be a humanitarian enterprise.

George Bush altruistically launched a humanitarian relief effort to the Horn of African nation in the twilight of his presidency by airlifting food supplies to Somalia in August 1992. The television coverage of starving Somalis pulled at American hearts. To alleviate mass hunger in the chaotic country, the Pentagon led the multinational Operation Restore Hope, which presidential candidate Bill Clinton endorsed, too. Approved by the Security Council, the United States answered the call to help relieve the plight of millions of people, not to engage in a shooting mission against the clan factions, which were locked in bloody conflicts. Operation Restore Hope brought in food from neighboring Kenya and cleared away the street gangs, who tried to block its distribution throughout much of the country.[8]

Before leaving office, Bush set in train a series of plans to withdraw most US military personnel and to turn over the relief program to the United Nations. On the eve of Clinton's inauguration, the US Defense Department staged a withdrawal of several hundred Marines, who were followed by other departing military contingents over the next months.

Finally in May 1993, Clinton's Pentagon, as scheduled by George Bush, transferred command of the international force to the United Nations' Operation Somalia and brought home all but some 5,000 military personnel. UNOSOM had a total force of 30,000 troops from UN member states. The State Department signaled completion of the American mission in Somalia, before it reversed itself in mid-summer.

Rather than decamping, the new government in Washington deepened America's commitment to the desolate land by joining with the United Nations in an ill-conceived nation-building project. The fledgling Clinton administration took up the UN's cause to bring order to a clan-based anarchic society. Somalia was an especially dangerous country because during the Cold War both Moscow and Washington poured in small arms to back their clients. Warlords jockeyed for power using foreign weapons against each other. During Restore Hope, the clan chieftains stood aside when the outsiders handed out food to their followers. However, they were averse to surrendering their automatic rifles to international militaries. To bring peace and order to Somalia demanded pacification of its warring factions. Clinton's America did not shirk from its new mission. Secretary of State Warren Christopher cabled his diplomatic corps: "[F]or the first time there will be a sturdy American role to help the United Nations rebuild a viable nation state."[9]

One step led to the next, and US forces soon embarked down the path of "mission creep." In a matter of weeks, US military units crossed the line from passive roles to hot-pursuit operations against Somali peace-breakers, who killed their own countrymen and UN troops. Mohamed Farrah Aidid, the leader of the Habar Gidir clan, especially attracted attention from the UN's secretary general, Boutros Boutros-Ghali. He held the notorious clan chief responsible for the 1991 overthrow of the Somali military leader, Siad Barre, which threw open the country to instability and conflict. UN troop assaults on Aidid's militia begot reprisals on the multinational forces during mid-1993. In one deadly attack in June, Aidid's henchmen killed twenty-four Pakistani UN peace-keepers. The day following the ambush, the Security Council ordered the arrest of those responsible for the killings. US forces soon took up the chase for Aidid and his lieutenants.

Retired US Admiral Jonathan Howe, who served as Boutros-Ghali's envoy to Somalia, put a $25,000 price on Aidid's head. Next, he urged the Pentagon to dispatch its elite military forces to hunt down the Habar Gidir leadership in order to restore peace to the clan-torn country in the wake of more firefights and US casualties at the hand of Aidid. The Defense Department deployed its US Army Delta Force operators and Army Rangers to undertake man-hunting missions in what was named Task Force Ranger. Before the end of the October 3 battle, about 100 personnel from the two classified Army units, plus scores of soldiers from the 10th Mountain Division took part in the firefight and rescue mission, known as Operation Gothic Serpent.

Aidid reacted to America's stepped-up attacks by escalating his reprisals on the UNOSOM peacekeepers. The local US commander, Major General Tom Montgomery, requested M-1 Abrams battle tanks and other armored vehicles to protect supply convoys. Despite reservations about the direction of Washington's policy, General Colin Powell, chairman of the Joint Chiefs of Staff, went along with the request, "a soldier backing soldiers," as he phrased it.[10] Les Aspin, Clinton's secretary of defense, turned it down just days before the fateful commando raid in Mogadishu. After the "black hawk down" debacle, Aspin loyally took the fall for the decision, although it is quite possible that he first consulted with the White House on such a weighty issue.[11] In the meantime, the seaside capital became a battleground between American military units and Aidid militiamen, who the special operators referred to as "Skinnies" or "Sammies."[12]

Back in Washington, members of Congress greeted news of skirmishes with unease. One subcommittee held hearings and summoned Madeleine Albright, Clinton's representative to the United Nations, to testify. There, Albright defined "assertive multinationalism" as US par-ticipation with the United Nations in military operations against Somali criminals, gangs, and renegade clan lords. The future secretary of state justified this robust societal engineering as necessary for "rebuilding Somali society and promoting democracy in that strife-torn nation."[13]

Task Force Ranger mounted a daylight operation to apprehend a couple of Aidid's subordinates meeting in downtown Mogadishu on Sunday, October 3, 1993. Planes and helicopters were mustered, along with "Humvees" (thin-skinned Jeep-like vehicles) and troops for the close-in mission. The raid planners considered it a routine one-hour venture, like many operations before it. Some of the soldiers carried only a few spare ammo magazines and traveled without canteens, as suitable for an in-and-out foray. Unexpectedly, the snatch force encountered fierce resistance just after it took Aidid's lieutenants into custody near the landmark Olympic Hotel. "Mog," as US troops called it, rose up in arms against the commando party, which ran into trouble when one, and then another, MH-60 Black Hawk helicopter crashed onto the city streets after taking hits from a fusillade of ground fire.

An armed citizenry encircled the US forces as they fought to return to the Mogadishu airport outside the sprawling city. While over 1,000 Somalis shot at the American column, others retrieved weapons from fallen comrades to pass along to those ready to take their place. Women and children acted as spotters for the Somali combatants. The Dantesque scene was urban warfare at its worst, with Somali gunmen firing from every direction amid smoke, burning buildings, and dead bodies. After a lengthy delay, a hastily assembled relief column reached the besieged American forces early the next morning enabling the shot-up band to escape the city some fifteen hours after the street fight erupted.

3.2 Consequences and Lessons from Mogadishu

The human costs of the star-crossed expedition stood out sharply. American casualties numbered 18 dead and 73 wounded. Estimates of Somali dead ran somewhere between 500 and 1,000 killed. Measured on the yardstick of a much smaller force fighting off a huge number of assailants, the US troops displayed enormous courage. Nor can the fortitude shown by the Somali resistance be undersold, for the local fighters engaged America's best in a raging gun battle in confined spaces.

Tactically, the Battle of Mogadishu represented a US military victory, for the encircled and hard-pressed troops accomplished their mission of seizing the Aidid sub-chiefs and fought their way out of a death trap with heroism and grit. But politically and internationally, the Clinton administration suffered a grievous blow to its reputation and America's image.

In the years following, when it came to the projection of US power abroad for humanitarian reasons, the Clinton presidency found it difficult to dispel the grim legacy of the Mogadishu tragedy. The events stiffened the White House's natural hesitancy to intervene overseas, no matter how dire the humanitarian plight. The Oval Office feared "another Somalia" when contemplating military actions to halt a blood bath or undo an injustice as in Haiti, Rwanda, or the Balkans.

Somalia suffered a catastrophe as well. The disproportionate numbers of dead and wounded demoralized the Aidid faction and the capital's residents. Many faithful Muslims were dismayed by the desecration of a fallen American's body dragged through the streets, as a dead dog. Many inhabitants feared retribution for killing US troops. Some contacted UN officials to avoid the Pentagon's wrath. Others simply left town before being hit by a counterattack, which never came. A worse fate befell Somalia in time. The Clinton administration abandoned the forlorn land to the tender mercies of warlords, criminal gangs, and Salafi-jihadi militants, who exacted a high price on the Somali people. Washington's retreat, as it turned out, proved to be only temporary.

With the US military's departure, the desiccated nation soon reverted to violent instability that would abet its role in the terrorist bombings of the American embassies in Tanzania and Kenya in 1998. Its descent into chaos allowed Islamic factions to fight one another and to threaten terrorism against the West. This danger prodded US Special Operations Forces and CIA field officers to return to Somalia to combat the terrorism and buttress the local government, as will be described in Chapter 6. Before those developments, the Somali disaster influenced Washington's policy toward faraway countries in the Caribbean, Central Africa, and Balkans.[14]

President Clinton put the best face possible on his inglorious retreat. First, he blamed the United Nations, even though it was disingenuous to hold the international body responsible for US military actions. Neither Task Force Ranger nor the larger Quick Reaction Force (used to rescue special operations troops from missions gone bad) had ever come under UN command. The Pentagon controlled its own military operations. An under-siege White House opted for Mark Twain's advice to never blame itself until it exhausted all other possibilities.

Finally, the Oval Office turned to peacemaking in Somalia. Clinton dropped the goal of arresting Aidid. He even tasked the US military to fly him to a peace conference with other Somalis in neighboring Ethiopia. Instead of perpetuating the conflict, he pledged to assist the Somalis to "reach agreement among themselves so that they can solve their problems and survive when we leave."[15] Two months after the commando raid, the United Nations also abandoned its manhunt for Aidid and freed eight of his compatriots.

For his part, Aidid boasted that his clan bested America's matchless fighters in urban combat. He took credit for the US retreat from Somalia as well. His self-proclaimed victories did him little lasting good; he died in a gunfight in 1996. But he lived long enough to see the US warships weigh anchor and sail off with the American ground forces in late March 1994. The Horn of Africa slipped from the Pentagon's radar for a few years, and Somalia traveled backwards into anarchy. Les Aspin was among the last casualties of the special operations thrust into the heart of Mogadishu. When a US Senate report found the secretary of defense and the president at fault for the calamitous military operation, Aspin dutifully resigned. His deputy, William Perry, took over from the ineffectual and digressive former civilian head of the Armed Forces.

Operation Restore Hope, begun in a burst of altruism by George H. W. Bush, racked up some humanitarian achievements. Half of Somalia's 10 million people were at risk due to starvation in late 1992. Some 300,000 died earlier that year, and another 3 million fled the ravished country prior to the UN-backed intervention. UNICEF vaccinated over 700,000 children. In this more secure environment, farmers returned to their fields under military protection and the famine ended. Estimates of the number of Somalis saved from starvation as a result of the humanitarian mission run between 100,000 and 250,000 lives.[16] Still, Warren Christopher overstated Washington's contribution to Somalia when he asserted: "We leave the country in a lot better shape than [when] we went in."[17]

For the United States, it was not a costless altruism, however. Some 100,000 US troops served in Somalia during the course of Restore Hope, while 30 died and 175 suffered injuries. The exertions, hostile fire, and casualties undermine the notion that the Somalia operation can be written off as an irrelevant MOOTW as General Shalikashvili dismissively did.[18] Moreover, the Joint Special Operations Command (the action arm of the US Special Operations Command) took away valuable lessons from the Blackhawk Down incident for conducting man-hunting raids.[19]

The aftermath of the Battle of Mogadishu held long-term consequences for US foreign policy. Because enemies of the United States interpreted its pullout as an ignominious retreat, they sensed the tactics employed in Somalia's capital could be utilized in other settings. In short, Washington signaled weakness when it did not pursue Aidid and deal his faction a deadly payback. Could the killing of a relatively few US military personnel compel the world's sole superpower to retreat?

The Iraqis, Osama bin Laden, and others thought so. They based their strategies on America's casualty-averse sensibilities. Prior to the American-led invasion of Iraq in 2003, for example, Saddam Hussein's Fedayeen trained themselves to inflict repeated "Mogadishus" on the invading forces.[20]

Years after the ferocious street battle, information surfaced that bin Laden had lent aid to Aidid's militia before the Black Hawk Down incident. Clinton's flight from the ravished seaside city increased bin Laden's status in the Middle East and led him to execute more sensational and murderous terrorism.[21] One major strategic lesson emerges from the commando raid into the heart of Somalia's largest city. Like the Panama intervention and the future Iraq War, it called attention to the repeated failures of the United States to deploy sufficient force to accomplish its goals and to anticipate things not going according to plan.

For the Special Operations Forces and the Pentagon itself, the Battle of Mogadishu was never forgotten. The close-in urban combat on that sweltering afternoon was studied and re-studied for tactical lessons and takeaways over the next twenty-five years. It became a defining firefight for training purposes, martial inspiration, and personal heroism. It was mined for both positive guidance and negative practices in conducting military actions in civilian-packed urban terrain. It enjoyed a near-constant reference, even to gun battles conducted two decades later in the populated downtowns of Afghanistan and Iraq.[22]

Before pulling out the US expeditionary force, the Clinton administration felt compelled to engage in a show of military strength while backing out of Somalia. Away in California to promote health-care reform when news broke about the urban gunfight, the president vented his anger: "How could this happen?"[23] Americans recoiled in horror at the graphic scenes on their TVs of a dead helicopter pilot's body being scourged and dragged through Mogadishu's dusty streets by a frenzied mob. Congressional figures demanded accountability from their commander in chief, who appeared out of touch with his own policies. Clinton lacked the stomach for more military action. Instead, he called off further pursuit of Mohammed Farrah Aidid, the clan chieftain who the United Nations held responsible for much of Somalia's violence.

For appearances, the White House went along with the Pentagon's recommendation to boost America's military might off the Somalian coast to act as covering force for the exiting troops. The military brass ordered up a reaction force of 1,700 soldiers and further 3,600 US Marines stationed on board a flotilla off the coast with the USS *Abraham Lincoln* aircraft carrier. The DoD ratcheted up its presence until its forces surpassed 10,000 troops. Their mission switched from aggressive patrolling and disarming the warring factions to defending United Nations forces and their compounds. But their uppermost assignment centered on force protection for the American military in the chaotic country.[24] If another street battle broke out, Defense wanted more than sufficient troops on hand.

The last Marines and soldiers left the volatile land on March 25, 1994, without the usual fanfare of an official flag-lowering ceremony. Some 19,000 United Nations troops remained to keep order. One officer in the 10th Mountain Division who was involved in the rescue of the embattled Army Rangers in the Battle of Mogadishu observed: "This was the Wild West or pretty close to it."[25] The United Nations pulled up stakes two years later, leaving the chaotic land prey to clan lords, indigenous Salafis, and al Qaeda terrorist instigators.

3.3   Rwanda and the Responsibility to Intervene

The story of Rwanda's genocide is not one of war, regime change, and stabilization operations like those that preoccupy this volume. Rather, when the portals to hell opened in the Central African country, Washington looked the other way, refusing even to label the mass atrocities as genocide, lest the term could trigger the United Nations to intervene to protect the Tutsi population from being hacked to death by Rwanda's majority Hutu people. Had the Security Council voted to intervene in the lush, coffee-growing nation, then the United States would have, quite possibly, been called upon to lead, organize, and logistically support a combat-like incursion for humanitarian purposes. Neither the White House nor the Pentagon wanted to wade into the merciless savagery engulfing Rwanda, whether unilaterally or together with other powers. Just as it had re-deployed Naval and Army units from Somalia months after the Black Hawk Down episode, the Clinton White House shrank from another intrusion into a complex and murderous conflict; by the end of June, 1994, when Rwanda's murderous rampage ended, "at least half a million Tutsi were dead."[26]

The antecedents to the mass killings stemmed from an ancient inter-ethnic feud between the two main indigenous communities. In contemporary times, the Hutu and Tutsi had been at each other's throats in murderous vendettas before and after the country's independence from Belgium in 1962. The horrendous atrocity that whipped across Rwanda in 1994 exploded with the assassination of the country's president, Juvénal Habyarimana, whose plane was struck by a missile in early April. Before his death, the Maryland-sized country of seven million people had been edging toward a cataclysmic civil war. Virulently anti-Tutsi tribesmen within the larger Hutu community organized machete-wielding militias and indoctrinated young members with their blind hatred of the minority Tutsis. The UN and neighboring states attempted to head off the building animosity between the two groups by holding meetings with government officials in Tanzania. Advocating moderation and calling for balanced ethnic representation in the ruling party, the conveners hoped to avert a repeat of earlier ethnic bloodbaths. The powder keg ignited with Habyarimana's death, as his missile-struck plane neared the suddenly darkened Kigali airport.

Once reports of the genocidal killings circulated beyond Rwanda, outside countries reacted differently. France dispatched soldiers to the mountainous country not to halt the carnage, but only to evacuate French citizens and other Western nationals. Paris responded because the Hutu militiamen murdered ten Belgian soldiers in a United Nations contingent. At the end of April, the Security Council voted for Resolution 912, which required the extraction of nearly all international peacekeepers from the country. Its passage came in spite of desperate pleas from the in-country United Nations military head, General Roméo Dallaire, a Canadian officer, for some 5,000–8,000 additional troops to halt or at least slow the rate of homicides.

By the first of May, the Clinton administration was deliberating on how to form, organize, and reimburse an intervention into Rwanda from neighboring states. The president and his top officials had ruled out any American military intercession. Nothing resulted from plans to involve the nearby African countries, for they mostly lacked the peacekeeping capacity to deploy abroad and to protect the Tutsi, who were fleeing into Tanzania and Zaire (now the Democratic Republic of the Congo). Later, some 1.7 million Hutu refugees flocked into Zaire when they were pursued by vengeful Tutsis. The White House ducked for political cover as the UN Secretary General Boutros Boutros-Ghali amplified his calls for interdiction of the rampaging militias. Recalling Somalia, President Clinton uttered his defense for inaction: "Lesson number one is, don't go into one of these things and say, as the US said when we started in Somalia, 'Maybe we'll be done in a month because it's a humanitarian crisis'.... Because there are almost always political problems and some-times military conflicts, which bring about these crises."[27]

When the drumbeat of condemnation reached a crescendo against the Clinton presidency for its obstinate inaction in the face of the harrowing genocide, it finally resolved to take a minimal step. The Oval Office ordered the Pentagon to enter the filthy and starving Zarian refugee camps. Some 4,000 US troops deployed bearing fresh water, food, and medical supplies at a cost of about $400 million. Although the American forces performed useful humanitarian services to the clusters of destitute people, they were barred from protection duties. Still haunted by Black Hawk Down, the Defense Department voiced objections to sending troops for military action. The DoD even refused to jam the extremist Hutu radio broadcast, which inflamed their militias to commit savage attacks on defenseless populations. Washington feared that even this innocuous activity would lead to the first step down a slippery slope to greater involvement in the spreading horror show.

What finally halted the pitiless violence was the resurgence of the Tutsi's Rwandan Patriotic Front. The RPF rallied its forces, fought, and turned the tables on the Hutu militias. Once mobilized, Tutsi formations marched into Kigali and put to flight the Hutu community. Tutsi resistance created another humanitarian nightmare. This time it was the fleeing Hutu who suffered coldblooded atrocities at the hands of their ethnic opponents. In time, the Tutsi imposed a severe peace on the turbulent land.

Although Clinton's America refused to intervene militarily, its foreign policy was greatly shaped by the Rwandan crisis and later Bosnia's Srebrenica massacre in 1995. To stop future mass killings, the United States and other Western governments embraced the liberal international mandate known as the Responsibility to Protect (R2P). This R2P standard demanded that the international community protect populations subject to mass murder, human rights violations, and ethnic cleansing. Rescuing at-risk peoples soon "morphed into the more ambitious strategy of removing the source of the problem by actively promoting liberal democracy in other countries."[28] By exporting democracy into illiberal lands, the Western world, as the argument ran, ensured the protection of peoples, even minorities, because democratic governments, by definition, protect all their citizens. Democracies also facilitate peace with likeminded countries and promote prosperity – all causes dear to the hearts of liberal interventionists after the Berlin Wall.

The fruition of this democracy campaign took place in the George W. Bush presidency. On the eve of the Iraq invasion, the forty-third president spoke about democratic promotion: "The world has a clear interest in the spread of democratic values." He went on to explain "because stable and free nations do not breed ideologies of murder."[29] Like his predecessors, Bush's views were influenced by Woodrow Wilson's ideas and by the successful democratization of defeated Germany and Japan after World War II. The Bush Doctrine provided a fresh and forceful ideological impetus to Washington's invasions and occupations in Iraq, Afghanistan, and other nations. In sum, the Rwandan nonintervention helped midwife an interventionist course for the United States, to be explored later in this book.

3.4   Haiti and Hesitancy

If the Clinton administration managed to avoid Rwanda's blood-soaked imbroglio, it proved much less successful escaping intervention into Haiti's political travails. Distance had something to do with different outcomes. Rwanda is nearly 7,000 miles from the East Coast of the United States, whereas Haiti is on Florida's doorstep. History also figured greatly in determining Washington's approach to the Caribbean island. Located on the western third of the island of Hispaniola (the Dominican Republic occupies the larger eastern share), Haiti is second only to Cuba in having a more tortured history with the United States among South American countries. Over the decades, Haiti moved in and out Washington's consciousness. President Woodrow Wilson deployed US troops in 1915 to occupy the island nation. The Wilson White House espoused a mission to restore democratic rule to the unruly nation, which was the poorest in the entire Western Hemisphere. Over a period spanning five presidencies, the United States occupied the country until Franklin Roosevelt extracted the military in 1934, as part of his Good Neighbor policy toward Latin America. Thereafter, Haiti only occasionally flicked on Washington's political radars, as it resumed its history of corruption, repression, and tyrannical rule by the mostly mulatto elite until the early 1990s.

At that time, political events in Haiti rekindled American concerns and hopes for island's fortunes. A democratic government unexpectedly came to power, which unleashed prospects for political reform before it was abruptly overthrown by a military junta. Arising out of Port-au-Prince's slum, Jean-Bertrand Aristide was a young Catholic priest who challenged the ruling clique. Aristide headed the Lavalas Movement (meaning "flood" in the Creole tongue, signaling that the movement would wash away everything in its path) that championed the destitute and marginalized. A charismatic and savvy campaigner, Aristide captured 67 percent of the vote for president in December 1990. Once in office, Aristide overreached his authority and alarmed the Haitian elite with his neo-Marxist speeches. The Vatican defrocked the political newcomer for his embrace of liberation theology. His pursuit of societal reordering unnerved wealthy Haitians who conspired to oust him in a military coup in 1991.

Nearly overwhelmed with the challenges from the collapse of communist rule in the Soviet Union, the dissolution of the Warsaw Pact, and the Persian Gulf War, the George H. W. Bush administration reacted minimally to the ouster of a democratic ruler on a small Caribbean island. Washington condemned the military regime, offered Aristide and his political circle asylum in the United States, and froze Haiti's assets in American financial institutions to keep them out of the junta's hands. The Bush administration also authorized a monthly payout of $1 million from the Haitian bank deposits to support Aristide in exile. None of these slender efforts convinced the new Haitian rulers to resume democracy. If anything, the minimal steps incited criticism of the Oval Office by presidential candidate Bill Clinton in the run-up to the 1992 election. Clinton zeroed in on Bush's policy of repatriating Haitian asylum-seekers who braved seaborne passage to the United States in flimsy boats. If he won the White House, the Arkansan presidential aspirant proclaimed: "I wouldn't be shipping those poor people back."[30]

After settling into the presidency, Clinton reversed himself, abandoning his campaign statements and tightening his predecessor's constraints on the entry of the Haitian boat people. He grew apprehensive of a political backlash against an inflow of immigrants from the impoverished island. Furthermore, the new president ordered a naval blockade to intercept craft off the Haitian coast and to transport the migrants to out-of-the-way settlements in Panama.

Clinton turned to the United Nations to broker a deal with the Haitian regime. He arranged for talks on New York City's Governors Island and for support from the UN and the Organization of American States for negotiations. Signed on July 3, 1993, an agreement stipulated democratic elections, professionalization of the Haitian security forces, and the return of Aristide to the presidency by October 30th. The Security Council also set up the United Nations Mission in Haiti to preside over the implementation of the deal. But UNMIH did not assume its duties until after Clinton sent the US military into Haiti fifteen months afterward. Then, UNMIH recruited military personnel from twenty-four countries and extended its mission until 1996, when it pulled completely out of Haiti. Before the United Nations involvement on Haitian territory, however, many political twists and turns overtook the Clinton administration.

Long story short, the Haitian regime sent vocal protestors to welcome the landing of the USS *Harlan County* in Port-au-Prince on October 11th. The amphibious warship transported 200 US soldiers and Canadian Mounties as part of a larger training and advising contingent. The rowdy protestors shouted "Somalia, Somalia" at the docking vessel, just a week after the Black Hawk Down incident occurred. The crowds' chanting reflected the world's awareness of the American setback in Somalia and of how it could be utilized to shape nefarious political ends elsewhere. Worse, much worse, than the Mogadishu retreat was Clinton's command to the *Harlan County* to turn around and sail away from the noisy demonstrators.

To offset images of this humiliating rout, the White House decided to re-impose sanctions, which it had previously lifted as a reward to the Haitian regime for accepting the Governors Island bargain. Clinton's foreign policy team had no appetite for another military expedition into a hot, chaotic, and hostile seaside city. The Department of Defense likewise displayed no enthusiasm to land troops in "another Somalia" environment. James Woolsey, the director of the Central Intelligence Agency, raised red flags about putting US armed forces in the seething island state. Complicating matters was the fact that members of the junta had been on the CIA's secret payroll.[31] Congressional members of the president's own Democratic Party got cold feet about putting troops in harm's way for so little payoff. Even normally hawkish Republican lawmakers joined the anti-intervention chorus. Kansas Senator Bob Dole, the minority leader, threatened anti-interventionist legislation if Clinton moved to deploy US forces.

Bill Clinton, with few options, returned to the United Nations, where the Security Council imposed tough economic sanctions on the wayward Caribbean nation. The sanctions eroded the already marginal standard of living, deepening poverty and disrupting growth sectors such as tourism and light industry. As the economy deflated, Haitians again took to frail craft for the perilous passage to the Florida coast. By early summer 1994, about 5,000 desperate people left Haiti each week. The US Navy intercepted overloaded boats and transported their occupants to the American naval base on Cuba's Guantanamo Bay. Insulated by wealth and position, the Haitian elite escaped the ravages of the embargo. Indeed, the junta and its cronies took advantage of scarcities in food, gasoline, and other necessities to jack up the prices paid by the poor.

Undeterred by the harsh conditions of Haitian life, the Clinton administration threatened even tighter penalties on the economy unless General Joseph Raoul Cédras (and the other two junta chiefs) stepped down by January 15, 1994. Unimpressed by the scare tactics, the general ignored Washington's red line. Clinton tried another scheme to induce the junta to leave power with promises of amnesty. He even went so far as offering to elevate likeminded Haitian political figures to power as a way to placate the military triumvirate and its political backers. Aristide joined Cédras in dissing on this half-baked proposition. The White House looked impotent and out of touch with the realities of the Caribbean state's politics.

Aristide made matters worse by assuming the demeanor and trappings of a prince in the wings, akin to the eighteenth-century Prince Charlie waiting across the English Channel in France for an insurrection to place him on the throne. The Clinton White House fanned his self-regard.

Top officials courted him. The Pentagon gave him a twenty-one-gun salute as a head of state and an exclusive briefing with William Perry, the secretary of defense. Aristide was not to be appeased. He hired professional lobbyists and cajoled influential figures to assist him in returning to power in Haiti. The exiled president was not alone in this quest.

Aristide's foremost American backers included the Black Caucus in the US House of Representatives and liberal Democrats in both legislative chambers. Their political capital rose as the November 1994 congressional elections loomed closer. President Clinton keenly recognized the importance of the African-American community to the mid-term vote and two years later to his own political fortunes. Thus, the former Catholic priest's clout rose behind the scenes as the upcoming election neared.

Caught between the rock of the fleeing refugees and the hard place of the Black Caucus, the Clinton administration finally moved, albeit haltingly, toward a military solution to its dilemma. At the end of July 1994, the White House returned to the Security Council to obtain authorization for a multinational armed incursion to restore democracy in Haiti. UN Resolution 940 authorized the "use of all necessary means" to return the exiled Haitian leader to his elected post. Still, the White House dithered, placing its hopes on a CIA organized $12 million "secret enterprise" to bribe "friendly elements" in Haiti's military to overthrow the junta. It was a conspicuous failure, since no one took up the offer.[32] The months of indecision finally came to an end.

Washington combined military power with forceful diplomacy. The Pentagon readied for what it termed a "forcibly entry" operation while the White House sent a trio of representatives to Port-au-Prince to parley with the junta about the "modalities" of its exit. The president selected former chairman of the Joint Chiefs of Staff Colin Powell, former president Jimmy Carter, and US Senator Sam Nunn (Democrat, Georgia) to persuade the Haitian army chiefs to allow an uncontested US military entry onto Haitian soil. The delegation arrived on September 17th with thirty-six hours to complete its mission. The junta wrangled for a while but eventually gave into Washington's demands. The Pentagon got its "permissive environment" demand, which meant no armed resistance to DoD's intervention. In return, the junta escaped punishment by a grant of exile to Panama. The strongmen also got to keep the ill-gotten gains they had looted from the island's population.

Operation Uphold Democracy rolled out on September 19, 1994. The onslaught of US warplanes, warships, and warriors overwhelmed Haiti's poorly armed and trained army and police of 7,000 personnel. Since the defenders of the western portion of Hispaniola Island lacked tanks and other modern weapons, they put up no resistance to the invaders who peacefully occupied their country, much as the Haitian generals had commanded. The Pentagon deployed some 20,000 troops, who either parachuted down to Haitian soil or disembarked from the sea. Off shore, the US military brass sailed two aircraft carriers – USS *America* and USS *Dwight D. Eisenhower* – with Special Operations Forces and other combatants on board. After months of dread over a possible "Mogadishu syndrome," the intervention bordered on the anticlimactic. Ordinary Haitians hoped the presence of US soldiers might improve their lot. Those expectations were soon dashed. Not quite a month after its heavy-footprint incursion, Washington returned Aristide to the presidency amid the cheers of his well-wishers in Port-au-Prince.

The Haitian chapter of American foreign policy resembled other Washington regime changes in the post–Cold War period. The United States went on to mount invasions, depose strongmen, and impose democracy. During the East-West competition, Washington relied on CIA operatives to collude secretly with disgruntled in-country army officers or politicians to dislodge anti-American regimes, as in the coups of 1953 Iran, 1954 Guatemala, and 1973 Chile. During the containment era, Washington favored leaders friendly to the United States and averse to communism, regardless of their skimpy democratic bona fides. The post-Soviet period marked a step up in the overt use of force to remove adversarial leaders from power and implant democratic governance for peace and stability, to wit, Noriega in Panama, Cédras in Haiti, and subsequently Saddam Hussein in Iraq, plus the Taliban in Afghanistan. The incursions garnered mixed success.[33]

Unlike the Soviet era, American presidents now openly celebrated their regime-change wins. In Bill Clinton's case, he flew to the battered republic seven months after the US military intervention to revel in the adulation of celebratory crowds. The American president, in turn, exalted in "bringing back the promise of liberty to this long troubled land."[34] Less than a year later, in his 1996 State of the Union address, he ignored the rising instability on the island and declared "the dictators are gone and democracy has a new day."[35]

The interactions between US combat personnel and the Haitian population were peaceful, unlike the hostile receptions in hot zones, such as Afghanistan, Iraq, Somalia, and other insurgent-besieged countries. The Defense Department learned, or at least re-learned, lessons in its Haiti operations that were applied on other battlefields. One official study noted how the skills and temperament of Green Berets won over the rural peoples. It observed: "Generally, however, in rural areas across Haiti, Special Forces found the populace receptive to their presence, a fact that contributed to a relatively high sense of satisfaction that Haitians were actually benefiting from the American presence. Through constant, low-level interaction, bonds of trust and understanding formed."[36]

Operation Uphold Democracy restored President Aristide to power. But when it came to reestablishing genuine democracy, it was a bust. Haiti's torturous past soon re-manifested itself in corruption, street protests, and political violence. Prior to that disastrous turn of events, the United States had extracted itself from the island's political morass. In March 1995, Washington turned over its Haiti operations to the UNMIH, which had been formed by the Security Council in 1993. Still, the Pentagon contributed 2,500 troops to UNMIH for training and development projects. The entire UN contingent numbered close to 7,000 peacekeepers and police officers from 24 countries. The United Nations Mission in Haiti concluded its assignment in mid-1996, by which time the United States had spent $3.2 billion on the entire Haitian enterprise. All's well that ends well might sum up the relief felt by the Clinton West Wing to be out of the Caribbean country.

Years later, President George W. Bush felt compelled to force out Aristide, whose dishonest second election, pervasive corruption, and political violence threatened to destabilize the island republic. The White House and the French government orchestrated a coup and exile of the Haitian president in 2004 amid the island population's relief and joy. The tiny military contingent of US Marines and international troops soon turned over their stabilizing role to UN peacekeepers, who lingered until 2017, in part, due to a devastating earthquake. This second Haitian intervention represented the last time the United States marched into a South American country.

3.5   The Balkan Wars: Ethnic Conflict and Noninterventionism

Washington might ignore political turmoil less than a hundred miles off its coast for months with only fluctuating domestic pressure for action, but it could not indefinitely detach itself from a raging humanitarian nightmare thousands of miles away in the heart of Europe. The disintegration of Yugoslavia with its attendant multiethnic atrocities and border-changing ramifications proved nearly impossible for the reigning superpower to ignore indefinitely. Located in southeastern Europe, Yugoslavia and the larger Balkan lands had been at the vortex of several momentous historical events. In the 1990s, the Balkans once again took center stage in a macabre drama.

Sitting at the crossroads of East and West Europe as well as the Middle East, the Balkans formed one of those planetary cockpits of major power intersection, interference, rivalry, and conflict. Matching the external dangers were homegrown perils deriving from rivalrous nationalism and religious hatreds rooted in historical turmoil. So factious, quarrelsome, and bloody were the internal feuds that the area gave rise to the vintage term of *Balkanization* to describe the nature of the bitterly fragmented lands. In the Balkans, as Faulkner noted about the American South, the past was not dead; it was not even past. Historical defeats or wrongs bit deeply in present-day consciousness. Outside powers exacerbated the internecine tendencies of the turbulent neighborhood by interfering, intriguing, and generally turning it into a veritable powder magazine before World War I. The collision of foreign interests formed the backdrop to the assassination of the archduke of the Austrian-Hungarian Empire in 1914 by a Serb nationalist in Sarajevo. The murder ignited World War I. When the guns fell silent, the victors presided over the formation of Yugoslavia out of a half a dozen small territories from the defunct Ottoman and Austrian-Hungarian Empires.

Yugoslavia suffered through the 1939–1945 war under an iron-fisted German occupation that fanned nationalistic divisions in pro- or anti-Nazi camps. After World War II, the former communist partisan Josip Tito succeeded in keeping together the various political entities. Marshall Tito issued a new constitution in 1963 establishing a socialist federal country comprising six republics – Croatia, Bosnia and Herzegovina, Macedonia, Montenegro, Slovenia, and Serbia. The Serbian state claimed two semi-autonomous sub-states: Vojvodina and Kosovo. Tito's death in 1980 stirred separatist solvents that ate away at Yugoslav unity. Yugoslavia's espousal of communism did little to erode the ethno-nationalistic furies of southeastern Europe. When the Soviet Union vanished, the cobbled-together Yugoslavia soon fell apart.

Balkan history returned with a vengeance in the post-communist interval. Yugoslavia reached a hinge-point in December 1990, when Slobodan Milošević, a onetime communist functionary, won the election to Serbia's presidency, on a platform of Serbian victimhood and persecution dating back to the thirteenth-century defeat at the hands of Muslim invaders.[37] Extreme nationalism was the catapult that flung Milošević to power. But it alone could not be responsible for his retaining office. Once in power, Milošević lost little time in exploiting Serbian ethno-nationalism to consolidate his increasingly authoritarian rule. Capitalizing on perceived Serb grievances, he resorted to demagoguery and heavy-handed tactics to make the Serbian republic the dominant player within the Yugoslav federation of twenty-four million people.

Croatia, Slovenia, and other republics pushed back against Belgrade's grab. Milošević lit the fuse, and the rickety federation turned into the heart of darkness. Serbian militias went to work "ethnically cleansing" adjoining precincts with systematic rape, summary executions, and intimidation to put non-Serb residents to flight from lands claimed as Serbian provinces. What the Balkan communities didn't know about revenge wasn't worth knowing. In time, the Serbs suffered the same fate as their victims when Croatians and Muslims copied their dehumanizing tactics. Their actions, all in all, ripped up the Yugoslav map.

Americans and Europeans alike recoiled from the pictures of widespread atrocities not seen in the West since World War II. No outside power was eager to enter into the hellish cauldron to halt the killing, raping, or "cleansing" of peoples from their ancestral homes. The massacres drew on the apocalyptic scenes of pestilence, war, famine, and death from the dreaded Four Horsemen in the book of Revelation. Neither of the two US administrations that served during the height of what came to be known as the Bosnian War, evinced any appetite for sending military forces into the hostilities. Both major political parties – Democrats and Republicans – disagreed on nearly everything; but they shared an antipathy to wading into messy civil wars since Vietnam.

3.6   Avoiding a Fourth War in Europe

The George H. W. Bush administration, which was in office when the Bosnian conflict broke out, strove to keep America from becoming entangled in another European conflict. In his memoir, Secretary of State James Baker recorded that he fully agreed with Bush's judgment that America must not "fight its fourth war in Europe in this century," taking note of the two world wars and the Cold War.[38] Commenting on the lack of any vital American interest in the fragmenting Yugoslavia, Baker colorfully phrased the US position: "We don't have a dog in this fight."[39] Both officials were comfortable with the European Community (now the European Union) taking up the responsibility to handle the crisis. Not long after, Washington acknowledged a stake – stability – in dealing with the fragmenting Yugoslavia.

The Europeans, for their part, initially bristled at any perceived assumption of American leadership in resolving the conflict. The rotating president of the European Community, Jacques Poos (Luxembourg's foreign minister), voiced Europe's newfound independence from American tutelage since the Soviet threat evaporated. Poos grandly proclaimed: "This is the hour of Europe, not the hour of the Americans."[40] As we shall see, the Europeans, in the last analysis, proved unable on their own to solve the unfolding tragedy in Yugoslavia's breakup. Nor was Jacques Poos' position the prevailing one. One British diplomat spoke for Europe when he expressed "the hope has been all along that the Americans would come in, would see that it's in their interest to have a peaceful Europe and avoid a Balkan conflagration."[41]

At first, American diplomacy tried to preserve Yugoslav unity as the best way to prevent the unpredictable consequences of the nation's disintegration. But in mid-1991, Slovenia and Croatia declared their independence from the federation. To compel Slovenia to return to the fold, the central government deployed tanks and aircraft, to no avail. The Slovenes quickly defeated the Serb-dominated Yugoslav National Army (JNA). Next, Milošević sent Serb militias and the JNA to grab territory from the eastern Krajina region of Croatia by using ethnic cleansing operations. Serbian atrocities caused an international furor.

The United States joined Britain, France, and other European nations at the United Nations to impose a Yugoslav-wide arms embargo as means to reduce the mass murder among the combatants. It failed and backfired vis-à-vis its intentions. Since Serbia possessed the bulk of the JNA's arsenals and their arms, it was largely unaffected by the weapons sanctions. Additionally, Belgrade had established weapons pipelines with international arms companies that enabled it to amass new weaponry and munitions. Indeed, the arms shut-off hurt Serbia's foes worse than Belgrade. The UN sanctions, if anything, emboldened Milošević to strike harder at the Croatians and Muslims in Bosnia.

United Nations participation led to false hopes by the United States, European Community, and the under-siege Balkan entities that the international body would reconcile the warring parties. The passing of the Cold War opened the prospect that the Security Council might fulfill its historic mission to arbitrate disputes dispassionately and fairly. But pursuing their own interests, the members deadlocked. The Security Council squabbles among the United States, Russia, China, and other powers paved the way for America alone to expand its role as international stabilizer and global arbiter of crises. By the early 2000s, Washington's predisposition to intervene stiffened resentment against American actions by other states, as we shall see. In the Bosnian case, Europeans grew to acquiesce to US engagement.

In the meantime, the Bosnia War disabused world capitals of the notion that the great powers sitting in the Security Council could adjudicate conflicts free of national interests. Specifically, Russia emerged as Serbia's main champion. The two nations shared the Orthodox faith and their wartime alliance against the Third Reich. Moscow also bristled at American and West European interference in its near-abroad – its nearby sphere of influence. This attitude represented an old – even pre-Soviet – quest for dominance over bordering countries.

Now in the Balkans fighting, the West was again pushing against the Kremlin's interests by singling out Serbia for condemnation. To be accurate, both France and Britain shared sympathies for Serbia because of its anti-Nazi resistance during the war. In time, Serbia's brutality against the Croats and Muslims turned Paris and London away from their wartime embrace. American elite public opinion generally favored the Balkan underdogs – the Bosnian Muslims, or as they were called, Bosniaks.

The conflicting loyalties and competing interests among the contending powers produced a minefield rendering outsiders fearful to enter. Their standoff lay open space for the Serbs to exploit. The Yugoslav national army and militias laid siege to the Croatian cities of Vukovar and the scenic Dubrovnik on the Adriatic coast. The heavy loss of life and destruction of historic buildings prompted the United States, Britain, France, and other nations to advocate for demilitarization of Dubrovnik and the insertion of United Nation peacekeepers. Serbia and Croatia accepted the proposal in late 1991. Three months later, 12,000 UNPROFOR (UN Protection Force) soldiers took up their posts. Soon the international force rose to 39,000 troops from over 40 nations. Their role became controversial as UNPROFOR members often served more as hostages to Serb gunmen than genuine peacekeepers to civilian Bosniaks or Croatian populations.

The Balkan maelstrom soon worsened and drew in other peoples from the splintering Yugoslavia. The territory of Bosnia and Herzegovina – a tiny republic that last enjoyed statehood as a medieval kingdom – undertook a referendum on reestablishing its own sovereignty. Made up of mainly Bosniaks and Croats, the vote recorded a 99 percent count for independence. Outraged by the plebiscite, the Bosnian Serb minority stayed home. As their fellow citizens celebrated their proposed return to statehood, the Bosnian Serbs set up their own mini-state, Republika Srpska, which subscribed to a radical Serbian nationalism to justify the killing and expelling of non-Serbs from their territory.

After three former republics – Croatia, Slovenia, and Bosnia-Herzegovina – gained membership in the United Nations, Serbia struck with ferocity against the Bosniaks, particularly in the city of Sarajevo, which hosted the 1984 Winter Olympics. Encircled and almost cutoff from the outside world, Sarajevo endured artillery shelling, sniper fire, and near-starvation for over three agonizing years. The besieged city exhibited scenes of damnation and agony reminiscent of Rodin's Gates of Hell. The bloody strangulation cost some 11,000 lives, of whom 1,500 were children. In the crucial dimension of world opinion, Sarajevo won a moral victory in its David and Goliath struggle. Before the Sarajevo siege finally precipitated an international military intervention into the Balkans, the European governments addressed the festering wound with rounds of meetings, consultations, and conferences as an overly diplomatic way to stanch the flow of blood. The Europeans substituted distillatory diplomacy for meaningful action. Nothing changed on the ground, except casualties rose.[42]

The Europeans stayed clear of involving the American-led NATO – the one military force capable of halting the bloodshed. London, Paris, and Berlin aspired to handle the crisis on their own. Leaving out the transatlantic alliance, thus left out the United States. To be sure, both Bush and Clinton administrations were just as reluctant to employ NATO, since such action meant that the United States would assume the ultimate responsibility for a military campaign to restore peace in the fractious Balkans. Another factor sidetracked a resort to NATO forces. At this early stage in the post–Cold War period, Americans and Europeans largely thought of the Euro-Atlantic military alliance as merely an anti-Soviet defensive partnership. In time, it attained a wider perspective, even sending troops beyond the European continent to Afghanistan and Iraq along with the US interventions.

With NATO benched and European diplomacy absorbed in often pointless foreign ministry talks, unproductive mediations, and official sit-downs, the Serb's deadly Sarajevo encirclement tightened. Bosnia-Herzegovina writhed with Serbian imposed agony, for which there appeared no end. Europe looked helpless. Some of its leaders worried about the blowback from the separating Yugoslav mini-states on their own populations, especially in Spain's Catalonia and Britain's Scotland.

Even though the Bush and then the Clinton presidencies assumed a stand-off posture, they did prod the Europeans to act especially after the Serbs laid siege to Sarajevo, a city of a half-million residents. In addition, President Bush secured the passage of UN Resolution 757 through the Security Council, which imposed economic sanctions on Serbia in May 1992. In June at the G-7 summit of major industrial nations, the White House obtained measures clearing the way for humanitarian relief to the encaged Sarajevo. Attending the July meeting of the Conference on Security and Cooperation (now known as the Organization for Security and Cooperation in Europe) in Helsinki, George Bush proposed doing "all we can to prevent this conflict from spreading."[43] The attendees, however, enacted no real measures to halt the widening conflict.

George H. W. Bush lost his bid for a second term in the November 1992 election to William Jefferson Clinton, governor of Arkansas. As a lame duck president, Bush ordered large-scale airlifts of food, shelter, and heating fuel to Sarajevo, along with smaller Muslim communities outside the embattled capital in a bitterly cold December. His humanitarian efforts differed from his nearly coterminous food-relief intervention into Somalia in that large numbers of US troops did not flow into Yugoslavia. Combined with ground-dispensed aid, the Balkan relief saved an estimated 100,000 lives from starvation and exposure. But the relief and diplomacy brought no cessation to the localized genocides or to the larger Balkan conflict.

3.7   Clinton Takes Up the Cause, Slowly

When Clinton walked into the White House, he faced a diminished Bosnia and an unworkable plan to create ten canton-like enclaves within the rump state. The young president rejected the territorial scheme and ditched his tough campaign rhetoric toward Serbia. His secretary of state, Warren Christopher, went on CBS' Face the Nation television program to proclaim the administration's new political line: "[T]he United States simply doesn't have the means to make people in that region of the world to like each other."[44] Soon the commander in chief confronted other seemingly intractable quandaries in Somalia, Haiti, and Rwanda, while Bosnia had become a sparrow among hawks.

Put on the defensive by European and domestic critics for its wavering posture, the Clinton West Wing considered using airpower against the Serbs. It ruled out the employment of a ground-force presence, because Colin Powell, the chairman of the Joint Chiefs of Staff, objected to placing American GIs in harm's way until the US government arrived at "a clear political objective." Reflecting on his service in the Vietnam War, the Army general, like many of his contemporaries, was wary of stepping on a slippery slope into a protracted, complex civil war. His view did not go unchallenged. Madeleine Albright, then America's representative to the United Nations, memorably retorted: "What's the point of having this superb military that you're always talking about if we can't use it?" Powell responded that US forces were not to be treated as "toy soldiers" that are "moved around on some sort of global game board." He pleaded for "tough political goals" first; then the armed forces "would accomplish their mission."[45] Albright remained unpersuaded and autobiographically noted that "the lessons of Vietnam could be learned too well." Avoiding similar quagmires, she wrote "was not a sufficient strategy in a messy and complex world."[46] Ultimately, Albright's outlook prevailed when Powell, the Bush holdover, left the chairmanship at the end of his term.

Faced with a murderous conflict spilling over the Balkans, Clinton's foreign policy team worried about instability. They dreaded the prospect of neighboring states being dragged into a wider conflagration similar to the chain reaction that led to World War I. Moreover, the fierce fighting raged close to NATO member states, Washington's foremost alliance and a bulwark of transatlantic cooperation for four decades. These facts aroused American anxieties. It was still tenable for the United States to stay aloof but it was becoming less comfortable for the White House.

The Clinton administration's first major initiative to come to grips with Balkan tragedy ran up against determined European opposition. This option called "lift and strike" advocated lifting the arms embargo on the Bosniaks so as to level the playing field with the far-better-armed Serbs and threatening to air-strike Serb military positions. First broached during the 1992 election campaign and embraced by candidate Bill Clinton, the lift and strike proposal was carried to America's European partners by Secretary of State Christopher in May 1993.

The British, French, Germans, and Russians flatly rejected the lift and strike proposal, because they feared Serb retaliation against UNPROFOR, the 39,000-troop peacekeeping force, formed by the Security Council in early 1992. They told the White House to put skin in the game by deploying US ground troops before wielding air strikes against Serb militias. In reply, the Clinton administration blamed the Europeans for not adopting tougher measures.

The Europeans responded by pressing the Security Council to pass a resolution establishing "safe areas" in Bosnia-Herzegovina for the Muslim-populated municipalities of Sarajevo, Bihać, Goražde, Srebrenica, Tuzla, and Žepa. Resolution 824 carefully skirted the term "safe havens," which under international law declared immunity for refugees. The UN action did proclaim the safe areas to be "free from armed attacks and from any other hostile acts."[47] The safe areas' reputation for protecting life suffered a body blow at Srebrenica as will be described in Section 3.8.

Even the minimal progress in standing up safe areas was undone when the Bosnian Croats, who made up 17 percent of Bosnia-Herzegovina, turned against the Bosniaks. They formed their own mini-state, known as Herceg-Bosna, in the western strip of Bosnia-Herzegovina. The inhabitants tried to ally with the larger Croatian state before the Dayton Accord drew the boundaries for all of Bosnia. Though nominal partners against the Bosniaks, the Serbs and Croats still hated each other. In fact, they called each other by their World War II designations. The Serbs were remembered as pro-communist Chetniks, who eliminated non-Serb populations. Others recalled the Croats as members of the Nazi-linked

Ustashe (fascist police). The Bosnian Muslim-Croat breakup did not last, as the United States and its European allies pressured them to reunify as a means to isolate the Serbs. The negotiations point up how significant, in the last analysis, diplomacy proved to the overall settlement in 1995. But it was diplomacy backed up with a sword's point.

Before Dayton, persistent bloodshed and insecurity in Bosnia-Herzegovina gradually changed the tide. The infamous shelling of Sarajevo's open market by Bosnian Serb gunners in early 1994 shifted the stance of the Clinton administration. The stern reaction to the killing of sixty-eight people with a Serb mortar round was a straw in the wind, indicating that the United States and the West would no longer idly stand by in the face of Serb atrocities. Washington, joined by Paris, secured a ten-day ultimatum from NATO, requiring the Bosnia Serbs either to cease firing and remove their gun positions from the highlands surrounding Sarajevo or to get heavily bombed. Radovan Karadžić, the Republika Srpska leader, gave into the demands. Next, the Clinton White House prevailed on Boris Yeltsin, the Russian Federation president, to dispatch 400 troops from UNPROFOR to replace Bosnian Serb fighters in their encircling hilltop redoubts.

Together with this diplomatic arm twisting, the Serb forces got a sobering taste of US military capacity in the wake of the mortaring the market. As the Cold War receded into memory, NATO recorded its first hostile military action in forty-five years, not against the defunct Soviet Union but Serbian aircraft. Two US F-16s, flying under NATO colors, shot down four Republika Srpska warplanes for breaching the "no-fly" zone in central Bosnia-Herzegovina that the United Nations declared in 1992. More than a year later, in June 1995, a surface-to-air missile downed one F-16 fighter over Bosnia-Herzegovina but the US Air Force pilot (Scott O'Grady) ejected and was rescued by US Marines.

In April 1994, American diplomats convinced their NATO partners to engage in limited bombing against Serb attackers of Gorazde, one of the UN-designated safe areas, where 65,000 people were huddled for security. Concerned about setting a precedent with the air strike, NATO claimed the so-called pinprick attack was justified to protect twelve UN peacekeepers inside the city's perimeter. Despite the minimal bombing, President Clinton hailed it: "This is a clear expression of the will of NATO and the will of the United Nations."[48]

The American leader spoke too soon. Washington's arm-twisting for more aerial bombardments caused the British and French to dig in their heels against subsequent air strikes. London and Paris threatened to drawdown their soldiers, who made up the largest contingent in the

UN "blue helmets" peacekeeping forces, if the Clinton administration kept calling for NATO air attacks.

During the balance of 1994, the United States pursued two diplomatic initiatives that reordered the Balkan chessboard. First, Washington won over Croatia and Bosnia to reestablish their anti-Serb alliance. It dangled rewards of integrating both states into the Western economic and political structures, while threatening both with ostracism and exclusion if they failed to come together. The mixture of carrots and sticks worked. Both governments agreed to participate in the Muslim-Croatian Federation. Uneasiness persisted between the two ethnic communities but open warfare ceased. Croatia removed its troops from Bosnia-Herzegovina and halted military backing for the tiny enclave of Herceg-Bosna. The arrangement permitted arms to reach the Bosniaks through Croatia without the prior "weapons tax" imposed by Croatian border guards, who skimmed off a large percentage of the arms.

Some of the imported weapons had a highly unexpected origin. With the approval of President Clinton in 1994, Iran set up a covert arms pipeline through Croatia to the Bosnian Muslims. The White House reasoned that the weapons were needed to balance the contest for the Bosniaks, as the Serbs enjoyed an arms monopoly. The secret authorization, nevertheless, double-crossed US allies in Western Europe and contravened international agreements to stop all weapon shipments. It also added to fears about inroads by radical Islamists to set up terrorist bases within the Bosnian Muslim community. Indeed, Osama bin Laden visited with and offered aid to the Bosniaks. Mujahedeen from Afghanistan and the Middle East journeyed to mountainous country to fight alongside their co-religious brethren.[49] After the Dayton Accord, the Clinton administration divulged the underground deliveries from Iran, an unyielding US adversary since the late 1970s.[50] Clinton's gamble paid off, and the region largely escaped from becoming a major terrorist hub in Europe. The Dayton settlement required foreign Muslim fighters to leave, and the local Bosniaks mostly rejected their radical appeals.

The second major American overture in the Bosnian political scene aimed to induce Russia to join the peace process along with West European countries. Because it was Serbia's main patron, Russia was crucial to moving its client toward resolving territorial disputes and ultimately to peace. Due to Russian political and economic weakness, Moscow offered little opposition. Yeltsin's Russia teamed up with the five-nation Contact Group, which also included Britain, France, Germany, and the United States. Like the nineteenth-century European conferences, the Contact members aspired to impose a peace settlement and draw boundaries for the warring states. At its July 1994 meeting in Geneva, the Contract Group laid down its borders for the Balkan combatants, which demanded territorial concessions from each. It was for the Bosnian Serbs and Bosniaks alike an easy decision to reject the borders as they satisfied neither.

The rejections, in fact, opened a fissure between the Republika Srpska and Serbia (along with Montenegro). The Serbian leader Milošević insisted his counterpart Radovan Karadžić in the Serb mini-state accept the Group's map, for he needed an end to the choking sanctions enacted by the United Nations. The political differences between the two Serb chiefs grew personal and raw. At the Dayton talks, the division played into the hands of the American diplomats.

Prior to the Dayton meeting in 1995, other developments worked to break the logjam. President Clinton felt the heat from his potential rival in the next year's presidential election. Republican Robert Dole, the US Senate minority leader, faulted Clinton for adhering to the European-backed arms embargo for all Yugoslavia. Dole's stance compelled Clinton to announce that the United States would no longer enforce the unpopular arms cordon, even if it would not formally end sanctions. Clinton's public climb-down eased the way for greater military intervention, as the White House inched away from its previous policy of letting the Europeans take the lead. Political changes within Britain's and France's top political leadership realigned both with a tougher posture toward the Belgrade government.

3.8   Entering the Balkan Cauldron

The last straw ending the disastrous international hands-off policy came from an event in the Balkans itself. Serb regular forces and militias assaulted Srebrenica ("place of silver") in July 1995. Although designated as a safe area and guarded by 400 Dutch UN peacekeepers, the enclave paid an exorbitant price when Serb gunmen rounded up and mowed down about 8,000 men and boys from the refugee population. This coldblooded atrocity transformed the dynamics of the Bosnian War. Srebrenica stood out as the worst massacre in Europe since World War II, as a colossal disgrace for the United Nations and its Dutch peacekeepers, and as a harbinger of even greater casualties and political instability engulfing the broader region, potentiality triggering a major war. This drift toward a wider calamity was confirmed when Žepa, another safe area, fell to local Serb militias two weeks later.

Despite the horrors associated with Muslim territorial losses in Srebrenica and Žepa, the local population's departures paradoxically made peace more achievable. The forced expulsion of Bosniaks enabled the drawing of boundaries between ethnically exclusive communities in Bosnia-Herzegovina. The July 1995 fighting mostly left Bosnia's Muslims in one area and Serbs in another sector.[51] The downside of territorial shifts was the resulting Serbian triumphalism.

Propelled by a false sense of history being in their corner, the Serbs fatally turned their guns on Bihać in the northwest frontier of Bosnia-Herzegovina. Bihać differed from the other designated safe areas in its close proximity to Zagreb, the Croatian capital. Being an hour's drive to the seat of their government provided cold comfort to the alarmed Croatians, who mounted a devastating counterattack against the Serbs. In late summer, the refitted and retrained Croatian army crushed the Serb forces and recaptured the Krajina pocket in Operation Storm. Surprising the Pentagon and the CIA, the Croatians next smashed into western Bosnia-Herzegovina. In Belgrade, Milošević turned a blind eye to the Bosnia Serbs, for he had other fish to fry. Serbia's dictator decided not to stick his neck out because he feared that intervening on behalf of his Serbian brethren would strengthen the United Nations commitment to its sanctions. Economic hardship endangered his hold on power, as discontent deepened among the citizenry.

A word must be said about the unexpected metamorphosis of the Croatian military. The Clinton state department lifted a page from Vietnam and other wars by training indigenous fighters to conduct military operations in lieu of GIs. This new version used a private firm rather than Pentagon military trainers. The State Department licensed a private American company, Military Professional Resources Incorporated (MPRI), based in Alexandria, Virginia. Retired US officers and NCOs worked with the ramshackle Croatian forces. MPRI shaped up Croatia's disorganized army into a force capable of integrating advancing infantry, air strikes, and artillery barrages in what became described as textbook coordination and maneuver warfare.[52]

Two consequences flowed from the novel approach. First, the American-trained Croatian armed forces vanquished the heretofore invincible Serb military – a myth the Serbians broadcasted to enhance their prowess on the battlefield. The revamped Croatian army dramatically reordered the war, shattering Serb dominance and opening the region for a possible peace settlement. Second, Washington's strategy of Croatian blitzkrieg warfare had downside consequences. It violated the UN ceasefire and resulted in a new round of atrocities, as Croat soldiers paid back the earlier atrocities committed by their Serb enemies. Fresh waves of refugees – this time Serbs – took to the roads for safety. Some Croatian officers were indicted for war crimes during the counterattack.

Thanks to their victim status after years of Serb brutality, Croats generally got less scrutiny for their sword-and-fire tactics.

The United States and MPRI also came under scrutiny for their role in training the Croat armed forces. Both tried to defuse the charges of complicity with the Croatian troops by maintaining that their instruction contained lessons on democratic values and proper battlefield conduct. The defense was less than convincing, but world interest turned soon enough to the end of the fighting and the negotiations at Dayton.[53] The Croatian victory also pointed toward the war's end.

The Clinton White House took heart at the turnaround on the long-stalemated battlefield in mid-1995. It now figured that the Bosnian War could be brought to a peaceful termination. President Clinton himself personally interceded. Months earlier, he appointed a former foreign service officer and Wall Streeter, Richard Holbrooke, to serve as Washington's point man in the Balkans. An indefatigable negotiator, the new assistant secretary of state for European affairs undertook shuttle diplomacy among the regional capitals. The US foreign policy team mounted a major diplomatic effort in the summer. Misreading the tea leaves, the Serbs surrounding Sarajevo lobbed another mortar round into city, killing thirty-eight people. Washington interpreted the attack as a calculated affront to its orchestrated peace initiative and hit out at the provocation.

It struck back with Operation Deliberate Force. Scores of Tomahawk missiles and sixty warplanes assaulted from the aircraft carrier USS *Theodore Roosevelt*, flying from the Adriatic Sea and from a US airbase in Italy. British and French artillery joined in the barrage on Bosnian Serb fortifications, radar sites, and storage facilities. Washington was willing to launch air strikes but opposed to fielding land forces, which might incur casualties. Occurring at the same time as the Croat and Bosniaks' counter-offensive, the NATO bombardments functioned almost as air support for the ground campaign. By the time Washington prevailed on the warring parties to break off fighting, the Serbs lost about 25 percent of the land they had held in Bosnia-Herzegovina.

The Bosnian Serbs encircling Sarajevo hunkered down to ride out the bombing blitz. But Milošević, the Machiavellian strongman, realized the dangers to his survival. He prodded Holbrooke to call off the shelling, which stopped after two weeks. NATO bombing and pressure from Milošević forced the Bosnian Serb government in Pale to lift the Sarajevo siege. Pale also surrendered to Belgrade's demands for "virtually total power over the fate of the Bosnian Serbs" in negotiations with the United States.[54]

The air strikes marked a visible reinvigoration of American diplomacy in the Atlantic alliance, which had languished for much of the Bosnian

War. Seeing that the altered facts on the ground shifted the diplomatic prospects for a settlement, Washington convened a Geneva meeting in early September 1995 of the Contact Group, plus representatives from parties in the conflict. At the summit, the Muslim-Croat Federation received 51 percent of the former Bosnia Herzegovina republic. The Republika Srpska settled for 49 percent of the territory. Setting the exact boundaries was left to a future conclave. Advised by Holbrooke's team, the White House worked to engage and reassure Boris Yeltsin, the Russian president, in the upcoming peace talks by sending the leaders of Croatia and Bosnia-Herzegovina to make Moscow a stakeholder in the deliberations.

Finally, the United States secured Moscow's assent to deploying Russian peacekeeping soldiers in any prospective bargain among the warring sides, thereby anchoring Russia's participation in the future deal. Thus, Russian and American troops would cooperate for the first time since World War II. US foreign policy advisers chose Hyde Park, President Franklin Roosevelt's former residence, to host the mid-October Clinton-Yeltsin talks, because the Russian president, like many of his countrymen, considered America's thirty-second president a Soviet ally during World War II.[55] Clinton also assuaged Yeltsin's aversion to the presence of NATO and the US defense forces into what was Russia's orbit. Later, Washington applied the lessons learned from the Balkan settlement to calm Yeltsin about the 1996 invitations to Hungary, Poland, and the Czech Republic for NATO membership. NATO's joint-peacekeeping mission to safeguard the Dayton Accords celebrated three firsts for the Atlantic alliance: (1) its first joint operation deploying non-alliance troops, the Russians, and others outside the organization; (2) its first post–Cold War mission; and (3) its first out-of-area military operation.

Washington, therefore, laid the military foundation for what was anticipated to be contentious negotiations among the Balkan players, beginning on November 1, 1995, at Wright-Patterson Air Force Base in Dayton, Ohio. Indeed, Holbrooke and his team shuttled from room to room to negotiate with delegates because face-to-face talks would end in shouting matches. Selected for its relative remoteness from the Washington media circus, to minimize leaks about the deliberations, Dayton hosted the twenty-one-day meeting, which nearly broke down in acrimony over the Contact Group's allocation of territory. At the conclusion, Bosnia-Herzegovina hung onto its allocated 49 percent, even if some of it was unpopulated areas filled with scrub bushes and rocks.

The Dayton Accord was signed in the Élysée Palace in Paris on December 14, 1995. It ended the worst hostilities in Europe since World War II and the worst war crimes in the West since the

Holocaust. The Bosnian War claimed about 140,000 lives and displaced two million people from their homes. Eight months before Dayton, the freewheeling Holbrooke termed the Balkan agony the "greatest collective security failure of the West since the 1930s."[56] As for Holbrooke's role, like a master of Rubik's Cube, he managed to fit in all the squares without any popping out at Dayton.

The next step to stanch the flow of blood necessitated military enforcement of the peace accord in what became a *pax*-NATO. US troops crossed the Sava River from Croatia into Bosnia-Herzegovina to assume their peace-soldiering duties on December 31, 1995, in what was to have been a one-year commitment. Washington extended the deadline nine times until late 2004, when the European Union took up the mission. Twenty thousand US troops participated in the Implementation Force, which comprised a total of 60,000 soldiers. IFOR differed from most peacekeeping missions, where UN forces strolled among reconciled populations. IFOR, instead, behaved like an army of occupation among hostile inhabitants. Its heavy armaments and sheer large numbers moved William Perry, the US secretary of defense, to brand IFOR as "the biggest and toughest and meanest dog in town."[57] As violent incidents and acts of hostility tampered off, IFOR became redubbed as the Stabilization Force, or SFOR, to more accurately reflect its softer-edged role.

On the heels of the American-led humanitarian intervention, a different type of military operation got underway. It was a pursuit of over 160 war criminals, mainly civilian or military leaders, who ordered atrocities against Croats or Bosniaks. The guilty also included the Bosniaks, who tortured and killed Serbs. The apprehensions of those accused of war crimes went beyond the normal cops-and-robbers arrests that police officers conduct against lawbreakers. Because the perpetrators were under heavy guard and secreted from one safe house to another, routine law enforcement procedures seemed insufficient. The Pentagon dispatched Delta Force operators and members of SEAL Team 6 to the Balkans for the manhunts. They acted on informant tips and CIA intelligence. Along with French, German, and Polish commandos, the American super-elite teams made numerous arrests for the International Criminal Tribunal for the former Yugoslavia.[58]

At The Hague, those guilty of mass killings received extended jail sentences in what turned out to be the most effective round up of the blackest villains of that age. Although American generals and politicians over-scripted the deployment of military forces to southeastern Europe to avoid military casualties, US troops in all branches experienced combat-simulated environments. The mocking designation of MOOTW fails to recognize the usefulness of the exercises, not to mention all the training gained from fielding forces to distant airbases, seas, and land redoubts. Special Ops teams honed their manhunting skills, preparing them to take down al-Qaeda figures and other terrorists in the post-9/11 world.

Vindicated and empowered by its progress in Bosnia, Clinton's White House decided the next year to enshrine democracy promotion in its 1996 National Security Strategy. Three years before, Anthony Lake, the National Security Adviser, had broached a "successor doctrine to containment" in a speech at Johns Hopkins University. He argued for a policy to "enlarge the family of democratic market economies."[59] Incorporating Lake's ideas, the new National Security Strategy called for international engagement and democracy enlargement because they stood "to improve the prospects for political stability, peaceful conflict resolution, and greater dignity and hope for the people of the world."[60] It clearly sets forth one of the themes of this book that post-Wall America sought to reshape the world in its democratic image by political persuasion or military means after the USSR disappeared.

Peace temporarily descended over the war-torn Balkans. The cessation of hostilities could only be a short-lived tranquility so long as ethnoreligious tensions simmered just beneath the surface and Milošević remained in power. Before the next violent chapter opened, United States had dispelled the widespread perception of its waffling and indecision. President Clinton moved beyond the "ad hocism" that characterized his first years in office. American leadership no longer appeared ineffectual and supine. American military power, in fact, ensured stability and peace in a conflict-shattered patch of southeastern Europe. Perhaps just as important, Euro-American tensions abated after the worst period since the Suez Crisis in 1956. Ambassador Holbrooke commented on the turnaround when he wrote: "Washington was now praised for its firm leadership – or even chided by some Europeans for the too *much* leadership."[61] That newfound leadership role was soon tested.

3.9   Kosovo: The Second Balkan War

The United States reaped little more than a respite following the Dayton Accord. Indeed, it seemed as if America simply segued from the Bosnian War to the one in Kosovo. The tiny Serb-ruled province would occasion the fiercest air campaign since the Persian Gulf War. Yet the Connecticut-sized entity was noticeably absent from the intense negotiations in Dayton for sound reasons. Bringing Kosovo into the deliberations was viewed by Washington as a certain deal breaker. It was too hot a political potato to handle, given the other nettlesome matters. At the twilight of his presidency, George H. W. Bush warned Slobodan

Milošević not to widen the Bosnian War into Kosovo or the United States would resort to military force.[62] That threat and the Serb's own motives postponed the day of reckoning.

The Serbian dictator and his compatriots regarded the territory as the birthplace of the Serbian nation. It was the revered site of the epic fourteenth-century battle in which Serbian knights fell to the invading Turkish hordes, ushering in centuries of draconian Muslim rule and forced conversion to Islam. By the end of the twentieth century, Kosovo's population of nearly two million people was close to 90 percent Muslim Albanian. Its Orthodox Christian Serbs were a decided minority despite their nearly mystical attachment to the land-locked province. Their brethren in Serbia and Bosnia-Herzegovina shared in the ethnic-religious affinity to Kosovo. The Serbs, therefore, vehemently opposed an independent and sovereign Kosovo.

Soon after keeping Kosovo off the Dayton table, President Clinton's foreign policy officials returned to the Kosovo issue as well as the maligned Milošević dictatorship. They first selected non-military methods to weaponize against the Belgrade government. Economic sanctions designed to change the behavior of governments became coercive instruments with all American presidencies after the fall of the Berlin Wall. In Clinton's case, Washington barred the return of the rump Federal Republic of Yugoslavia (FRY) (Serbia, Montenegro, and Kosovo) to membership in the International Monetary Fund and the World Bank for its ongoing misrule in Kosovo. This decision excluded the FRY from borrowing funds desperately needed to rebuild and adapt its aging economy to the post-Soviet era. West European governments, however, preferred economic and diplomatic engagement with the recalcitrant Serbia as means to peacefully undermine Milošević's rule while making the tyrant irrelevant in an increasingly globalized world. Washington, instead, hung tough toward the Serb regime, as it did against Cuba, North Korea, Iraq, and Iran.

Kosovo may have seemed a tranquil island during the Bosnian hurricane, but its domestic politics smoldered beneath the surface, leading to a political eruption. Its aspirations for national sovereignty rekindled with the Berlin Wall's collapse.[63] One of the first manifestations of a budding nationalism cropped up with the formation of the moderate Democratic League of Kosovo (made familiar by its Albanian initials, LDK) in December 1989. Its academic orientation was emphasized with the selection of its first president, Ibrahim Rugova, a professor of Albanian literature, by his colleagues in attendance at the initial meeting. The Serb authorities and security forces recognized the LDK's moderation by allowing it to function openly.[64] Like the democratic movements forming in Central Europe at the same time, the moderate LDK endorsed a peaceful transition from the crumbling communist edifice to free elections and democratic rule. Political unrest developed slowly, in part, thanks to the LDK's monopoly over Kosovar politics.[65]

The LDK's restraint and reformist agenda did not sit well with more rebellious and nationalistic voices within Kosovo, who hated their Serb masters. These disgruntled Kosovars formed small independent cells that began surreptitiously to coalesce into a movement that became known as the Kosovo Liberation Army (KLA). Kosovars were radicalized by the Dayton Accord, for it left Kosovo in Serb hands. When the European Union diplomatically recognized the Federal Republic of Yugoslavia (in which Kosovo was included), it froze the status quo without addressing the Kosovars' longings for freedom. Next, the Belgrade government exacerbated tension by settling Serbs in Kosovo from areas ethnically cleansed by Croatian forces. The arriving "colonists" presence further inflamed Kosovar resentment.

KLA gunmen fired on Serbian security forces and arriving Serbian settlers. Isolated attacks gave way to a spiraling insurgency. The Kosovo conflict differed from the Bosnian set-piece battles of entrenched positions and sieges against the safe areas and Sarajevo. In Kosovo, the KLA mounted hit-and-run ambushes rather than defending trenches and artillery. Like insurgents the world over, they committed atrocities, dispersed, and melted into the population or hid out in the sticks after attacks. The insurgents benefited from fleeing into neighboring Albania, where they regrouped, trained, and rearmed. Milošević's forces struck back at their shadow enemy with heavy-handed tactics of mass reprisals against suspected insurgents and their livestock. With heaps of irony, Milošević, who promised the United States another Vietnam if it invaded Serbia, found himself mired in his own insurgency-plagued morass in Kosovo.

As violence flared, Western capitals paid closer attention to the Muslim-dominated enclave. Grabbing international headlines served one of the KLA's objectives. Another was to portray its struggle as one worthy of American and European sympathy and intervention. The killings, refugee-clogged roads, and grandiose proclamations did, in fact, spark unease in Washington, London, and Paris. KLA pronouncements about fashioning a Greater Albania from unhappy Albanians in Montenegro and Macedonia, plus Kosovo, also heightened anxieties in Western foreign ministries. They feared that the KLA terror campaign would draw in neighboring states, igniting the Balkan tinderbox. The Milošević regime played up Western fears. It characterized the KLA as an Islamist terrorist network with pan-Albanian ethnic intentions.

Despite Western apprehensions, Osama bin Laden more than once reflected on the difficulties of insinuating a substantial number of militants into Orthodox Serbia or Catholic Croatia.[66]

The United States, in response to Milošević's blood-and-soil nationalism, reestablished the Contact Group (again with Britain, France, Germany, Russia) to confront the new crisis. The Western members slapped sanctions on the FRY but Russia conducted business with it as usual. Again, Moscow deemed Serbia, with its Orthodox religion and Western hostility, as a partner, not an adversary. The Kremlin also regarded NATO advancements eastward into its near-abroad with anger and loathing. Nor could the United States corral its NATO allies into a military intervention against Serbia to halt Belgrade's murderous policies in Kosovo without United Nation's authorization. The Clinton administration knew that Russia and China, as two of the five permanent members on the Security Council, were certain to veto any military action. Washington tried diplomacy with Richard Holbrooke as the US representative to the UN. Holbrooke's peacemaking summit between Milošević and Rugova boomeranged when the LDK leader appeared to appease the truculent, steely Serb leader. The KLA got a boost from Rugova's setback because Kosovars now saw the militant faction as their best bet for sovereignty. So did Milošević, who dug in his heels.

With few real cards to play, the Clinton White House turned back to the threat of military power. At the urging of the United States, NATO's defense ministers convened in Brussels in mid-June 1998 to plan for armed action against Serb security units in Kosovo. As it turned out, Milošević was less than impressed. He had become blasé to the West's lines in the sand, which Europe blurred with lengthy meetings, procrastination, and overall hesitancy to deploy military forces. He banked on the European aversion to the use of military action without Security Council approval. Washington did gain the European Union's cooperation in prohibiting international business with the FRY and barring airlines from landing at airfields in Serbia and Montenegro.

In a politically risky gamble, the Clinton administration prodded NATO to at least opt for a display of airpower to warn the Serbian ruler. The member states went along with Washington's pleas. NATO lofted eighty warplanes under restrictive guideless on June 15, 1998. So as to avoid transgressing Serbia's air space, Operation Determined Falcon directed that the military aircraft jet over neighboring Albania and Macedonia. The Serb ground forces paid the thundering planes little heed as they went about their business of menacing Kosovars.

Russia did take notice, for it resented the Atlantic alliance's breach of its sphere of influence. The Clinton state department strove to keep Boris

Yeltsin in America's corner, however. Although known as a hard drinker, Yeltsin was more amiable than other hard-line Russian civilian and military officials. Washington greased the wheels at the IMF for a $10 billion loan to the Yeltsin government just prior to the Russian presidential election, in which the onetime Politburo member won reelection for a second term. The Clinton bet paid off, as the United States and the Russian Federation agreed to share information on missile launches and to trim weapons-grade plutonium from their respective stockpiles. The US leader worked to co-opt his Russian counterpart to rein in Milošević's excessive bloodletting. Yeltsin agreed with Clinton "that Serb government must stop all repressive actions ... and pursue an interim settlement."[67]

The Washington administration was still divided on how to handle Milošević. Madeleine Albright considered the Serb tyrant as the root of the Kosovo crisis. The secretary of state bumped up against a cautious Defense Department, which wanted no part of slipping into another bitter insurgency a la Vietnam. After William Perry returned to Stanford University, the new secretary of defense, William Cohen, agreed with his risk-averse military chiefs and conveyed their thinking to the Oval Office. Not to be out done, Albright picked up the backing for military action from General Wesley Clark, the Supreme Allied Commander in Europe (SACEUR). The SACEUR also headed up NATO military forces. In time, Holbrooke joined the hawks, seeing the Serbian chief as an impendent to any settlement in Kosovo.

Meanwhile, NATO ambassadors meeting in Portugal adopted OPLAN 10601 on September 24, 1998, which closely mapped out an air operation to ensure Serbia's full compliance with UN Security Council Resolution 1199, which demanded all parties "immediately cease hostilities" while it reaffirmed "the sovereignty and territorial integrity of the Federal Republic of Yugoslavia."[68] Thereupon, the Pentagon readied aircraft in its European bases and deployed B-52 bombers to British airfields.

An iron ring was tightening around an isolated Serbia. Amidst the US military preparation, nonetheless, a domestic scandal deflected the White House's concentration on a miniscule enclave in the Balkans. US foreign policy took a backseat through much of 1998 because President Clinton faced a political crisis over a sexual encounter with White House intern Monica Lewinsky. Republicans in the House of Representatives impeached Clinton but the Senate in its trial of the president acquitted him of all charges on February 12, 1999. With the start of a new year and a new lease on political life, the Clinton foreign policy advisers doubled down on the raging Kosovar firestorm.

Having grown weary of the troublesome Milošević, the Kremlin signaled a dramatic reversal in its hard-and-fast defense of Belgrade. During
a meeting of the Contract Group the previous October, Igor Ivanov, the
Kremlin's foreign minister, made an astounding declaration. If NATO
went ahead militarily against Serbia without UN approval, then Moscow
would only publicly denounce the attack. In short, the Russian
Federation would stand aside without countering the Atlantic alliance's
military operation.[69] Armed with what seemed like a greenlight for a
NATO combat offensive, Holbrooke returned to bend Milošević to his
will. The wily autocrat agreed to NATO overflights to monitor ground
activities, to the presence of unarmed international observers from the
Organization of Security and Cooperation in Europe (OSCE) to protect
Kosovars, and to the pullout 4,000 paramilitary police.[70] In the end, the
2,000 OSCE monitors proved useless to halt Serb killings of Kosovars
and were withdrawn before the bombing started. The agreement did
temporally spare Serbia from an air bombardment – Milošević's goal.

Russia's pledge to stand aside emboldened the KLA insurgents, who
infiltrated back into their deserted positions. They also stepped up
attacks on Serb security forces, which infuriated Belgrade. To counter
the Kosovar inroads, the Serbs launched Operation Horseshoe in
December 1998. This bloody offensive multiplied murders, livestock
deaths, and torched farmhouses, resulting in a half a million Kosovars
fleeing their homes for safety in other parts of the province or neighboring countries. A Serb paramilitary unit, the Scorpions, committed its
share of atrocities. One particularly chilling incident took place near the
Račak village, where Serb killers shot to death some forty-five Kosovar
civilians. The international outrage about Račak turned into a rallying cry
for action.

Secretary of State Albright seized on the furor over the massacre to
push for measures against Serbia. She won over her peers in the Contact
Group to summon both the Milošević regime and the Kosovar leaders to
send representatives to negotiations to be held at a fourteenth-century
chateau in Rambouillet, a town thirty miles south of Paris on February 6,
1999. Both combatants agreed to attend out of fear of being excluded
from protecting their interests in a settlement. The Kosovar delegates
selected Hashim Thaçi, a founder of KLA, as their head, displacing the
moderate Ibrahim Rugova. Since Milošević feared arrest for war crimes,
he sent Serbia's deputy prime minister to the talks but called the shots
over the telephone from Belgrade.

The Rambouillet negotiations failed to reach a settlement satisfactory to
the Federal Republic of Yugoslavia because the accord granted far more
autonomy to Kosovo than Milošević deemed justifiable. His rejection

formed the basis of NATO's going to war against the FRY. The Kosovars, Americans, and British accepted the Rambouillet Accord, while the Serbs and Russians walked away. The accord outlined a 30,000-troop NATO administration of an autonomous Kosovo still within the FRY framework.

A particular bitter pill for Belgrade was the accord's Annex B, which authorized NATO troops, "vehicles, vessels, aircraft free and unrestricted passage and unimpeded access throughout the Federal Republic of Yugoslavia," not confined to just Kosovo.[71] Annex B, in Belgrade's view, conspicuously trampled on Serbian sovereignty. The terms were tantamount to a declaration of war. Henry Kissinger, President Richard Nixon's secretary of state, judged that "the Rambouillet text ... was a provocation, an excuse to start bombing."[72] Led by Thaçi, the Kosovo delegation signed the accord in Paris on March 18th. Boxed in by humanitarian considerations and West European expectations, Clinton's America fought to stabilize a turbulent region and to remove Milošević, who stood as an impediment to peace and democracy.

3.10   The White House's Home Campaign

The White House steeled itself for another round in the Balkans. President Clinton came around to the prospect of wading back into southeastern Europe. The Bosnian War schooled him on the area, players, and use of military power for political outcomes.[73] Weeks before the Paris signing of the accord, the West Wing waged a political offensive to line up congressional authority for an American-led NATO bombardment. It was not an uphill campaign, for Milošević and his atrocities were well publicized in the United States. Ground troops were ruled out because the president worried about casualties undermining support for the war. The Senate voted for air strikes by a bipartisan majority of 58-41 on March 23. Earlier in the month, the House voted 219 to 119 to authorize the dispatch of US military forces, after implementation of a peace settlement, as Clinton requested.[74]

Before sketching the conduct of the Kosovo air war, it is necessary to outline the justification for attacking a state that never directly threatened the security of its neighbors or the United States. Foremost among the two rationales for unleashing air strikes was the concept of preventive warfare. Like the firefighters resort to the "control burn" to contain a conflagration, the United States and its NATO partners sought to cauterize the Serbian wound before it sucked in outside states, leading to a major war in the Balkans. Russian, Bulgarian, Turkish, and Greek handwringing about the fate of their religious brethren during the explosive Kosovo crisis gave rise to fears of hostilities of a greater magnitude.

President Clinton voiced this apprehension as the bombs started to fall: "Let a fire burn there in this area and the flames will spread."[75]

A secondary justification for going to war over Kosovo sprang from humanitarian and democratic governance considerations. Media images of refugees and corpses galvanized anti-Serb sentiments. At the time, interventionist proponents defended the aerial bombardment by invoking the just war texts of St. Thomas Aquinas.[76] Milošević's obstinacy played into Albright's calculations and united his NATO opponents. The White House and NATO ginned up pro-war sentiment with only moderate success. American public opinion stood at just over 40 percent for the air campaign before its start. Once underway, support rose to 61 percent at mid-point before falling off as the air war dragged on for weeks.[77] One means used to build public approval involved the last-ditch peace bid by Richard Holbrooke, who visited Belgrade at the eleventh hour. The indefatigable mediator left empty handed; Milošević made no meaningful concessions. Secretary Albright's consistent hard-line stance toward Serbia led to wags calling the lengthy Kosovo bombing "Madeleine's War."

3.11   Kosovo's Lengthy Bombardment

NATO bombers, led by US warplanes, commenced their destructive attacks on March 24, 1999, without a Security Council resolution, because Russia and China pledged to veto the military operation. Labeled a humanitarian intervention, the ultimately 1,000-warplane operation first took out military infrastructure in Serbia and Montenegro. American airpower, the dominant force in NATO, operated from bases in Germany and Italy, from which F-15s and F-16s flew. Sailing in the Adriatic Sea, the aircraft carrier USS *Theodore Roosevelt* launched wave after wave of F-14 Tomcats while other surface ships and submarines fired Tomahawk missiles at heavily defended shore-based installations.

Three days after pulverizing the Serb's strategic military aim points, Operation Allied Force turned to bombing economic infrastructure and symbolic targets, including power stations, bridges, water purifying plants, industrial factories, and other civilian complexes or historical monuments.[78] Death estimates for those on the ground vary from a low of 489 people to a high of over 2,000.[79] NATO suffered no combat fatalities among its thousands of sorties. But Yugoslav ground-to-air missiles downed two American advanced fighters – an F-117 Nighthawk and an F-16 Fighting Falcon – out of which the pilots ejected safely and were rescued before falling into Serb hands. After eleven weeks, the Milošević regime threw in the towel and accepted the imposition of foreign soldiers in Kosovo.

Notwithstanding the massive destruction perpetrated on the FRY and NATO's ultimate, lopsided victory, the Kosovo air war encompassed flaws and organizational turmoil not apparent from the above sketch. To start with, the air campaign lengthened far beyond anticipation. Expectations were that Belgrade would capitulate not in a matter of weeks but days, as happened during the Bosnian War four years earlier. On a television news program, the first night of the bombing, America's top diplomat, Madeleine Albright, confidently predicted: "It is not something that's going on for an overly long time." The next day, in words she would later regret, the secretary of state reaffirmed the bombardment would be over in a "relatively short period of time."[80]

There were many explanations for the longer than envisioned air war. Execution of the operation was "hampered by uncooperative weather and a surprisingly resilient opponent." According to a thorough analysis prepared for the US Air Force, other lapses and shortcomings accounted for the less-than-optimal outcome. These included "persistence hesitancy on the part of US and NATO decision-makers that was prompted by fears of inadvertently killing civilians and losing friendly aircrews." Furthermore, there were, in the words of airpower expert Benjamin Lambeth, "sharp differences of opinion within most command elements over the best way of applying allied air power against Serb elements."[81]

Exponents of airpower nearly always advocate a massive opening onslaught rather than a gradual application of bombardment. Instead of delivering a knockout punch at the outset, Operation Allied Force dribbled out with some 400 planes before approaching 1,000 aircraft. For comparison, the Gulf War, a decade earlier, opened with over 2,700 sorties in the first twenty-four hours.[82] Frustrated with the operation's inability to hit entrenched and elusive Yugoslav Army positions, NATO's supreme commander, General Clark, requested 300 additional planes at the end of the third week of bombing, which brought the total up to near the final 1,000 level.[83] The United States committed 60 percent of the aircraft. In second place was France, which put nearly a hundred aircraft in the sky.

The allies' 40 percent contribution fell short of ensuring harmony among the participants. The major cause of disunity stemmed from target selection. The allies squabbled over the utility of striking dual-use civilian-military targets or army installations close to noncombatant populations. Before hitting such targets, US generals needed approval from their peers in the militaries of France and Britain. The French often stonewalled the process before eventually acquiescing. Overcoming Gallic objections resulted in frustrating and time-consuming appeals necessitating General Clark's personal intervention to secure a green light. The NATO supreme military chief sometimes second-guessed his own subordinates in their choice of targets, abetting the prolongation of the overall campaign.

A genuine philosophical division lay at heart of the Franco-American divide over the choice of targets designated for destruction. Since World War II's strategic bombing, American airpower doctrine advocated annihilation of an enemy's industrial capacity, not just obliteration of its strictly military sites. The US military wanted a sharp, short aerial campaign. France, on the other hand, embraced a limited-bombing roll out to minimize damage and to speed the postwar recovery, reconstruction, reconciliation, and return of Serbia to mainstream European political values of democracy and peace.[84] By contrast, a flattened Serbia might follow the resentful, bitter trajectory of post–World War I Germany, causing decades of problems in Eastern Europe. The Pentagon fretted that a lengthy operation allowed the Belgrade government to adapt and survive. A protracted conflict provided more opportunities for sharper inter-allied factionalism and for hotter anti-NATO protests, which had already been occurring in major cities around the world. Belgrade fueled the anti-bombing demonstrations by publishing a volume, *NATO Crimes in Yugoslavia*, replete with gruesome photographs of charred bodies and hair-raising accounts by survivors.[85]

On top of the increasingly controversial bombing campaign came a horrendous mistake. America's B-2 stealth bombers inadvertently dropped five 2,000-pound, satellite-guided bombs on the People's Republic of China's embassy in Belgrade on May 7th. The explosions killed three among the embassy staff and wounded twenty more. The supersonic jets intended their ordinance for a Serb arms center. The error was traced to the use of an old map, which failed to note the new location of the Chinese embassy. The Beijing regime dismissed the explanation and fanned street protests against the United States in China. The raucous demonstrators ended up imprisoning the US ambassador, James Sasser, in the American Embassy and damaging the building. President Clinton apologized for the mistake and reached a financial settlement with China for a new structure in Belgrade and for the three dead diplomats. Beijing, in turn, paid Washington $2.87 million for the rioters' damage to its embassy. The misjudgment remained a sore point in Sino-American relations for years.

As the air war dragged on, coalition relations fluctuated between highs and lows. Unlike the Persian Gulf War, where the United States dominated the coalition as the prime mover in orchestrating the intervention, the Kosovo War was fought by a NATO partnership from the outset. True, America was *primus inter pares*, but not the sole decision-making power. For the Gulf War, Washington organized the coalition. For Kosovo, NATO was in charge. The consensus-seeking format and collective decision-making almost guaranteed bickering, friction, and misunderstandings among the allies. Tensions simmering beneath the surface boiled over as the conflict lengthened and claimed more and more civilian lives and structures. Germany and France joined Greece and Italy in voicing disenchantment with the course of the air attacks. Paris, always sensitive to American "hyperpower," called for Washington's special tending. President Clinton cajoled Jacques Chirac, his French counterpart, to soothe relations with France. To ensure unity, Clinton involved himself in NATO's fiftieth anniversary summit in Washington in April. NATO hung together at the meeting despite tensions among the players. And as two analysts observed, the summit succeeded, "if only because it did not fail."[86]

The United States also ran into more formidable diplomatic troubles with Russia over NATO's eastward encroachments. Russian protestors demonstrated outside the US Embassy in Moscow. Members in the Duma spoke for sending "volunteers" and military aid to the FRY. The Kremlin even pulled its representative from NATO as a sign of opposition. President Yeltsin's government also appealed to individual NATO members to shut down the bombing. Strobe Talbott, the US deputy secretary of state who dealt almost exclusively with Moscow, later recalled that the Kosovo bombardment "was to be the most severe, dangerous, and consequential crisis in US-Russian relations in the post–cold war period."[87] When the April NATO summit sidestepped fragmentation, Yeltsin became more open to dealing with Clinton, especially since Russia wanted Western financial largesse to continue. Besides, the Kremlin held Milošević's intransigence, in part, responsible for inviting the prospect of NATO troops entering Kosovo. Russian officials preferred to defenestrate him but worried about a popular backlash. So, they looked for someone else "to accept the sword of surrender from Milošević," as one Russian higher-up colorfully phrased it.[88]

American and Russian interlocutors put together a mechanism to consult and to press Milošević to see that his best interests lay with a negotiated settlement. They brought on Finland's President Martti Ahtisaari from a non-NATO country to aid in talks. But since Moscow held the most clout with Milošević, it had to pull the laboring oar to convince him to cut his losses. The Serb leader resented NATO's insistence of a total withdrawal of his 50,000-troop army and paramilitary police. He also resisted acceptance of a NATO "at the core" peacekeeping force inside Kosovo at the end of the conflict. Failure to acquiesce meant that sooner or later NATO was going to march into Serbia.

As the weeks passed without a suspension in the aerial-delivered death and destruction, the Serbian people's morale sank. Their initial Serbian patriotic defiance of NATO bombardment buckled. War weariness and anxiety darkened the public's spirits. Lacking hope of victory, fearing the loss of Russian backing, and facing a likely war on Serbian soil, the Milošević regime grasped the available settlement terms.[89] There was no way to square the circle of retaining power and retaining Kosovo as part of the FRY. The Serb autocrat chose holding onto power.

More salient than the population's flagging morale in Milošević's decision to throw in the towel was the prospect of a NATO ground invasion into FRY proper. At the start of bombing operation, President Clinton ruled out a land intervention when he proclaimed: "I do not intend to put our troops in Kosovo to fight a war."[90] Clinton spoke to alleviate anxieties on the home front about casualties. His comments, no doubt, lessened Belgrade's worries, to boot. But air power alone seemed to falter in spite of almost daily reassurances from the Pentagon that Serbian capitulation was just a matter of time.

Desperation gripped the Clinton administration as the air campaign lengthened over weeks. The president publicly reversed himself on May 18: "[W]e have not and will not take any option off the table."[91] His National Security Council let it be known that it was looking at a land war. Finally, on June 2, the media reported that the president had scheduled a meeting the next day with the Joint Chiefs at the White House "to discuss options for using ground troops if NATO decides to invade Kosovo."[92] No ground intervention took place because Serbia quit the war on June 3, 1999.

The looming threat to deploy land forces proved to be the last straw for the Milošević regime.[93] The Belgrade leader knew a NATO land invasion would destroy his army and security forces. Without this pillar, his dictatorship would have succumbed to internal opposition, which existed since the early 1990s. The Clinton administration's mistake lay in not fielding land forces in neighboring countries at the beginning of the air war while hurling missiles and satellite bombs at FRY targets. Without a menacing land-based army, Serb generals could carry on their fight with the KLA with virtual impunity. The US error conformed to past cases of deploying insufficient power to conduct a mission in an expeditious and victorious way. In both Panama and Somalia, insufficient forces and firepower translated into trouble for the combat personnel on the ground. Similar failings took place in subsequent campaigns.

Milošević's acceptance of NATO's terms halted the air campaign on June 9th. The Security Council then passed Resolution 1244, which authorized the entry of NATO forces into Kosovo and placed the beleaguered province under United Nations supervision. The UN postponed pronouncing the final status of Kosovo, which left it in limbo for years. The same resolution set up the UN Interim Administration Mission in Kosovo. UNMIK facilitated the return of refugees, presided over civilian administrative functions, and coordinated humanitarian relief from governments and nongovernmental organizations. Before NATO bombs stopped falling, the Atlantic alliance needed to nail down a consensus on its occupation of Kosovo and the Serb pullout. To hammer out this agreement, the NATO representative, British General Mike Jackson, started negotiations with Serb generals in neighboring Macedonia on June 2nd. They reached an agreement in a week after the talks initially bogged down in a replay of earlier sticking points. The Serb signature on the Military Technical Agreement, which spelled out the cessation of hostilities, timetables for FRY withdrawal, and other tactical provisions, ended the eleven-week war.[94]

While explosions still rocked the Serbian countryside, the Russians pursued their own two goals. Moscow dreamed of an exclusive sector in Kosovo and its own military command outside of NATO control. Washington held firmly against these Kremlin demands. It opposed another divided county as came about during the Cold War, with Serbs migrating to the north and Albanian Muslims moving to the south.[95] Washington also believed unrealistically in an ethnically mixed Kosovo. Russian negotiators came around to a halfway solution to their extravagant notion of their own non-NATO military structure. The Americans opened a channel for Russian forces to report to the US command, not NATO. Because it had no love lost for Milošević, Moscow worked with Washington to rein him in but it had its own agenda as well.

When they least expected it, Moscow made an end run around the bargain it struck with the United States and its Atlantic allies. Two days after the Serbs signed the Military Technical Agreement, the Kremlin rolled the dice by rushing a contingent of 200 Russian paratroopers into Kosovo. The troops peeled away from the NATO-led Stabilization Force, which had been stationed in Bosnia and Herzegovina after the signing of the Dayton agreement. Breaking SFOR's mandate requiring four-months notification for a pullout, the Russians raced overland in military vehicles into Priština, Kosovo's capital city, where jubilant Serbs cheered what they saw as their liberators. Then the Russian soldiers barreled into the Priština airport, with the goal of carving out their own territorial sector, as the Red Army had accomplished by seizing Berlin in the closing days of WWII. Compounding Moscow's cavalier maneuver was Kremlin duplicity. Igor Ivanov, the Russian foreign minister, reassured Madeleine Albright that the Russian soldiers were not headed toward Kosovo, when, in fact, they were dashing toward the province.

Once at the Priština airport, the Russian military presence prompted an international confrontation. Both NATO and the Russians hastened to bolster their footholds at the airfield. The Kremlin prepared to fly more paratroopers but miscalculated its own political reach. Bulgaria, Hungary, and Romania denied Russia flyover authorization, thereby precluding the Kremlin's airborne option to strong-point its advance unit. The United States also held a weak hand; it had unwisely held back on transporting troops into Kosovo until after the Military Technical Agreement was signed. US General Wesley Clark, the military head of NATO, turned to two British companies under command of the British three-star General Mike Jackson, to obstruct the airport runways to prohibit any Russian planes from landing. After consulting with his higher-ups in Britain, Jackson refused to take "any more orders from Washington." When Clark replied that he and NATO Secretary General Javier Solana were ordering Jackson in the name of the Atlantic alliance, the British officer famously replied: "I'm not starting World War III for you."[96]

The crisis quickly passed as cooler heads intervened in London, Washington, and Moscow. NATO's 50,000-troop Kosovo Force rolled across the border from the Republic of Macedonia (now known as the Republic of North Macedonia) to take up peacekeeping duties in the turbulent province. A 3,500-strong military and civilian KFOR still maintains peace in Kosovo, albeit restructured and streamlined over the years to devolve responsibilities into local hands. A combination of airpower and land-war threats brought the Kosovo War to a close, but not before over 13,000 people lost their lives and well over a million fled their homes for safety.

The Kosovo War sealed Milošević's fate. As a Cesar Borgia–like figure dependent not on a pope but Russia, Milošević's lost power when his patron stood aside. The war's coda came with the American-engineered rejection of Milošević at the polls. The US Agency for International Development funded and assisted in organizing an opposition youth movement, which spearheaded the political campaign against the strongman.[97] It was not long after his election defeat and resignation from power that the "Butcher of the Balkans" found himself jailed in the UN war crimes tribunal at The Hague. The international court charged Milošević with genocide and war crimes in Bosnia, Croatia, and Kosovo. Before his trial concluded, he died in his prison cell from an apparent heart attack in 2006.

3.12   Kosovo: Consequences and Signposts

In the West, America's and NATO's resolution of a second Balkan crisis was scored a victory. A wobbly stability descended on the volatile region. The aerial intervention neutralized a political firestorm before it exploded into a conflagration that could have drawn in nearby nations. The fear that the Balkans could ignite another major conflict always lurked near the top of diplomatic concerns. Former critics saw President Clinton in a new light. Prior to the outcome in Kosovo, politicians and pundits faulted his policies for "strategic incoherence" and international "social work."[98] He was now credited with preserving Euro-American unity. A year later, Clinton received from Germany the Charlemagne Prize, the first for an American president.

Passing quickly from the international stage, the Kosovo showdown, nonetheless, was not forgotten among Russian leaders who opposed and distrusted the eastward advances of United States and NATO into their strategic backyard. Among other perceived political humiliations, the Kosovo confrontation represented one more nail in the coffin of the West's attempt at rapprochement with post-Soviet Russia. The East-West animosity intensified as the years passed, becoming deeply rooted with Vladimir Putin's assumption of the Russian presidency in 1999. Under Putin, Russo-American relations in some respects resembled a return to the tensions and competition present during the Cold War. In this second round of rivalry, power politics and geopolitical interests, not ideology, accounted for much of the hostility.

Inside Kosovo, the ethno-nationalistic hatreds never abated. Serbians and Albanians remained at swords point. Each saw the other as a vile race-apart. The West's dream of a multiethnic nation fizzled amid centuries-old ethno-sectarianism. Twenties years after the air campaign terminated, Serb and Albanian officials fruitlessly conferred on redrawing the Serbia-Kosovo border to separate the communities as means to bring peace between them. For years Washington persisted in brokering a genuine peace between the two Balkan states. In 2008, Kosovo announced its independence from Serbia. Over 100 capitals recognized its sovereignty; but Belgrade and Moscow refused. Priština and Belgrade did agree to work toward normalizing their economic relations in 2020 via a deal brokered by the Donald Trump administration.

Like a tropical storm, the Balkan wars arose suddenly, blew fiercely, and then subsided leaving thousands of dead, much destruction in their wake, and fears throughout Europe that others might demand redrawn borders. Russia remained aggrieved at the United States – a dangerous residue from the wars. Kosovo is still home to over 600 US troops in an unsettled dispute.

Despite the relative, short-term success of the Kosovo engagement, Clinton's America strove to stay clear of stabilization operations in Sierra Leone and East Timor. The president came in for criticism for wearing out the US military with what critics termed as international "care giving" or global policing. Additionally, the Balkan wars chastened the White House about the arduousness of meshing military and diplomatic approaches in complex environments to attain peace and stability. The man from Hope, Arkansas, however, never renounced humanitarian interventions nor stepped away from his inaugural Wilsonian rhetoric.[99]

When violence, for instance, erupted in Sierra Leone, Washington did broker the short-lived Lomé Agreement, which established the UN Assistance Mission for Sierra Leone. When the agreement broke down in 2000, Washington was only too glad to have British paratroopers wade into the chaos, suppress the drug-crazed teenaged gangs, and jail the militia leader. In East Timor, the United States handed off leadership of the UN-authorized International Force East Timor (INTERFET) to Australia. The Pentagon aided the UN force with air and sea lift along with communication capabilities. Staffed by soldiers from Australia, Britain, New Zealand, Canada, and other countries, INTERFET took up the mission to safeguard the Catholic East Timorese from the rampaging Muslim militias and regular Indonesian troops. INTERFET's effectiveness in restoring order encouraged Clinton officials to hail the effort as an example of regional cooperation and of outsourcing the duties of international policing, although the United Nations, in the words of one observer, "did less than the decently minimal."[100]

After Bill Clinton's presidency, America's role in leading humanitarian assistance around the world morphed into that of a global cop to hunt down terrorists, while still pursuing democratic and altruistic goals. This new chapter in US defense and foreign policies brought no cessation in its global-spanning interventions.

4 Afghanistan
Regime Change and Building Society in the Graveyard of Empires

> In Afghanistan, the Americans have all the wristwatches but Afghans have all the time.   Prevalent saying among US troops

> It is wise in war not to underrate your opponents.   Liddell Hart, *Strategy*

The September 11, 2001, terrorist attacks on the Pentagon and the Twin Towers of the World Trade Center dramatically transformed America's global interactions, security policies, and ways of waging war. Despite numerous signals from the al Qaeda terrorist network and urgent warnings by some George W. Bush officials, such as Richard Clarke, the NSC counterterrorism coordinator, the United States was woefully blindsided by the "martyrdom" operation and caught unprepared as well on how to strike back. Terrorism changed the nature of overseas military missions from humanitarian expeditions to heavily armed interventions against determined adversaries. These new wars of regime change and occupation differed vastly from the preceding decade of military do-good relief missions as in Somalia, Haiti, Bosnia, and Kosovo. America now had a wily and ruthless enemy. Al Qaeda's "planes operation" on the American homeland ended Washington's "holiday from history," jarring top officials and average citizens back to the hard, cruel reality that the United States was not exempt from the vicissitudes of human affairs.

The plane-hijacking jihadis, who crashed commercial airlines into iconic American buildings and a western Pennsylvania field, proved that the United States with its two vast oceanic moats was still vulnerable to mass-casualty violence, something avoided during the entire Cold War. These suicidal terrorists lacked the technological and computational skills of the digital era. Yet their religiously fired hatred of America sufficed to overcome deficiencies in high-tech weapons or raw firepower. It was a lesson that saw repeated applications in the years ahead.

Another lesson the United States came to learn was the blowback incurred from walking away from a turbulent nation. Abandoning Afghanistan after the Soviet Union's 1989 pullout left the high-altitude country to the tender mercies of the Taliban rulers, who invited in

Osama bin Laden to plot and execute mass murder around the globe from his mountain fastness. Only a handful of State Department and CIA officials advocated for an American presence in Kabul after Moscow departed. They were anxious about instability, drug exports, and the seeds of terrorism. One departing undercover officer wrote in 1992 that "foreign extremists may want to move in" resulting in Afghanistan "becoming a training ground and munitions dump for foreign terrorists" and "at the same time the world's largest poppy field."[1] The fears turned out to be prescient.

Osama bin Laden, who the Clinton administration had in its gunsights more than once, emerged as the leading culprit for the 9/11 terrorism. The scion of a wealthy family in Saudi Arabia, bin Laden financed his fellow mujahedeen (holy warriors) fighting in the Soviet-Afghanistan conflict. After the Red Army retreated from a war-shattered Afghanistan, bin Laden had helped establish al Qaeda ("the base") with other radical Islamists to carry on the war against apostate Muslim rulers, America, and the West after the Red Army retreated. He perceived the Soviet Union's downfall primarily a result first of its death "like Kipling's Tommy Atkins on Afghanistan's plains." To bin Laden, the United States was the next superpower to be defeated: "Having borne arms against the Russians in Afghanistan, we think our battle with America will be easy by comparison," as quoted by terrorism expert Michael Scheuer.[2]

After the terrorist assaults on Manhattan and the Pentagon, bin Laden's Afghan sanctuary became the immediate target of Washington's retaliation, when the Pashtun-majority Taliban rulers refused to surrender the fugitive.[3] Diplomatic pressure from Saudi Arabia, one of the few countries to recognize the Taliban takeover in 1996, went nowhere in convincing Kabul to jettison bin Laden. Motivated by radical interpretations of Sunni Islam, the Taliban ("students") movement unseated the former mujahedeen leader and replaced him with one-eyed Mullah Mohammed Omar, their founder and a veteran of the anti-Soviet War. Once in power, Mullah Omar installed the Islamic Emirate of Afghanistan and strictly enforced the Sharia, or Islamic law. As ardent practitioners of the ethnic Pashtun's *Pashtunwali* (a traditional tribal code of ethics) that governed hospitality among other behavior, the Taliban regime was bound by the ancient practice not to surrender guests to their enemies.[4] Also, Mullah Omar was beholden to al Qaeda for its help in consolidating control over parts of the country. Besides, host and guest viewed the world through the same radical and violent Islamist prism. Thus, the Kabul regime rejected Washington's demands that it handover Osama bin Laden for an indictment on terrorism charges.

Both Afghan rulers and the Washington government misjudged the cost to be incurred by honoring this custom over the next two decades. Any US commander in chief walking in Bush's shoes would have ordered an attack on Afghanistan to deprive al Qaeda of its mountain sanctuary. Left unmolested, al Qaeda was certain to stage another September 11 cataclysm. Retaliation for nearly 3,000 dead souls also figured in the calculation to strike back. This new chapter of large-scale military interventions, first into Afghanistan and then Iraq, was accompanied by deploying small US military formations into a score of countries to hunt terrorists or to train locally based partners to wage counterterrorist missions. This topic is explored in Chapters 6 and 7. Following a different trajectory, the Afghan and Iraqi wars went from military invasions to prolonged occupations, to troop-intensive counterinsurgency operations, and to societal reengineering programs to build Westernized societies and representative governments.

In some sense, the US armed intervention into Afghanistan constituted a military and diplomatic reengagement of the high-terrain nation. During the 1980s, the Ronald Reagan presidency aided the anti-Soviet resistance fighting the Red Army's 1979 invasion and military occupation intended to shore up a communist regime in Kabul. When the Islamic mujahedeen fought Soviets, they were supplied with munitions and money by the United States and Saudi Arabia, which funneled their assistance through Pakistan's shadowy Inter-Service Intelligence (ISI). The ISI trained some 90,000 fighters (mostly Afghans but also volunteers from other countries). Among those ISI trainees was Mohammed Omar, the future Taliban leader of Afghanistan. The Central Intelligence Agency aided the mujahedeen, many of whom later joined the Taliban. They subsequently fought other Afghan militias and then the US expeditionary forces.

As the USSR faltered in its war, the Reagan administration played the key role in brokering a diplomatic settlement with the Mikhail Gorbachev government, which paved the way for the Kremlin's withdrawal. Afghanistan and Pakistan signed the Geneva accord. Then Washington and Moscow entered into the agreement as guarantors.[5] Once the Soviet forces exited from Afghanistan, Washington administrations also disengaged from the country.

The George H. W. Bush government struck a deal with Moscow, which agreed to cut off arms transfers to its former Soviet puppet in Afghanistan, Najibullah Ahmadzai, who was booted from power in 1992. Four years later, the Taliban killed and hanged him from a traffic pole. His removal opened the floodgates to an intra-warlord conflict. Unexpectedly, the Tajik and Uzbek forces captured Kabul. For the first time in 300 years, the Pashtuns lost possession of the capital. The Taliban, made up mostly of ethnic Pashtuns who represented well over a third of the Afghan population, fought back. Supported by the ISI, the Taliban militia overran Kabul in 1996. The ethnic Tajiks (about a quarter of the Afghan population) hung onto a sliver of land in the Panjshir Valley northeast of the capital. The Tajik-dominated Northern Alliance (officially known as the United Islamic Front for the Salvation of Afghanistan) fought the Taliban and collaborated with the US-led coalition in the war against the Mullah Omar.

Neither the outgoing Bush administration nor the incoming William J. Clinton one lifted a finger to arrest Afghanistan's slide into civil war and anarchy. Absent the Cold War, which gave prominence to all sorts of players on the East-West chessboard, Washington simply did not care about a former Soviet pawn, even though it sat on the world's largest opium-poppy crops, from which flowed hundreds of tons of refined heroin to European consumers. Diplomats and CIA officers cabled the State Department and Langley that the country's instability readied the conditions for Islamic fundamentalism and terrorism to take root. The Washington establishment knew better and turned its attention to other pressing matters in the former Yugoslavia, Haiti, and Rwanda.

For almost a decade, the White House sent neither an ambassador nor a CIA station chief to Kabul, not until autumn 2001 after its invasion.[6] As such, pre-9/11 Afghanistan, like Somalia and Iraq, underscored the lesson that in the age of terrorism the wages of neglect and abdication can bite back. Decades afterwards, this realization made it hard for US military and civilian policymakers to abruptly pull up stakes and leave countries beset by Islamist militancy, for they sensed the dubious consequences from a retreat.

By 1996, Afghanistan populated American counterterrorism radars. The CIA established a special center to track Osama bin Laden and to analyze intelligence about his al Qaeda network now both resident in a compound in Kandahar. The little-known Saudi emerged from obscurity three years earlier, because of his ties to the terrorists who truck-bombed Tower One of the World Trade Center in New York in 1993 by placing explosives inside a rental van in the garage. This wake-up call killed six people but soon slipped from the headlines. Alarmed by terrorist threats over the years, President Clinton appointed Richard Clarke, a CIA terrorist expert, to head an interagency outfit known as the Counterterrorism Security Group in 1998. Additionally, the CIA's Counter-terrorism Center concocted plans to snatch or kill bin Laden in his Kandahar hideout. The proposals met with skepticism in the Pentagon, which questioned their actual feasibility.

Al Qaeda's 1998 bombing of the two US Embassies in East Africa intensified the search for effective defenses against the elusive terrorist front and its charismatic chief. The Clinton Pentagon's retaliatory missiles missed their targets. The failure left the attack against the US diplomatic offices in Kenya and Tanzania not only unavenged but also inviting another terrorist incident. One was not long in coming with the attempted sinking of the USS *Cole* in Yemen in October 2000. Berthed in the natural port of Aden for refueling, the Arleigh Burke–class missile destroyer was struck by two al Qaeda militants in a skiff loaded with explosives. The blast tore a forty-foot hole in the warship, killing seventeen sailors and wounding another thirty-nine. Determined to send a signal of recovery, the US Navy repaired the ship and returned it to active service. Much less determined was the resolve to prevent another terrorist assault.[7]

Before the climactic 9/11 attack, the United States underwent a presidential election between Texas governor George W. Bush and Al Gore, who was President Clinton's vice president. The national campaign contributed almost nothing to preparing the United States for an era of war and more war. One incongruity in Bush's subsequent incursions into the Middle East and South Asia stemmed from his campaign pledges to spare the US armed forces from multiple deployments abroad and especially nation-building endeavors. Candidate Bush derided the outgoing Clinton government for wearing out the Pentagon with peace-soldiering duties. Condoleezza Rice, soon-to-be incoming President Bush's national security adviser, took aim at Clinton for "the 82nd Airborne escorting kids to kindergarten" in the Balkans.[8] Not without irony, the Bush administration plunged America's fighting forces into full-blown nation-restoring and democracy promotion in Iraq and Afghanistan. Before that ironic deduction consciously sunk in, America went to war.

In office just eight months, Bush turned to the legislative branch before taking action against the 9/11 jihadis. Congress overwhelmingly passed the Authorization to Use Military Force a week after the horrific destruction of the Twin Towers in Lower Manhattan. The AUMF granted the commander in chief "authority under the Constitution to take action to deter and prevent acts of international terrorism."[9] Given the massive scale of death and destruction, the passage of the Joint Resolution seemed almost beside the point. The AUMF, in fact, did largely slip from everyday consciousness for over a decade despite its not infrequent usage. During the presidencies of Barack Obama and Donald Trump the authorization was applied to a wide range of Salafi jihadi networks other than in Afghanistan with few serious questions from Capitol Hill.

With congressional authorization in hand, Bush rallied his fellow citizens to fight back against the attackers, while eschewing Islamophobia in his public utterances. In his series of speeches right after al Qaeda hijackers seized control of the four passenger airliners, the American leader made abundantly clear that the battle was against terrorists, "who are traitors to their own [Islamic] faith," not "our many Muslim friends" or the larger Muslim world.[10] Intended or not, dividing probable enemies into camps of jihadi foes and Muslim friends constituted a clear military strategy. Historically, the great captains almost always strive to reduce the ranks of adversaries by playing them off against each other.

4.1   Forming Coalition Rings

Coalition warfare also formed a basic strategy of the American way of war, for it brought allied military muscle to the cause and lessened international opprobrium for acting unilaterally. For the Bush administration, as for previous Washington governments, lining up a wide collection of allied states imparted justification and legitimacy to an assault on Afghanistan for sheltering al Qaeda. The White House moved swiftly to patch up strained relations with the People's Republic of China (PRC) after the Hainan incident in April when Chinese warplanes forced down a US reconnaissance aircraft on a South China Sea island. Washington wanted no adverse votes from the PRC in the Security Council.

The president and his foreign policy team moved to broker concentric inner and outer rings of states circling the bull's-eye – Afghanistan. The closest-in nations were asked to serve as bases for the US war on the alpine state. Outer-lying countries were requested to grant permission to overfly military aircraft and to curb the flow of funds to al Qaeda. The Oval Office and the State Department acted to harness not only NATO partners but also nations beyond the usual US allies in Western Europe. Colin Powell, the secretary of state, served as *the* point man for assembling the anti-Afghanistan coalition. But George Bush called the Russian President Vladimir Putin himself. He also spoke with the leaders of China, Britain, Germany, France, and Canada.[11]

A non-frontline state, yet a critical partner was Saudi Arabia because of its premiere oil fields, leadership in setting petroleum prices, and centrality in the Islamic faith with two of the holiest Muslim shrines on its soil. Riyadh's role in the spread of Islamist terrorism, nevertheless, was abhorrent for a US ally. Private Saudi citizens subsidized the extreme Wahhabism of the Islamic faith in madrassas throughout the Muslim world. Money also flowed to terrorist outfits like al Qaeda. That fifteen of the nineteen airline hijackers were Saudis on 9/11 cast the desert king-dom in a sinister light. By ignoring the consequences of its citizens flirting with violent extremists, the Saudi government soon witnessed its chickens coming home to roost. Salafi terrorist attacks took place in the desert kingdom. This compelled Riyadh's volte-face from sometime terrorist backer to terrorist scourge. Saudi Arabia's reversal also exer-cised influence on its Gulf neighbors to rein in their sponsorship of Salafi jihadism, as the United States embarked on its international campaign against terrorism.

In another outer-ring play, the US administration engaged the Russian Federation, which had many grievances against its *glavny protivnik*, or main adversary, reminiscent of Soviet times. Moscow bristled at US meddling in its border nations in Eastern Europe. The Kremlin also resented Washington's complaints over its human rights abuses. The Federation was exceedingly irked by the NATO bombing two years earlier of Serbia for its harsh rule in Muslim Kosovo. It interpreted the Atlantic bloc's interference through the lens of a Muslim-Western con-flict. So, US-led NATO airstrikes on behalf of Muslim Kosovars placed Russia and America in opposing camps. Washington's impending Afghan attack now realigned the two powers against a common foe.

For an air and land surge into Afghanistan, the Pentagon needed Russian cooperation. Its invasion plans banked on flyover rights and on freedom to operate from bases in nearby countries. President Bush achieved an unexpected breakthrough with the new Russian leader, Vladimir Putin, a much more hard-nosed and calculating personality than the outgoing Boris Yeltsin. In time, Putin drove Russo-American relations into the political freezer. Before that downturn, Moscow gave a green light to Tajikistan and Kyrgyzstan to work with Washington. Counterterrorism cooperation between the two major powers remained good throughout the Bush presidency despite the Kremlin's land, sea, and air invasion into the Republic of Georgia in 2008.[12] No doubt, Putin recognized that America's fundamentalist Muslim enemies in Afghanistan were also his enemies in Russia's Chechen Republic. Anything that inflicted harm on the extremist Taliban militants stood to benefit similar Russian counterterrorism efforts against Islamists in the Caucasus.

Three Central Asian nations – Tajikistan, Turkmenistan, and Uzbekistan – shared borders with Afghanistan. Of the three, Uzbekistan was located closest to the American-friendly Northern Alliance, an effect-ive anti-Taliban foe. The Pentagon obtained expanded usage of the Uzbek's Karshi-Khanabad airfield (called K-2 by US airmen) in return for millions of dollars and military equipment. The Department of Defense deemed K-2 as critical for Combat Search and Rescue (CSAR) missions. Without CSAR, a downed pilot might be harmed or used as a Taliban hostage on the international stage. Just after the US invasion into Afghanistan, the DoD stationed over a thousand troops from the 10th Mountain Division in Uzbekistan to defend against anticipated attacks into the mountain-top country. American-Uzbek ties strengthened as then-President Islam Karimov faced his own terrorist perils with the Islamic Movement of Uzbekistan (IMU). The IMU found sanctuary in Afghanistan to stage assaults on Uzbek forces, which Washington financially and militarily backed until relations soured between the two countries a few years afterward.

The United States also entered into cooperative agreements with Turkmenistan and Tajikistan, although both lacked the close proximity of Uzbekistan to the Afghan allied forces fighting the Taliban. Even the more distant Kazakhstan and Kyrgyzstan agreed to link up with US Armed Forces. Moscow thus stood aside while Washington negotiated limited cooperative deals with its former Soviet republics.

Bush's America recognized that the "most pivotal nation we recruited was Pakistan."[13] It shared a 1,600-mile border, known as the Durand Line, with the Islamic Emirate of Afghanistan. Dealing with Islamabad was anything but easy. Washington and Islamabad drifted apart after the Soviet Union's breakup. The Clinton administration, moreover, deepened the rift when it replaced Pakistan with India as America's main partner in South Asia. This realignment embittered the Islamic Republic of Pakistan, for it and India had been venomous rivals since the independence of both from British rule in 1947. Amid this twin-state duel was Afghanistan, in which Pakistan's Inter-Services Intelligence had long run clandestine operations. The ISI trained and funneled US arms to the mujahedeen fighting against the Soviet occupation. After the USSR defeat and withdrawal, the ISI backed the Taliban as a way to ensure Kabul remained friendly to Pakistan and hostile to India. Pakistanis often referred to Afghanistan as their strategic depth vis-à-vis India.

Winning over General Pervez Musharraf, Pakistan's military ruler, to the American cause in Afghanistan took a combination of arm-twisting and blandishments, plus Powell's considerable skill of talking military man to military man. Powell labored to convince Musharraf to grant landing rights for US and allied aircraft, to open airspace for bomb-laden warplanes destined for Afghan targets, and to assume a friendly posture for other American requests. The Islamabad government made available two bases – Pasni and Jacobabad – for intervention into the landlocked country. Washington waived sanctions imposed on Pakistan as well as India for their testing nuclear weapons and rescheduled Islamabad's debt payments on $379 million. Despite Washington's additional billions of dollars in aid to Islamabad's coffers, the ISI never broke its ties with the Taliban. The spy agency smuggled weapons and other supplies over the border into Afghanistan. Crucially, the ISI never fully revealed information on the whereabouts of the Taliban or al Qaeda.[14]

Still, America's top diplomat made real progress in swinging Pakistan into Washington's column. Despite the backdoor channels between the Taliban and Pakistan's spy agency, Islamabad presented itself as much more friendly to the United States than during the latter days of the Clinton presidency. President Bush acknowledged Powell's pivotal role in Islamabad's reorientation, when he thanked the retired general because he "single-handedly got Musharraf on board."[15]

An unanticipated surprise greeted Bush's bid to engage Iran, America's most implacable adversary in the Middle East since the Islamic clerics overthrew its close ally, Mohammad Reza Shah Pahlavi, in 1979. Once in power, the ayatollahs orchestrated hate-American rallies where crowds chanted their vitriol toward the Great Satan – the United States. Sharing a border with western Afghanistan, Iran feared and loathed the Sunni Taliban rulers in Kabul. Iran, like Russia, supplied arms to the Northern Alliance for its battle against the Salafist-dominated Taliban. Tehran despised Taliban militants for their deadly reprisals against Afghanistan's Farsi-speaking Shiite minority. What's more, the Taliban regime ignored the rampant drug smuggling across the common border into Iran, whose youth suffered from widespread heroin addiction. Little wonder that Tehran acquiesced to an American invasion in its backyard. The ruling mullahs hated America but they delighted in seeing it sweep away Kabul's Sunni zealots.

4.2   Preparing for Invasion

A day after the 9/11 attacks, NATO invoked the defense clause within its founding treaty for the first time. The ambassadors to the Euro-Atlantic bloc released a statement from their hastily arranged meeting: "if it is determined that this attack was directed from abroad against the United States, it shall be regarded as an action covered by Article 5 of the Washington treaty." Article 5 made clear that "an armed attack" against any signatory of 1949 treaty "shall be considered as an attack against all of them." The drafters of NATO's collective security framework had in mind a Soviet tank offensive deep into Central Europe. But the post-9/11 conveners affirmed its new applicability "today, in a world subject to the scourge of international terrorism."[16]

Three weeks after the Twin Towers crumbled into toxic ashes, NATO authorized collective action after being presented with "clear and compelling proof" of al Qaeda's role in crashing commercial jetliners into the Twin Towers and the Pentagon. After studying satellite photos, financial records of fund transfers, and other classified intelligence, George Robertson, NATO's general secretary, concluded that "it is now clear all roads lead to al Qaeda."[17]

The Bush White House went all out to get NATO's green light for its counteroffensive. It asked the North Atlantic Council, NATO's decision-making body, for access to its member state's seaports, airports, and airspace to fly through. NATO also sent troops to relieve US forces from peacekeeping duties in the Balkans. As the military intervention got underway in Afghanistan, NATO took over air defense operations from the US Air Force. This freed up America's AWACS (Airborne Warning and Control Systems) stationed over the Atlantic, allowing them to fly over South Asia where their sophisticated radar and tracking capabilities managed air operations in Afghan skies. The European contribution was more symbolic than substantive. After all, America was under terrorist threat, not imperiled by long-range, supersonic bombers flying from Soviet airfields in Smolensk or Belaya in Siberia.

When it came to choosing close NATO invasion partners, Washington turned out to be unexpectedly picky, given the enthusiasm within the Atlantic alliance for combat roles. The DoD was uninterested in a rainbow force of varying competencies. Multilateralism counted in sentiment, but not too much in practicality. By late September, as the Pentagon began implementing its invasion plans, NATO members let it be known that they expected fighting assignments in the operation.

Donald Rumsfeld, the secretary of defense, had different ideas for waging expeditionary warfare. He worried about an unwieldy armada of behind-the-curve European military units holding back the lethal, fast-paced, and ultra-high-tech strike force envisioned by the Americans. US commanders held many NATO forces in low regard. Even for Cold War–type missions they were woefully unprepared to wage modern tank warfare. NATO countries notoriously underfunded and under-trained their militaries. As a practical matter, the West European defense forces were still largely entrenched against a Red Army sweep across the continent, not to engage in an agile, fleet-footed, and quick-moving campaign. At its early October NATO meeting in Brussels, European officers were still in the dark about their role in the Afghan intervention. America's deputy secretary of defense, Paul Wolfowitz, commented about NATO participation: "if we need collective action, we will ask for it."[18] DoD civilian planners sidestepped an outsized operational role for NATO in the invasion phase. They recalled the complex consensus-based structure to reach approval for bombing runs during the Kosovo campaign that frustratingly delayed or obstructed the execution of flights. Reaching agreement among nineteen countries amounted to waging a war by committee. The Bush war planners were determined not to repeat Kosovo.

So, rather than running the operation through NATO, the Pentagon and White House pulled together a small coalition for the opening stage of the war. Chafing at the American control over military decisions, one French official alluded to "washing up the dirty dishes" following the Americans doing "the cooking and prepare what people are going to eat."[19]

US military officers professed confidence that British and Australian elite commando units were up to the arduous and fast-paced maneuver warfare they had in mind for the opening onslaught. Soon after the initial blitz, Poland (a new NATO member) announced the dispatch of ground troops and eighty members of its GROM commando unit. By early 2002, Denmark, France, Germany, Italy, and Norway joined in Operation Anaconda. Many US allies sailed warships into the Arabian Sea, including Japan and the Netherlands.

By the start of hostilities in the Afghan war, Washington's diplomatic outreach to foreign powers netted positive results. President Bush exalted: "More than 40 countries in the Middle East, Africa, Europe, and across Asia have granted air transit and landing rights." Even without participation by a single Arab government in the Afghan offensive, the US president still asserted: "We are supported by the collective will of the world."[20] Months into the intervention, Washington looked to NATO with much less disapproval, as it needed land forces for stabilization, peacekeeping, and governance in the prostrate country. Once the incursion bogged down into a Taliban-led insurgency against the foreign occupiers, regular NATO and other international troops were welcomed, as will be noted.

4.3   Entering the Afghan Theater with a Different Type of Invasion

Afghanistan was on the receiving end of a different type of invasion than the United States executed in its recent incursions into the Kuwait-Iraq theater, Panama, Haiti, Bosnia, or Kosovo. Each of those conflicts were preceded by fairly lengthy preparatory periods, as the Pentagon marshaled its land, air, and sea assets. Plans, training, and munitions build-ups evolved over months. The DoD telegraphed its objective well before the opening hours of the assault. Each was also largely reliant on American battalions rather than local militia. President Bush's and the American public's impatience for a fast-tracked strike against the al

Qaeda terrorists and their Afghan allies dictated a swift and innovative counterattack strategy.

Equally important in devising an Afghan battle plan was the country's formidable topographical and human terrain features. From a military strategist's perspective, Afghanistan presented daunting challenges. Mountainous, landlocked, distant, and lacking a modern network of roads and airfields, the impoverished state was not easily accessible by outside powers. Its desiccated flatlands kicked up dust in the summer and blew icy winds in winters. Its uplands beheld rugged mountains, forested ravines, rocky outcroppings, and caves, many of which sheltered warrior bands for centuries. Tourists saw postcard beauty. Invaders perceived forbidding geography.

The human terrain was even more treacherous. Inured to hardship, persistent fighting, and clan rivalries, the Afghan irregulars were no slouch in ambushes, hit-and-run raids, or surprise skirmishes, no matter how out-of-date their weaponry. Indeed, their fierce resistance to the military presence of Victorian Britain and Soviet Russia earned Afghanistan the epitaph as an imperial graveyard. It was often stated that Afghanistan might be easy to invade but it was next to impossible to hold. Its inhabitants never quit defying their occupiers. Little of this bleak history crossed the minds of the post-9/11 war planners. They thought in terms of regime change, revenge against al Qaeda, and in a smash-and-dash invasion with the political void filled by caretakers from the United Nations.

For all but a handful of scholars, diplomats, and CIA professionals, Afghanistan was a tabula rasa. The Islamic Emirate of Afghanistan's governance differed from the pattern across much of the neighboring political landscape. Where nearby Arab and Persian states were governed by centralized top-down regimes, whether monarchies, theocracies, or dictatorships, the Kabul government's writ ran intermittingly in the countryside. Warlordism traditionally played a defining role in the nation's history particularly after the pro-Soviet Afghan regime in 1978 tried to extend Marxist doctrine into the villages. The Red Army's march into the country the following year deepened the opposition to central authority. And the rural rebellion against the occupation further fragmented the Kabul-countryside connection.

Perched at 6,000-foot altitude, Kabul was a capital that ruled in name only over the powerful regional warlords. These chieftains filled the governance vacuum spawned, in part, by the elevated terrain, which inhibited travel, and by the violent Soviet intervention, which destroyed the country's remaining political institutions. The Taliban, more of an ideological movement than a coherent ruling apparatus, clumsily and brutally administered the machinery of government in the days after seizing Kabul.

Nor had Afghanistan's titular rulers over the centuries blended the disparate ethnic communities into a homogenous nation. Afghanistan's estimated population of twenty-five million at the time of the 9/11 attack was splintered into ethnic groups, made up of about 38 percent Pashtun (known also as Pathans), 25 percent Tajik, 19 percent Hazara, and 6 percent Uzbek, along with smaller percentages of Baluch and Turkmen peoples.[21] The Islamic faith bestowed less unity than might be expected because of the divisions between the Shia and Sunni sects. Most Afghans fell into the Sunni camp, but the Hazara practiced the Shiite version of Islam. All this ethnic and religious factionalism later befuddled Washington's well-meaning efforts to unify, modernize, and pacify the contentious country.

Afghanistan's devastating 1980s anti-Soviet insurgency, its show-stopping topography, and its ethno-nationalistic rivalries constituted liabilities that were well-known to the CIA hands laying plans for the US incursion. The spy agency's familiarity with the rugged country dated back even before Moscow's jackbooted control. As the mighty Red Army – the victors of Stalingrad – bogged down fighting a tribal insurgency, Washington started working through Pakistan to arm the mujahedeen fending off the infidel intrusion. The CIA under President Jimmy Carter's direction supplied aged Lee-Enfield rifles circa World War I. His successor, Ronald Reagan, surpassed this minimal backing, and the CIA finally handed over the famed Stinger ground-to-air missiles in 1986. The shoulder-fired rockets downed scores of Soviet Hind helicopter gunships, a particularly lethal platform against the mujahedeen. Together with enhanced training and expanded logistics, the Stringer was a key variable in the USSR's defeat.

Ronald Reagan and his inner circle dreamed of turning the tables on Moscow for all its assistance to North Vietnam during the Southeast Asia war. A fortiori, the West Wing realized the centrality of the Soviet-Afghan War to the Reagan Doctrine. This game plan called for aiding insurgencies fighting newly installed pro-Soviet regimes in Afghanistan, Angola, Cambodia, and Nicaragua. Its purpose was to roll back Soviet gains in Third World countries and to tax Moscow's ability to sustain its earlier victories.[22] Years before Moscow's military infestation of the inhospitable nation, CIA operatives recruited and subsidized Afghans who recoiled at the growing atheistic Soviet influence over the regime in Kabul. Once the Red Army scurried out of Afghanistan in 1989, Soviet Russia as well as the Bush and Clinton presidencies lost interest in the forlorn country.

As lower Manhattan lay smoldering, President Bush summoned to Camp David what became a war cabinet made up of Pentagon's top civilians, CIA officials, military brass, and presidential aides. The commander in chief signed "exceptional authorities" that conferred broad powers to the CIA to destroy al Qaeda. These powers were normally labeled as presidential or intelligence findings; the Bush version was called a Memorandum of Notification. Days later, Bush also approved two memoranda transferring legal authority to Langley for covert operations aimed at the terrorist band. America's forty-third president differed from his predecessor. Whereas Bill Clinton bound himself up with a law-enforcement approach requiring forensic evidence, criminal justice procedures, and courtroom due process, Bush perceived the conflict in terms of blunt force, preemptive military strikes, and covert action.[23] The Bush White House also put in place defensive measures to police the nation's borders, pursue likely terrorists within the country, and, of course, erect a new cabinet agency, the US Department of Homeland Security.

Any intended American counterstrike would be enabled by DoD's existing web of bases in the Persian Gulf region. The Pentagon's airfields and harbors in Saudi Arabia, Kuwait, Turkey, and Bahrain bristled with warships, warplanes, and battalions, numbering around 15,000 troops in the region. In addition, naval flotillas made up of aircraft carriers and other warships cruised the Arabian Sea and the Persian Gulf. The aircraft carriers ferried fleets of bomb-bearing fighters and attack helicopters within striking distance of Afghanistan.

At the Camp David meeting, the attendees pored over the Defense Department's order of battle for hitting back at the Afghan terrorist bases. September 11 acted as a form of deck-clearing for the mustering of new tactics. Unlike countless other adversarial countries and possible contingencies, the Pentagon had no pre-drafted battle plan to take off the shelf, tweak, and execute for an Afghan campaign. So, the military brass first put forward an unimaginative conventional plan. It called for six-months or more to build up military forces, to lay in combat matériel, and to set up air and ground transport in the lands neighboring Afghanistan. This lengthy preparation conformed to the pre–Persian Gulf War formula; but it sat adversely with George W. Bush, who sought a quick strike-option against al Qaeda.

Hugh Shelton, the outgoing Joint Chiefs of Staff chairman, offered formulaic air-bombardment schemes involving cruise missiles and manned bombers, with a SOF component.[24] Appointed by President Clinton, Army General Shelton's strategy bore a striking resemblance to the former Arkansas governor's lackluster approach following al Qaeda's vehicle bombing of the US embassies in Nairobi and Dar es Salaam. In those suicide assaults, US casualties numbered 12 dead, and African deaths reached 212, with thousands wounded. In retaliation, the Clinton administration merely fired cruise missiles at suspected al Qaeda camps in Afghanistan and a pharmaceutical plant outside Khartoum, Sudan (wrongly accused of manufacturing VX nerve agent). Inside and outside government, experts wrote off this minimalist plan as completely ineffective.[25] In the Afghan case, war planners were struck by the paucity of targets to hit in the impoverished country. One official was quoted as saying that it would be like "bombing them up to the stone age" thereby flipping General Curtis LeMay's famous quotation.[26]

President Bush ruled out a repeat of the ineffectual Clintonian missile launches. When telephoned by Tony Blair the day after 9/11 about an immediate counterattack, Bush replied to the British prime minister that he did not want to "pound sand with millions of dollars in weapons" just to satisfy a need for retaliation no matter how empty.[27] The American leader and his high-level appointees favored "boots on the ground" that ensured al Qaeda's destruction and ouster of the Taliban regime for hosting the bin Ladenists. As it turned out, Operation Enduring Freedom did include a heavy bombing component to destroy the Taliban foot soldiers hunkering down in trenches or tramping in the open.

Bucking standard military strategy, Bush went with a CIA game plan that harkened back to missions run by the agency's World War II forerunner. Like those earlier operations, the military and intelligence planners opted for unconventional warfare tactics of using the local forces, shored up by airstrikes, to go on the offensive against Taliban regime. Sketched out in the White House Situation Room two days after the jihadi attack on America and then elaborated upon at Camp David on September 15, the intelligence agency's strategy took advantage of the on-the-ground realities in Afghanistan. George Tenet, the CIA director, called for the agency's veteran field officers to infiltrate the snow-capped land. The first covert team entered Afghanistan on September 26 in Operation Jawbreaker; others soon followed, reaching about ninety operatives by the time the Taliban were chased from power in December.[28]

Once on the ground, the Agency's field operators linked up with anti-Taliban militias and regional warlords. The CIA professionals set up the Northern Alliance Liaison Team (NALT) to collaborate with the local leaders of which Fahim Khan (who replaced the recently assassinated charismatic Ahmed Shah Masood) was among the first. Joined by Special Forces A Teams (normally two officers and ten sergeants), the NALT's CIA officers and Green Berets worked with the Taliban resistance to step up their effectiveness, coordinate airstrikes, and subsidize their payrolls with millions of dollars handed out in wads of $100 bills. Their mission was to utilize anti-Taliban fighters in order to topple Mullah Omar who founded the Islamic Emirate of Afghanistan in 1996.

Operation Enduring Freedom represented a role reversal for Washington, which usually propped up beleaguered anti-communist governments fighting Marxist-inspired guerrillas during the Cold War, such as in South Vietnam, Nicaragua, El Salvador, and Bolivia. This time Americans would be enabling the rebels. George Tenant underscored the irony when he stressed: "We would be the insurgents" against an unpopular ruling faction.[29] As such, the Special Forces and CIA teams busied themselves with upgrading the military skills of their proxy fighters from the Hazara, Tajik, and Uzbek ethnic communities grouped within the Northern Alliance. The alliance had fought the Taliban even before it lost the capital in 1996.[30]

President Bush embraced the CIA strategy because it accelerated the American counterstrike against al Qaeda. Congress, media, and the public urged an immediate response to the 9/11 atrocity. The Pentagon's first-draft answer seemed plodding by contrast. As ingenious as the intelligence agency's scheme was, it was not really a new way of attacking an entrenched foe. An earlier version was tested during the Allied liberation of Nazi-ruled France in World War II. The Office of Strategic Services, the predecessor of both the CIA and the Green Berets, parachuted small teams into France to work with local resistance groups against the Third Reich's occupation. After the US and Allied troops waded ashore on Normandy's beaches, American and British intelligence services quickened the insertion of arms and advisers into France to create havoc among the retreating Germans.[31] Working with the underground French resistance, they sabotaged railways, blew up repair facilities, and ambushed German patrols so as to disrupt the Reich's defenses.[32] Throughout the war, British and Americans enabled proxies elsewhere in Europe against the German army and in Asia against the Japanese militarists.

The US Central Command refined and honed the CIA strategy for invading Afghanistan. More in line with America's traditional military operations was the incorporation of overwhelming airpower. The Air Force and Navy warplanes flew wave after wave of sorties to destroy the Taliban and protect the CIA-Special Forces groups, together with their Afghan allies. The US Air Force combat controllers and others used lasers to zero in close-air support, which devastated the Taliban militias on open plains or fortifications. The Northern Alliance conducted most of the ground fighting together with the side-switching warlords such as the Uzbek-chief Abdul Rashid Dostum, Tajik-leader Ismail Khan in the north, and with Gulbuddin Hekmatyar in the south. The anti-Taliban militias were trained and mentored by the Green Beret personnel. The Green Beret's Operational Detachment A-team 555 (the "triple nickel") took over Bagram, the sprawling former Soviet base, which facilitated the US air campaign and then the fall of the Taliban regime in late 2001.[33]

Regular American troops arrived with the deployment of the 10th Mountain Division and the 15th Marine Expeditionary Unit. As the scope of the conflict escalated into a widespread territorial battle, the Pentagon and Central Intelligence Agency agreed that the command of field operations "would migrate over time from the CIA to Defense," as Donald Rumsfeld sketched in his memoir. The DoD supremo reasoned the Pentagon was a much larger department better suited to commanding disparate forces scattered over the countryside.[34]

An increasingly militarized CIA stayed involved in the land war, gathering intelligence and crossing into the classic remit of the Green Berets by standing up and training proxy units. Its ultrasecret Special Activities Division (SAD) specialized in paramilitary operations such as assisting and mentoring proxy fighters – a mission at the heart of the Special Forces' repertoire. Operating under the vague rubric of OGA (other government agency, an open-secret euphemism for the CIA), SAD also subscribed to the Green Beret methodology of relying on host-nation recruits to engage the enemy. The jostling Green Berets and SAD did not always see eye to eye about how to wage the battle, but their differences never greatly impeded the war effort.[35]

Those engaged in building "partner capacity" with local allies often cited T. E. Lawrence (better known as Lawrence of Arabia). Because he was an Arabic-speaking scholar, the British Army posted Lawrence to the Arab Revolt fighting against the German-allied Ottoman Empire, which ruled the Levant when World War I broke out. During the revolt, Lawrence liaised with the British headquarters in Egypt and participated in battles against the Turks. His much-quoted insight ran: "Do not try to do too much with your own hands. Better the Arabs do it tolerably than you do it perfectly. It is their war, and you are to help them. Not win it for them."

This pithy comment became part of the counterinsurgency (COIN) catechism. Even the meticulously drafted 2006 *U.S. Army/Marine Corps Counterinsurgency Field Manual 3–24* approvingly cited Lawrence's maxim.[36] Almost ignored totally was the fact Lawrence was an insurgent during the 1916–1918 Bedouin rebellion, not a government participant in a counterinsurgency campaign suppressing the Arab rebels. Thus, his counsel was directed to help the offensive rebels, not defensive counterinsurgency measures.[37] In the Afghan invasion, the United States turned to indigenous proxies for offensive actions to overthrow the Taliban regime. As such, these operations approached Lawrence's offensive role in the Arab Revolt against Turkish rule. Once in occupation mode, the US military turned again to local recruits to defend the elected Kabul government against the Taliban insurgents. No matter the confusion, Lawrence's advice about letting the locals take ownership stood the test of time.

4.4   The Bombing War Commences

Sustained bombing commenced on October 7, eleven days after Langley inserted its first covert operatives into the Panjshir Valley in northeastern Afghanistan. As bombs and cruise missiles struck their targets, helicopter-borne Green Berets off-loaded and promptly went native wearing local dress, growing beards, and riding horses. The disparity between modern and medieval times could not have been starker. Troops from the 5th Special Forces Group galloped into battle on horseback in picturesque cavalry charges alongside their new Afghan compatriots.[38] Horse-mounted Green Berets (supported by combat controllers from the Air Force) keyed in bombing coordinates on their laptops while high-performance jets overhead hit targets on forested slopes. This air cover helped level the playing field, for the Taliban possessed captured Soviet tanks and artillery that outgunned the pro-US militias.[39]

Operation Enduring Freedom marked another time the Eisenhower-era B-52s were used in combat since the Vietnam War. Flying 3,000 miles from their temporary island base on Diego Garcia in the Indian Ocean, the hulking Stratofortresses delivered precision JDAMS (joint direct attack munitions, pronounced "Jay-dams") on Taliban frontline positions at Bagram airfield, Kabul, Mazar-i-Sharif, Taloqan, and other northern urban centers. Navy and Air Force warplanes, such as F-18 jets, B-1 bombers, and AC-130 Spectre gunships (converted from cargo planes) joined in pummeling the Taliban positions, killings a score of enemy militiamen in virtually every swoop. The lopsided and relentless air bombardments broke the fighting will of the enemy combatants. They ran away, retreated to their villages, and tried to blend back into rural life. Unbeknownst at the time, these same retreating hordes would adapt their tactics and return years later to wage a deadly insurgency, which on occasion outflanked the one-sided advantage enjoyed by the Pentagon and its allies with advanced-tech weaponry.

Much of the punishing air war was initially directed at the dusty city of Mazar-i-Sharif, sitting just forty miles from the Amu Darya River separating Afghanistan from Central Asian countries. Seizing the city of 200,000 inhabitants opened a beachhead, through which a pipeline of resupply and weaponry could flow from US bases in Uzbekistan. Possession of Mazar-i-Sharif also aided the Northern Alliance in cutting Taliban supply lines to western Afghanistan and opening a gateway to Kabul. By late November, the country's northern tier had fallen to the Northern Alliance and auxiliary factions led by Abdul Rashid Dostum, the ethnic Uzbek warlord.

Betting on the Afghan warlords was expedient in the short term but disadvantageous in the longer term, as they had their own parochial interests at heart. One of the most egregious examples was Gulbuddin Hekmatyar, who commanded the HIG (Hezb-i-Islami, or Islamic Party), which he had formed when the Soviets invaded. He went from anti-Soviet mujahedeen, to opponent first of the US intervention and Hamid Karzai, to exile in Iran, to sometime-collaborator with bin Laden and the Taliban, before receiving a pardon in 2016 from Ashraf Ghani, the Afghan president, in return for signing a peace deal.

After the fall of Mazar-i-Sharif, the locus of the fighting shifted southward to Kandahar, the spiritual birthplace of the Taliban movement. When Afghanistan's second largest city fell to moderate Pashtuns and other ethnic militias in early December, the Taliban forces lay prostrate. They suffered an estimated 10,000 battlefield deaths, roughly 20 percent of their militia army. Another 7,000 surrendered while still others switched sides, observing the time-honored Afghan tradition. While the Western attackers regretted noncombatant casualties, they could not halt them. Precision bombing technology and military guidelines prohibiting indiscriminate firing contributed to the figure of 700 deaths, lower than anticipated for the intervention phase.

This in itself served to limit ill-will among the Afghan population toward the outsiders who now strode their land. Great numbers of Afghan civilians celebrated the demise of the austere and barbarous Taliban theocracy with its many puritanical commandments. These people warmly greeted their foreign and domestic liberators for ending the Taliban's religious strictures on everyday behavior. Once more they played music, clipped beards, removed veils, and watched soccer games on television. By this point, the Mullah Omar regime had dissolved.

The Taliban leaders took flight first to the Tora Bora cave complex, southeast of Kabul, before escaping over the border to Pakistan. The al Qaeda and Taliban foot soldiers defected in droves. Terrorized by the bombing, the militants deserted their cause just as Macbeth's thanes fled his bloody kingship. The slender number of Special Ops forces, regular US troops, and their Afghan auxiliaries raised the question whether their small footprint was inadequate to close the frontier to bin Laden's bolt into Pakistan.

Once in Pakistan, the world's most wanted fugitive and his entourage enjoyed sheltering furnished by the ISI and even officials inside the Islamabad government. It would be ten years before the CIA tracked bin Laden down in the military town of Abbottabad in northern Pakistan and the US Navy SEAL Team 6 administered long-delayed justice to the terrorist ringleader in May 2011. In the interlude, he served as a global symbol for radical Islam's war with the United States and the Western world. Even after bin Laden's death, Pakistan continued to serve as safe haven for the Taliban, al Qaeda, and other anti-coalition militants.

There wasn't much the United States could do about Pakistan's sanctuary-granting stance. It relied on Islamabad for truck transport of vital arms from the seaport of Karachi to Afghan bases. The Pakistani government closed this artery over a US airstrike that killed twenty-four Pakistani soldiers in 2012.[40] For several months, the Pentagon ran supplies through Central Asian countries to bypass Islamabad's shutdown, although this route cost more and moved slower. From time to time, the George Bush and Barack Obama administrations sent drones and Special Operations commandos to kill insurgents along the Afghanistan-Pakistan borderlands. But Washington wanted for the means to seal the boundary. Frustrated with American ground actions and air strikes, which killed civilians along with militants, Musharraf temporarily closed border crossings several times, thereby holding up equipment and supplies to US and NATO combat units.

The invasion phase – cum indigenous fighters – of Operation Enduring Freedom lasted until spring 2002. Up till then, the US contingent numbered a mere 450 Special Operations Forces and CIA paramilitary officers. They harnessed local manpower for the assault on Kabul's motley AK-47–wielding bands. Some 15,000 Afghan fighters organized under the Northern Alliance got abundant air cover from US Air Force and Navy warplanes. In less than three months, the United States and its coalition partners expelled the Taliban rulers. As the author of *Imperial Grunts* summarized: "America's initial success rested on deftly combining high technology with low-tech unconventional warfare."[41]

As the beginning phase passed, the battlefield beheld a mini-surge of thousands of regular Army and Marine grunts, as stabilization operations commenced. At this point, Pentagon expenditures in casualties and cash were comparatively small. US military deaths numbered less than a dozen. Operational costs reached the slender amount of $12 billion in a defense budget of $357 billion for 2002 before ballooning to $711 billion in the full tide of the wars in Iraq and Afghanistan. The initial tiny figures included the largest ground battle yet in the Afghan invasion.

Operation Anaconda (to squeeze to death enemy forces) in early March 2002 fielded regular Army and Marine units, along with elements from the Special Operations Forces. Together, they were arrayed against an estimated 2,000 Afghans, Arabs, Chechens, and Uzbeks, who chose to stand and fight. So tenaciously did they resort to close-quarters combat with the superiorly armed invaders that US commanders called in the B-52 bombers to rain down strings of JDAMs on Taliban bunkers below. The defenders selected what they held to be an impenetrable redoubt, since Taliban militias defeated Soviet troops there with heavy casualties during the 1980s. The Anaconda Operation did not repeat the Soviet debacle.

The battle took place in the Shah-i-Kot Valley, which bordered Pakistan. The US forces and their allied Afghan fighters went up against a resolute foe. Fought in extreme cold weather conditions, the battle raged for days, marking a controversial helicopter landing of SEALs into a hot zone, where they were met by a fusillade of ground fire. Blending different SOF units with conventional soldiers, not widely seen since Vietnam (except for brief actions in Grenada and Panama), in an extended ground action reinitiated tactics that were later duplicated often in Afghanistan and then in Iraq. SEALs, Green Berets, and regular military forces worked together to take on the Taliban militias.

Anaconda recorded high casualties for the defenders as deadly American firepower decimated their ranks. Estimates range from 100 to 1,000 militants killed in action, depending on the source.[42] Armed mostly with Soviet-made AK-47 rifles and rocket-propelled grenades but also heavy machineguns and mortars, the Taliban managed to knock out four or five (depending on the account) MH-47 Chinook helicopters, damage Apache gunships, and kill eight US servicemen, while wounding over seventy in a snafu-filled battle.[43]

A large number of al Qaeda and Taliban fled over the border after the battle. Bin Laden may have been part of this exodus; other reports held that the terrorist mastermind escaped weeks or even months earlier to a Pakistani haven. In addition to failing to capture bin Laden, the US internal after-action reports criticized American coordination and execution of the complex operation with "lots of moving parts," as related by Army General Tommy Franks.[44] The Taliban's losses and their mass exfiltration across the Pak-Afghan border marked the last big-scale battle fought between the two antagonists. This miniature Waterloo taught, or retaught, the indigenous Afghan defenders the lesson to avoid set piece conventional-type clashes with a twenty-first century military force.

Adapting to the new battlefield realities, the Taliban turned to insurgent warfare, using roadside bombs, assassinations, and hit-and-run raids. By waging a low-intensity war with murky battle lines, they turned the table on their adversary's reliance on high-powered weaponry. Tommy Franks, the CENTCOM commander who oversaw both the Afghan and Iraqi interventions, was too quick to pass judgment on Anaconda when he wrote that "the last al Qaeda sanctuary in Afghanistan had been destroyed. And it would never be rebuilt."[45] There would be other al Qaeda sanctuaries hidden within the mountainous land, albeit smaller but still lethal to the United States and its allies.

4.5   Military and Political Developments in an Unsettled Land

Not unlike the US military offensive, the political reconstruction got off to a good start before colliding with the realities of Afghanistan's decentralized, ethnic, and traditional politics. Historically, Afghanistan never fully evolved into a unified nation, necessary for effective governance. Moreover, the Soviet Union's savage occupation further divided the ruling elites, as it gave birth to an Islamist resistance to atheistic communist doctrine imposed by the Kremlin's puppets in Kabul.

Two Washington shortcomings, however, diminished America's fortunes for duplicating its well-documented success in recasting post–World War II Germany and Japan into model democracies. First, the unanticipated early collapse of Taliban rule caught the United States unready to standup an indigenous civil government acceptable to broad swaths of the population. The new chairman of the Joint Chiefs of Staff, Air Force General Richard B. Myers, mused about hostilities lasting for a year or more. Instead, the Pentagon and the White House beheld a political vacuum created by the panicked disintegration of the Islamist regime in two months.[46] Being unprepared for the sudden flight of the Taliban rulers, including Mullah Omar, the United States resembled a tug-of-war team that reeled when the other side dropped the rope.

Years later in the dead of night, when the Taliban returned to pick up the fight, they found their American foes were pulling against one another in how the intensifying insurgency should be fought. Exponents of heavy firepower crossed swords with proponents of classic counterinsurgency, who believed in winning hearts and minds of the population to marginalize and defeat the Taliban's guerrilla warfare tactics. Even the American ambassador entered the dispute. Karl Eikenberry, a retired three-star Army general and Afghan veteran, cast doubt on the scrupulousness and political capacity of the Kabul ministries to fulfill the vital governing role in waging a counterinsurgency campaign.[47]

The second shortcoming stemmed from the Bush administration's preliminary predisposition against involvement in postwar Afghan governance. Presidential candidate George W. Bush left little doubt about his distaste for plunging the US armed forces into nation-building as the Clinton government undertook in Somalia, Haiti, and the former Yugoslavia. A week into the Afghan campaign, President Bush again made his feelings clear to his advisers: "I don't want to nation-build with troops."[48] The president reflected the realpolitik thinking of his father and that of security adviser Condoleezza Rice, who shared the political realism of her mentor Brent Scowcroft, Bush senior's national security adviser.[49]

Ergo, the top levels of the Bush administration gave little thought on what to do with Afghanistan once the Pentagon unseated the Taliban rulers. Washington, therefore, grabbed the helm of invasion without a compass for governance. On October 7, three days prior to the start of the heavy bombing campaign, at a National Security Council meeting in the White House, the president's chief security adviser was caught off guard by a question about the makeup of the next Kabul government. The commander in chief asked Rice: "Who will run the country?" She confessed that not a lot of thought had been given to the post-invasion phrase.[50]

Later, at the impending fall of Kabul to the US-led coalition, Colin Powell asserted: "We will turn it [Afghanistan] over to Brahimi and the United Nations."[51] The secretary of state was referring to Lakhdar Brahimi, the Algerian diplomat, appointed to be the UN's special representative to Afghanistan by Kofi Annan, the world body's secretary general. At the end of November, Donald Rumsfeld was likewise dismissive of a post-incursion role for his Pentagon. The secretary of defense thought it "highly unlikely" that uniformed Americans would serve in "a semipermanent peacekeeping activity in the country."[52]

Indeed, Washington did strive to pawn off the war-plagued, destitute nation to the international community. The UN Security Council passed Resolution 1378 on November 14. It called for the United Nations to play a "central role" in establishing a transitional administration and to deploy peacekeeping forces to nurture stability. Under prodding from Washington officials, the United Nations convened a meeting of Afghan opposition figures in Bonn, Germany, as the war still raged in the southern tier of the desolate land. After deliberating, the participants signed the Bonn Agreement, which set up a provisional government since no agreed-upon state administration existed since 1979 when the USSR invaded. The summiteers tried to overcome the deadweight of history. They created an interim administration, set forth a framework for basic civic functions, and mapped out a democratic path.

The attendees chose Hamid Karzai, a member of the Pashtun ethnic community who had standing in the Popalzai tribe of the influential Durrani Pashtuns, to be head of the transitional government. Karzai had had run-ins with Kabul during the Taliban's tenure. Karzai, who spoke English, had earlier served as deputy foreign minister. Most significantly, Karzai was acceptable to the Northern Alliance despite his Pashtun lineage. Russia and Iran also gave their approval along with Washington and its allies. The conferees spread ministerial seats among ethnic groups for inclusivity to make up for the lack of electoral democracy.

President Karzai also engaged unsavory military chieftains in administration, such as Abdul Rashid Dostum, so as to reconcile them with the new central government. This practice was a two-edged sword; it also cut at the central government's effectiveness. Warlords mobilized their own militias and ruled their own independent fiefdoms, undermining Kabul's writ. Afghanistan's factionalized nature meant that regional warlords, with no enduring loyalty to a central authority, tore at the very concept of nationhood. Their armed militias and financial resources made them powers unto themselves. Having their own agendas, they ran counter to central authority. So weak was Karzai's rule in the countryside that he was known as the mayor of Kabul.

To aid Afghanistan's stabilization, the United Nations passed a resolution at the end of 2001. It stood up the International Security Assistance Force (ISAF), whose primary duty centered on developing Afghan security forces to ensure public safety. The international unit began with a force of 5,000 international soldiers to restore order in Kabul. Over time, ISAF moved beyond the capital's precincts, only to encounter a resurgent Taliban in the countryside.

As the Iraq War began, NATO assumed leadership of ISAF, which ostensibly took command of the Afghan war in mid-2003, except where the fighting was most intense – along the eastern border with Pakistan. That war zone fell under independent American control, which was fine with the NATO members, for they strove to skirt combat and casualties. Even as the ISAF footprint covered more territory beyond the capital starting in 2006, its commander, British General David Richards, regarded his mission primarily as a peacekeeping operation.[53]

ISAF's responsibilities transitioned to Afghan military and police forces beginning in 2011. Its main purpose shifted to enhancing Afghanistan's counterterrorism capabilities. The Afghan security units took the lead in operations in much of the country by summer 2013. At the end of the following year, the beleaguered country's Afghan National Security Forces assumed full responsibility for security operations. The

ISAF mission ended. International forces transitioned into a largely non-combat role by January 1, 2015. Operation Resolute Support provided equipment, training, and advisement to Afghanistan military, police, and intelligence.

Civil society's economic and political development was accompanied by widespread corruption, particularly in Kabul's government ministries. The Security Council passed Resolution 1401 in March 2002 that formed the UN Assistance Mission in Afghanistan (UNAMA). The UNAMA served to integrate various UN and nongovernmental reconstruction and humanitarian activities. A handful of countries took up the job of instructing and professionalizing the country's rudimentary judiciary and police forces. The Pentagon undertook the herculean task of constituting a national military, known as the Afghan National Army.[54]

The interim government, formed during the Bonn conclave, took office with Hamid Karzai's swearing-in ceremony inside the Kabul Interior Ministry's cavernous hall on December 22, 2001. Authority was transferred to Karzai by the last internationally recognized president, Burhanuddin Rabbani, whose tenure the Taliban militias cut short in 1996. The handover looked auspicious with its peaceful Western decorum. Appearances outside the capital city also seemed pacific. Attacks from the Taliban's rearguard tapered off before re-materializing four years later as a full-blown insurgency that unleashed countless urban bomb blasts and village murders.

The Bonn Agreement gave the temporary Karzai administration six months to convene a *loya jirga*, a traditional council for many of Afghanistan's leaders. The agreement also charged the new rulers with drafting a constitution and holding nationwide elections within two years. Meeting in June 2002, the *loya jirga* of some 1,550 delegates named Karzai president for a two-year term.

To jump ahead, Hamid Karzai won election as president against a score of other candidates in October 2004. His victory, though, was marred with accusations of fraud and corruption by his opponents. More than a year later, in December 2005, the first democratically elected parliament in over thirty years convened. In spite of these democratic milestones, Afghanistan was plagued with the curse of resilient Taliban militants. Subsequent exercises in consensual government ensued over the years. The incumbent Karzai won a second and final term in 2009. He stepped down in 2014 after the election of Ashraf Ghani, an anthropologist-turned-politician. In spite of the orderly transfer of power, Afghan democracy continued to be afflicted by repeated assassination attempts on both presidents and by governmental dysfunction, pervasive corruption, financial scandals, voter fraud, and intimidation at the polls.

4.6   From Laser Airstrikes to Suicide Bombers

Bowing to the dire political reality in Afghanistan, President Bush cast off his administration's reluctance to undertake reconstruction, nation building, and democratic governance. Just weeks after the rout of the Taliban government, Bush committed the United States to a partnership with the Karzai government, in his words to "ensure security, stability and reconstruction for Afghanistan, and foster representative and accountable government for all Afghan women and men."[55] This new dispensation was to be nurtured without an army of occupation, unlike America's showcases of democratic restoration in Germany and Japan, where American military occupiers lingered for years.

What provoked the change of thinking among Bush officials to pick up the nation-building mantel, where earlier they dismissed the idea? Why not just settle for their spectacularly rapid and thorough unseating of the Taliban regime, followed by an "offshore" overwatch? Stripped to its essentials, the Pentagon and the CIA could have carried on their remote war of proxies, aerial strikes, and commando raids, much as the United States took up later in its small-footprint conflicts in Africa and the Middle East to contain, if not defeat, jihadi terrorists. There is no on the road to Damascus answer. Rather, the decision grew out of the same basic American altruism and Wilsonian impetus for advancing progress and democracy as occurred in Somalia, Haiti, and the Balkans. In her memoir, Secretary of State Rice wrote that even before America's counterattack on Afghanistan, "we felt an obligation to leave them [the Afghan people] better off than when we had come."[56] Admitting to changing his mind, President Bush took a little longer to warm up to the prospect of civil reconstruction and social engineering. In January 2002, he reassured Karzai that he could "count on America as a partner ... that we would not abandon his country again." The commander in chief reflected that "we have a moral obligation to leave something better." Bush was not all heart and no head, however. Writing about his White House years, he penned that "terrorists took refuge in places of chaos, despair, and repression." Thus, "we had a strategic interest in helping the Afghan people build a free society."[57]

So as to avoid the appearance of an army occupation, like the Soviet Union undertook, the Pentagon brass deployed a small military footprint. Unwittingly, this decision meant the United States had insufficient troops on the ground to seal the Pakistani border or finish off the remnants of the fleeing Taliban.[58] Bush's America couldn't rectify this misjudgment, because it was gearing up for war in Hussein's Iraq.

Still, Bush associated his occupation-lite policy with the famed Marshall Plan, which is credited with rebuilding post-1945 Europe and securing democracy in the face of communist subversion. In a speech at the Virginia Military Institute, George Marshall's alma mater, in April 2002, the American president praised the legendary former general for "the peace he secured" after World War II.[59] Bush asserted that the plan known for "rebuilding Europe and lifting up former enemies showed that America is not content with military victory alone." He added that Marshall's vision had ignited a "beacon to light the path that we, too must follow."[60]

Despite the lofty rhetoric recalling one of the most hallowed names and notable secretaries of state in American history, Bush soon turned away from the Afghan disarray and fixed on his impending war in Iraq. That second Bush war shortchanged the unstable Afghan peace in military as well as economic resources. Neither congress nor the executive branch ever backed a Marshall Plan–like reconstruction, although they spent more money over the next two decades than the European Recovery Program, much of it went to Afghan security forces. The Bush administration's preoccupation with the Iraq War, which turned into a raging insurgency and sectarian civil war in the years following the 2003 invasion, shifted America's focus away from the Afghan slow-burning brushfire to the Gulf nation. Iraq's mushrooming terrorist insurgency drew military forces, financial resources, and Pentagon bandwidth away from the low-intensity conflict simmering in the faraway Afghanistan.

By going into Iraq and turning a blind eye to the reemergent Taliban threat, the United States missed an opportunity to deal a lethal blow to an adaptable and resilient adversary. Over the years, the Taliban's resurgence was motivated as much by Pashtun dignity and revenge as religious fervor for the loss of their 300-year centrality in the governance of Afghanistan. First the Soviets, and then the Americans, radically altered what "the Pashtuns considered to be the 'natural' order in Afghanistan."[61] Constituting nearly 40 percent of the population, the Pashtuns' aspirations to rule had to be recognized in any political settlement for the country. Pashtun dominance was such that historian Thomas Barfield wrote that Afghanistan could be glossed over as the "land of the Pashtuns" rather than that of the Afghans.[62] In short, the Taliban militants were not the men to beat their swords into ploughshares.

Another, more tactical, factor contributed to the Taliban's comeback in the countryside. At first, US and allied forces thought their street patrolling and armed presence, as in Bosnia and Kosovo, would suffice to restore a peaceful order. Some US commanders came from the ranks of conventional combat divisions. They took charge of their territorial zones with military precision and disciplined efficiency. Green Berets, on the other hand, favored a grassroots interaction with village leaders to win them over to the new dispensation. Steeped in the costly lessons of Vietnam, the Special Forces soldiers resolved to leave aside conventional tactics. Instead, they lived among the villagers, wore similar dress, shared their hardships, supplied basic amenities, and trained them in self-defense techniques.

Above all, they worked to protect the rural populations from insurgent attacks or intimidation, which is at the heart of classic counterinsurgency. US Green Berets referred to these efforts as Village Stability Operations (VSO) in which they strove to help local populations gain security, governance, and development. Military practitioners summarized COIN as implementing a "clear, hold, and build" formula. This catch-phrase summarized the strategy of clearing insurgents from the land, holding territory, and building up the government's capacity to deliver civic services to the populace.

The population-centric approach put them at odds with the regular Army brass, which initially disdained or misunderstood the nature of counterinsurgency.[63] In time, most American and allied ground forces utilized the VSO methods. This close-in approach concentrated on relationship building, while undertaking minor rectification activities such as repairing roads, furnishing electrical generators for lights, and treating injuries or medical conditions, so as to swing the population toward the local authorities and the central government in Kabul. Green Berets went about their business without upsetting traditional life and customs.

Foreign armies hold few cards in the contest to win over the "human terrain" to the counterinsurgency side. The resident populations see them as uncouth and murderous invaders The local insurgents speak the language, understand the culture, and share a nationalistic affinity with their fellow citizens. Outsiders are intruders. In the Afghan case, most of the international forces were also non-Muslims, which helped the local gunmen rally villagers against the foreign infidels in their midst.[64] Those who resisted were killed by the Taliban. Utilizing their advantages, a rejuvenated Taliban slipped back into Afghanistan from their sanctuaries in Pakistan. By 2006, the Taliban were once again a force to be reckoned with in the southern provinces.

As ISAF pushed southward in 2007 from their peacekeeping patrols into Pashtun-majority lands, it ran into an active Taliban insurgency. Some non-American ISAF commanders quickly placed constraints and conditions, or "caveats," on their soldiers' movements. The purpose of caveats was to stave off casualties by minimizing exposure to hostile fire.

This practice lessened flexibility and, more importantly, decreased available military personnel for combat activities. The Pentagon opposed most caveats. The business of war was already restrained by tight rules of engagement (ROE) for ISAF and US Forces in Afghanistan or USFOR-A. The ROEs only allowed troops to use their firearms, if they came under fire first or when no civilians were near enemy shooters so as to spare noncombatant lives.

To confront returning Taliban, Washington had already persuaded NATO to move out its exclusive European arena and to assume the leadership of the International Security Assistance Force in August 2003. By the second half of 2006, ISAF transitioned from defending just Kabul to a nationwide presence. As such, it ran into the Taliban's swelling insurgency, which was being felt even in northern areas by 2008. ISAF's primary objective was to train, advise, and build the Afghan government's newly formed security forces so they could take up the role of protecting the population and reducing the territory being used for terrorist sanctuaries. The NATO-led ISAF permitted the United States to focus its resources on fighting the raging war in Iraq and taking up the security slack in many parts of Afghanistan.[65]

At the height of ISAF's strength, its American contingent numbered 90,000 troops together with NATO country forces of 38,000 and some 4,000 non-Atlantic alliance service members for a total of 132,000 personnel.[66] US generals served as ISAF's commanders as well as heading up the US Forces-Afghanistan. The Pentagon furnished the bulk of resources as well as combatants for both commands. The all-American USFOR-A operated in the eastern part of Afghanistan, where it faced a rising tide of Taliban ambushes, roadside bombs, and suicide detonations, particularly in Helmand province, home to Afghanistan's booming poppy industry. As the United States focused on a worsening war in Iraq, Taliban fighters slipped back into Afghanistan from their refuge in Pakistan. They were joined by Hezb-i-Islami (HIG), the Haqqani network (HQN), foreign fighters, local warlords, and criminal gangs.

Like countless guerrilla armies before them, the Taliban insurgents summarily shot government officials and installed their own representatives. These functionaries adjudicated local disputes, extorted "taxes," and meted out punishment for disloyalty or tipping off the central government with intelligence about the Taliban. The parallel governments enabled the insurgents to administer territory pried from the Kabul authorities. By exploding huge bombs in the capital and other cities, they kept the population on edge and distrustful of official promises of security. The Taliban's re-conquest was well underway as George W. Bush left the White House.

Since Afghanistan lacked functioning government institutions, the United States practiced what became known as a "whole of government" approach for its muscular societal reengineering in a barren landscape. America's new charges needed economic development, new hospitals, modern farming, a working court system, labor regulations, business data, and a host of societal institutions that were deemed essential to the ultimate pacification of the wild and woolly countryside. The implementation proved grueling in overcoming a stubborn rural war and improving life in communities reminiscent of the Old Testament.

This whole of government philosophy was to underpin a fully resourced counterinsurgency campaign. Military commanders and top civilian administrators contended that non-military problems undercut US pacification efforts against the insurgents. Under the rubric of nation building, the White House employed Defense, State Department, Agency for International Development and the departments of Agriculture, Commerce, Justice, and Labor to transform Afghanistan's volatility and violence into a stable mini-America.[67] Getting various American government agencies to collaborate and integrate their programs proved daunting in Afghanistan, Iraq, and other theaters. One authoritative study concluded that, despite years of practice, the "challenges of collaboration in complex environments and the need to engage networks in the Whole-of-Government approach ... shows no sign of diminishing."[68] Modernization proceeded in urban centers, as the populations embraced Westernized fashion, consumption, and mores. Rural areas, on the other hand, lagged in economic and political development as the Taliban menaced villagers and security forces with bombings and small-arms fire.

So as to counter the growing bloodshed in the countryside, the United States redoubled its classic counterinsurgency practices. To pacify the rural provinces, where the vast majority of Afghans live, Washington adopted methods to build popular legitimacy for the provincial and district governments by boosting their capacity for effective governance, together with constructing schools, roads, and dams. The purpose was not for the US military and their civilian technicians to win hearts and minds for the American cause but to win them for the Afghan political leadership. Decades of distrusted, abusive, and corrupt officials made the task almost a lost cause from the get-go.

Washington introduced Provincial Reconstruction Teams (PRTs) to work at the district and provincial level. The civilian-military PRTs sought to enhance the defense of villagers while trying to improve local governance, agriculture production of non-poppy crops, and economic development. They also worked to demobilize and reintegrate militants back into society. Unlike the civilian-led PRTs in Iraq, the Afghan variety were under command of military officers, which some observes contended skewed the priorities away from civic projects.[69]

Although the United States provided the bulk of the personnel and resources for the PRTs, it transferred the supervision of the teams to the NATO-headed ISAF by late 2006. Composed of between 100 to 125 members (roughly half were military to protect the teams), their civilian experts came, in part, from the US Agency for Development, plus other government branches. All but three of the twenty-five PRTs were American staffed and funded by Washington, along with some of its international partners. The PRTs opened health clinics where they delivered first-aid and vaccinations. By 2011, they incurred President Karzai's wrath for creating institutions separate from the central government. Over time, the United States phased out the PRTs. Overall, their record was mixed. Clearly, the PRTs failed to interdict the Taliban's spreading violent subversion and territorial dominance, if not physical control. But this was not their failing alone.

The entire American military enterprise veered toward defeat. Less than four years after their innovative intervention, US forces encountered severe headwinds from an intensifying insurgency ripping across Afghanistan that was only eclipsed by an even fiercer sectarian civil war in Iraq. President Bush passed a losing war to his successor, who in turn handed over a "forever war" to his successor.

5   The Iraq War
Changing a Regime, Building Democracy, and Fighting an Insurgency

<hr>

> But, in my opinion, there is no such thing as a preventive war.   Dwight
> Eisenhower, Remarks at the Carnegie Institute, Pittsburgh, 1950

> Wars begin where you will, but they do not end where
> you please.   Niccolò Machiavelli

After the devastating 9/11 attack, fear and mistrust lay at the bottom of
the controversial US decision to go to war against the Republic of Iraq.
A Gresham's Law of decision-making functioned when a catastrophic
event drove out sound thinking about implications of casting the die for a
second war. The George W. Bush administration feared another calamitous sneak attack hitting America – this time with weapons of mass
destruction. It singularly distrusted Saddam Hussein's Iraq because of
Baghdad's past nuclear-arms quest, history of regional conflict, suspected ties to terrorist networks, and war-like rhetoric. Washington's
apprehension and Baghdad's provocations conspired to make a second
conflict almost inevitable. Once the Bush White House decided on war,
it viewed an occupation of Iraq, as Michael R. Gordon and Bernard
E. Trainor describe in their book *The Endgame*, "as a strategic opportunity and even a moral crusade" to implant democracy, reflecting a new
"freedom agenda."[1]

In the course of the earlier Persian Gulf War, the world learned of
Iraq's budding nuclear program at Tuwaitha, just outside the capital.
International arms inspectors shut down this nuclear site along with
some lesser facilities. The site's very existence, nevertheless, fueled anxiety about the extent of Iraq's nuclear know-how, potential atomic
weapons stockpile, and malign intentions. Misgivings about the country's capacity and agenda for amassing nuclear weapons deepened over
the next decade. President Bush senior and Bill Clinton had lined up
international arms inspections to ferret out any Iraqi WMD facilities.
Over and over again, Hussein thwarted the inspectors. His threatening
behavior and the 9/11 terrorism combined to create a well of foreboding

and suspicion. As a consequence, the Bush administration took counsel of its fears.

Although Dick Cheney was a moderating voice against seizing Baghdad when he was defense secretary at the time of the Gulf War, he became an outspoken advocate for the 2003 Iraq War as George W. Bush's vice president. Like his boss, Cheney believed war and invasion were necessary to safeguard the United States from a pending nuclear threat. In the August before the US invasion, speaking before the Veterans of Foreign Wars in Nashville, Cheney thundered that "there is no doubt" that Iraq possessed weapons of mass destruction. He added that defensive wars are unwinnable; "we must take the battle to the enemy." He justified his uber-hawkishness, as did the president, on the need to safeguard American lives. Cheney sounded the administration's mantra that the "president and I never for a moment forget our number one responsibility: To protect the American people against *further* attack."[2]

A faulty U.S. government intelligence assessment about Saddam Hussein's likely possession of the most lethal weapons of mass destruction reinforced the perception of a genuine threat. In sum, George W. Bush could have dodged a regime-change war that led to occupation, insurgency, and a costly stabilization campaign, as his father had done. When no nuclear arms were uncovered, many Americans lost faith in the war and the White House. The dubious reasons for going to war against Iraq, therefore, generated much belated controversy.

Historically, fear has led to other disastrous wars. Fear contributed to a ruinous war between ancient Athens and Sparta according to Thucydides, the fifth-century BCE historian.[3] The multiple reasons for the start of World War I remain debatable to this day. Fear, nevertheless, featured predominately in the participants' decisions to fight. Wilhelmine Germany, in part, went to war in 1914 out of the dread for a rising Russia and a declining Austrian-Hungarian Empire – Berlin's chief European ally. Britain entered into the Great War against Germany at the prospect that the Kaiser's defeat of France would pave the way for German hegemony over the Continent. Two decades afterward, Imperial Japan bombed the US fleet at Pearl Harbor to preempt American naval power from threatening its Asian conquests.

In the Iraq case, the American people shared in their government's war decision to deal with the worries about Hussein's Baghdad. Just days after the US intervention, a CNN/USA Today poll recorded a whopping 72 percent of Americans expressed support for the attack.[4] That no nuclear WMD turned up inside Iraq dissolved the administration's *casus belli* and turned Americans in large numbers against the war over time.

The disclosure that the Baath regime had no megadeath bombs also dispelled the feelings of anxiety that characterized the immediate pre-war period, making the war seem pointless thereafter.

Once its original case fell apart, the Bush White House evangelized the cause of democracy as an unassailable and noble justification for war.[5] The administration's post-hoc pretext for intervention – so as to substitute liberal democracy for an oppressive despotism – never resonated widely with the public. In the 2006 midterm elections – nearly three years after the US invasion – the Democratic Party won both houses of Congress for the first time since 1994, in part because of dissatisfaction with the Iraq War.

But before the war, Salafi-jihadi terrorism in Manhattan and Washington generated a war psychosis that crowded out clear and dispassionate judgments about what America's policy should be toward Iraq. Enough uncertainty and trepidation hung in the air to contribute to the deeply flawed 2002 National Intelligence Estimate (NIE) on Iraq's mass destruction weaponry. The rushed ninety-two-page NIE relied on existing "off the shelf" prior assessments and was produced in what Senator Robert Byrd (Democrat, West Virginia) characterized as a "war fervor" atmosphere.[6]

Osama bin Laden's "planes operation" stirred a pervasive fear and even desperation that other attacks were in the offing. Even the full-blown assault on al Qaeda's Afghan sanctuary never eliminated this angst in key members of the George W. Bush administration that the country faced another 9/11-scale attack.[7] Coming into office, the president and Colin Powell, the secretary of state, first worked at keeping "Saddam in his box" with more sanctions. Later Bush wrote: "9/11 hit, and we had to take a fresh look at every threat in the world."[8]

Leading up to the Iraq invasion, the political mood was thick with talk about the first-strike options to counter nuclear threats. Policymakers, pundits, and academics differentiated between preventive wars (launched to destroy a potential threat) and preemptive military strikes (executed to head off an imminent attack). Bush officials articulated the two definitions, sometimes interchangeably, and for Iraq generally endorsed the preventive option. But the administration's *National Security Strategy* of September 2002 argued: "We must deter and defend against the threat before it is unleashed .... The United States will, if necessary, act preemptively."[9] Proponents of the Bush doctrine, including defense hawks and neoconservatives (a political movement that broke years earlier with pacifist wing of the Democratic Party), lauded the proactive approach toward Iraq. They believed Hussein always had his sword half out of its scabbard.[10] Detractors of Bush's rush to war condemned the White House for ramming through its case with murky, even false, intelligence on Iraq's nuclear and chemical arms capabilities.[11]

Not a few critics judged the president harshly over the issue of phantom nukes. They chanted that "Bush lied and people died." Even a caustic detractor of the Bush administration's war decision, like Michael Mazarr, acknowledged that the president must have felt "an insistent compulsion to protect the American people from further attack."[12]

The war against the Baath regime was blamed on the neoconservatives inside the Bush administration and outside it, particularly at the American Enterprise Institute, a think tank in the District of Columbia. The neocons, for the most part disenchanted former Democrats, lined up against Iraq, which they held accountable for many ills in the Middle East. Within the Bush entourage, nearly a dozen neocons served in various capacities, with political clout inside the top civilian ranks of the Defense Department. They backed a war against the Baathist regime to replace it with a democratic government.[13] So virulent ran their animosity that detractors accused them of being infected with Iraqnophobia, a pathological hatred of the Gulf nation. While the neo-cons were politically influential, they could not have prodded George W. Bush to war without the United States suffering a catastrophic terrorist blow, which generated uncertainty about other potential threats and rallied the nation behind its commander in chief.[14]

Some commentators forgave the Bush foreign policy team for getting the WMD intelligence terribly wrong but not their actual handling of the Iraq War, which suffered from mismanagement and mistakes after the masterpiece invasion phase.[15] Whatever the judgment on the rationale for America's entry into the Iraq War, an inescapable verdict endures about its strategic value. In the last analysis, it was a mistake. There are historical judgments that persist over time – Munich's 1930s appease-ment failed; America slid down the slippery slope into the Vietnam War; and now America got it wrong about the Iraq War. The cost in blood and treasure exceeded all expectations. One poll from the Pew Research Center fifteen years after the start of the intervention recorded that nearly half (48 percent) of Americans regarded the decision to use military force against Iraq as a wrong decision.[16]

Nothing looms on the horizon that might change the widely shared view that the United States made a grievous error in going to war against Saddam Hussein. For all his faults, the Iraqi autocrat was a counter-weight to the aggressive theocracy in Iran.[17] His ouster meant that the United States was now left to directly confront Tehran's machinations in the Middle East. Some will respond that without the US and allied invasion, Hussein would have sooner or later turned again to nuclear arms. True, he might have. But we will never know for sure what history would have brought since Bush came into the Oval Office with other concerns.

Rather than obsessing about Hussein, the incoming Bush administration was warily eyeing an emerging People's Republic of China (PRC). The former Texas governor and his national security adviser Condoleezza Rice believed that a rising China posed a challenge. The president lambasted Bill Clinton's project to form a strategic partnership with the PRC. Six months into office, President Bush declared China a "strategic competitor."[18]

A year earlier, while campaigning for candidate Bush, Stanford University professor Rice wrote in *Foreign Affairs* that China sought "to alter Asia's balance of power in its own favor."[19] The foreign policy adviser disputed Clinton's romanticized view of China as a benign trading partner. In Bush's second term, Rice – now secretary of state – leaned on Beijing to resolve the nuclear arms threat posed by rogue North Korea, again postponing a reckoning with the PRC's trade practices. But in 2000, Rice expressed no urgency about Iraq or North Korea as rogue states because they lived on "borrowed time, so there need be no sense of panic about them." To deter them from rash activities, the soon-to-be national security adviser recommended "classical deterrence," not war.[20]

Pre-9/11, the Bush administration encountered a grave international crisis with China, a mere three months after it first held the reins of office. A Chinese pilot foolhardily sideswiped his jet fighter into a US reconnaissance aircraft, resulting in a forced landing for the American plane on Hainan Island. Chinese authorities detained the twelve crew members for eleven days and stripped the spy plane of its advanced surveillance equipment, before returning it in pieces months later. Upon recovery of the EP-3, US authorities found a note under the front seat in English: "Thank you." Other Chinese thefts of America's advanced technology were subtler.

This fleeting high-stakes drama was overtaken by the immediacy of the horrific events on America's eastern seaboard. The Bush foreign policy team shelved its burgeoning counter-China stance. It had a new, urgent threat to confront. Thereupon, the United Stated first launched the war on terrorism in Afghanistan, then invaded Iraq for WMD, and next set out to strike at Salafi-jihadism globally.

5.1   Saddam Must Go

Given the decade-long roadblocks encountered by UN nuclear-weapons inspectors to uncover atomic arms in Hussein's Iraq, it was not out of the question that Baghdad was hiding weapons of mass destruction.[21] By advertising Iraq's putative nuclear capacity to keep Iran in check, Hussein himself underscored the assumption that Baghdad possessed atomic weapons.[22] The authoritarian leader bragged about his nuclear capability to intimidate Iran and other enemies. As a result, Hussein lifted himself on his own petard, while inviting the Baathist regime's destruction.

Saddam Hussein's years of obstructing arms inspections heightened fears among senior Bush officials as American and allied intelligence findings concurred that Baghdad possessed a developing nuclear-weapons capacity to match its chemical and biological cache.[23] The existence of megadeath arms and Hussein's willful intentions to employ them raised the stakes to the level that the Bush administration felt compelled to conduct a preventive war. The president himself believed that "time is not on our side." Convinced he was in a race against a duplicitous Hussein, Bush vented, "I will not wait on events, while dangers gather" in his 2002 State of the Union Address.[24]

Inside and outside the Bush administration, the false assumption prevailed that Saddam Hussein also had links to al Qaeda. But George Tenet, the CIA director, repeatedly denied possession of any reliable intelligence confirming collaboration between al Qaeda and Iraq in his statements to the commission on the 9/11 attacks. The Agency concluded in June 2002 that there were few substantiated contacts between al Qaeda jihadis and Iraqi officials. Thus, the intelligence chief objected to speeches and interviews, in which Bush appointees suggested a Hussein–bin Laden working pact.[25] At some remove from the American incursion, the Defense Department's own inspector general issued a declassified report in 2007 that spelled out that "the Hussein regime was not directly cooperating with al Qaeda before the U.S. invasion."[26]

Once convinced of Hussein's nuclear culpability, George W. Bush could not be dissuaded from war, even by the towering figure of Colin Powell. The former four-star Army general revealed years later his interaction with Bush: "I didn't say to him, 'I oppose this war.' Because it wouldn't have worked."[27] All lay plain and clear before Bush – regime change, denuclearization, and democratization became the order of the day.

Others in the administration also held warlike views about the Iraqi tyrant. Populating this anti-Hussein clique were a half dozen civilian officials in Donald Rumsfeld's Pentagon, chiefly Paul Wolfowitz, who harbored a deep animus toward Hussein. Ahead of serving in the second Bush administration, Wolfowitz had acted as the intellectual catalyst making the case for removing the Iraqi strongman because his policies destabilized the Middle East during the 1990s.[28] Vice President Cheney jumped quickly into the hawkish camp. His prodding of the intelligence establishment to find Iraq had nuclear arms later came under close scrutiny.[29] Days after 9/11, they agitated for war against Hussein to get rid of him, when Bush's closest aides were drawing a bead on al Qaeda and its Afghan lair.[30]

In the post-1991 years, Washington carried on hostilities against Iraq with air-to-ground missile attacks. So, relations between the two antagonists were anything but peaceful. Both Bush (41) and Clinton mounted massive air bombardments of Iraqi military targets, when Hussein hamstrung UN arms inspectors searching for nuclear or chemical plants. Both US administrations kept up air patrols to destroy Iraqi air defense radars and missile sites. They fired salvos to protect a semiautonomous Kurdistan in the country's north. For its part, Baghdad flaunted its hindrance of UN weapons inspectors, threatened neighbors, and backed Palestinian attacks on Israel.

In 1998, the US Congress passed a bipartisan Iraq Liberation Act that called for the removal of Hussein from power, authorized $97 million to fund Hussein opponents, and set up Radio Free Iraq to broadcast anti-Baghdad information into the dictatorial state. After its passage, America's official Iraq policy was regime change. By the time President Clinton left office, nonetheless, his administration had spent less than $3 million from the dedicated budget. Doing hardly nothing to subvert the Iraqi regime, Clinton's America was still at daggers drawn with it, when the two-termed president vacated the White House in early 2001. His successor made up for lost time.

5.2   Gearing Up for a Second War against Iraq

The Afghan War had just begun when, during the Thanksgiving holiday at the White House, President Bush requested war plans for Iraq from Donald Rumsfeld. The Defense Secretary, in turn, commanded Army General Tommy Franks to begin planning for an armed intervention. The CENTCOM chief updated Op Plan 1003, the Top Secret operational strategy that resembled the 1991 Kuwait operation. Like its predecessor, the off-the-shelf plan called for a large ground force, in this case a minimum of 500,000 troops. Again, the war planners envisioned a massive buildup of military matériel in neighboring states to feed a nearly insatiable demand for arms, ammunition, and fuel by the invading army.

The size of the land force dismayed Rumsfeld. The former corporate titan put his stock in a lighter, faster, and highly lethal force that would crush an adversary with "shock and awe." He pushed his officers to cut the force drastically. Over the next year, Franks and his staff whittled down the number of the invading American troops, ultimately reaching 145,000 US soldiers and Marines for invasion. The next largest contributor was Britain with over 40,000 combatants. Other nations made much smaller commitments to the more than a quarter million invading troops.[31]

Unlike the Persian Gulf War, there was no sizeable Arab contingent. Most Middle Eastern governments opposed the US incursion and ouster of Hussein.[32] Saudi Arabia, the Arab lynchpin in the previous war, feared a rise in Iran's malign presence regionwide unchecked from an intact and muscular Iraq. Egypt and Syria also joined the desert kingdom. History bore out their forebodings. Other Arabian Peninsula sheikdoms stepped into the breach created from Riyadh's absence by granting airfields and forward bases.

CENTCOM laid plans for land and air assaults into Iraq. It poured concrete for buildings, expanded runways, and erected storage facilities in Qatar, Kuwait, Oman, and the United Arab Emirates. On its island base in Bahrain, the US Fifth Fleet geared up for the upcoming war. Not all states in the neighborhood were cooperative, however. Syria, Yemen, Jordan (gave covert assistance), and other Arab states publicly abstained from the attack. Accounts of war preparations among the Persian Gulf states and military plans regularly popped up in the news media by spring 2002.[33] Operation Iraqi Freedom (OIF) was still a year away but the military buildup steamed ahead.

Not to be left behind, the Department of State organized workshops during summer 2002 for experts and exiles for its Future of Iraq Project. The participants considered the post-Baath Party political order and government institution. They made recommendations to deal with corruption and police abuse. The thirteen volumes pinpointed post-intervention problems but the reports were not a formal blueprint for restoring civil society.[34] In his memoir, Rumsfeld dismissed the Future of Iraq Project, because its "broad concepts" did not "constitute postwar planning in any sense of the word. There were no operational steps outlined in them nor any detailed suggestions about how to handle various problems."[35]

As the Defense Department readied for Operation Iraqi Freedom, the White House pursued a diplomatic track, while publically foreswearing war talk. Returning from Moscow after signing the Strategic Offensive Reductions Treaty (to limit both countries' nuclear arsenal) with the Russian Federation in May 2002, President Bush told German and French leaders: "I have no war plans on my desk, which is the truth."[36] The American leader's reassurances hardly allayed French and German skepticism. So ramped up was the media reportage of America's military mobilization in the Gulf that the *Financial Times* characterized it in a clever recasting of one of Churchill's most memorable quotes: "Never in the field of human conflict has so much war planning been revealed to so many by so few."[37]

As part of its campaign to win political support for war with Hussein's Iraq, the administration rolled out the doctrine of preventive war. George Bush laid the cornerstone during a West Point commencement address. Speaking on the banks of the Hudson River on June 1, 2002, he departed from previous US administrations' policy of containing and deterring Iraq's threats. Instead of waiting for "threats to fully materialize," America would take "preemptive action when necessary." In careful language he announced a "strike first" strategy.[38]

Bush returned to the preventive war theme in earnest that autumn. Officials repeatedly sounded the WMD alarm. The national security adviser uttered a memorable characterization of the fledgling doctrine. While giving a CNN interview, Condoleezza Rice replied: "We don't want the smoking gun to be a mushroom cloud," alluding to a nuclear explosion.[39] In mid-September, George Bush spoke to the General Assembly, beseeching the United Nations to enforce its myriad resolutions against the Republic of Iraq. He pointedly raised the prospect of war: "If the Iraqi regime wishes peace, it will immediately and unconditionally forswear, disclose, and remove weapons of mass destruction, long-range missiles, and all related materials."[40]

The United Kingdom entered into the contentious issue by shoring up estimates made by US agencies. Prime Minister Tony Blair came out in favor of the US course of action against Saddam Hussein. London released a sensational dossier, Iraq's Weapons of Mass Destruction, which purported to prove that Baghdad was pursuing WMD. A year later, the dossier was exposed as an egregious fraud. But in the run-up to the Iraq War, it buttressed the Bush administration's case against Hussein.

At nearly the same moment, the US National Intelligence Estimate unveiled its report on Iraq. The NIE presented a summation of the American intelligence community's findings. Its report assessed that Baghdad possessed biological weapons and held chemical stockpiles of 500 metric tons with more in production. This assessment turned out to be totally bogus. Two years later, the presidential Commission on Intelligence Capabilities of the United States Regarding Weapons of Mass Destruction concluded: "These assessments were wrong."[41] This clarification was little comfort to a nation already at war over grossly inaccurate WMD appraisals.

Fall 2002 also marked the release of National Security Strategy by the White House as mandated by the 1986 Goldwater-Nichols Act. The Bush strategy outlined a new formula for preventative attack. Foreshadowed in the president's West Point speech, the strategic document set forth an offensive posture toward terrorists and rogue states that red flagged Hussein's Iraq. The report let it be known that even absent approval of the international community, the United States would still exercise "our right to self-defense by acting preemptively against such terrorists to prevent them from doing harm against our people and our country."[42]

With the doctrinal foundation behind it, the Bush White House turned to rousing domestic and international consent for an Iraqi intervention. To win over the American public, George Bush went into campaign mode by delivering speeches and statements. In his Cincinnati speech, he warned that Iraq "could have a nuclear weapon in less than a year."[43]

Just before the legislative branch voted on the Authorization for Use of Military Force Against Iraq Resolution, the administration released a declassified edition of the National Intelligence Estimate, which was shorn of the caveats, dissent, and doubts about Iraq's WMD capabilities present in the classified version. The declassified text came close to policy advocacy, for it endorsed the White House's version of the Iraq threat without any of the skepticism in the classified NIE.[44] Public opinion polls reflected widespread approval for Bush's muscular approach. On the eve of the Iraq War, one opinion poll showed 71 percent of the respondents endorsed the president's forceful disarmament policy.[45]

The US Senate and House overwhelmingly authorized the president to wield military power "as he determines to be necessary and appropriate" against Iraq in a vote in the second week of October.[46] Congress, therefore, granted wide latitude to the nation's commander in chief to use preventative military force against the Baath leadership. Some Democratic legislators cynically endorsed the White House's initiative because they had missed out on the widespread popularity of Gulf War's victory in 1991. Others were genuinely opposed to Hussein's gross human rights abuses and dangerous provocations. Republicans overwhelmingly backed their president. Later, as disenchantment with the war worsened among the general public, the lawmakers contended that Bush misled the nation about Hussein's WMD stockpiles.

With domestic support nailed down, the White House turned to the United Nations for its endorsement of the invasion. The Security Council proved a far tougher nut to crack, although most members acknowledged that the Baath regime was progressing toward chemical, biological, and, perhaps, nuclear armaments. Led by France, China, and Russia, the council opted for two votes: one to determine Iraq's "material breach" of the various UN arms control resolutions and a second vote to decide the course of action. Washington favored one vote. If the council found a material breach, then that vote automatically would trigger a resolution authorizing the United States and other powers to resort to "all means necessary," or, in other words, war. Once the two-step procedure was reluctantly accepted by the Bush mandarins in mid-November, the council sent the UN Monitoring, Verification and Inspection Commission (UNMOVIC) team into Iraq to uncover secret WMD sites, with a report deadline set for January, 2003.

Meanwhile, preparations for OIF proceeded apace. American troops, weapons, and military stores flowed into several of the Arab Gulf countries. To be near the frontlines, CENTCOM (headquartered in Tampa, Florida) opened a satellite installation in Qatar. General Franks moved his war-fighting command to the new nerve center. The perception grew that America was going to war no matter what was uncovered by the international arms inspectors.

Both UNMOVIC and the UN's International Atomic Energy Agency complained about Iraq's grudging cooperation during their search for megadeath arms. Crucially, they reported simultaneously that no prohibited weapons had been discovered before the late January deadline. Both agencies pleaded for more time to do their work. At the time of the inspectors' reportage, President Bush delivered his second State of the Union address, at which he presented a US intelligence assessment that the Baath regime possessed large quantities of anthrax and botulinum toxins. The US leader also argued that Hussein never accounted for "30,000 munitions capable of delivering chemical agents."[47]

All the administration's strident assertions about WMD dissolved into hot air after the land incursion turned up no useable nuclear, chemical, or biological weapons, outside of a cache of deteriorating 1980s chemical artillery shells. This realization contributed to the public's unhappiness with the Iraq War. In the course of the lead up the US invasion, the Bush government's assertions about Hussein's arms of mass destruction dampened opposition to the war. But the Bush White House's relentless march to intervention never muzzled opponents, who staged public demonstrations in Europe as well as America.

To win over the UN Security Council's opposition, Bush's America dispatched the nation's top diplomat to make the administration's case against Iraq. Former Army general Colin Powell delivered a riveting presentation that commanded global television viewership. The secretary of state's case later fell apart upon close examination. Under intense scrutiny, his arguments collapsed over time, as the underlying intelligence proved inaccurate. Powell felt betrayed by his own administration. His reputation suffered with this "blot" on his record.[48]

At the time of the UN speech, Powell met with no success among the permanent Security Council members, nor with Germany. Only Britain stood with the United States. The Atlantic divide was the most bitter in years. Academic Robert Kagan expounded on the political culture: "Americans are from Mars and Europeans are from Venus."[49] So steep was the split that the Bush foreign policy team did not press for the second council vote, knowing that it was a lost cause. Instead, they decided to act without the UN by pulling together a coalition of willing partners to topple Saddam Hussein, who exuded a conquistadorial optimism and a false sense of security from attack.

5.3   Operation Iraqi Freedom: America's Cakewalk War

Twelve hundred miles from George Bush's bête noire in Baghdad, the Afghan war was heating up. There was something Napoleonic to starting another war before finishing the old one. Fighting in Afghanistan and Iraq was also accompanied by a growing worldwide conflict against terrorism. Stealth and secrecy defined this war known for its below-the-radar drone strikes and commando-style raids by America's shadowy Special Operations Forces in the Philippines, Somali, Yemen, and other states. None of these smaller hostilities greatly suffered from Washington's re-focus to Iraq as did Afghanistan.

Long before soldiers rushed forward and battle tanks clanked in a second war on Iraq, American and British warplanes obliterated targets below their wings. The Anglo-American air forces had patrolled over northern and southern no-fly zones since the end of the Persian Gulf War. These air incursions, as related in Chapter 2, were to protect first the Kurds in northern Iraq and then later, and much less effectively, the Shiite population from the Iraqi dictator's murderous police. The zones prohibited Iraqi flyovers. Over the following decade, the warplanes strafed radar installations and missile batteries on the ground. In the lead-up to Operation Iraqi Freedom, the Pentagon and the Royal Air Force accelerated their continuous bombing campaign. From June 2002 until the American-led invasion started, the Anglo-American pilots flew over 21,000 sorties and struck 349 terrestrial targets, encompassing air defense installations, command-and-control nodes, and fiber-optic communication networks.

In the course of the first days of intense land warfare, the air campaign turned on Hussein's army with some 1,800 airplanes on station. From this armada, the coalition lofted some 1,000 warplanes in the air each day. Overall, the Anglo-American aircraft struck Soviet T-72 tanks, armed personnel carriers, and artillery pieces – blowing them all to smithereens. Iraq's Bronze-Age horde ran full-force into a twenty-first century, information-age military. The conventional war recorded a one-sided American-British victory.[50]

Speaking from the Oval Office, Bush addressed his fellow Americans the evening of March 19, 2003, to announce Operation Iraqi Freedom, forty-five minutes after the commencement of bombing strikes in and around Baghdad to decapitate the Baathist regime. Hussein survived the attacks. The US president proved to be far more prescient than he imagined when he postulated that fighting in the days ahead "could be longer and more difficult than some predict."[51] Poor intelligence largely accounted for the failed decapitation airstrikes. The failure pointed to an inauspicious prelude to a war that was to be a "cakewalk," as character-ized by one of its ardent advocates.[52] The quick victories in Panama and the Persian Gulf war instilled a false sense of optimism before the Iraq infestation.

America's invasion strategy incorporated basic geopolitical consider-ations about geography, terrain, and the Republic of Iraq's defenses. Initially, the Defense Department planned for a two-front war, with armored columns thrusting deep into Iraq from the country's north and south. Such a dual offensive would have compelled Iraq's disorgan-ized armed forces to split resources and wage war against two widely separated, fast-paced mechanized sprints. The defense secretary held that a variant of the World War II Germans' blitzkrieg warfare – armored tanks, mechanized infantry, close-air support to punch through enemy frontlines – would make up for a smaller ground force. Whereas the Persian Gulf War recorded close to 700,000 troops, counting allies, OIF reached a total of 284,500 US and coalition troops a month after the start of the invasion.[53] Rumsfeld wholeheartedly believed that his prized smaller army's lethality, speed, mobility, and awesome firepower would outweigh any advantage of sending larger forces. The defense secretary threw out the phrase "shock and awe" to convey the devastating blow that was to befall Iraq's Republican Guards.

Opening a northern front depended on permission for access across Turkey by the Ankara government. The recently elected Justice and Development Party spurned Washington's $26 billion aid package for the 4th US Infantry division to transit from Mediterranean ports to Iraq's northeastern corner. Occurring just weeks prior to the Iraqi D-Day invasion, the close parliamentary vote killed plans for the northern land-based attack. The DoD quickly substituted an airborne entry of special-forces teams and regular troops to link up with the Kurdish irregulars in northern Iraq. The eighty-ship flotilla carrying equipment for the Army division off the coast steamed from Turkish waters to Kuwait, where it joined the fight four weeks after the start of the incursion. In retrospect, the Turks' rejection caused no appreciable disruption in the seizure of Baghdad, the original destination of the planned fast-rolling northern and southern pincer columns. Even without the heavy-duty force from the north, the capital fell three weeks after American and British armored vehicles crossed the frontier into Iraq.

The US military implemented a relatively conventional attack strategy as it took account of Iraq's riverine features. Iraq's ancient name of Mesopotamia means in Greek "the land between two rivers." War planners mapped approaches alongside the Tigris and Euphrates Rivers for battle tanks and other high-tonnage vehicles to storm Baghdad.

Their operational orders called for the Army's Third Infantry Division to barrel up the west side of the Euphrates. Its famed "thunder run" advanced the column toward the capital's gates. Meanwhile, the 1st Marine Division rolled up the plain between the two famed rivers. Just before American military units reached Baghdad, some 25,000 British soldiers laid siege to Basra, the country's second largest city, which thereby guarded the Marine's right flank from any potential Iraqi counterattack. The Anglo-American commanders coordinated their simultaneous offenses into both urban areas to discombobulate further the overmatched defenders.

Based on the US Army's AirLand Battle doctrine, the offensive, which also borrowed from Germany's blitzkrieg tactics, stressed tight coordination between ground forces and airstrikes. This 1980s–1990s strategy was rehearsed in the European theater to turn back a Red Army onslaught. In Iraq, the Pentagon's ground attacks launched with massive firepower, speed, and maneuverability. Main battle tanks and armored infantry carriers sped into Iraq from their staging areas in Kuwait. Highly trained crews and superior weapons' technology all but guaranteed the lethality of the fast-moving armored forces. When they collided with Hussein's Republican Guards, the Iraqis were crushed in mismatched encounters that resembled computer war games. Cobra II, the official designation of the Pentagon's attack plan, turned out to be an unmitigated disaster for dictator's forces.

As the armored pinchers closed in on Baghdad and other urban centers, a host of unconventional operations unfolded to attain other objectives of the invasion. These may seem like "off Broadway" missions but each fulfilled vital purposes. US Navy SEALs, British Special Boat Service crews, Polish GROM (Thunder) commandos, and other elite warfighters captured offshore oil platforms to prevent their destruction. Equally vital, if less splashy, Special Operation Forces operating in the western Iraq desert neutralized Scud missile batteries and seized the H1 and H2 airfields before they could launch rockets on Israel. Had the Jewish State been assaulted, its justifiable retaliation against Hussein's bases might have destabilized the Arab Middle East at a time when Washington hoped for neutrality among Iraq's neighbors.[54] British coalition forces also prevented Hussein saboteurs from torching all but a handful of oil wells in the coveted Rumaila oilfields.

Twenty days from the ground war's kickoff, Abrams tanks accompanied by Bradley Fighting Vehicles smashed through Baghdad's flimsy defenses, overran their hastily built redoubts, and infested palaces pushing aside the outmatched defenders. The Army's Third Infantry Division battered its way into central Baghdad. The 1st Marine Division crushed the overwhelmed Iraqi defenders in hasty-dug trenches around buildings. The Leathernecks rolled over their inadequately trained adversaries. The swift defeat of Republican Guards and Special Republic Guards no doubt spared civilian lives. Oil wells were also spared and excessive damage minimized. Secretary of Defense Rumsfeld seemed vindicated by his insistence that a small invasion army go toe-to-toe with Hussein's 400,000 soldiers. Rumsfeld's shock-and-awe strategy didn't just prevail over the opposing armored forces; it stomped them.

OIF's combat operations all but stopped on April 14. Back in Washington, the DoD's spokesperson declared: "The regime is at its end and its leaders are either dead, surrendered, or on the run."[55] Standing on the deck of the USS *Abraham Lincoln* off the coast of San Diego, George W. Bush announced the cessation of major military actions six weeks after invasion's rollout. Following a photo-op landing in a small airplane, the president stood in front of banner emblazoned with "Mission Accomplished." That glib conclusion soon haunted the Bush administration as Iraq plunged into bloody insurgency. To his credit, the commander in chief never uttered the phrase. If anything, he correctly argued that "the war on terror is not over," by way of highlighting the intractableness of battling terrorism.[56]

The dreaded battle of Bagdad never occurred, despite armchair generals' predictions of another Stalingrad. CENTCOM commander Franks later reflected that the only observers taken by surprise at the sudden victory were "the cable news folks, like Al-Jazeera and CNN."[57] Other dire projections also fell by the wayside, such as the fear of biological weapons. In fact, Hosni Mubarak, the Egyptian president, warned Tommy Franks that Saddam Hussein "has WMD – biologicals, actually – and he will use them on your troops."[58] At the opening stages,

US soldiers and Marines temporarily donned protective suits in the sweltering heat to protect against chemical and biological weapons. But Hussein's army never fired its aged mustard-agent artillery shells.

The gloomy forecasts of massive casualties also failed to materialize. Two inside-the-Beltway pundits made predictions of thousands of US dead and wounded that turned out to be far off the mark.[59] Actual American casualties came in at eighty-nine killed in action and another forty-nine from accidents (including friendly-fire deaths) by May 1st. British military deaths numbered forty-two, of which nineteen resulted from accidents. Iraqi military casualties were the subject of conjecture. Estimates varied from 5,000 to 20,000 deaths.[60] Iraq's civilian deaths were a matter of guesswork also. One plausible estimate placed the figure at 3,240 deaths.[61] In World War II, for comparison, some 35,000 French citizens died in the lead-up to the Allied landing at Normandy and to the assault itself from "bombing, strafing, and artillery strikes."[62] The 1944 invasion witnessed much heavier and longer battling than the Iraq attack phase. Compared to modern warfare death rates, the troop body count during the Iraqi invasion was decidedly lower than it could have been. Advances in military medical care explain the smaller figures. Swift evacuation (inside the "golden hour"), usually by helicopter, of wounded troops to field hospitals, distribution of blood-clotting bandages, and one-hand tourniquets at the squad level greatly contributed to fewer body bags going home.

Three months after the Republican Guards were ignominiously defeated, General Franks retired from active service after overseeing interventions into Afghanistan and Iraq. The CENTCOM job fell to his deputy, General John Abizaid, a West Point graduate and Arabic speaker, who took up the reins of a far different type of warfare than his predecessor faced. As in the Afghan incursion, the conventional US campaign came to a sudden halt against a vanquished foe. Unlike the mountainous country, the transition to an insurgency in the Mesopotamian desert arose rapidly; indeed, its first signs appeared as US armored units raced toward Baghdad.

Even before the army-on-army conflict ground to a halt, irregular Fedayeen Saddam forces clashed with coalition military columns rushing toward Baghdad. The Fedayeen enjoyed a loose relationship with the dictatorship but the paramilitaries fell short of a government auxiliary guard. They did torment the regime's domestic opponents while it let them profit from gangsterism. Once the American-led incursion neared Baghdad, its trailing supply trucks fell prey to the militias, which operated from pickup trucks bristling with AK-47 rifles, RPGs (rocket-propelled grenades) and mounted 50-caliber machine guns. The

Fedayeen harried supply lines with guerrilla-style attacks, catalyzing the insurgency that was underway by June. The dearth of what the West Wing called "rear-area security" raised "an early indication that the military's Phase IV (post invasion) plans were lacking," in the words of Rice, the president's national security adviser.[63]

5.4   A Disorderly Occupation and a Return to Self-Rule

On the heels of the coalition's successful invasion came disorder, widespread looting, and violent demonstrations by Iraqi citizens. These outbursts contributed to the budding resistance to what the population grew to consider a foreign occupation. The initial sense of relief from Hussein's vile authoritarian rule evaporated quickly. The expectation that American service personnel would be greeted as liberators – like the marching troops down the Champs-Élysées in 1944 after the liberation of Paris – proved to be fleeting. Events soon illustrated the ancient Greek maxim that hubris is followed by nemesis.

Iraqis' disenchantment, in part, arose from several misfires in the post-invasion governance. Little, if any, careful thought had been given to a post-Hussein Iraq. This state of affairs is all the more startling in the wake of the Afghanistan intervention, which also suffered from an inadequate blueprint for running the mountainous country once the Taliban were chased from power. In the Afghan case, Washington officials passed off the governance issue to UN auspices. The acerbic wrangling over prewar Iraq with France, Russia, and, to a lesser degree, China precluded a similar handoff to the United Nations. The United States was much more in charge of the Iraq War without a Security Council–authorized international coalition.

The Pentagon's limitations were seen early on when Shiite residents, who had been oppressed and excluded from power under Hussein's Sunni-run autocracy, erupted in protest. They ransacked the former ruler's palaces and mansions occupied by his two brutal sons and their unscrupulous henchmen. The looters totted off cars, appliances, paintings, and furniture. Mixed with the scavengers were some 100,000 hardcore criminals released from prison by Hussein the previous fall so as to disrupt any foreign-imposed presence. The released convicts formed or joined gangs, which were responsible for bloodshed and lawlessness.

Urban populations speedily became dissatisfied with the American-instituted rule. Everything that went wrong – shortages in food and gasoline, interrupted electricity distribution for the essential air conditioners, petty crime – fell at the occupiers' doorstep. Unreasonable expectations sapped the initial gratitude toward the foreigners who had helped residents pull down Saddam Hussein's statue in Firdos Square in central Baghdad in early April. Populations quickly tire of foreign occupations, even when they liberate them from tyrannical rulers.

Here we come to the root causes of Iraq's swelling opposition to its international liberators. Two main factors were so closely entwined they cannot be disentangled completely, but for clarity sake must be treated separately. First, among the mistakes that surfaced almost immediately was the inadequate number of boots on the ground to maintain order in the aftermath of the military intrusion. All told, OIF introduced over a quarter of a million military personnel into the country then at a population of twenty-five million inhabitants. Compared to other pacifications, the numbers came up short. Contrast Iraq's ratio of 8 military occupiers per 1,000 inhabitants to the 18–20 per 1,000 in Bosnia or 16 per 1,000 in Kosovo. When Britain fought insurgencies in Malaya and Northern Ireland, it deployed 20 troops per 1,000 residents. In vanquished 1945 Germany, the Allies imposed a whopping 100 soldiers per 1,000 citizens. Later, the Army and Marine Corps official field manual for waging counterinsurgency recommended a minimum of 20 military occupiers for each 1,000 inhabitants.[64] The paucity of uniformed personnel hampered the US counterinsurgency.

When vandals and looters ransacked business establishments, museums, and Hussein's palaces, American soldiers stood watching the chaotic scenes. When an Iraqi citizen inquired why a Marine officer atop a tank did not intervene to stop the disturbance, he answered: "We just don't have enough troops."[65] Even post-invasion decisions contributed to the shortages. For instance, Pentagon chief Rumsfeld "off ramped" the First Cavalry Division from duty in Iraq. Thanks to the precipitous fall of Baghdad to US forces, the Defense Department pulled the plug on deploying an additional 16,000 military personnel.[66] This decision turned out to be a mistake.

The brewing scandal over deficient military strength ricocheted loudly back in Washington. Prior to the Iraq invasion, the US Senate Armed Service Committee asked General Eric Shinseki, the Army chief of staff, how many troops were needed. He replied: "something on the order of several hundred thousand soldiers" for "posthostilities control" on account of "ethnic tensions."[67] Even with the general's thirty-eight years of military service, his assessment was dismissed by Paul Wolfowitz, the deputy secretary of defense. At a House Budget Committee session, the civilian appointee characterized Shinseki's estimate as "quite outlandish" and "wildly off the mark." The outer E-Ring civilians objected to the idea that more troops were needed for the occupation than the pell-mell offensive into the country. Defense Secretary Rumsfeld joined with his deputy in stating: "The idea that it would take several thousand US forces I think is off the mark."[68] Long story short: events vindicated Shinseki and other skeptics about the wisdom of going light into Iraq.

Now we come to the second, even more glaring failure of the Bush foreign policy mandarins. No competent postwar governing apparatus came in the baggage trains of the invading armies to assume the civilian duties of the displaced Hussein dictatorship.[69] Nor were there plans to keep on the job those lower-level bureaucrats who could issue or stamp everyday paperwork. Instead, routine civil functions largely ceased with the Baath Party's implosion. Mundane jobs such as garbage collection, street cleaning, and traffic management screeched to a halt.

A mere two months before the invasion, the Pentagon established the Office of Reconstruction and Humanitarian Affairs (ORHA), which anticipated a post-apocalyptic nightmare in the wake of discharged nuclear, chemical, or biological weapons. Rather than mass military and civilian casualties or horrific scenes of rampant typhoid and cholera cases, ORHA ran into disorder from the sudden onset of governmental entropy. Its commander, retired Lieutenant General Jay Garner, laid tentative plans to use existing Iraqi ministries to run the country. But the former Army officer's uneasy tenure was cut short. As ORHA struggled to come to grips with unanticipated political issues, the White House switched not only the rider of its civil structure but also the horse itself. It sacked the retired three-star general in charge of ORHA, replacing him with L. Paul Bremer III as its presidential envoy. Washington additionally ditched ORHA entirely and created the Coalition Provisional Authority (CPA) to tackle the break down in governance.

The White House placed the CPA under Bremer's thumb. Bremer's professional background as a twenty-three-year State Department foreign service officer and a manager in a consulting firm lacked command or governing experience. He was new to the Middle East to boot. In short, the Oval Office miscast him for an exceedingly difficult job. For all his paucity of qualifications, Jerry, as his friends called him, functioned with exceedingly wide latitude from Washington. According to Donald Rumsfeld's undersecretary of defense policy, the Pentagon chief "didn't want to use a five-thousand-mile screwdriver" to micromanage the CPA.[70] Later, it will be discussed how the secretary of defense misconstrued post-invasion issues.

The CPA head took up residency within Baghdad's Green Zone, a four-square-mile fortress-like compound where he ruled like an imperial proconsul. Surrounded by fourteen-foot-high concrete barriers and guarded by heavily armed troops, the Green Zone's masters seized

Hussein's Republican Palace and many Baath administrative buildings. The new tenants used them as the seat of the military occupation's command and control. Outside was the Red Zone, where a ferocious insurgency was mushrooming under the victor's radar. In a short time, the insurgency gave rise to a replay of the Vietnam War debates about the proper tactics to defeat a low-intensity conflict.

Operating from within protected confines, Jerry Bremer issued a series of far-reaching and controversial diktats to reshape Iraqi politics and society, which resulted in unintended consequences. One of his earliest blunders occurred when he disbanded the badly mauled Iraqi army on May 23. He reasoned that this decision made clear to people that Hussein was not returning to power. This decision put trained and armed military men on the street with plenty of time on their hands. Had they received pay in return for some civic duties, like trash removal or debris clearing, their grievances might have been assuaged. In the 1990s Bosnia incursion, the allied Stabilization Forces mandated that soldiers from the various ethnic communities report for duty each day in return for pay. As a consequence, they peacefully whiled away their time playing cards and downing shots of the local slivovitz. More recently in Afghanistan, the US-initiated Ministry of Defense placed some 100,000 militiamen on its payroll for a couple of years. It funneled the funds through a miscellany of warlords, who padded their ranks to collect extra money. Back in Iraq, the CPA chief acted according to his own lights, opening the floodgates of rebellion to disgruntled former soldiers.

The discharged Iraqi soldiers, connected by the Baath intelligence network, abetted the start of a countrywide insurgency. Soon the intelligence system fueled a fulmination of killings from disparate terrorist groups, criminal rings, and insurgent fighters

Matters were made worse when the CPA instituted a severe de-Baathification initiative that was modeled on post–World War II Germany's de-Nazification procedures to bar Hitler's officials from holding government positions after 1945. To purge Hussein's henchmen, Bremer established a De-Baathification Council, whose members were mostly from Kurdish and Shiite communities, thereby exacerbating sectarian and ethnic hatred. The council carried out personnel cuts well below the upper tier of Baath officialdom. It hacked away some fifty thousand civil servants, who only carried party membership cards as a means to get a job in the country's bureaucracy. Angry and vengeful, the unemployed found themselves on the street. Almost immediately, the government ground to a halt.

Last but not least, Paul Bremer pushed aside Iraqi political leaders cultivated by Washington planners prior to the invention. Among the prominent figures were Ahmed Chalabi of the Iraqi National Congress, Ayad Allawi of the Iraqi National Accord, and Abdul Aziz al-Hakim of the Supreme Council for the Islamic Revolution in Iraq, plus two leaders of the two main Kurdish parties. Among the most actively eyed by the Pentagon as a possible leader was Chalabi, a secular Shiite, US-educated Iraqi banker, who "became a central figure in the story of the US invasion and occupation of Iraq," according to Douglas Feith, the under secretary of defense for policy. But the Lebanon-based businessman crossed swords with the CIA, which he criticized as incompetent. The Agency, in Feith's words, "produced an amazing volume of reports written to make him look ill informed, ill motivated, unskillful, and untrustworthy."[71] As a result, the senior DoD civilians dropped Chalabi from active consideration, when it became apparent his prospects were nil.

In his memoir, Rumsfeld revealed his pique at the Department of State and the Agency for their "desire to ensure that Chalabi not have a leadership role in postwar Iraq may have led both organizations to oppose the exiles generally .... Regrettably, because of State Department wariness of the Iraqi externals, the United States did little to include them in planning for the postwar period until after Saddam's regime had fallen."[72] Post-invasion planning, therefore, fell victim to inter-department wrangling inside the Beltway.

Instead of devolving power and responsibility into Iraqi hands, Bremer grasped control for himself. As a concession, he formed the Iraqi Governing Council, made up of a score of political figures, to serve as sounding board, not to run the country. In other, recent interventions, such as Panama, Haiti, and Kosovo, the United States lost no time in turning over power to local figures and in scaling down its military presence.

The CPA chief believed he knew what was best for the vanquished nation. He held the council members in low regard, writing later in his memoir that the Iraqi leaders "couldn't organize a parade, let alone run a country."[73] Many on the council, in fact, did go on to win elections and participate in governing Iraq. By entrenching the CPA in the details of running the country, Bremer exposed the agency to a well of derision, all of which undercut the US military's stabilization operations. The capture of Saddam Hussein in late 2003 and his hanging death three years later brought no cession to the pervasive instability.

Frustration fed the budding insurgency. In retrospect, the populace's expectations were unrealistic given that years of damage from UN and US sanctions had crippled civilian infrastructure, including electricity production for air conditioners. But the foreign caretakers were cut no slack by the irked population. Outsiders also scored the CPA with failing marks. One on-the-spot observer noted that the CPA's "obsession with control was an overarching flaw in the US occupation from its start to finish."[74] Troops in the field likewise dismissed the CPA with the quip that its acronym meant "Can't Produce Anything." Whereas the CPA enjoyed little acclaim, America's soldiers were honored with a picture of three military personnel on the front cover of *Time* at the end of 2003 as the magazine's Person of the Year. Not since 1950 had the weekly accorded the armed forces a similar accolade. The tribute also reflected the American public's approval of the war at the time – a high-water mark soon to slump amid heavy casualties and repeated missteps within a society torn asunder by multiple and overlapping conflicts.

The political stumbles by the Coalition Provisional Authority axed its tenure. Realizing the increasing burden of presiding over an unruly populace, the White House searched for a way out of the morass. The United States pressed for a temporary constitution and a caucus-selected transitional parliament to return sovereignty to the Iraqis. Washington reached out to the United Nations, which it had spurned on its march to war. It wanted the Security Council to pass a resolution endorsing the transfer of authority to the interim Iraqi government. To gain the Council's sanctification, the Bush administration made concessions to Iraq's representatives. On paper, the semi-sovereign rulers got authority to oversee the police, to manage the economy, and to decide political questions. The Defense Department retained the right to conduct offensive military operations as its local commanders saw fit.[75]

Only now, with the legal necessities in place, could the United States move toward reestablishing Iraq's independence. A barebones ceremony ensued in a nondescript room within the Green Zone where the Iraqi Governing Council held its meetings. CPA Administer Bremer and Ayad Allawi, Iraq's interim prime minister, signed the transfer documents, conferring self-rule to the Baghdad government on June 28, 2004. The onetime proconsul did not stop to bid adieu his former subjects. Immediately after the five-minute *pas de deux*, Ambassador Bremer boarded a plane to return to the United States after ruling Iraq for fourteen months. No brass band, no fanfare, or no flag-lowering ceremony accompanied the momentous event to hand back a country's sovereignty. Neither Bremer's departure nor Iraqis setting inside Hussein's ornate palaces ushered peace into the turbulent land.

5.5   An Insurgency Wrapped in a Civil War inside a Sectarian Struggle

The proliferating insurrection against the military coalition's presence initially took on a bewildering nature that reflected Iraq's complex ethnic, sectarian, and political composition. The blood feud between Sunni and Shia dated from the death of the Muslim prophet Muhammad in 632 CE when a succession struggle forever cleaved the factions into hated enemies. Iraq's bitter defiance was anything but a straight up fight between a united Iraqi rebellion and the US-directed Coalition. Arrayed against American and allied combatants were Sunni fighters, some of whom came from Baath Party's military, while others arose from the ranks of Salafi-jihadism. These Islamic extremists flocked to Osama bin Laden's local al Qaeda branch, which was headed by the bloodthirsty Jordan-born Abu Musab al-Zarqawi, who was determined to ignite a Sunni-Shia civil war, while also killing coalition soldiers.

Still other insurgents arose from fertile Islamist conditions in the city of Fallujah, west of the capital on the Euphrates. They linked up with al Qaeda elements but remained in separate militias. Yet other Sunni discontents joined criminal gangs to take advantage of the extreme lawlessness to smuggle, extort, and kidnap for ransom. From the Shiite community rose up so-called Special Groups, often trained, armed, and guided by operatives from Iran's security forces. They were as interested in killing Sunnis as foreign soldiers. The Salafist Sunni jihadis, for their part, staged their share of targeted sectarian assassinations, random murders, and suicide bombings, which elevated Shiite-Sunni animosity to barbaric levels.

By summer, just months into the US-led invasion, CENTCOM confronted open rebellion that morphed into not just one centrally controlled conflict but multiple insurgencies that reflected the patchwork of secular and sectarian movements that attacked the American and allied occupation with sniper fire and IEDs (improvised explosive devices), usually in roadside bombs made from artillery shells with a detonator attached. Iraq's fractured ethnic and sectarian communities lay at the root of the multifaceted resistance that spurred a frenzy of killing, all of which complicated assessments and defenses. To rewrite Churchill: the complex Iraqi insurgency was a riddle wrapped inside an enigmatic civil war. Within Iraq, the Shia made up 60–65 percent (versus 15–20 percent Sunni Arabs and 17 percent Sunni Kurds) of the population. Once liberated from Hussein and his tyrannical Sunni-dominated regime, the Shiite residents struck out at the Sunnis and coalition forces.

The Shia swept to power in the December 2005 parliamentary elections. Four months later, Nouri Kamal al-Maliki (a Shiite apparatchik) became prime minister after a cabinet shuffle. Holding power in Baghdad, Maliki soon sought revenge against the Sunni citizenry. His henchmen formed death squads who killed thousands of young men and dumped their bodies on the streets. Excluded from power and indiscriminately killed by the new rulers, the Sunni militias struck back at their Shiite oppressors as well as the non-Muslim intruders.

While Maliki officials appeared to be cooperating with their American overlords, the Shiite government was in realty a murderous faction participating in the civil war, not a neutral entity attempting to bring peace to the violence-stricken land. As a consequence of the Sunni-Shiite conflict, battling soared between the two sects, while members of both ethnic communities still attacked American and Coalition forces with rifle fire and IEDs. Two locations sustained the heaviest bloodshed from insurgent murders – the Shiite Sadr city, a district in Baghdad and the so-called Sunni Triangle, bounded by Tikrit in the north, Ramadi in the west, and Baghdad in the east.

Not all the deadly encounters between US-led coalition forces and insurgents were short, sharp exchanges of gunfire. The Sunni Triangle city of Fallujah was the scene of two epic battles. In the first battle of Fallujah in April 2004 (following the killing and mutilation of four contractors from the private security company Blackwater), the US Marines fought to the center of the city to take down the killers only to be ordered to turn it over to the Baathist-controlled Fallujah Brigade designated by the Iraqi Governing Council, which had replaced Bremer's CPA.[76] The American commanders ordered a unilateral withdrawal from Fallujah because of the mounting civilian toll and criticism from the IGC and other groups.

The insurgent bands still in Fallujah lost little time in throwing up defenses in preparation for the next American assault to clear Fallujah of ex-Saddam Fedayeen irregulars, al Qaeda in Iraq terrorists, Army of Mohammed militants, Ansar al-Sunna fighters, and others who also had their headquarters in Fallujah. Foreign mujahedeen flooded into the belea-guered city from the Middle East, Chechnya, Libya, and the Philippines

The second battle for Fallujah pitted dug-in militants against attacking American and British infantry accompanied by Special Ops teams. The pitched urban combat called to mind the close-quarter conflict inside Hué city of Vietnam War fame. Fought in November and December, 2004, the second brawl for the west-central Iraqi city in al Anbar province ended up as the biggest battle of the Iraq War. Rather than shooting-and-running as in so many skirmishes, the Iraqi resistance of some 1,500 defenders stood their ground in well-prepared trenches, tunnels, and firing positions. Hunkering down in fixed redoubts, however, was worse than a fool's errand; it was virtual suicide against the weight and volume of American firepower from the heavens.

The US Air Force delivered intense close air support, using A-10 Thunderbolts, F-16 Falcons, AC-130 helicopter gunships, and even

B-52 bombers from the island of Diego Garcia in the Indian Ocean. Some 11,000 US Marines and Army infantry spearheaded the assault, plus 2,000 Iraqi security forces, and 850 British troops from the Black Watch regiment. The actual battle raged for over a week and then smoldered another six, while the attackers mopped up isolated pockets of resistance and disarmed booby traps left to kill and maim. The US Armed Forces suffered ninety-five fatalities and its allies about fifteen deaths.[77]

Chastened by US troops and their unsparing weapons, the few survivors resolved to rely in the future on hidden IEDs, ambushes, and snipers. Like insurgents in Afghanistan and the Philippines, they learned to stay clear of set-piece shootouts with US forces. As Mao Zedong instructed, the guerrilla fish must learn to swim in the population sea for survival.[78] Other lessons bobbed to the surface in time. By then, Bush's America understood it was in a quagmire.

5.6   The Strategy War within the Iraq War

Not a few defense intellectuals reasoned that the "shock and awe" offensives would prevail over almost any foe. Psychologically shocked by the "killing technology," they would give up after a "demonstration of US precision firepower." Retired general Bob Scales scoffed at the notion: "Al Qaeda, the Taliban, and ISIS have long put paid to the idea." The former Army officer lamented that inside the Beltway techno-warriors still continue to "seduce and spawn other firepower-centered silliness." The big-ticket weapons platforms (high-technology ships, planes, and missiles), in his view, drain money and energy from the "Soldiers and Marines who engage daily in the bloody business of close combat."[79] Indeed, there was an abundance of intense combat left in Iraq and other theaters. In a word, the jihadi insurgents adapted by waging war with guerrilla tactics.

Washington seemed adrift as Iraq plunged into scenes of surreal bloodletting with running street battles, roadside explosions, and sniper killings. At the heart of the failing occupation stood Washington's indifference, ineptness, and gross lack of planning for a post-Hussein Iraq. Not since the Reconstruction era after the American Civil War had the United States so fumbled a military occupation that sought to protect and lift a despised and powerless people out from under a repressive society.

The planning and execution of the first three operational stages – Phase I: Set the conditions, Phase II: Initial operations, and Phase III: Decisive operations – proceeded on track. There were logistical glitches – some advancing units outran their supplies in fuel and ammunition – but the incursion was absent any calamitous setbacks. In fact, the superb execution of the US ground blitz to Baghdad brought into sharp relief the failures in Phase IV: Post-conflict stability operations to calm the violence-filled nation.

Donald Rumsfeld, according to author Fred Kaplan, was disinterested in Phase IV operations. This stabilization phase fell well short of the high drama of the preceding battles that crushed the Republican guards. By contrast, the fourth stage dealt with returning captured domains to civilian control, running down enough hospital beds, handling prisoners, and caring for refugees.

Before the intervention into Iraq, the defense secretary embraced the high-tech RMA or revolution in military affairs. His belief in the theory was strengthened by the rapid third phase of decisive operations, which he relished. As sketched in Chapter 2, the hugely lopsided US victory over Iraq in 1991 contributed to renewed interest in RMA. The proponents of this proposed game-changer held that US dominance on the battlefield through advanced "smart" weapons and information technology inaugurated a military transformation of historic significance. Skeptics called attention to RMA's shortfalls and overblown assumptions, made painfully clear with insurgencies in Iraq, Afghanistan, and many other countries.[80]

In Rumsfeld's worldview, an insurrectionist Iraq did not lend itself to being "shaped by [the weaponry] transformation and had nothing to do with his broader vision of American power." So, he "had lost all interest in Iraq" and its post-invasion need for civilian governance and normal stability.[81] Simply put, the Pentagon leader had no appetite for conducting an intricate campaign to defeat an insurgency that he partially blamed the US intelligence services for not predicting.[82]

Rather, he favored a rapid withdrawal from the phantasmagoria of sectarian, ethnic, and radical Islamist bloodshed engulfing Iraq.[83] Rumsfeld was not shy about pressing his Army commander in Iraq to withdraw from the Mesopotamian quicksand. The DoD chief favored a quick turnover of authority to the United Nations as happened Afghanistan. He also pushed for holding Iraqi elections and for drafting a constitutional framework – all aimed at returning the conquered country to its own sovereignty and leaving. He wrote afterwards about his approach: "I wanted to give Iraqis concrete assurance that the occupation of their country was going to end – and soon."[84]

In this enterprise, the outspoken DoD boss pressed against an open door in the US command of the Iraq War. Both General George Casey Jr. and the CENTCOM chief John Abizaid were on board with redeploying from Iraq. They believed, with justification, America's original liberating presence had turned into an unwelcome army of occupation. Taking charge of the Iraq War in June 2004, Casey, officially the commander of the Multi-National Force – Iraq, at first opposed the introduction of many of the standard practices of counterinsurgency warfare. He backed a hasty stand-up of Iraq's own security forces to replace US and Coalition forces. The four-star Army general wanted to avoid a dependency syndrome. Casey held that American soldiers must leave after protecting and assisting the Iraqis to elect and form a government of their own.

Like Rumsfeld, Casey placed great store on the three elections in 2005 to bring peace. The January vote was to fill 275 seats in national legislature. Some 60 percent of the population defied threats from terrorist networks and cast their ballots, dipping their index finger in purple ink so as to foreclose another vote. Next, Iraqis voted in a referendum to approve the constitutions drafted by the national legislature. Finally, twelve million Iraqis, 70 percent of the population, turned out in December and elected a government under their new constitution. This electoral progress gave a green light to Generals Abizaid and Casey's "plans to turn over more responsibility to the Iraqi Security Forces month by month and reduce US troop levels gradually."[85] But however commendable, even the best of these specific electoral actions were but small upward steps on an escalator that was going down.

The political hopes for the new year were dashed in February by the bombing of the Shiite's Samarra Golden Mosque. The destruction of the shrine's famous golden dome ignited a retaliatory fury by Shiites against Sunni mosques and citizens. US officials and others pointed fingers at the local branch of the al Qaeda terrorist group for the attack on the al-Askari mosque. The explosion widened sectarian killings and turned a new chapter in its savagery. Foreign Muslim recruits infiltrated across the Syrian border to join the local al Qaeda cell, Sunni militias, or criminal groups. From the east, Iranian youth flocked into Iraq and Shiite militias. Many joined up with the renegade Shiite cleric, Muqtada al Sadr, whose Mahdi Army militia engaged in protests and violence. Allied with the Shiite-dominated government in Baghdad, death squads prowled the capital's streets with guns and electrical power drills to torment, torture, and murder up close their despised Sunni quarry.[86]

The strife persisted unabated into 2006, upending President Bush's "strategy for victory in Iraq," whereby Washington planned to turn over security to the Iraqis as the American presence shrank. As a consequence of the new reality, General Casey temporarily introduced a handful of counterinsurgency tactics in his operational plans. But he never felt comfortable with overseeing a full-fledged COIN campaign. As the struggle in Iraq descended into a Hobbesian war of one against all, Casey returned to his former assumptions about the war and the proper American strategy. He argued that the multisided fighting within Iraq made counterinsurgency operations useless, because the DoD was fighting not a one-on-one battle against a single insurgent group but a puzzling array of sectarian militias, tribal armies, and criminal gangs.[87]

The faltering Iraq War sparked a closed-door debate in the Pentagon among the combatant commanders and service chiefs in May 2006. Rumsfeld's "idea was to bring as many of the forces as he could back to the United States."[88] Casey was in accord on the futility of remaining in the violent and chaotic country. Thus, he advocated for an expeditious exit. This understanding was among the first signs – but far from the last – of America's building propensity for disengagement no matter what. Other military service chiefs opposed it.

5.7   The Rise of the COINdinistas

America's occupation stumbled toward a debacle by mid-2006 as the capricious violence worsened. As a consequence of the metastasizing insurgency, the ground beneath General Casey's strategy began to shift. An emerging coterie of active and retired military officers, civilian experts, and academics espoused counterinsurgency tactics. Marines and soldiers both conducted COIN operations in Vietnam. Afterward, this population-focused strategy was studied in West Point's Social Science Department and tepidly applied during the "military operations other than war" in Somalia, Haiti, and the Balkans during the 1990s."[89]

Derided as COINdinistas (formed from COIN and the leftist Sandinistas who seized exclusive power in Nicaragua in the 1980s), the proponents of a counterinsurgency campaign ignored the derision from conventionally minded officers. As students of military history, they looked for lessons in Britain's Malayan insurgency, America's Vietnam War, and El Salvador's rural war. The COINdinistas extracted key principles from the past conflicts to influence what became a war within the wars in Afghanistan and Iraq for the proper strategy.

The counterinsurgency exponents pored over the basic texts of waging irregular warfare, particularly former French army officer David Galula's *Counterinsurgency Warfare: Theory and Practice*. The British army officer known as Lawrence of Arabia, who wrote *Seven Pillars of Wisdom*, famously observed: "War upon rebellion was messy and slow, like eating soup with a knife."[90] This fabled metaphor encapsulated the wickedly problematic task of waging counterinsurgency warfare. Eating soup with a knife became a slogan among the COINdinistas. Along with book learning, they drew lessons from their firsthand experiences in other interventions and combat tours in Afghanistan to propose a strategy to defeat the insurgency.

The iconoclasts battled military traditionalists, whose conventional tactics they believed killed far too many innocents to win over hearts and minds for an American-backed government in a faraway capital. The counterinsurgency advocates placed the protection of the population at the apex of their revolutionary doctrine. Defending the local people from attack and intimidation, according to the COINdinistas, would gain their trust and lead to information that the counterinsurgents could use to kill or capture their elusive adversary. Counterinsurgency, in their interpretation, amounted to "20 percent military action and 80 percent political," an observation drawn from Galula, the French COIN theoretician.[91]

The rising star David H. Petraeus, a US Military Academy graduate, career soldier, Princeton PhD, and commanding officer of the 101st Airborne Division during the 2003 offensive on Baghdad, emerged as the leader of the growing COINdinista rebels. As the Pentagon's fortunes deteriorated in Iraq, like-minded officers converged with Petraeus and his faith in COIN to address the cascading insecurity. Among his closest acolytes were a cadre of once-and-future general officers, including H. R. McMaster (a COIN practitioner in Iraq and author of *Dereliction of Duty*), William Hix (Special Forces background), and Peter Chiarelli (COIN adherent who worked as General Casey's deputy). Another officer, John Nagl, retired as a lieutenant colonel from the Army but his book *Learning to Eat Soup with a Knife*, attained wide influence among the COINdinistas. Another officer, who like Nagl left the Army without a star, was Peter Mansoor (General Petraeus' executive officer). As a college professor, Mansoor wrote that there were two surges that reversed the tide and calmed Iraq's violent waters: "the new concept for employment of forces and the surge of [American] forces."[92] Together with these officers and think tankers, Petraeus forged an informal network of a like-minded rebels against the Army's conventional mindset.

Petraeus joined with US Marine Corps officers to publish a counterinsurgency field manual. It enthusiastically embodied their understanding of how to win rural insurgencies, when it expounded the new operational culture: "Soldiers and Marines are expected to be nation-builders as well as warfighters."[93] COIN, therefore, called for buildings along with bullets. Despite the COIN cadre's passion, not every officer embraced their concepts. With gumption and some guile, Petraeus pushed the new manual through the Army bureaucracy and it was printed and uploaded on the Fort Leavenworth's website in mid-December 2006. This doctrinal guide gained admirers and detractors at a time when the Iraq War was hurtling toward an American defeat. As the cliché holds: timing is everything in life. Hence, the manual's new thinking and Petraeus' advocacy of it as a strategy to turn around the faltering war aced the three-starred general another star and a promotion as the new commander of Multi-National Force – Iraq. He relieved Casey, who Bush kicked upstairs to be Army chief of staff.

Leaving out the US Marine Corps contribution to development of COIN in Iraq would amount to an incomplete account. From its storied expeditionary campaigns in Central America and the Caribbean during the late 1890s through the early 1930s, the Marines stowed away a trove of experience in combatting insurgents. Over the years, Marine officers gathered, analyzed, and published lessons from their experiences in the so-called Banana Wars. Much of the wisdom gleaned from waging what were termed non-kinetic operations to protect the civilian population and to enhance their living conditions was distilled into the 1940 *Small Wars Manual*. This volume offered information, insights, and lessons for the writing of the 2006 counterinsurgency manual. The earlier Marine service in Vietnam was also relevant to Iraq and Afghanistan.

The 1st Marine Division's General James Mattis recommended that his grunts and officers read the manual prior to deploying to Iraq as a pacification force in 2004. A four-star officer who went on to be secretary of defense (2017–2018), Mattis later reflected that his Marines concentrated on trying to "turn down the cycle of violence" in Iraq. He recommended a double-pronged approach of "promoting governance, economic development, and essential services" along with "neutralizing the bad actors." Like Petraeus, Mattis instituted foot patrols so Marines became familiar with the residents, and they with the Marines. He, too, subscribed to the people-centric tactics and advised "young Marines" engaged in the excitement of battle: "Be careful. Don't allow a single innocent person to be injured. We are the good guys."[94] Because of the Marine Corps' historically embraced counterinsurgency warfare, it was spared the same bureaucratic stonewalling of a COIN strategy as within the Army hierarchy.

5.8   The Quagmire Worsens in 2006

The months leading up to the changes in military leadership, counterinsurgency strategy, and turnaround in the war were loaded with portentous events. Among the most injurious to the American cause happened at the US-operated Abu Ghraib prison where degrading treatment, but not torture, of Iraqi inmates cast a dark cloud over the whole interventionist enterprise. US military police and intelligence officers committed human rights violations that resulted in ten separate investigations, a presidential apology by George W. Bush, and the speeded-up departure of the ranking Iraq commander, Lieutenant General Ricardo Sanchez, for mishandling the war effort. His replacement, General Casey, soon aligned with Rumsfeld by beating a drum for withdrawal from Iraq as the most realist policy in face of the spiraling hit-and-run attacks.

The skyrocketing violence, particularly in the Sunni triangle throughout 2006, awakened the White House as well as the Pentagon to the fact that the United States faced the prospect of defeat. The unremitting bloodshed made Anbar province a vortex of murder and fear. By virtue of its geographical location, sharing borders with Syria and Jordan, Anbar was central to pacifying Iraq, as foreign youths came into the strife-ridden country, mainly through Syria, to join a modern-day jihad against the infidels.

The Shiite-dominated government struck back at the Sunni gunmen with their brand of grisly atrocities. It turned to its own death squads or to Iran's Special Groups, militia factions trained and subsidized by Tehran' Quds Force, a clandestine arm of the Islamic Revolutionary Guard Corps.[95] Iran infiltrated its terrorist trainers and facilitators into Iraqi territory to commission violence through its local proxies against US forces and the Sunni population. The Special Groups wielded with particular effectiveness EFPs (explosively formed penetrators or projectiles) that pierced the US up-armored vehicles and killed their crews. At the head of the Quds Force, Iranian general Qassem Soleimani was responsible for the deaths of hundreds of US soldiers and Marines in a strategy to displace Washington's influence in Iraq.[96] In the end, Bush's troop surge checkmated the Special Groups, but his efforts, nor those of subsequent administrations, never froze out Iranian political influence in Baghdad. The ayatollah regime gained sway over Iraq's government either through its co-religious Shiite politicians or through its Iraq-based militias.[97]

Another signpost among many of America's impending failure was evident in the congressionally empaneled Iraq Study Group, chaired by James A. Baker (former secretary of state) and Lee H. Hamilton (former Indiana Congressmen). Formed in March 2006 with ten politically prominent Americans, the bipartisan commission reported out its seventy-nine recommendations in early December. The drafters of the report observed: "the situation in Iraq is grave and deteriorating."[98]

The recommendations called for a more sustainable Iraq policy by reemphasizing the training of the Iraqi army, stepping up Special Operations targeting of al Qaeda Central as well as its Iraqi offshoot, and seeking a regional approach to peace. In retrospect, the Iraq Study Group represented Congress' desperate attempt to extricate the United States from what appeared as an unsustainable and unwinnable war. The study group's findings reflected a mix of contradictory and dubious recommendations. It called for a "diplomatic offensive" with such hostile states as Iran and Syria, both of which aided the insurgents attacking American troops. In sum, its recommendations looked like a last-ditch effort to get the United States off a sinking ship.

Ironically, the panel proposed expediting Casey's and Abizaid's strategy, whereby US armed forces trained Iraqi troops, transitioned the frontline fight to them, and pulled out American personnel first from combat roles and then from Iraq all together, as quickly as possible.[99] The White House greeted the recommendations tepidly. Others, inside and outside the administration, judged them as a thinly veiled retreat under fire.[100]

What killed off the Iraq Study Group's pessimism was the insurgents' decreasing murder rate seen by the end of 2007 and beyond. The downturn in bloodshed was visible and measurable in daily records as time passed. Monthly civilian deaths plummeted from over 1,700 in May of that year to just over 500 by December. The fatalities dropped to around 4,000 annually in the years from 2009 through 2011.[101] What caused casualties to shrink? Briefly, three broad variables transformed the battlefield. These can be summarized as new tactics, new allies, and a new infusion of US boots on the ground. Each will be subsequently fleshed out.

5.9   The Turnaround

By summer 2006, the Pentagon, White House, and the American public knew the Iraq War was trending badly, even headed toward a disastrous end. The US Armed Forces casualties soared to more than 800 fatalities annually from 2004 through 2006. Iraqi civilian deaths during the same time frame spiked from over 11,000 in 2004 to 29,000 in 2006.[102] Congress looked to the Iraq Study Group to fend off the voters' wrath. For the Republican members, this turned out to be a forlorn hope; they lost seats in both the House and Senate in the November 7, 2006 midterm election. The Democrats picked up thirty-one House seats to gain control and they won enough seats in the Senate to take over that chamber, too. Commentators attributed the Republican losses to dissatisfaction with the Iraq War as well as Washington financial and political scandals laid at the feet of the administration. President Bush, like the sorcerer's apprentice, ran afoul of a politico-military deluge that his invasion unleashed.

The Republican election setbacks prompted a number of personnel changes in the beleaguered Bush administration. Under criticism from a score of retired generals and from Capitol Hill for being an ineffective defense secretary, Rumsfeld immediately resigned in the wake of the election returns. Former Director of Central Intelligence Robert Gates replaced him. CENTCOM commander Abizaid announced the relinquishment of his position a month after the election. He retired from the Army the following March, after serving longer as head of the Middle East command than any of his predecessors. Admiral William J. Fallon, the first naval officer to head CENTCOM, enjoyed a less than successful tour.

Heralding the most change for the conduct of the Iraq War were two other shake-ups in leadership and strategy. General David Petraeus, the counterinsurgency guru, stepped into Casey's vacated position at the head of the multi-national Coalition in Iraq. The other key job went to Ambassador Ryan Cocker, who had served in Afghanistan and Pakistan. He became the US representative to Iraq. There, he was particularly effective in negotiating with the Iraqi foreign ministry for an overall strategic agreement and a SOFA (status of forces agreement) governing the operation and conduct of American and UN forces within a newly sovereign Iraq. The SOFA expired on December 1, 2011, which set up a convenient deadline for the Obama administration to withdraw, as subsequently described.

Promoted for his fourth star, Petraeus returned to Iraq where earlier he had led the 101st Airborne Division and overseen extensive counterinsurgency cum nation-building practices in the city of Mosul. In that assignment, the infantry general had tested his theories about combatting insurgent warfare with its clear, hold, and build strategy to first expel insurgents, then hold the land, and finally distribute government services to the populace.[103] Winning over the hearts of the population with security and non-military public services to include medical clinics, clean water, electricity, and schools lay at the crux of the Petraeus' COIN formula. His effective voice for an overhaul in US ground strategy landed him the command of the Multi-National Force – Iraq at a time when the Bush administration committed to a new battle plan and 28,500 additional combat personnel to salvage the failing war.

The rationale for revamping strategy and surging more troops into Iraq gathered momentum in 2006, when the Bush White House scrambled to reverse the downward trajectory of the conflict. Retired Army Vice Chief of Staff General Jack Keane championed a study from a Washington think tank that advanced a plan to secure the population in greater Baghdad by posting nearly 30,000 additional soldiers and Marines in the capital and environs with the explicit mission of safeguarding the inhabitants. Toward the end of the year, George Bush weighed various options, selecting in the end General Keane's recommendation.[104]

President Bush broadcasted his announcement of "The New Way Forward in Iraq" at the start of 2007. In his nationwide address, he noted how the Baghdad Security Plan possessed "the force levels we need to hold the areas that have been cleared" (of terrorists and insurgents). Popularly known as "the surge," this commitment of "more than 20,000 additional American troops to Iraq" enabled a new strategy. The commander in chief made it clear he gained "a green light" from Iraq's Prime Minister Nouri Kamal al-Maliki for US combat troop to enter and secure Shia neighborhoods. Acknowledging that the Shiite-dominated government had previously opposed Coalition deployments within Baghdad, Bush now locked in al-Maliki's cooperation. Bush announced: "Here is what he told his people just last week. The Baghdad security plan will not provide a safe haven for any outlaws, regardless of [their] sectarian or political affiliations."[105] The passage of time and events demonstrated that al-Maliki dissembled.

By doubling down on a winning strategy rather than drawing down US armed forces, as some of his generals, many advisers, and all Democratic voices insisted, President Bush represented a profile in courage. Holding fast in extremis helped balance negative feelings for his erroneous judgment in getting the country into the Iraq War in the first place. Still, no second act of presidential backbone is ever likely to recast the historical judgment of his detractors, who charged that the forty-third commander in chief mistakenly pushed America into an "unnecessary war."[106]

Buried within Bush's surge speech was a game-changing revelation: "Recently, tribal leaders have begun to show their willingness to take on al Qaeda." He added: "our commanders believe we have an opportunity to deal a serious blow to the terrorists." The American leader's observation turned out to be understatement of a momentous turning of the tables against the local al Qaeda franchise and other terrorist networks.[107]

With less fanfare, the White House announced a change in command for the Iraq War a week earlier than the televised rollout of a new strategy. It broke the news of General Petraeus' return to the combat theater as the overall commander. The new four-star Army officer backed both the personnel surge of 28,500 troops to reinforce the already present 132,000 US personnel and the newly devised pacification playbook. General Petraeus moved his forces out of large, fortress-like bases to small, dispersed fighting positions to live among the Iraqi civilians. The swelling ground forces fanned out on foot, rather than in armored vehicles, to patrol streets, to protect residents, and to get acquainted with the locals in order to gain their trust and, in time, information about their common al Qaeda enemy. To proponents of "the Surge," the key to a falloff in killings came from the US reinforcements and the doctrinal switch from conventional to classic counterinsurgency tactics. Petraeus' command must be factored into the altered conditions that brought about an ebbing in the daily murder rate as 2007 progressed. For his role in the turnaround, Petraeus was dubbed a savior general of the Iraq War.

The infusion of five Army brigades into Baghdad and its suburbs, plus 4,000 Marines in more than three battalions, realigned the military balance in the Wyoming-sized Anbar province, located in the country's western reaches. Their concentration on population-protection tactics coincided with an even more dramatic sea change. Reacting to years of al Qaeda's ruthless and homicidal rule, including forced compliance to premodern Sharia religious codes, the sheiks within the Sunni community rebelled in what was termed the Awakening movement. This Sunni revolt against al Qaeda, thugs, and common criminals cropped up by mid-2006. The US commander in Ramadi, Anbar province's capital, reached out to the disaffected Sunni population offering protection in return for intelligence to enable his soldiers to hunt down and eliminate the gunmen.[108]

Led by Abdul Sattar Abu Risha, some forty other sheikhs signed an Emergency Council declaration to cooperate with the Multi-National Force – Iraq to drive out the Islamic State of Iraq (ISI). The Islamic State of Iraq grew from the local al Qaeda offshoot and the merger with other groups after Zarqawi's mid-2006 death. The September 14, 2006, signing furthered the coinage of Sheikh Sattar's Sahawa (*Sahawa al-Anbar*) term for the uprising. Almost exactly a year later, ISI militants killed the key US ally with an explosive device planted near his house in Ramadi. By that time, the Sunni Awakening had become a force to reckon with among the tribesmen in the flat, desert Anbar jurisdiction. By their violent excesses and restrictive strictures, the Salafi-jihadis drove the sheiks and their followers into the arms of the US military forces.[109]

The sheiks resented the extremists' imposition of strict rules that demonstrated a contempt for local Sunni norms and societal customs. They bridled at extremist demands for men to grow beards and women to wear Islamic dress. Prohibitions on smoking or drinking alcohol irked them. Likewise, they were put off by the nearly gratuitous barbarity from the puritanical Salafists. They vehemently opposed their daughters marrying ISI members. They also pushed back against the takeover of their smuggling and illicit business enterprises by the ISI militants.[110] These grievances formed the basis of the resistance against the Islamic State of Iraq.

An early rendition of the Awakening phenomenon dates from May 2005, when the district of al-Qaim revolted against Islamist militants because they beheaded a popular police chief.[111] Basically, the Awakening was rooted in the choice between localism versus outside interference. In briefest terms, the Awakening entailed a voluntary changing of sides by the Anbar Sunnis. They went from fighting the American pacification to waging war against the Islamic State of Iraq, which they grew to perceive as more inimical to their well-being than the US occupation.

The on-scene Coalition forces facilitated this side-switching by their former Sunni foes. They willingly engaged them, welcomed volunteers to the American side, and paid most others $300 monthly for their service. They protected their neighborhoods from Salafi militants. The US forces took advantage of Sunni discontent, put 100,000 Iraqis, many of them former insurgents, on their payrolls, and allied with them against their mutual jihadi foes. The Iraqi-American alliance stabilized Anbar, which led to other Sunni stand-downs in the once rebellious land. Over time, US commanders managed to have a few thousand of the volunteers integrated into the regular Iraqi Security Forces overseen by the Ministry of Interior.[112] Skipping ahead briefly, the inclusion of Sunni males within the Iraqi national army never proceeded adequately, however. The Shiite government in Baghdad actually barred most Sunni recruits from its national forces. Prime Minister Maliki, in fact, turned the Iraqi army into a Shiite militia and used it against the Sunni community, as noted in Chapter 7.

Now the question of what caused the battlefield transformation presents itself. It is a topic, perhaps, better to introduce than resolve definitively. By 2008's end, nearly two years after the start of the troop surge and redrawn tactics, US fatalities fell to 314 from the previous year of 904 killed. Deaths declined to 58 in 2011, the year President Obama withdrew all US combat forces from Iraq.[113] By then a dispute had broken out among military officers, think-tank analysts, and academics about the correct explanation for the dramatic turnaround in the insurgency.

One school of thought argued that the credit goes exclusively to the Surge to include the infusion of over 28,000 troops and the correct application of counterinsurgency techniques.[114] Protecting Baghdad's civilian residents with concrete walls, US military personnel and Iraqi allies formed linchpins of the Surge strategy. Another school emphasized the Anbar Awakening uprising against the ISI jihadis. The Anbar Sunni sheiks and their followers deserve the lion's share of the credit for turning the tide.[115] Yet another camp attributed the decrease in the casualties to the burning out of the insurgency and the "cleansing" of opponents.

A journalist wrote: "the killing stopped because there was no one left to kill."[116] This statement is factually wrong and superficial. Still, others interpret the reduction in deaths to the combination of the Surge and the Awakening working at the same time.[117] Three professors writing in an academic journal argued plausibly for a "synergistic interaction" between the Surge and Awakening to explain the reduction in violence in 2007. Both "were necessary; neither was sufficient." This synergy produced "something new that neither could have achieved alone." The trio perceived a uniqueness in the Iraq case study by noting that "U.S. policy thus played an important role, but Iraq provides no evidence that similar methods will produce similar results elsewhere without local equivalents of the Sunni Awakening."[118] To this historian, the multi-causal explanation resonates most persuasively, as does its unlikely replication in a future war.

Whatever explanation one accepts, the victory did pull America's chestnuts out of the Iraqi fire, salvaged George Bush's presidency, and restored a modicum of luster to the US commander in chief's reputation even with his bad call on Saddam Hussein's phantom nuclear arms. It also spared the Defense Department from a humiliation akin to Vietnam in the popular mind. As noted by one scholar, the president's surge-strategy decision set forth the "boldest stroke of his presidency."[119] Snatching victory from the jaws of defeat in Anbar also weighed heavily in Barack Obama's 2009 decision to "surge" military forces to Afghanistan, described in Chapter 7.

George Bush's roll of the dice paid off as the orgy of sectarian killings steadily contracted during the remainder of his presidential tenure. Other measures also figured in the drop-off in military casualties, of which 60 percent of the nearly 4,500 deaths resulted from IEDs. Man's best friend, K-9 dogs trained to sniff out bombs, saved countless troops from death, wheelchairs, or disfiguring burn-blasts. Even greater numbers skirted these cruel fates when Robert Gates, who replaced Rumsfeld, made it a top priority to ramp up the manufacture of the V-bottomed Mine Resistant Ambush Protected vehicles, which largely shielded the GI occupants from the fiery blasts of the roadside-planted IEDs. Gates stepped on toes, pushed, and bullied until belatedly the United States shipped some 27,000 MRAPs to Iraq. Not until mid-2008 did adequate supplies accrue for the bulky protected transports to be sent to Afghanistan.

One unsalvageable problem rested with the billions of dollars misspent, wasted, or vanished (down the proverbial rat hole) for nation-building projects in the war-ravaged country.[120] To get Iraq on its feet along with futile attempts to "buy" peace and stability among a distraught population, the United States spent heavily on electricity production, schools, clinics, and water treatment plants. Worthwhile expenditures existed next to foolish outlays. Paid-off contractors left buildings unfinished. Outside walls stood without roofs, doors, or windows in hastily erected classrooms. Only a profligate nation could overindulge in such ruinous pursuits.[121]

Over a dozen years after the Iraq invasion, the US Army itself published a sobering, two-volume study of the war that amounts to an official and comprehensive account. The work honestly recounts the well-known mistakes made by the Pentagon and the White House. Among the blunders covered are the failures to prepare adequately for the post-invasion phrase, to have adequate numbers of US troops on hand for stabilization, to maintain the Iraqi army as constabulary force, to react quickly and correctly to popular demonstrations leading to an insurgency, to retain low-level Baath Party members for running the bureaucracy and to understanding sectarian bloodshed. To be sure, there were many bright spots in Army's handling of a pervasive insurgency. Officers such as H. R. McMaster in Tel Afar, Sean MacFarland in Ramadi, and David Petraeus as overall commander distinguished themselves.[122]

Of all the conflicts summarized in this book, Iraq stands out in many ways as an exception to the other hostile actions. It consumed substantially higher costs in lives and money. Nearly 4,500 Americans lost their lives and possibly half a million Iraqis suffered the same fate. The financial expenditures reached between one and two trillion US dollars. In a gross strategic miscalculation, the incursion removed Iraq from checkmating the sinister ambitions of next-door ayatollah Iran, whose power-seeking tentacles now extend deep into Shiite-dominated Baghdad as well as into Lebanon, Syria, Yemen, and the Persian Gulf.

The immense expenses of the Second Iraq War (2003–2011) sobered the American people. The deeply rooted feelings among Americans and their political elites that the war was a grave mistake contributed to the disengagement sentiments, if not isolationist thinking, which arose in President Bush's second term, plus the Obama and Trump administrations into the Joseph R. Biden's White House term. Tactically, the Iraq War contributed to the switch in gears away from social engineering projects of nation building and democracy promotion to a tighter focus on killing militants or standing up indigenous forces to tackle the terrorist problem, as will be described in Chapter 6.

5.10 America Temporarily Withdraws from Iraq

The Pentagon celebrated the pacification of Anbar Province on September 1, 2008, with a parade down Main Street in Ramadi, the provincial capital, in which the US military commanders formally handed off peacekeeping duties to the Iraqi Army and police. The brief ceremony capped one of the most stunning turnarounds in the Iraq War. The transfer of authority replicated similar transitions in eleven of Iraq's eighteen provinces. Attacks on American and allied forces in Anbar receded more than 90 percent over the twenty months since the start of the surge.[123] The Islamic State of Iraq was on the ropes. After an airstrike killed al-Zarqawi, the leadership passed to another foreigner, Abu Ayyub al-Masri, until the Egyptian's 2010 death in a safe house. These foreign jihadi leaders repulsed Anbar's residents by their strident fundamentalism, designation of the locals as apostates, and their wanton killings of Iraqis. Now the Salafi-jihadis had lost almost all their support where they once enjoyed loyalty and respect.

The Ramadi turnover on that hot autumn day in 2008 coincided with the start of America's Great Recession, which shrank the economy, turned the American public inward, and led to the election of Barack Obama to the presidency. The Illinois US senator ran on a political platform of ending the Iraq War by withdrawing US combat forces. Before then, other events occurred along the exit route (see Chapter 7).

The sharp turnaround in the Iraq War enabled President Bush in late 2008 to agree to a timetable for retiring all US troops, among provisions for soldiers' legal protection from Iraqi civil crimes.[124] This status of forces agreement called for the United States to retire its military forces from Iraq's major cities by summer of the next year and to pack up all its combat troops and leave the country before 2011 ended. Those two milestones occurred after Obama walked into the White House, and after campaigning on a nation building at home slogan.

During his campaign for the White House, Barack Obama articulated his disengagement prescription for the Iraq War, which he opposed from the start. Five months before George Bush ordered US Armed Forces to invade, the Illinois state senator delivered a dissenting speech: "I don't oppose all wars. What I am opposed to is a dumb war."[125] In his speech accepting the Democratic Party's nomination for president in mid-2008, he voiced again his repeated theme that Iraq was "a war of choice" and that it was unnecessary to waging a global anti-terror campaign "by occupying Iraq."[126]

Once in office, the new commander in chief traveled to Camp Lejeune in North Carolina to stand before thousands of camouflaged Marines so as to outline his timetable to extract thousands of American military personnel from the largely stabilized country. Obama directed that the bulk of these forces would be on their way home by August 2010.

His schedule called for the remaining 35,000–50,000 "transnational forces" to leave before the conclusion of 2011.[127]

The new American leader assumed his duties with more than a smidgen of skepticism about the US military brass. Writing about Iraq in his post-presidency memoir, Obama wrote how the "military prided itself on accomplishing a mission .... In Iraq that had meant an escalating need for more of everything: more troops, more bases, more private contractors, more aircraft, more intelligence, surveillance, and reconnaissance (ISR). More had not produced victory."[128] This skeptical mindset motivated him to retrench from Iraq and then slash the number of American forces in Afghanistan after an initial troop buildup rather than accede to further personnel requests from his generals.

The DoD's Iraqi deployment must be measured as more than just a military occupation. Army and Marine officers functioned like town mayors; they restored public services; they brokered local disputes; and they expended funds to construct projects and undertake government functions. Their Commanders Emergency Response Programs authorized a total of $4 billion in small amounts over a seven-year period to carry out these humanitarian and civic duties. As a consequence, American service members wove themselves into Iraq's political life by working with tribal sheiks, village elders, politicians, and military representatives.[129] They went a long way toward stabilizing and reconciling a malevolent environment.

High-ranking US officers unsuccessfully pressed the Malaki government to integrate Sunni irregulars into the national army and security forces to bridge the Shiite-Sunni divide and unite a fractured country. The American leave-taking rekindled the unchecked inter-sectarian pathologies. The day after the last US soldier packed up and left, the sectarian parties were at each other's throats. The Shiite-dominated government ordered the arrest of a Sunni vice president for running a "death squad that assassinated police and officials."[130] The accusations and anti-Sunni actions convinced the increasingly marginalized population that government institutions were being directed against the minority by the Shiite majority. Their pool of resentment underlay a fresh explosion of beheadings, shootings, bombings, and other grisly atrocities by a resurgent Salafist-terrorist movement soon enough in Syria as well as Iraq.

To preside over the end of the US war in Iraq, the White House dispatched Leon E. Panetta, the defense secretary who replaced Gates, to close out the nearly nine-year conflict. Standing in a concrete fortified courtyard in the Baghdad airport, Panetta enumerated the economic, terrorism, and democratic issues still ahead. Then the Pentagon leader uttered glittering generalities about America's future supportive role: "the US will be there to stand by the Iraqi people as they navigate those challenges to build a stronger and more prosperous nation."[131] Panetta's parting remarks sounded like pretty typical fare for the occasion. His perfunctory words seemed more predictive than intended as the US Armed Forces returned to defend Iraq from a vicious Salafi-jihadi rampage in less than three quick years.

6   America's Small-Footprint Wars
Asia, Africa, and the Middle East

Big countries don't fight small wars.   Attributed to the Duke of Wellington

Long may the barbarians continue, I pray, if not to love us, at least to hate one another.   Tacitus

In the approximately ninety minutes that it took the suicidal jihadis to crash commercial jets into the Pentagon and the Twin Towers, US security policy and even the conduct of warfare underwent a profound transformation. Combating terrorism demanded new tactics that differed from large-scale conventional wars of massed aircraft carriers, tanks, and brigades. Twenty-first-century America faced threats emanating from a chain of non-state terrorist networks. The state-less Salafi-Muslim extremists set up shop in ungoverned corners of the world's poorest countries, such as the Philippines, Afghanistan, Somalia, Yemen, Mali, Niger, and others to include cells within the urbanized Western world. New strategies and nontraditional forces were needed. Employing yesterday's balance-of-power stratagems to hold violent extremists in check amounted to futility. The fight had to be taken to the terrorists.

6.1   The Bush, Obama, and Trump Counterterrorism Campaigns across the Globe

During the George W. Bush administration, US military forces went from a conventionally armed Goliath of the Cold War to a lithe and lightly armed David, whose Special Operations Forces could take down the shadowy terrorist circuits with their counter-networks. This SOF focus in no way diminishes the contribution of the other branches of the US Armed Forces. The conventional Army, Air Force, Navy, and Marines all served in the wars in Afghanistan, Iraq, and the planetary struggle against Salafi-terrorism. For example, the Army deployed tens of thousands of soldiers to far-flung battlefields; the Air Force lofted strike aircraft for ground-cover operations and for airlifting troops and equipment; the Navy launched transport ships and attack warplanes on

176

terrorist targets; and the Marines fielded infantry and raiders. In short, the war on terrorism could not have been waged without what the Defense Department labeled as combined arms. In this chapter, the spotlight is on the micro-battlefields of counterterrorism, which by its nature relies on small numbers of Special Operations Forces and air strikes from drones or piloted aircraft instead of regular ground forces.

The Bush White House rolled out the global war on terrorism (GWOT). Fought under the rubric of GWOT, this multi-fronted campaign closed in on Islamist terrorists far afield from the wars in Afghanistan and Iraq. Small numbers of American forces soon found themselves battling Salafi militants in Africa, Asia, and the Middle East to forestall terrorist attacks on the homeland. This conflict marked the ascendancy of Joint Special Operations Command (JSOC) over the far-flung campaign to kill or capture violent extremists. The Defense Department oversaw the painful birth of JSOC after the failed 1980 hostage-rescue operation inside Iran. That debacle, caused in part by failed helicopters and faulty coordination among the military's various branches, which lacked an adequate centralized command, convinced the military brass to act on the recommendation of Charles Beckwith. The Army colonel had led the recently organized Delta Force in the aborted Operation Eagle Claw to free fifty-two US Embassy staff members held by Iranian "students" and militants. To avoid future failures, Beckwith petitioned the Joint Chiefs of Staff to establish JSOC to coordinate and execute commando-type raids to free hostages and eradicate terrorist nests.

Half a decade afterward, Congress enacted legislation to establish USSOCOM, or the US Special Operations Command, placing it under a four-star military officer and supporting it with a separate budget to protect its funding from pillaging by the Army, Navy, and Air Force. The larger SOCOM entity presided over JSOC, which functioned as the ultra-secretive action arm of the parent command. For its part, JSOC oversees, among other units, the US Army Rangers, Navy SEALs, Delta Force, Intelligence Support Activity (ultra-secret signals intelligence unit known by many names), and the 160th Special Operations Air Regiment (nicknamed the Night Stalkers for its daring helicopter penetrations). The Special Operations Command supports the subordinate JSOC, which carries out a host of highly classified missions. JSOC, for example, handled the high-profile raid to kill Osama bin Laden in spring 2011, after the CIA uncovered the arch-terrorist's secret compound in Abbottabad, Pakistan.[1]

The GWOT set out to stamp out Salafi-jihadi cells. For part of this mission, the Pentagon enlisted and enabled other armies. The

Department of Defense had conducted Foreign Internal Defense (FID) missions to instruct and equip allied militaries dating back to the Cold War. US military forces first assisted NATO countries and then other nations around the world to resist communist internal subversion and external aggression. Now FID was updated. The DoD armed, professionalized, and advised foreign armies in the arts of counterinsurgency and counterterrorism. The application was named the "Indirect Approach" since US troops fought indirectly through their partners. FID saved American lives and, perhaps, dollars while wisely involving locals in their own fight.

The usage of Indirect Approach terminology waned as the military spoke more about special warfare, an umbrella term for all operations conducted "by, with, or through" indigenous forces. Whatever the nomenclature, Defense personnel forged tight relationships with resident auxiliaries, who they empowered with instructions, weapons, intelligence, air cover, and even cash. To Churchill, transport was the stem that made possible the bright colored flower of victory. To the Pentagon, partnering with local forces figured as the root to countering terrorists.

Another way of eliminating violent extremism fell to the Special Operation Forces who fought a twilight struggle wreathed in secrecy and in association with intelligence services. Spec Ops teams staged high-tempo, lethal assaults to capture or kill militants while scooping up as much information from computers or notepads as possible in order to prepare for the next raid. To target the amoeba-like multiplying and dividing terrorist groups, Army Deltas and Navy Seals placed a premium on F3EA (Find, Fix, Finish, Exploit [intelligence], and Analyze information). In a word, counterterrorism is man-hunting. Defeating spectral terrorist networks called for counterterrorist networks made up of intelligence personnel of various stripes to locate and track their targets. Intelligence operatives worked sources who divulged secrets for money or revenge against terrorists. They passed their information to kinetic units to carry out attacks.[2]

Coming into office, President Barack Obama made mostly rhetorical changes or a "shift in emphasis rather than a truly substantive move" in the Pentagon's war against Salafi extremists.[3] The Obama White House discarded Bush's phrase about a global war on terrorism and replaced it with a campaign known as "countering violent extremism" to combat the sub-state Salafi-jihadi networks. The fresh designation masked a continuation of the preceding tactics, including kinetic actions such as drone airstrikes or SWAT-type raids on violent Islamists. The new president was no laggard when it came to applying deadly force to bringing terrorist to justice, although he had a penchant for micromanaging operations.

Additionally, Obama renounced his predecessor's policies of water-boarding and other enhanced interrogation techniques (sleep deprivation, binding limbs in stress positions) used on terrorist suspects in CIA-operated black sites around the world, although the Bush administration had largely emptied the prisons. At least one expert speculated that Obama officials understood that their allies in the Middle East "would continue to engage in such activities" with the knowledge that when "those techniques happened to produce useful intelligence, the United States could still benefit from it."[4]

A foremost exponent of an intelligence-driven approach to bringing down terrorists was the hard-charging Army General Stanley McChrystal, a West Pointer, who rose through the ranks in the Rangers and Special Forces. In Iraq, Ranger McChrystal conducted Direct Action (or Direct Approach) tactics of his parent unit. These tactics simply meant engaging head-on the nation's adversaries. In Iraq, he pioneered a swift integration of information from the Defense Intelligence Agency, CIA, and other intelligence entities by breaking down bureaucratic stove-piping among intelligence-gathering communities so as target terrorists in real time. One of McChrystal's intel coups resulted in the bombing death of Abu Musab al-Zarqawi, the head of what became known as al Qaeda in Iraq.[5]

The general's close-in combat tactics during what Delta squads called "Baghdad SWAT" gutted al Qaeda elements from the Iraqi capital and suburbs at the height of the sectarian civil war. Casualties, particularly among the Army's Delta teams (which had overall responsibility for Iraq, whereas the SEALs predominated in Afghanistan) were high, although not publically disclosed.[6] Running deadly sweeps against Islamist bomb makers, moneymen, and terrorist plotters, McChrystal's command dismantled much of al Qaeda's operational infrastructure in Anbar Province.[7] Along with the Anbar Awakening and US troop surge, the battlefield fierceness and Agincourt courage of the Special Warfare fighters contributed to the turnaround in the fortunes of the Iraq War in the late 2000s.

Later in his career, the four-star general espoused classical counterinsurgency warfare with its concentration on population protection and emphasis on working "by, with, and through" local partners to create security forces. In this method of warfare, America's partners pull the trigger, while the US troops fight indirectly by training, advising, and equipping the host nation's soldiers. Involving indigenous manpower was seen as a force multiplier for the stretched American units. Forming ties with resident fighters also lessened local aversion to the presence of foreign soldiers.

In the course of the Barack Obama administration, the Pentagon dropped the indirect approach terminology for more encompassing designation of "Security Force Assistance" (SFA). The SFA concept covered "partnering with foreign governments, organizations, and fighters to counter national security threats" in the course of counter-insurgency and counterterrorism missions.[8] The name was new but the US strategy of assisting allies to modernize and build up their armed forces dated back decades. In its contemporary application, DoD terms the effort "train, advise, and assist" missions to bring on board partners in the fight against Salafi-jihadi militants.[9]

The terrorist ecosystem festered in lands that proved veritable suction pumps, in which the vacuum created by anemic or even absent government authority laid bare vulnerabilities for jihadi penetration. To protect a growing number of security threats, the US military and State Department turned to in-country opponents of the militants. Partnering with allied forces became the hallmark of America's low-visibility, light-footprint wars in the earth's backwaters. The Defense Department's strategy boiled down to preventing the Salafi-jihadis from establishing hubs capable of exporting international terrorism. The US Army stood up Security Force Assistance Brigades to expand training and mentoring beyond the Green Beret's smaller-scoped activities. Initiated during the Bush presidency, refined by Obama's Pentagon, and carried on by the Donald Trump administration, the partnering formula has kept another 9/11 attack at bay. America's withdrawal from Afghanistan and other fronts could jeopardize this viable strategy.

6.2   The United States Returns to the Philippines

The United States returned to the Republic of the Philippines to wage a low-profile war on terrorists just before the September 11th shock. Faced with rising numbers of kidnappings in the south of the Philippine archipelago, in 2000, the Manila government asked the then Pacific Command (now Indo-Pacific Command, or INDOPACOM) for assistance. PACOM responded by sending troops to the scene from the Special Operations Command, Pacific to offer counterterrorism instructions to Filipino light infantry units. The Pentagon also resumed the Balikatan (translated as "shoulder-to-shoulder") military exercises with the Armed Forces of the Philippines (AFP). Earlier American-Filipino cooperation lapsed after the Cold War when anti-Washington sentiments flourished in the Pacific islands.

The Filipinos felt strongly about their national sovereignty. The island nation fought and lost a bitter insurgency to the United States in its bid for statehood at the turn of the twentieth century. According to historian Brian McAllister Linn, the 1899–1902 Philippine war was the "most successful counterinsurgency campaign in U.S. history."[10] The war consolidated Washington's rule for nearly half a century. Near the end of World War II, the US and Filipino forces together liberated the islands from Japan's cruel occupation. The Philippines gained full sovereignty from American colonial rule in 1946.

Independence brought neither internal peace nor sectarian harmony to the Philippines. The island's history set the stage for its contemporary conflicts. Four centuries of Spanish colonialism and Catholicism posed nearly 90 percent of the population against Muslims, particularly in the southernmost isles where Islamic settlements resisted Madrid's rule dating from 1521 when Magellan landed in the 7,000-island archipelago. The Spanish colonialists encountered Muslim inhabitants, whose forbearers made landfall three centuries earlier on Mindanao, Palawan, and Sulu. Relations between Muslims and Christians alternated between periods of tolerance and conflict. The rise of Islamic militancy in the Middle East during the 1970s infected the Philippines, too. The Muslims, who numbered over ten million inhabitants, or approximately 11 percent of the population, hated their Christian rulers in faraway Manila.

In modern days, the Philippine authorities struggled to extend governance and public services to distant and neglected locations. Thus, poverty, underdevelopment, and underemployment compounded the Islamic-Christian animosity. These same dire socioeconomic conditions also gave birth to communist opposition in 1930s. The communists joined in the resistance to Japan's 1940s occupation and then resumed their opposition to Manila in the 1950s. The rural communist attacks lasted decades before dwindling but not totally dying out, leaving Muslim militants the main threat in the nation of 100 million inhabitants.

Prior to the Pentagon's return in 2000 to assist the AFP against the upstart Abu Sayyaf Group (ASG), the island government contended with earlier Muslim movements. These parties yearned for autonomy from Manila's repressive and negligent rule. The Moros, as Muslims were known locally, originally resisted the US claim to the islands after the Spanish-American War. Decades later, the Moro National Liberation Front (MNLF) took up arms against the central government. When the MNLF reached a settlement with Manila for the Autonomous Region of Muslim Mindanao in 1987, its ideological purists split with its parent body to establish the Moro Islamic Liberation Front (MILF). Decades afterward, the MILF entered into peace negotiations with central authorities. But other Muslims resisted Manila's entreaties.

The salient point in this summarized history is that the southern islands stayed rebellious even before the onset of al Qaeda's attacks. The US role remained minimal until linkages could be established between acts of Filipino terrorism and Islamic millenarianism emanating from east of Suez. Washington feared terrorism launched from the Philippines either from native bands or Middle Eastern networks hiding out in the island's paddies and jungles.

The US Indo-Pacific Command, one of the six geographical combatant commands that divide up the world for DoD responsibility, initiated the joint Balikatan military drills with the Philippine military. Its debut maneuvers took place just a year before a high-profile abduction that riveted attention on the Muslim southern islands. On May 27, 2001, an obscure extremist band, Abu Sayyaf, kidnapped an American missionary couple – Martin and Gracia Burnham – along with others from a tourist resort on Palawan Island and whisked them over the Sulu Sea to hideouts on Basilan Island off the Mindanao coast.

Abu Sayyaf swore fealty to Osama bin Laden. Its name honored the Afghan jihadi Abdul Rasul Sayyaf (meaning roughly "the bearer of the sword"). Abu Sayyaf owed its early funding to a Saudi businessman, who married one of Osama bin Laden's sisters in the 1990s. Mohammed Jamal Khalifa oversaw commercial enterprises and an Islamic charity in the Philippines where he allegedly funneled money to Muslim extremists.[11] After fleeing to Madagascar, he met death a decade later.

Abu Sayyaf went on to infamy. More bandits than religious practitioners, Abu Sayyaf members intimidated, murdered, raped, and kidnapped for ransom. A well-placed journalist wrote that Abu Sayyaf thugs knew little of the *Koran*, Islam's holy book. Asserting holy warrior status, nevertheless, they "sexually appropriated several of the women captives (who were taken with the Burnhams), claiming them as 'wives.'"[12] Radicalized Muslims in the past used Islam as a religious cover for nefarious deeds, as exemplified by the Barbary pirates along the north African coast of the Mediterranean Sea.[13] In contemporary times, the Islamic State of Iraq and Syria (ISIS) carried out terrorism, beheadings, immolations, sexual slavery, and abductions-for-money in the name of religion.

6.3   Operation Enduring Freedom: Philippines

Abu Sayyaf's allegiance to al Qaeda Central put the start-up group squarely in DoD's crosshairs. Like other terrorist outfits, it craved the limelight. Its erstwhile leader, Aldam Tilao, often sought media attention decked out in a colorful bandana and wearing Oakley sunglasses for press photographers.[14] In time, Tilao's (or using his nom de guerre Abu Sabaya, meaning "bearer of captives") thirst for headlines contributed to his undoing. Before his death, he brought the US military down hard on his compatriots.

President George W. Bush offered his Philippine counterpart, Gloria Macapagal Arroyo, military assistance to combat the Burnham abductors. The island president accepted the offer but attached some strings to the US role. Due to decades of American colonial occupation, Manila was hypersensitive to any infringement on its sovereignty by the presence of foreign troops. It imposed restrictions on American armed forces operating under the DoD's newly created Joint Special Operations Task Force – Philippines. The JSOTF-P's Visiting Forces Agreement, negotiated and signed by both governments, barred US Defense personnel from engaging in direct combat with Islamist insurgents, unless attacked. The agreement also specified a relatively small US Armed Forces contingent at around 600 personnel, including both warfighters and support troops.

Activating the partnering approach, Special Operations Forces and CIA paramilitary officers got the behind-the-lines assignments for intel briefings, training, advising, and mentoring the Filipino security forces. This cooperative arrangement required "buy in" from the Manilla government, which demanded that the AFP shoulder the "trigger-pulling" roles. Thus, SOF and CIA personnel concentrated on laying plans for man-hunting operations rather than heavy-duty patrolling.[15] SOF cadres kept at least "one hill" behind the point of conflict. Special warfare weighed most heavily on the Green Berets to build rapport with the host-nation's military.

Headquartered in Zamboanga, the old center of Spanish colonial rule on Mindanao, JSOTF-P funneled arms and military resources to the Filipino-armed forces. The White House deemed this offensive an extension of its Global War on Terrorism but it used the official title of Operation Enduring Freedom – Philippines. The "enduring freedom" counterterrorism effort originated with the start of Operation Enduring Freedom in the Afghanistan war in 2001. Later, DoD activated affiliated campaigns such as OEF – Philippines (OEF-P) and OEF – Trans Sahara, after uncovering ties between al Qaeda Central in South Asia to other jihadi fronts.

Enduring Freedom – Philippines got underway in earnest during January 2002. It proved effective by enabling the Filipino forces to kill a string of Abu Sayyaf chiefs and scatter the followers to outlying islands. To fulfill its promised assistance to Philippine special forces and conventional units, the Defense Department rotated American special operation personnel through JSOTF-Philippines command for six-month tours on average. US casualties from hostile fire were very rare, numbering less than a dozen KIAs over a ten-year period, including other locations – except Afghanistan and later Iraq.[16]

In addition to working "by, with and through" Manila's army to shoot Islamist terrorists, the JSOTF-P did "wage peace" among civilians. A handful of Special Forces labored to alleviate the Muslims' hardships with walk-in medical, dental, and veterinary clinics. They engaged in small-scale construction projects to access water or to build helipads in the countryside. Thus, the hard-edged counterinsurgency attacks were matched by goodwill endeavors to win over the inhabitants to a distant government. Often, however, the social services to include schools, medical clinics, veterinarian facilities, and electrification failed to offset official corruption, fraudulent elections, government ineptness, and thuggish police. This was classic hearts-and-minds stuff, but its application by Special Forces had to be genuine and without cynicism, as journalist Robert D. Kaplan stressed.[17]

Initially, the American instructors taught basic soldiering to their Filipino students, such as marksmanship and fire-and-maneuver tactics to improve their infantry skills. In time, they worked at higher echelons to improve battalion and brigade operational capabilities. Not insignificantly, US advisers moved the AFP away from indiscriminate attacks that often harmed noncombatants. They carried out proper population-centric approaches to spare civilian casualties and regain their trust on behalf of Manila. In less violent zones, Philippine armed forces integrated police officers into counterterrorism operations to gain information as they were often closer to the people than the soldiers.

Lasting peace and tranquility seemed at hand in the southern Muslim domains before long. Indeed, OEF-P was viewed as a showpiece for the Pentagon's turnaround of the Philippines from a heightened terrorist threat. A trio of RAND Corporation analysts conducted an assessment of US Special Operations Forces' activities for the years 2001 to 2014. The three researchers concluded their study on a note of praise: "OEF-P contributed to the successful degradation of transnational terrorist threats in the Philippines." The key findings homed in on the drop in Abu Sayyaf Group attacks, fewer militants in its ranks, and polls showing "reduced support for the ASG and a substantial majority reporting satisfaction with Philippine security forces." The upbeat report card lauded the US presence for the "increased Philippine security forces' capabilities at the tactical, operational, and institutional levels."[18]

In another report undertaken by the Center for Naval Analysis, the authors also extolled the US counter-extremism mission on the Pacific islands. Entitled "Operation Enduring Freedom-Philippines: Civilian Harm and the Indirect Approach," the study examined the military support delivered by JSOTF-P to the AFP in order to assess the effectiveness of the Indirect Approach. The authors concluded: "While US direct action operations alone can make short-term gains against global terrorism, a US kinetic approach is unsustainable in itself. Partners are essential in the struggle against violent extremism, and partners may require the United States to adopt an indirect approach to a common challenge."[19] The apparent effectiveness of the Philippine partnership accentuated the Pentagon's long-standing predisposition for working by, with, and through the armed forces of allied states, as spelled out it is Security Force Assistance strategy.

The American-engineered stability, so lauded by US officers and experts, came a cropper with the sudden and havoc-wreaking takeover of Marawi, a Mindanao city, by the resurrected Abu Sayyaf Group. It switched its tactics, along with its allegiance from al Qaeda to the Islamic State in Iraq and Syria, before infesting the urban center. Led by Isnilon Hapilon and inspired by the Islamic State, the militants overran the city of 200,000 residents in May 2017. Since its terrorism in the early 2000s under the leadership of Hapilon, who died in the Marawi siege, the ASG carved out a reputation for being the most violent of Muslim factions with a rash of kidnappings, murders, and even beheadings in the Pacific country.

ISIS recognized Hapilon's prominence by naming him emir of Southeast Asia. For its part, Abu Sayyaf proved itself a worthy acolyte to the Islamic State with gruesome deeds and a doctrinaire mentality. For instance, Abu Sayyaf disavowed the Moro movements that made peace with the Manila government in return for some autonomy over the Muslim-populated southern islands. ASG's ties to the Islamic State boosted the profile of both terrorist networks. The Islamist conquest of Marawi attracted foreign Muslim jihadis, who flocked to Mindanao from the Middle East, Malaysia, Indonesia, and elsewhere.[20] Abu Sayyaf militants strove to turn Marawi into the seat of a Southeast Asian caliphate.

The Pentagon went into high gear to aid the embattled Philippine military. The United States hurried small arms to the besieging Philippine forces, furnished intelligence, and deployed surveillance drones, such as the MQ-1C Gray Eagle. The unmanned aircraft handed off real-time video streams of Marawi's streets, buildings, and Muslim fighters. US troops also trained and mentored the AFP for the trial by fire of urban warfare.[21] The battle to retake Marawi lasted five months and claimed the lives of more than 1,000 people, including some

800 militants and about 70 AFP soldiers. Much of the city lay in ruins afterwards. The urban center's sudden fall to ASG shattered the complacency in the DoD as well as the Manila government. Even after routing the militants, apprehension persisted about how strong a foothold the Islamic State had gained in southeast Asia.

The central authorities always looked for ways to divide and decrease their enemies. They had struck and signed a bargain in early 2019 for greater autonomy with the Moro Islamic Liberation Front, which provided for a temporary parliament with an election in 2022 for new representatives. The agreement also called for decommissioning of MILF members, which entailed Manila buying their weapons and training them to help local peacekeeping forces. This process made headway until the onset of COVID-19 and fresh threats from Islamic State terrorists.[22] The central government's extension of more self-rule was intended to placate local grievances that fueled Islamist terrorism. Despite the peace agreement with Rodrigo Duterte's government, bombings and killings persisted in the Muslim-majority islands, including the detonation of a Catholic church in Sulu province at the start of 2019, which stood apart from the rest of the southern region by rejecting the accord.[23]

ASG's reborn militancy and piracy off Sabah, Malaysia, and the Sulu archipelago attracted foreign fighters as far away as Bangladesh, Pakistan, and the Middle East along with recruits from Muslim Southeast Asia. What is more, the destruction of ISIS' caliphate in Syria and Iraq resulted in jihadis fleeing to the Philippines in search of a new religious home.[24] Given the Philippines' history, it is unlikely that the country has seen the last of terrorism and insurgency. This prognosis all but ensures that US forces will continue to partner with the Philippines unless Manila decides to back out of the defense agreement with Washington.

6.4   Interminable Wars in the Horn of Africa: Somalia and Yemen

On the other side of the world, the Horn of Africa presented a vexing set of terrorist-insurgencies at the same time the Defense Department was returning to the Philippines. Both Somalia in the Horn and Yemen on the Arabian Peninsula harbored al Qaeda operatives who worried American intelligence agencies. Both of these desperately poor countries succumbed to bloodshed, chaos, and disruption by Salafi extremists. They became terrorist havens and launching pads for murderous attacks beyond their borders.

The Pentagon stood up the Combined Joint Task Force-Horn of Africa (CJTF-HOA) (it was later folded into the US Africa Command) to counter threats from al Qaeda in 2002. Based in the tiny nation of Djibouti, CJTF-HOA eventually housed some 4,000 US military personnel. Djibouti, which faces the Red Sea where it joins the Gulf of Aden, benefited from its strategic location and relative safety from the nearby turmoil. Formerly a part of the French empire, the parched enclave is home to less than a million inhabitants. The US Navy took over the former Fort Lemonnier, an old French Foreign Legion outpost. It lengthened runways, constructed barracks, and built military facilities. The installation became a regional hub for the CIA and SOF to monitor, assess, and pick off terrorists in the surrounding neighborhood under a shroud of secrecy.

At the start of the GWOT, one of the Agency's Predator drones fired a Hellfire missile into a vehicle traveling Yemen's backroads, killing an al Qaeda sub-leader and five others in November 2002. Coming soon after the first air-to-ground killing in Afghanistan, the Yemen missile firing set a precedent for this novel method of getting rid of hard-to-reach antagonists. Except for official combat zones, such as Afghanistan and Iraq, the CIA took charge of the cloak-and-missile campaign in low-profile conflicts in Somalia, Pakistan, and elsewhere. Overall, CJTF-HOA focused on prevention and deterrence of terrorism for export.[25] Nearby Somalia offered up a worst-case illustration of an ungoverned, violent, and politically torn country that became a terrorist incubator.

Somalia never returned to the era of Mohamed Siad Barre's enforced passivity after a popular uprising ousted the decades-long military dictator from power in 1991. Fierce clan rivalries, criminal gangs, and throat-cutting assailants stalked the France-sized country. The lawlessness produced hunger and then starvation among the population. The breakdown of order, in turn, motivated George H. W. Bush to dispatch US Armed Forces to assist nongovernment agencies in feeding the destitute. This intervention led to "mission creep" and the so-called Black Hawk Down incident during Bill Clinton's presidency, as described in Chapter 3.

Clinton's decampment left the fractured society defenseless from radicalization possibly underway since 1992, when Osama bin Laden reportedly distributed funds to Mohammed Farah Aidid, the clan chieftain who eluded American capture before the Battle of Mogadishu. Bin Laden interpreted Clinton's retreat far more significantly than the White House or news media did. In 1996, he issued a fatwa that revealed his contempt for Clinton's America:

When tens of your soldiers were killed in minor battles and one American pilot dragged in the street of Mogadishu, you left the area in disappointment, humiliation, and defeat, carrying your dead with you. Clinton appeared in front of the whole world threatening and promising revenge, but these threats were merely preparation for withdrawal. You had been disgraced by Allah and you withdrew, the extent of your impotence and weakness became very clear.[26]

The American public and media outlets quickly moved on from the cruel Mogadishu streets to other things. Somalia might be publicly forgotten but it was far from being a pacified, stable, or terrorist-free country. If anything, it lay open like the Aristotelian vacuum abhorrent to nature and to human nature, too. Salafi-jihadis soon infiltrated its political sphere.

Al Qaeda perceived President Bush's 1992 humanitarian intervention into Somalia as a "catalytic event" in Islam's growing clash with the United States. Osama bin Laden's exiled band, residing at the time next door in the Sudan, fixed its hatred, more and more, toward its "far enemy" in the United States and away from its "near enemy" in the apostate monarchies and corrupt dictatorships in the Muslim world. That refocusing figured in the September 11th terror attack in the following decade.[27]

6.5   The Americans Return to Somalia

Since the Black Hawk Down incident, Somalia drifted off the radars in government offices back in Washington, none of which displayed any eagerness to wade back into the convulsed land. The Pentagon especially hung back over concerns about being drawn into a quagmire. Despite the desire to wash its hands of what appeared to be a hopeless economic and political "basket case," the Clinton White House authorized the CIA in the mid-1990s to mount undercover operations inside Somalia. Officials feared that without some forceful counter presence the country would become a haven for international terrorism.

The Agency stepped up its covert counterterrorism activities following the twin truck-bombings of the US embassies in Dar es Salaam and Nairobi in 1998. Some intelligence reports suggested that al Qaeda facilitators trekked through Somalia to the bombing sites prior to the East African attacks. Additionally, a US criminal indictment of Osama bin Laden cited that al Qaeda had sent operatives to Aidid, the notorious warlord, who trained Somalis to shoot down the two Black Hawk helicopters in 1993.[28]

Somalia had all the prerequisites for a terrorist sanctuary – lawlessness, ungoverned spaces, and a predominately Muslim population that was hard pressed to eke out a subsistence living. Yet these failed-state conditions also made it tough going for al Qaeda members who, in the words of a West Point report, "fell victim to many of the same challenges that plague Western interventions."[29] Al Qaeda overcame difficulties by resorting to its own version of working "by, with, and through" anti-Western clans. The bin Ladenists transferred bomb-making skills and funds to the Somali jihadis.

To head off terrorist threats, the CIA's Special Activities Division inserted agent-handlers into Somalia to recruit local sources for information about terrorist plotters. Operating out of the Mogadishu airport, SAD case officers paid their warlord contacts to kill terrorist cadres or to turn them over to American custody for incarceration in CIA-run "black sites" (i.e., prisons) around the world.[30] The CIA also collaborated with the Somali government's National Security Agency, which it trained and funded to round up Salafi gunmen. The terrorists weren't so easily suppressed, nevertheless.

Besides the two embassy bombings in East Africa, a series of jihadi attacks alarmed the Pentagon about countries in the Horn of Africa region. Al Qaeda militants orchestrated the bombing of the USS *Cole* in nearby Yemen's Aden harbor. Two years later in November 2002, militants crashed a vehicle and detonated bombs in the Paradise hotel in Mombasa, Kenya, killing over a dozen people. Almost simultaneously, others fired two surface-to-air missiles to down a charter jet bound for Israel as it lifted off from Mombasa airport. The aircraft escaped harm because the missiles missed their target.

By the time of the Kenyan hotel assault, Somalia had come under renewed Defense scrutiny. The rise of homegrown Salafi-jihadis and the presence of al Qaeda facilitators prompted the Joint Special Operations Command to put Special Ops teams back into the country after the 9/11 attacks. Given recent Somali history, Pentagon planners exuded no enthusiasm to return conventional US boots on the ground to the country.[31] As in Afghanistan, CIA field officers preceded America's elite covert troops again into Somalia. Created to conduct stealthy actions, JSOC had worked with the CIA in the former Yugoslavia to arrest war criminals for trial before international jurists.[32] The experience gained by the CIA to collect intelligence, vet information, and hand it off to SEAL Team 6 or Delta Force was used again when the CIA-SOF collaborated in the combat zones of Afghanistan, Iraq, Yemen, and Syria. Rather than taking suspects into custody for prosecution in international courts, the secret warriors launched drone airstrikes or commando-style raids to kill or capture insurgents to obtain intelligence for further counterstrikes.[33]

Somalia's endemic violence precipitated a Hobbesian void in which no central government could accumulate enough authority to extend its writ even within the capital's precincts. Repeated attempts to form an effective government ended in failures over the years. Finally, a group of political figures banded together to form the Transitional Federal Government (TFG), meeting in neighboring Kenya due to widespread violence at home. Although often harried by terrorist attacks, the TFG received international recognition in 2004 as an interim governing authority in hopes of establishing peace in the conflict-torn country. Eight years later, in 2012, the Somali Federal Government superseded it as a more organized governing structure.

6.6   Insecurity and the Rise of Salafi Movements

Inside Somalia, a desire for personal safety drew people toward one or another of the Islamic Courts. These Salafi institutions capitalized on insecurity felt by communities. The Sharia-dispensing courts broadened their mandate from settling spats to providing education, health care, curbing street crime, and funding charities. The courts also acted as a police force, paid for by local business in "taxes" collected by the militants. The courts consolidated their support, even though they barred attendance to Hollywood movies and forbid watching soccer matches on television. The courts also meted out severe punishments such as amputating hands for theft or stoning for adultery. Several courts banded together as the Islamic Courts Union (ICU). The ICU extended its brutal sway over most of southern Somalia including Mogadishu and other major cities by 2006. It reopened Mogadishu's airport and harbor to travel and commerce. Overall the ICU delivered a semblance of order that won over residents fed up with hoodlums and crime.

Backed by CIA professionals and local businessmen, some warlords and clan chieftains organized themselves against the Islamic Courts Union. These anti-extremists formed the secular Alliance for the Restoration of Peace and Counter-Terrorism (ARPCT) and went on the offensive against the ICU and terrorist figures. The Agency's paramilitaries secretly funneled cash payments to the ARPCT and offered bounties for terrorist plotters. ARPCT handed over a senior leader, Gouled Hassan Dourad, who headed a terrorist network allied with al Qaeda, to US authorities. Stepping up a counterterrorism offensive, the George W. Bush administration identified a miscellany of al Qaeda explosives experts and facilitators who were sheltered by Somalia's radical Islamists.[34] Washington also deployed US warships off the coast in order to utilize AC-130 gunships against suspected "high value" Somali and al Qaeda militants. The ICU fought back.

As part of its 2006 sweep into Mogadishu, the ICU put to flight the CIA's proxies. The Agency's setbacks resulted in the State Department and Pentagon taking control of Somalia policy. The CIA's fumble held other ramifications. The ICU onslaught worried not only the fragile TFG, now seated in the central city of Baidoa, but also the capitals in other nations in the Horn of Africa. Nearby governments dreaded a chain reaction of spreading conflict through the Red Sea region. Ethiopia feared rekindled conflicts within its borders resulting from the ARPCT's expulsion from the Somali capital. Considered a Christian country, Ethiopia had a large minority Muslim population that ICU fighters might inflame against Addis Ababa. By late 2006, reports surfaced about Ethiopian soldiers slipping across the Somali border to train TFG recruits to fight the Islamists. Next came evidence of the Ethiopian army directly engaging ICU militants.[35]

Rolling the dice, the United States backed Addis Ababa's decision to unleash its army on the ICU to displace it from Mogadishu and wide swaths of Somali real estate. Washington was loath to see a terrorist foothold take root that could endanger the Middle East and beyond. Weeks before the Ethiopian offensive, JSOC shifted some Special Operators from war theaters in Iraq and Afghanistan. It also moved close–air support aircraft to its Djibouti hub so as to pursue al Qaeda militants. Since the Cold War, DoD had worked with Ethiopia, established listening posts and bases on its territory, and considered Addis Ababa a reliable partner in an Islamic neighborhood. The 9/11 attack only tightened America's partnership with the Horn of Africa nation. For years, the Defense Department had a hand in training Ethiopian troops and believed they were adequate for the mission.

DoD officials subscribed to a partnering approach by harnessing "American commandos (i.e. SOF units) and the use of the Ethiopian army as a surrogate to root out Al Qaeda operatives." JSOC's helicopter gunships rendered close-air support to the advancing soldiers and struck at suspected militants. This American-Ethiopian partnership offered a "blueprint" for "terrorism missions around the globe," according to Defense Department representatives.[36] Similar sentiments were often uttered by US military officers in the Philippines and elsewhere.

When questioned by members of Congress about its authority for attacks within a country not declared a war zone, such as Afghanistan or Iraq, the Pentagon had a ready answer about its shooting missions in Somalia. Marine General Peter Pace, the chairman of the Joint Chiefs of Staff, replied that the authority to hunt down and kill terrorists around the world derived from congressional power given the George W. Bush administration on the heels of 9/11. Over time, this justification was trotted out by all subsequent presidential administrations. Occasionally, members of the legislative branch vainly called for either a new or revised authorization to use military force.[37]

The Ethiopian ground intervention in early 2007 saved the Transitional Federal Government from displacement. It also overran much of ICU's resistance, with some assistance from TFG fighters. A coordinated offensive by Ethiopia's tanks, jet fighters, and helicopters chewed up and expelled the Islamic Courts from its Mogadishu occupation in a three-week battle.[38] Not a few of the capital's residents were pleased to see the ICU in retreat. Some pro-ICU clans, nonetheless, favored the status quo.

By large and large, however, the city's denizens had little love for the Ethiopians, who they regarded as non-Muslim occupiers. Wisely, the Ethiopian army pledged to return home speedily.[39] Rank-and-file TFG forces undermined their cause by looting and harassing their fellow citizens during the onslaught. Thus, Ethiopia's occupation backfired, but not before its intervention chased away the ICU militants.

The ICU militias fled to the southern parts of the country. Some took up temporary positions in the city of Kismayo before being expelled to the borderlands alongside neighboring Kenya. The ICU remnants were knocked down but not out. Washington looked to consolidate the TFG's fragile grip on the capital and other areas of the country with financial aid, air-strikes, and diplomatic assistance from abroad. The State Department appealed to the African Union (the successor to the failed Organization of African Unity) for peacekeepers. It founded a Somali Contact Group (African and European countries with the United States) to fashion a unity government and to deploy an African-staffed stabilization force to replace the withdrawing Ethiopian soldiers.

The African Union founded AMISOM (African Union Mission in Somalia) in 2007 for a six-month trial. Its mandate has been renewed at six-month intervals until the present. The UN Security Council endorsed AMISOM and financed it as a peacekeeping force that also defended the Transitional Federal Government from ICU attacks. Fearing casualties, Uganda, Kenya, and a few other close-by states reluctantly committed less than 2,000 troops into the lawless land at first. Thanks to American lobbying, African states eventually dispatched over 20,000 troops to AMISOM.[40]

To help stabilize Somalia, the United States turned to other nations and other means. It relied on Israel – long-time ally of Ethiopia – to assess the needs of the Northeast African country and to coordinate relief.[41] The State Department hired DynCorp International, a private company that worked on military contracts in Afghanistan and Iraq, to train and transport African soldiers for peacekeeping duties in Somalia.[42] In short, the Bush administration searched for another indirect way of managing a failed state so as to limit terrorism. Shoehorning the ICU into a southern quadrant helped to make other regions somewhat safer from shootings and bombings. But sequestration of the extremist movement contributed to the rising instability in neighboring Kenya. Militants committed not infrequent terrorism on Kenyan targets, including the mass-casualty rampage on Nairobi's posh Westgate Mall in 2013.

The Ethiopian incursion resulted in at least one unintended consequence. Under intense pressure from the attacking military, the Islamic Courts Union fractured. One faction, Hizb al-Shabaab ("the party of youth"), broke off from the parent organization and staked out an uncompromising brand of radical Islam. The radical youth movement both displaced ICU militias and welcomed their scattered militants to its ranks. Al-Shabaab pledged fealty to al Qaeda, exterminated moderates, and murdered randomly with bullets and car bombs in Mogadishu and other urban centers. Almost from its inception, al-Shabaab singled itself out as the chief terrorism movement inside the chaotic Horn nation and America's main antagonist. The US State Department declared al-Shabaab a Foreign Terrorist Organization in 2008.

Another US adversary, the Islamic State in Somalia (IS-Somalia, also known as Abnaa ul-Calipha), made an appearance in 2015 within the mountainous areas of the northern, semi-autonomous Puntland territory. Swearing loyalty to Abu Bakr al-Baghdadi's Islamic State of Iraq and Syria, the smaller Salafi-jihadi group boasted of terrorist attacks beyond its northern operating pocket. IS-Somalia also collided with al-Shabaab fighters, who retained the upper hand in most of the desolate country.[43]

One defector from the splintered ICU in time played an unlikely role in bringing a measure of order to some of the lawless nation. Known as a moderate in the ICU, Sheikh Sharif Sheikh Ahmed came in from the cold to lead the TFG through its transitional status to become the Federal Government of Somalia. He was a member of the Hawiye clan, one of the country's four main clans, which carried considerable political clout. The TFG parliament voted Sheikh Ahmed its president in 2009. He headed the secular government until the presidential contest in 2012, when he peacefully handed over power to his successor. During his tenure, Sheik Ahmed managed to engender political order in the topsy-turvy government. Blocks away from its protected buildings, the neighborhoods suffered frequent bombing deaths. Besieged though it was, the Federal Government served as a rally point for anti-terrorist clans, businesses, and ordinary people.

6.7   America Responds to Terrorist Threats

To combat the rising jihadi network, both the Bush and Obama administrations waged a beefed-up counterterrorism campaign from the shadows. Southern Somalia became the epicenter of classified manned and unmanned air strikes, as well as Special Operations raids. Special Ops forces sported unique skills, honed in ferreting out Colombian drug lords and Balkan war criminals, to track down and remove al-Shabaab gunmen from the battlefield.[44] The special warfare operators sharpened these man-hunting skills in Afghanistan and Iraq, as the wars in both theaters intensified.

Unlike the partnering approach in the Philippines, JSOC assumed a hands-on kinetic posture in Somali CT operations. Collaborating with CIA field operators, they identified targets, verified "kills" by collecting DNA evidence (cutting off the fingers of dead suspects), and entered the fight on the ground and from the air. Make no mistake about life in Somalia. Without the US military and intelligence presence, the Horn country would have fallen to al-Shabaab's Salafi rule.

Adapting lessons learned in Iraq and Afghanistan, JSOC pursued Somali high-value terrorists. General Stanley McChrystal assigned one unit an overwatch function to coordinate counterattacks. In Afghanistan, he gave SEAL Team 6 and the 75th Ranger Regiment a similar role; and in Iraq, Delta Force got the job. In Somalia, McChrystal assigned the Intelligence Support Activity (ISA, the super-secret intelligence signals unit also known as Task Force Orange and Gray Fox, among other names).[45] ISA's high-tech monitoring and human intelligence gathering capacities enabled it to zero in on hiding Islamist militants.[46]

During George W. Bush's second term, his Defense Department formed the US Africa Command (AFRICOM), the newest addition to DoD's geographical commands around the globe. AFRICOM subsumed the still-operational CJTF-HOA under its command in 2007, when it was formed. AFRICOM was charged with maintaining military ties with African nations and cooperating with the African Union. By 2020, AFRICOM deployed over 6,000 US military personnel, of which slightly over 10 percent went up against the Somali insurgents in what had become the America's longest and most intense undeclared conflict in Africa.

As the al-Shabaab threat worsened in the middle 2000s, numerous American-born or naturalized Somalis living in the state of Minnesota joined up with the terrorist network. To meet the danger, DoD threw more resources into the Indian Ocean country in 2011. The Obama White House turned to a greater use of drone attacks to spare ground commitments in Somalia and other theaters.[47] ISA's uncanny reconnoitering and tracking capabilities bolstered the White House's airstrike strategy.

America's total air dominance across Somalia aided its piloted aircraft and aerial-drones as they struck the unprotected ground-bound militants in a passel of deadly attacks. The Pentagon also employed Tomahawk missiles fired from US warships off the Somali coast. One such attack felled Aden Hashi Farah Ayro, an al Qaeda operative who served as a Shabaab military commander. Tracked for weeks by communication intercepts and satellite imagery, Ayro's death came in May 2008.[48] Eighteen months later, in September 2009, JSOC's Little Bird helicopters flying from another American warship along the Somali coast took out a senior al Qaeda figure, Saleh Ali Saleh Nabhan. After a burst machine-gun fire into Nabhan's fleeing vehicle, SEAL Team 6 members landed to collect DNA samples and information from the four corpses, one of which was confirmed to be Nabhan.[49] US forces killed Ahmed Abdi Godane, the emir of al-Shabaab and an al Qaeda loyalist, in a Hellfire-missile strike in September 2014.

As the Somali government consolidated its power under the protective wing of US bombardments, AFRICOM treated it as a credible institution and its representatives as partners, despite reoccurring claims of corruption and criminality. The international intervention and partnership with the governing assembly managed to retrieve Somalia from the jaws of defeat at the hands of the religious extremists. Defeat looked likely in the early 2010s, when the insurgents controlled around 60 percent of the country. The Joint Special Operations Command and AFRICOM aligned with the AMISOM to fight back by aiding the emerging Somali National Army (SNA). The SNA was initially trained by AMISOM instructors from East African countries. In more recent years, the United States headed up the training.

In the second decade of the twenty-first century, JSOC lengthened its footprint outside the capital city into smaller hubs in such urban centers as Kismayo and Baledogle, both of which had airfields. The drone campaign from these outposts stayed veiled in layers of classification, while the number of attacks mounted. Unlike Yemen and Pakistan, where few US ground actions took place, Somalia beheld numerous US commando-style raids. Surrounding Somalia, the US Armed Forces ramped up the quality and number of its installations in Ethiopia, Kenya, and the Seychelles Islands to confront surging terrorism within the Horn country. During the Obama administration, its officials acknowledged that there were "up to" 120 US personnel stationed inside Somalia.[50] US troops increased fivefold under Donald Trump. This figure did not take count of a sizeable contingent of private contractors hired by the departments of State and Defense.[51]

Under the Barack Obama administration, the United States initially entered into an unusual contract with a nonprofit entity to train Somali recruits. Bancroft Global Development turned to former SOF contractors to assemble and prepare a light infantry force known as Danab, or the Lightning Brigade. Starting with a pilot platoon in 2012 before reaching battalion size, Danab is the only unit within the overall Somali National Army framework fully capable of lethal, offensive operations. Plans call for the Danab to expand to five battalions of 500 troops each. Presently, it relies on US personnel for intelligence and logistics.

Professional observers highly rated Danab's performance in contrast with some regular Somali units as being riddled with graft, ineptness, low morale, and subpar performance. They saw the Lightening Brigade as a model for a functioning modern society. One expert contended: "Danab's significance is both operational and symbolic, that is, showing that with proper training, equipment, and mentoring, multi-clan, meritocratic units are possible."[52] Setting up a national security architecture, therefore, pointed to future civil society dimensions from the Danab example. Killing terrorists still topped the list but alleviating inter-clan strife scored second. The Pentagon recognized Danab's importance by partnering the US Army's 2nd Security Force Assistance Brigade (SFAB) with the elite Somali force in July 2020. Formed in 2018, the SFAB prioritized soldier-to-soldier interaction to build counterterrorism capacity, not unlike the Green Beret mission, except for larger and regular militaries. Almost two decades into the global fight against terrorist networks, the Army set up these 900-troop training brigades solely to build partner capacity in austere hinterlands.

Targeting upper level terrorists initially headed the list of counter-terrorist operations. Removing jihadi plotters and enablers from the battlefield, it was theorized, disrupted bloody schemes and impaired networks. But the ease with which they were replaced led to a reassessment. Years after 9/11, some anti-terrorist experts argued that striking at middle level cadre could be even more effective. Eliminating an expert bomb maker or well-connected financier might prove more destructive to network operations than the death of an in-charge cleric.[53] The debate was never completely resolved but counterterrorism killings still mostly focused on leaders.

The air-to-ground shelling did give rise to the unintended consequence of driving militants from the countryside into urban centers for safety. Their new locations spared them casualties. The American forces shied away from striking targets amid city populations out of fear of killing bystanders and alienating urban residents. DoD officials usually downplayed the death of innocent people and estimated few such deaths. Tragically, civilian deaths have been intrinsic to war. Historian Victor Davis Hanson estimated the number of French civilian deaths from

Allied airpower exceeded 70,000, a figure greater than those killed in fighting within France by the German occupation in World War II.[54]

Incoming President Donald Trump ramped up the Pentagon's CT actions. The new commander in chief approved the DoD proposal entitled "Principles, Standards, and Procedures," which confirmed the designation of Somalia as an "area of active hostilities." This new designation instituted "war-zone targeting rules" (similar to those used in the Afghanistan and Iraq conflicts), without a war declaration. The White House, hence, delegated decision-making on strikes to the Pentagon's combatant commanders. Somalia soon recorded an uptick in drone strikes, rising to at least 122 by mid-2019 from a total of 31 in Obama's two presidential terms.[55] In November 2017, the administration authorized military strikes on the Islamic State-Somalia branch, located mostly in the country's northern reaches.

By 2020, Somalia's Islamist extremists held sway in about 25 percent of the territory, mostly in the south, which was down from over twice that figure a decade earlier. Violence frequently flared even in the capital and other urban centers with suicide bombings and roadside explosions. Despite its setbacks, Shabaab was still able to carry out assaults in neighboring Kenya from its quasi-haven in the Juba River valley. One small-arms action struck a US airstrip on Manda Bay, where about 200 American troops trained and advised Kenyan forces, in early 2020. These attacks presented ongoing evidence of Shabaab's capacity to penetrate highly secured bases through bribery or brute force. Even so, Special Operations units, weathered repeated suicide bombings and heavy gunfire against their rural outposts.[56]

According to AFRICOM officials, they intended to "slowly degrade it [al-Shabaab], reduce it to manageable proportions" with air strikes. Since "al-Shabaab is not a monolith," the military pressure, so the argument went, could motivate some clans or sub-clans to strike deals with the Mogadishu government. Ultimately, the weakened insurgent militia, it was thought, would come to the negotiating table for relief.[57]

Testifying before the Senate Armed Services Committee in February 2019, Marine General Thomas Waldhauser described AFRICOM's strategy: "our kinetic activities … create opportunities for governance to take hold."[58] The AFRICOM commander supported "political efforts" in Somalia and elsewhere in Africa by devoting "significant energy and resources to assist the State Department."[59] These civilian activities nurtured stability by making local governments responsive to their citizens. Nongovernmental organizations, such as the Spirit of America, joined the efforts.[60]

One positive milestone was the reopening of a US Embassy in Mogadishu in October 2019, after nearly three decades when the country fell first into civil war and then under an Islamist grip. The reestablished embassy denoted progress despite reoccurring attacks from Salafi militants whose deadly presence seems indelible in another perpetual war zone. A little more than a year afterward, the outgoing Trump presidency retrenched all of the roughly 700 US military personnel from the embattled country to keep its word about ending the nation's forever wars. The relocated forces were stationed in neighboring Kenya, Djibouti, and onboard US naval ships offshore. Ever resourceful, AFRICOM started "commuting to work" by flying into Somalia to train and advise its partners in early 2021. Being out of country, however, entailed shortfalls in intelligence, surveillance, and reconnaissance, while making operations more complex and risky. Nonetheless, the operations could serve as a model to scale back the US ground-force presence in other light-foot engagements.

6.8   Yemen: An Endless Proxy War

Across the Bab-el-Mandeb from Somalia lies the Republic of Yemen at the southern tip of the Arabian Peninsula. The straits between the two states really separate little as both Somalia and Yemen are the two poorest countries in the Arab world and both are beset with deadly instability, which opened them to violent extremists bent on attacking the West. Desolate, distant, and desiccated, Yemen stayed off Washington's political radar until 2000, when two al Qaeda hit men exploded their skiff into the side of the USS *Cole* in the Aden harbor. Outgoing President Clinton refrained from retaliating for what was tantamount to an act of war due to inconclusive evidence of al Qaeda's role in the ship bombing. Months later, the CIA and FBI held the Afghan-based al Qaeda at fault. Autobiographically, Clinton reflected in his memoir that his "biggest disappointment was not getting bin Laden."[61]

George W. Bush authorized the CIA to conduct targeted killings of al Qaeda militants just days following the 9/11 terrorism. The presidential authorization led the United States not only to invade Afghanistan but also to strike within Yemen. A Hellfire missile launched from a Predator drone blew up an SUV carrying Abu Ali al-Harithi (a prime suspect in the *Cole* bombing) traveling across Yemen with other passengers in early November 2002. The drone lifted off from the Pentagon's base in nearby Djibouti. The Intelligence Support Activity tracked al-Harithi after an intercepted mobile phone call. His death and the method of its execution commenced a new way of war – surveillance, tracking, and airstrikes – practiced by the CIA and the Special Operations Forces to kill difficult-to-reach jihadis. Targeted-killing operations were repeated innumerable times across a dozen fronts in the years to come with near perfection of what the counterterrorism world called "decapitation."

Although Yemen was no stranger to political strife, it did not immediately become a battleground for Washington's global conflict with al Qaeda. Its durable president, Ali Abdullah Saleh, assured his American counterpart that he stood with the United States as a partner in the struggle against extremism. As a secular Arab ruler, Saleh was ipso facto an enemy of the Salafi-jihadis. Al Qaeda regarded secular Middle Eastern governments as an abomination. Thus, the Yemeni "pharaoh" had little choice but to throw his lot in with the United States or to stand alone against the tide of radicalized Islamists.

Saleh's marriage of convenience with Uncle Sam, which supplied arms and instructors for the Yemeni security forces, offered no immunity from rebellion in his fractured country. A Shia-linked insurgency erupted in mid-2004, when a dissident cleric, Hussein Badreddin al-Houthi, leader of the Zaidi sect (an offshoot from Shiite Islam), undertook a revolt against the national government in Sanaa. The Houthi rebels (upon taking the name from their religious head) took up arms, in their view, to defend their community against the central authority's Sunni-based hostility and discrimination. Their anti-Sunni stance brought them aid from Iran, which, in time, supplied drones and rockets to the rebels, along with small arms. So began a raging civil war that still rips apart the south Arabian nation.

Once under siege, the Saleh government appealed to the United States for more assistance. In response, the Defense Department stepped up its training mission to counter al Qaeda assailants. US Defense combatants also executed missile attacks and manned air strikes with assistance from the CIA, which supplied intelligence for targeting, often from Saudi Arabian sources. Then the order of battle changed in 2011 when the CIA took over the drone-strike program in Yemen from the military, because of the Obama administration's dissatisfaction with JSOC's mistakes and missed opportunities. The intelligence agency modeled its cloak-and-drone program in Yemen after its approach in Pakistan, another undeclared war zone that sheltered terrorist networks. There, CIA drones killed an estimated 1,400 Taliban militants by 2011.[62] Terrorist activities emanating from both countries worried Washington.

The separate al Qaeda branches in Yemen and Saudi Arabia merged in 2009 to form one movement, al Qaeda in the Arabian Peninsula (AQAP). The newly formed AQAP escalated terrorist attacks, accentuating the unstable security environment. Both the CIA and JSOC tried to strengthen their toeholds in the besieged land. As Yemen turned into a virtual al Qaeda outpost, a flurry of attacks with a US destination originated from the lawless land. Due to an intelligence tipoff from the Saudi Arabian government, toner cartridges filled with PETN explosives on American-bound cargo planes were intercepted and disarmed safely. In another plot, a UPS carrier exploded while in flight, killing the two crewmen.

Many lethal attacks were attributed to a leading AQAP bomb maker and to Anwar al-Awlaki, an American-born radicalized cleric who journeyed to Yemen to broadcast Islamist recruitment appeals and incendiary anti-US propaganda. His inflammatory preaching and videos motivated others to commit acts of terrorism, including US Army Major Nidal Hasan's shooting rampage at Fort Hood, Texas, in which thirteen people died. Al-Awlaki's effectiveness can be attested to by Washington's assortment of schemes to remove him. It eventually did after former Army general David Petraeus, the new CIA chief, transferred drones from Pakistan to a secret Agency base in Saudi Arabia.[63] From that site, CIA operatives fired more than one deadly missile.

The Republic of Yemen ran into the same Arab Spring shock waves in 2011 that seismically shook Tunisia, Libya, Egypt, and other Mideast nations. Long-ruling Saleh, like his neighboring tyrants, faced popular revolts in the streets. In an effort to placate his restive population, Saleh abdicated power in 2012 to his vice president, Abed Rabbo Mansour Hadi, who fared no better than his predecessor. Then, Saleh did the unexpected. In a total volte-face, he struck a deal with his onetime enemies, the Houthis, to oppose his successor in a sequence reminiscent of what a Plantagenet monarch would have done to hang onto power in medieval England. None of these maneuvers sufficed to calm the despot's troubled countrymen. The Houthis went from victory to victory, even storming and holding Sanaa in 2014.

Things became so chaotic and violent the next year that the State Department yanked out its embassy staff, the CIA extracted its officers, and even the Pentagon withdrew a Special Forces contingent (the next year JSOC reinserted SOF teams). Coming on the heels of Obama's withdrawal from Iraq and then his "nonintervention" into Libya, Washington's abandonment of Yemen cast doubt on the US administration's commitment to continuing counterterrorism missions.[64] The other options were unpalatable. Neither Barack Obama nor later Donald Trump favored replaying the massive Iraq-style invasion. But withdrawing under fire was not prudent.

Forsaking a terrorist-besieged nation also was no option at all. An unwelcome fate befell Iraq after the Obama administration pulled out all US ground forces in late 2011. Lacking a viable alternative to introducing land armies, the United States fell back on partnering with local recruits, who functioned as a force multiplier to small numbers of Green Beret trainers and mentors. These indigenous fighters were often the only ground-force presence posed against jihadi militants.

6.9   Saudi Arabia Intervenes in Yemen

In 2015, Saudi Arabia led a coalition of over a dozen countries in an air and ground intervention to strike back at the Iranian-allied Houthi militants. This coalition joined Yemeni soldiers loyal to the Hadi regime in a counteroffensive against advancing tribal militia, which had seized the country's capital. Made up principally of the United Arab Emirates, Egypt, and Jordan, plus the desert kingdom, the Arab military bloc went to war against Iran and its Houthi proxies to keep Yemen from becoming another fallen domino to Tehran's influence. The coalition deployed some 100,000 troops and scores of warplanes.

The centuries-old enmity between the two sectarian adversaries reached a new intensity in their military duel between Persian-Shiite Iran and Arab-Sunni Saudi Arabia. The Yemeni war became ever more vicious. Civilians – women, children, and the elderly – became not just collateral damage from misdirected aerial bombardments but actual targets. Saudi warplanes deliberately struck hospitals, schools, and funerals. From the ground, the Houthis replied in kind with drones, rifles, and bombs.[65]

Not to be outdone, militants from the Islamic State of Iraq and Syria network traveled southward to engage in terrorist acts in an already complicated war zone by attacking al Qaeda and the Sanaa government. The two Salafi-jihadi movements vied for favor among the Sunni population in Yemen, as in other untamed backlands.

The United States took sides in the ongoing Yemeni civil war by selling the Saudis, Emiratis, and their allies high-performance warplanes, instructing the pilots, and providing intelligence. The DoD also transferred tanks and armored vehicles to America's Arabian Peninsula allies. Washington and Riyadh shared an antipathy toward the mullah-ruled Tehran, whose terrorism and proxy militias (Lebanon's Hezbollah and Iraq's Shiite paramilitary battalions) unsettled the Middle East. Within the Yemen conflict, the Donald Trump administration, as in Somalia and Afghanistan, eased Obama's rules for CT missions, resulting in more air strikes against al Qaeda figures.

By purveying arms to the Saudi royals, the Trump White House came under scrutiny from the desert kingdom's legions of critics in Europe and the United States. They saw Trump as an abettor and enabler of a gross human-rights violator. Denunciations overhung the monarchy's

2018 murder of dissident journalist Jamal Khashoggi. Detractors called out Riyadh's role in war crimes committed against Houthi civilians. Hunger has been a weapon of war since Homer, and the Saudis implemented it anew against their foes. Washington politicians, columnists, and advocates derided the Trump administration for closing of the port of Hudaydah to accommodate its Saudi allies. This Red Sea harbor served as the major transit point for importing food to the starving Yemeni population. Truth be told, both sides disrupted food and water supplies to break their enemy's will. The East Coast media trained its ire on the White House for its part in the human tragedy. Trump felt the sting of the political backlash when Congress passed a bipartisan resolution calling for America to end its participation in the Yemen conflict and in its backing of the Saudis. The Oval Office vetoed the measure in April 2019.

A year earlier, the Pentagon sought to extract itself from the perception that it had a direct role in the conflict. Testifying before Congress, Marine General Joseph F. Dunford Jr., the Joint Chiefs of Staff chairman, stated that while the United States allied itself with the Saudi coalition, it was not involved in its "kill chain" inside Yemen.[66] Trump critics stayed unpersuaded and hostile to the Saudi partnership. For its part, the Trump government held fast to the Saudi alignment, perceiving a reliable ally against Iran's machinations and aggressions in the Persian Gulf and Levant.

Once the Houthis were seen as Tehran's proxies, the localized conflict became infused with geopolitical consequences for American interests. No one in DoD wanted to see an expansion of Tehran's Persian Gulf footprint. How the conflict turned out – victory or defeat – would impact American allies and, by extension, the United States itself. Withdrawing and leaving the country took on regional and international considerations over lost standing, reliability, and prestige.

The war persisted as the Iranian-backed Houthis and the Saudi-led coalition settled into a tit-for-tat cycle of attacks and retaliatory strikes over their shared border. In reprisal for coalition airstrikes, the Houthis flew drones and fired rockets across the poorly demarcated frontier, striking Saudi and Emirati airports and military installations. In May 2019, Houthi drones hit a Saudi oil pipeline, temporarily shutting down the two pumping facilities. Derided as backward and tribal, the Houthis unexpectedly turned to drones as their preferred weapon. Numerous drones and missiles struck at targets within Yemen as well as inside Saudi Arabia. Riyadh turned to defensive rockets to shoot down many – but not all – of the drones and incoming missiles. Saudi and US military authorities held Iran responsible for supplying drones to their Houthi proxies.[67] The war drew Yemen more deeply into the larger conflict between Iran and American allies Saudi Arabia and the Emirates.

The Yemeni civil war did not diminish the importance of the country in America's conflict with Salafi-jihadism. The US Central Command announced that another AQAP militant, Jamal al Badawi, fell to a precision strike in 2019. American authorities suspected Badawi of playing a role in the USS *Cole* attack eighteen years earlier. Ibrahim Hassan al-Asiri, the internationally feared AQAP bomb maker, and other militants similarly found themselves on the receiving end of air strikes in Yemen. Moreover, Yemen's location facilitated American-Saudi cooperation. The CIA enjoyed long and discreet ties with Saudi Arabia, the home of the Agency's secret drone base, from which it launched aerial strikes into Yemen.[68] The spate of aerial assassinations thinned AQAP's top ranks, but it remained the dominant Salafi-jihadi group, even over its chief rival the Islamic State of Yemen (an offshoot of the Islamic State in Iraq and Syria). For its part, JSOC's deployments reached into Somalia, Ethiopia, and the African Sahel as the fighting dragged on within Yemen.[69]

Nearby, AQAP fell short of supplanting its Islamic State rival in the Sinai Peninsula. Terrorism erupted in the Sinai enclave as the Arab Spring protests removed Egypt's Hosni Mubarak from power. The peninsula's extremists opted to stage bombings and killings under the ISIS banner as a "province" of the main network. Similar affiliations came to light further westward across the northern tier of the African continent. Israeli-Egyptian cooperation managed to contain the Sinai province militants, although from time to time Salafi-jihadis unleashed bloody attacks on Egypt's military forces or civilians.[70]

By the start of 2020, the Yemeni civil war slipped into a stalemate, as the Riyadh-orchestrated coalition ran out of martial steam against a much tougher adversary than expected, and the Saudi-backed Yemeni forces faltered. Then in April, the desert kingdom officials announced a two-week, unilateral cease-fire to jump-start peace talks brokered by the United Nations. The coronavirus pandemic motivated the peace gesture, the first such offer by any of the belligerent nations.[71]

Toward the end of the year, Yemen's government and Houthi rebels began an exchange of over 1,000 prisoners. Separately, the Houthis freed two American hostages. The swaps evolved from a 2018 piecemeal cease-fire that was honored more in the breach than observance. The prisoner exchanges signaled no end to the war, either. In fact, the Houthi fighters opened three new fronts in the Marib province, the Hadi government's last stronghold in northern Yemen. The Houthi militias also laid siege in the southwest to Taiz, the third largest city, and escalated violence in Hudaydah on the Red Sea. The Saudi air force replied with punishing strikes.

After defeating Donald Trump's bid for a second presidential term, Joseph R. Biden Jr. temporarily froze US offensive weapons sales to Saudi Arabia soon after stepping into the White House in 2021. Deeply dissatisfied with what he saw as the kingdom's no-holds-barred war against the Houthis, the incoming president called for a policy review of arms transfers. He also revoked the designation of the Houthis as a foreign terrorist organization. The new Oval Office occupant disapproved of Riyadh's indiscriminate bombing of Yemeni civilians. Joe Biden, however, stopped short of suspending US counterterrorism operations against al Qaeda elements in Yemen and of continuing sales of defensive arms to protect the Saudis from Iranian missiles, drones, and cyberattacks. The Biden West Wing also reversed Trump's delegation of authority to the combatant commander on air strikes in Somalia and returned to Obama's familiar pattern. Without any fanfare, Biden's National Security Adviser Jake Sullivan issued an order requiring the White House sign off on AFRICOM aerial attacks against Somalia militants, as means to reduce civilian casualties.

6.10   The Maghreb and Sahel Frontier Wars

Four years after 9/11, a Pentagon official referred to the Sahel as the next front in the war on terrorism.[72] It was a prophetic forecast. America's war on international terrorism returned Africa to prominence similar to what the continent experienced during the long Cold War. Although not a central front in the Soviet-American confrontation, the continent figured in each power's strategic calculations. Moscow and Washington worked to check each other from gaining dominant strategic influence. With the eclipse of the Soviet Union, Africa slipped for years from the Defense Department's threat assessments. When red flags returned to DoD's African maps, the continent's forbidding terrain stirred unease across the military command. It's vast steppes, scrublands, and sands could suck in and envelope regular armies pursuing elusive jihadis, who often looked the same as farmers, herders, or traders.

To the west of the Arabian Peninsula, across the Suez Canal, lies a vast expanse of desert that extends to the Atlantic Ocean. Often referred to as the Maghreb, it primarily includes Morocco, Algeria, Tunisia, and Libya. It is bordered by Egypt and the Nile River to the east and the Atlantic to the extreme west. Its northern edge fronts on the Mediterranean Sea, and its southern flank crosses scrubland until eventually blending into the humid and verdant tropical rainforest of sub-Saharan Africa. Nearly 2.5 million square miles, it is home to over 100 million people. The trackless lands improbably spawned such thriving medieval desert kingdoms as Ghana, Mali, and Songhai, where arts and culture flourished before the entities slid into obscurity in the wake of European colonial rule. Below the Sahara lies the semi-arid Sahel, a sprawling stretch of scrubland bordering the desert to its north and encompassing parts of Senegal, Mauritania, Mali, Niger, Chad and Burkina Faso, which make up a large swath of West Africa. Even the Sudan and Eritrea are often lumped into the Sahel band.

The post–World Trade Center fears returned Africa to the security analysts' worry list. The DoD added the US African Command to the five established geographical combatant commands during the Bush (43) presidency. But AFRICOM's counterterrorism strategy could not be a simple redux of the former East-West standoff. Combating Salafi-jihadis required a different approach than jousting with a superpower competitor. The Pentagon and Langley needed rigorously trained resident proxies to fight violent extremists on the ground.

The United States faced battlegrounds in Africa that afforded ideal landscapes for terrorists. They were mostly sparsely inhabited. Government control tended to be feeble or nonexistent. Administrative services were absent or scarce. Populations needed security, adjudication of disputes, and access to public services. Salafi-jihadi movements proved adept at meeting the locals' needs. With their mix of clerics and militants, they filled the voids in government jurisdiction and basic services. Armed and fierce, they also instilled fear and meted out harsh punishments for infractions of Sharia.

Often the American role went beyond coaching their partners how to win firefights in the African bush. Building partnerships intertwined Special Forces with the job of resolving blood feuds, providing civic amenities, and dealing with smuggling – skills not practiced by conventional soldiers. Halting terrorism meant first achieving peace so as to promote stabilization and governing institutions so that one day the Americans could leave and their hosts could run things themselves without resorting to mass violence, which opened a wedge for extremists to exploit.

The Maghreb and Sahel figured almost not at all on the Defense Department's military maps until the mid-2000s.[73] Today this zone of concern extends even further south to Nigeria, Cameroon, and into coastal West Africa, where their respective northern parts frequently fall prey to terrorism. Years ago, terrorist attacks were almost exclusively perpetrated by Boko Haram, an Islamist movement whose name in Nigeria's Hausa language means roughly "Western education is wrong or forbidden."[74] Allied with Boko Haram, extremists came from the Fulani ethnic community of pastoralists, farmers, and traders who have also attacked Christian villages in north central Nigeria, killing over 2,000 people in 2018.[75] Terrorist attacks in Nigeria, a country of over 190 million inhabitants, spread disorder and fear over its northern flank. Nowadays, West Africa endures jihadi attacks from several violent groups and criminal gangs.

The principal spark for the trans-Sahel's prairie fire unexpectedly arose not from the decade-long savage civil war in the north African nation of Algeria when a secular government fought off an Islamist assault in the 1990s. Inspired by Salafist teachings, the Islamists overplayed their hand with summary executions and predation that lost them popular support after they rose up over a canceled parliamentary election by the Algerian army. Instead, the catalyst came from the regionwide Arab Spring revolt.

6.11   The Maghreb Spark

The Arab Spring uprising got its start from a popular protest in Tunisia at the end of 2010. The Tunisian populace loathed and feared its avaricious regime. A lowly Tunisian produce peddler sparked an upheaval that culminated in the ouster of the long-serving despot, Zine El Abidine Ben Ali, and opened the door for a democratic revolution there. The popular revolt then surged throughout much of the Arab Middle East, sucking into its turbulent undertow Libya, Egypt, Syria, and Yemen, leaving political disorder and vulnerabilities for Salafi-jihadis in its wake.

Obama's America watched the Arab Spring street revolts topple adversarial and friendly strongmen alike from power with a mixture of concern, caution, and detachment. Uncorked by the upheaval, the fermenting political and sectarian issues poured onto the desks of unprepared Washington policy makers, who, it may be judged, let a good crisis go to waste for the advancement of democracy. When the storm subsided, the Arab Middle East had new dictators in Egypt and Yemen together with persisting violent turmoil in Libya, Yemen, and Syria. Alone, Tunisia took steps toward representative government. The Arab Spring, in short, unsettled the continent. Against a backdrop of lawlessness in Africa, radical Islam found fertile soil to sprout.

One ember that ignited Islamist extremism jumped from Libya's implosion. Since 1969, when Colonel Muammar al-Qaddafi usurped power from the decadent monarchy, the former Italian colony moved into the ranks of rogue states by sponsoring terrorism and pursuing WMD. Amid all the problems the onetime army officer caused internationally, he could be counted on for his vehement opposition against the spread of Islamic fundamentalism, which endangered his own one-man rule. While his renegade regime tottered, he made accommodations with the United States and Britain to turn over his WMD stocks and suspend the export of terrorism. None of his placatory maneuvers saved his corrupt and murderous rule from the tidal wave of the Arab Spring, which precipitated an anti-Qaddafi rebellion.

Obama's White House briefly spearheaded a United Nations–approved air campaign with Britain, France, and other nations to safeguard the Libyan population from Qaddafi's hobnailed crackdown. After five days of bombing, the Obama administration chose to "lead from behind" and limited its participation to refueling, intelligence provision, and logistics. Later, the Pentagon injected teams of Special Ops troops into Libya for counterterrorism operations and to train locals against Salafi militants. By that time, Libya was already on the path to societal breakdown and militia-ridden strife. Without US political stabilizing plans for the bombardment's aftermath, Libya conformed to the templet set in Afghanistan and Iraq as the American way of war. President Obama, for his part, garnered few laurels for his lancing of the Libyan boil, because he applied no follow-on treatment to stabilize the chaotic nation.

Even in death, Qaddafi still caused problems. His demise in 2012 at the hands of a mob accelerated political destabilization. As the regime imploded, the numerous rebel militias, which were divided by region, tribe, interpretations of Islam, and even neighborhoods, fought one another over the spoils of oil and power. Foreigners intruded into the multi-sided civil war, unlike their generally hands-off posture during the popular protests in Tunisia and Egypt. Qatar aided one faction with weapons and instruction. The British and French sent units to provide training and intelligence. The political meltdown left armed secular and extremist militias up against each other to this today.

To confront the Salafi-jihadi threat, the Pentagon secretly inserted about 100 Special Ops forces to combat the al Qaeda–linked Ansar al Sharia faction. ISIS-Libya also drew a lot of DoD attention, especially when its forces overran the city of Sirte until driven out by a JSOC-managed air campaign at the end of 2016. As the internecine war became anarchic, AFRICOM withdrew a small contingent of US Special Operators who ran counterterrorism missions in a handful of outposts across the northern half of Africa.[76] The drawdown of troops left in doubt the American strategy for Libya.[77] A far greater jolt came from the new Washington government.

After the Trump administration entered office, it unexpectedly reversed US policy. Formerly, Washington, along with the UN, and the Western powers, had backed the Government of National Accord (GNA). Based in Tripoli, the GNA had cultivated wide international diplomatic recognition. Even with the establishment's endorsement, the Oval Office switched its backing from the GNA to Libyan general Khalifa Haftar, whose eastern-based militias laid siege to Tripoli. At the urging of Saudi Arabia and Egypt, President Trump abruptly dropped the GNA for Haftar, who later also picked up Moscow's military assistance. Riyadh and Cairo viewed the Western-recognized Tripoli government as aligned with their regional rivals in Turkey and Qatar as well as with Islamic extremists.[78] Almost a decade after its dictator's passing, Libya was mired in instability and civil war. The decapitated al-Qaddafi regime, moreover, left open its arsenals, allowing arms to flow southward into the African Sahel states, sparking a witches' Sabbath of terrorism. The pipeline of weapons added to the combustibleness of societies below the Sahara, allowing Salafi-terrorist militias to arm and murder.

6.12   The Fire Spreads

The Pentagon watched with apprehension the ominous developments unfold in the Maghreb and Sahel arenas. It feared that budding terrorist sanctuaries might stage attacks on the American homeland à la Afghanistan in 2001. For security reasons, Washington recognized the necessity of deploying military and civilian personnel to combat international extremism and to foster stability in hopes of preventing the rise of Salafi-jihadi groups. It dispatched Special Operation Forces and military assistance programs. The State Department, Agency for International Development, and nongovernmental organizations worked to nurture civil society and to deliver government services.

The cratering of Qaddafi's Libya upended stability in neighboring Mali, a country named for its famed medieval empire. Disbanded ethnic Tuareg fighters from Qaddafi's military returned home to northern Mali. Like the returning knights in 1453 from the Hundred Years War in France, who fueled the political rivalries culminating in England's War of the Roses, the Tuareg soldiers seized control of the landlocked country's northern territory in early 2012. The former fighters garnered popular support, because the Tuareg community felt marginalized since Mali's independence in 1960.

Instability in the north didn't spare the capital city Bamako, which underwent a military coup by a Malian army general who took advantage of the Tuareg-induced chaos. In an extravagant case of mea culpa, the American general in charge of Africa Command blamed US military training. Army General Carter Ham stated that his command failed to instruct Malian troops on "values, ethics, and military ethos," resulting in their failure "to abide by the legitimate civilian authority."[79] Future instruction contained the admonition that soldiers must not usurp duly elected civilian governments.

The outbreak of turbulence in Mali, as in Libya, Syria, and Yemen, created opportunities for Salafi-jihadis to protect endangered communities and portray themselves as defenders of insecure populations. It should come as no surprise to outsiders that militants intentionally provoked violence in order to pose as protectors of at-risk villagers. Salafist movements like al Qaeda in the Islamic Maghreb (AQIM) and Ansar Dine ("defenders of the faith") soon prevailed over the tribalist Tuareg and instituted strict religious customs. The militants consolidated their hold by using mediation and arbitration in similar manner to the methodology employed by the Prophet Mohammed over fourteen centuries ago.[80]

At the request of the new Bamako government, France dispatched military forces in 2013 that ultimately reached over 5,000 troops in Sahelian Africa – the most of any US partner by far – with a mission to confront the creeping jihadism peril. As a follow-on, the French military activated Operation Barkhane (named after crescent-shaped sand dunes) to cooperate with regional governments against violent Islamist groups. Headquartered in N'Djamena, Chad, the French military soon expanded its direct support of allied governments along with the United States.

The US Air Force airlifted many of the French forces to Mali and Niger, both former colonies of France. A year later, in 2014, the central Mali town of Timbuktu harbored an underground AQIM training camp for the barbaric Boko Haram, which usually terrorized over 400 miles to the southeast in Nigeria. Before the French bombed the site in mid-January, recruits learned to repair Kalashnikov rifles and shoot the nearly ubiquitous RPG (rocket-propelled grenade, that is, a shoulder-fired explosive warhead). France also stiffened the Malian military in its advance to recapture lost territory by committing French warplanes and ground forces to the counterattack in the north. Overall, Paris played an unsung and pivotal part in retrieving Mali from the hands of militant Islamist groups.[81] Their "crusader" invasion posed a risk of retribution within France from its restive five million Muslim inhabitants, who represented an Achilles' heel for the French government.

At that time, Obama's America had sidelined itself because US laws barred the Pentagon from assisting the Malian army until a legitimately elected government replaced the interim authorities who tossed out the ineffective leader of the coup. The Obama administration, reluctant to get involved, grudgingly offered air transport for a mechanized unit from

France to Mali. Africa's potential for volatility in the age of radicalized Islam had become more visible to the White House when militants attacked the US consulate in Benghazi, Libya, killing the American ambassador and three other citizens in September 2012.

Advisers inside the Obama administration debated whether turning over actionable intelligence about al Qaeda made the United States a cobelligerent with France. In the end, the White House squared the circle by arguing that it was helping France rather than joining the campaign directly against the AQIM fighters.[82] The US military's unarmed Reaper drones furnished targeting information for a spate of French jetstrikes. Next-door Chad committed its elite fighting unit to the Mali conflict. Trained by US Special Forces, Chad's Special Anti-Terrorism Group fought the Malian militants to a standstill by hunting, chasing, and ambushing them in the country's northern mountains.[83]

As the Mali crisis unfolded, the Pentagon doubled-down on its strategy for combating the rising terrorist danger in the trans-regional Sahel and Maghreb. Similar to the formula pursued in other theaters, such as Afghanistan, Iraq, and the Philippines, the Pentagon strove to establish surrogate forces utilizing the indigenous recruits to tackle the Salafi-jihadis. The United States no longer looked to its own armed forces to do the heavy lifting in waging counterterrorism. Instead, it worked to minimize US boots on the ground by carrying out its missions "by, with and through" local partners. When it came to actual firefights, America relied on its partner forces to patrol, search, and shoot.

This light-footprint model was replicated across the desert and scrub terrain as threats surfaced. In Chad, for example, the Pentagon temporarily dispatched 80 US troops and surveillance drones in May 2014 to locate over 200 Chibok schoolgirls, who had been snatched in northern Nigeria by Boko Haram, which a year later swore a *bayat* (oath of loyalty) to the Levant-based Islamic State emir, Abu Bakr al Baghdadi, rather than al Qaeda. The abduction of Chibok students was followed by several other kidnappings for ransom that threw into sharp relief the integration of terrorism and criminality.

Mali and its neighbors secured no lasting peace even with the aid of US and European Union forces, the G5 Sahel states (Burkina Faso, Chad, Mauritania, Niger, and Mali) or MINUSMA (United Nations Multidimensional Integrated Stabilization Mission in Mali), a 16,000-strong entity of troops, police, and civilian experts, tasked with protecting population centers. The lagging security enterprise got some unexpected shoring up from Paris. Midway through 2020, European governments in the Czech Republic, Estonia, Italy, Sweden and other countries put commandos into the field to bolster the performance of the regional troops and to accompany them into combat. This task force, named Takuba (meaning "saber" in the local tongue), was the signature initiative of Emmanuel Macron, the French president, who advocated for a stronger European military capability in Africa.

All the while, jihadi groups kept exploiting local disputes among the Fulani ethnic community in order to boost their ranks and sway. Operating among the Fulani, whose roughly sixty million people span West and Central Africa, jihadi groups aligned with either al Qaeda or the Islamic State who sowed chaos and death. They targeted the Dogon and Bambara ethnic communities, along with those affiliated with the security forces in Mali. Long-standing grievances over stolen livestock, land, and water sharpened disagreements among the three groups.[84] All this violent strife earned Mali the dubious distinction of being the most dangerous United Nations peacekeeping assignment.

From the last years of the Bush (43) presidency to the present, Washington went from almost no military presence in Africa to operating a web of almost thirty small bases for training and surveillance purposes to combat the expanding jihadi incursions. Drones and manned aircraft flew from airfields in Niger, Cameroon, and Chad, along with flights from Somalia, Djibouti, Ethiopia, and Uganda.[85] Niger grew to be an AFRICOM hub for the roughly 1,200 US troops deployed in West Africa, some in secret outposts. In its Agadez region, the US Air Force constructed an airbase costing over $100 million and taking four years to complete. The seventeen-acre facility is host to military personnel and to a launch pad for drone flights starting in late 2019.

Much of this military activity remained unknown to the wider public. There were occasional media reports on counterterrorism operations. Generally speaking, nevertheless, armed actions were staged behind the curtain of secrecy. The media had to accept specific guidelines, such as not identifying SOF warriors by name or not mentioning the super-secretive SEAL Team 6 or Delta Force in its stories. They referred blandly to special operations forces without any specificity.

The curtain was pulled back briefly when an ill-fated patrol in Niger lost four Green Berets in a gun battle. Twice the size of Texas, the Republic of Niger bulked large in DoD worries because of its political and ethnic precariousness. Split between savanna and desert like other West African nations, it was the scene of sustained Special Forces' instruction and mentorship of Nigerien soldiers. The advising routine was broken when a team of eleven Special Forces troopers and thirty Nigerien soldiers stumbled into a fierce ambush in October 2017. Roughly 100 fighters from the Islamic State of Greater Sahara (ISGS) surprised the small American-led patrol near Tongo, a little more than a hundred miles north of Niamey, the capital. Affiliated with the Syrian-based Islamic State, the ISGS militants inflicted casualties on the joint detachment because, in part, it had no accompanying close-by air cover.

Placing fault for the four Green Beret deaths, high or low on the chain of command, took nearly two years to apportion blame. Eight Green Beret officers and a two-star Air Force general received official reprimands, which failed to mollify family members and others in uniform.[86] Then the State Department offered a $5 million reward for information leading to the arrest and conviction of militants responsible for the ambush of the US-Nigerien military patrol. Additionally, its Rewards for Justice Program put up the same amount for information about or the location of Adnan Abu Walid al-Sahrawi, the chief of the Islamic State in the Greater Sahara, the Islamic State offshoot, for his role in the shoot-out. Undeterred, the ISGS went on to wreak fearsome carnage among poorly trained and equipped government soldiers in Niger, Mali, and Burkina Faso.

In a sense, the national attention given these four Special Forces deaths pointed to public sensitivity over American casualties and protracted conflicts. US commanders, in response, made force protection a top priority in the Africa theater as well as others. Consistent over the last three American presidencies has been the policy of relying on local partners to wage counterterrorist operations. The broader picture of working to reduce injustices and venality needs wider official recognition. Government criminality, abuse of power, and official wrongdoing work like recruiting sergeants for Salafi-jihadism.

Washington pledged to "work with local stakeholders and civil society to mitigate the grievances that terrorists exploit."[87] After George W. Bush, other presidents shied away from astronomically priced infrastructure building so prevalent in post-invasion Afghanistan and Iraq. Many of these elaborate construction projects were never completed or fell into disrepair and malfunction with unskilled local staffs to tend them. Subsequent administrations stayed focused on restoring basic services and promoting good governance, not building hydroelectric dams, modern highways, high-tech facilities, or new hospitals, which were put up by giant American construction conglomerates under government contract. They concentrated on killing, capturing, and interrogating terrorists so as to preempt attacks on the US mainland. The Pentagon's more limited strategy of the forward defense did safeguard homeland security.

As the United States neared a national election in 2020, it was confronted again by Mali falling victim to another military coup. The Malian Armed Forces compelled President Boubacar Keita to resign. The mutiny upended the American democratic principle of the primacy of civilian authority. In reaction, Washington suspended military cooperation with the ruling junta except for intelligence sharing to facilitate counterterrorism operations.

Washington's official displeasure with the Nigerien military's overthrowing a democratically elected government stopped well short of a total suspension of their partnership. When SOF, including SEAL Team 6, mounted a successful hostage-rescue operation in Nigeria at the end of October 2020, the American troops enjoyed "cooperation from Nigerian and Nigerien authorities."[88] The dramatic raid recovered an American citizen taken from his farm in Niger. Parachuting near the half-dozen captors, the US force suffered no casualties in the predawn firefight in the Sahel region that witnessed an escalation of kidnappings and killings by affiliates of the Islamic State and al Qaeda, together with criminal enterprises. The swelling number of attacks necessitated American ties with governments under siege.

When Trump's Pentagon weighed the possibility of withdrawing from Western and Northern Africa so as to focus on strategic threats from Russia and China, the French pressed DoD to "continue its assistance – especially drone operations, aerial refueling, and intelligence support."[89] Paris convinced the White House to stay its counterterrorism course. On a broader canvas, America's interventionist response to terrorists' networks worldwide notched a prominent victory in successfully forestalling another 9/11 attack on the homeland. Critics, in time, called attention to the costs of this strategy, as it keeps the United States tied down in numerous small proto-wars, all of which were negatively impacted by the coronavirus pandemic. Yet the critics have no realistic plan to offset the risks a US pullout poses for the United States and its allies. So, the Departments of Defense, State, and the Agency for International Development slogged along to "degrade and contain" violent extremist organizations without an end in sight.

7   America's Larger Forever Wars
Afghanistan, Syria, and Iraq

The first, the supreme, the most far-reaching act of judgment that the statesman and commander have to make is to establish... the kind of war on which they are embarking; neither mistaking it for, nor trying to turn it into, something that is alien to its nature.   Carl von Clausewitz, *On War*

One day we're bombing Libya and getting rid of a dictator to foster democracy for civilians, the next day we are watching the same civilians suffer while that country falls apart.   Donald Trump, foreign policy address in Washington, April 27, 2016

The ultimate object of war is a stable peace.   Alexander the Great attributed to Aristotle

The wars in Afghanistan and Iraq both began as US regime-change invasions, became occupations racked by insurgencies, and turned into protracted stabilization campaigns. The opening military strategy concentrated primarily on removing the Taliban rulers and the Hussein dictatorship. The George W. Bush administration's senior appointees and military planners never envisioned long insurgency wars. Their assumptions were based on recent US interventions. In Panama and Haiti, the US military swooped in, executed its mission, and departed without undue delay. In the Persian Gulf War, the American-led coalition expelled Iraqi forces from Kuwait in a hundred hours. Even Somalia, with its intense Mogadishu firefight, entailed no lengthy stay.

Flowing from each of the 1990s regime changes was the expectation that American-style freedom would peacefully ensue. Even in Bosnia and Kosovo, the US military and partner contingents undertook stabilization amid generally peaceful populations, requiring only beefed-up street patrols. After the Berlin Wall, the US Armed Forces found themselves no longer saving the world from communism but rather executing decapitation campaigns and installing democracy without fighting insurgencies.

Elsewhere, George Bush (43) pulled out all the diplomatic stops to muscle through democratic transitions in the so-called color revolutions. Though few remember, Bush's America blessed, boosted, and backed the turn from dictatorship to democracy in the Republic of Georgia, Ukraine, and Kyrgyzstan during the three successive movements, respectively known as the Rose Revolution, Orange Revolution, and the Lemon Revolution. After the 2005 democratic election in US-occupied Iraq set off the "Baghdad Spring," Lebanon revolted against its Syrian overlords, who had dominated the Levantine country since 1976. Joined by France, the United States pressured Syria to leave the small Mediterranean state. These American victories sparked resentment from Russia and Iran for overturning their own desiderata. Their revanchist policies took shape a few years afterward.

America's regime-change policies at first ran smoothly after the Wall fell. Not unnaturally, Pentagon planners and White House staffers were conditioned to anticipate similar positive outcomes in Afghanistan and Iraq. In both nations, however, local men felt it was a humiliating grievance to be occupied by Western, non-Muslim armies. The cultural realities made for intense resistance. Therefore, the two countries went from hostile regimes to hostile landscapes – and then to forever wars. It was as if the wars in both countries constituted gravitational black holes enveloping troops, weapons, and resources. Once entered into, the United States found it nigh-impossible to escape or completely prevail over shadowy figures in the night.

Trying to avoid getting stuck, Barack Obama hastened to fulfill his campaign promise to drawdown all US ground troops from the Persian Gulf country. Referring to Iraq as a "misguided war," presidential candidate Obama pledged upon entering the White House to "safely redeploy our combat brigades at a pace that would remove them in 16 months" (i.e., by summer 2010).[1] Once out of Iraq, the White House would be free of George Bush's "dumb" war so as pursue the "good" war in Afghanistan until American forces there could also come home. On the campaign trail in 2008, Obama pledged to "make the fight against al Qaeda and the Taliban the top priority .... This is a war that we have to win."[2] The USFOR-A (US Forces in Afghanistan) would concentrate on the Taliban insurgency and al Qaeda jihadis.

President Obama's actual Iraq pullout timetable slipped a little more than a year, to the end of 2011. In any event, by the time US ground combat forces evacuated, the Iraqi countryside had calmed considerably from the tsunami of killings by Shiite death squads and Sunni jihadi insurgents, which peaked in 2006–2007. As the exit date neared, the Nouri Kamil al-Maliki government got cold feet at the prospect of a total American military withdrawal. It asked the Obama administration for a sizeable detachment of US troops to instruct and guide its reconstituted national army. Additionally, Baghdad petitioned for a small number of

Special Operations Forces to continue the pursuit of the dwindling al Qaeda fighters still operating in the outlying corners of the country. Various numbers were discussed, but in August the White House instructed its ambassador to start negotiations with the Iraqis to keep 3,500 combat troops on year-long tours and 1,500 Special Warfare soldiers, who would rotate in and out every four months, plus half a F-16 squadron and support personnel. The president dismissed larger numbers put forward by the Pentagon.

The sticking point remained a new status of forces agreement (SOFA) governing legal immunity for US personnel, if arrested for civilian crimes. The Obama White House's demand for parliamentary approval was judged by "a number of commentators" as "negotiating in bad-faith, making an offer that it knew would be politically toxic in Iraq."[3] In the end, no second SOFA was signed between Baghdad and Washington. As a result, all US combat forces cleared out of the country as prescribed by the Bush agreement.

A few military and civilian observers expressed their dark predictions about the dangers in tossing Iraq aside without a longer American presence.[4] Vindicating these apprehensions, the remaining 700–1,000 al Qaeda terrorists still active in Iraq crossed over the border and acted as a multiplying virus in the vulnerable body of Syria, which was engulfed in a civil war (see Section 7.2). Even within Iraq, things went from bad to terrible.

America's historical experience in staying put in Germany and Japan after World War II offered examples of how the US military stabilized former foes (along with the case of South Korea after the Korean War) and contributed to their economic growth and democratization. Instead, Obama's foreign policy team cast the country adrift. It did not save Iraq from a fresh wave of Salafi-jihadism. Nor did it save the Maliki regime from itself as the nascent democracy tilted toward majoritarian rule, reducing the Sunni population to minority status, and creating fertile earth for extremism to take root.[5]

Following the US Armed Forces' departure, Iraqi politics took a turn for the worse. Rancorous ethnic tensions broke out between Sunni and Shiite politicians in the country's political institutions, which sowed discord rather than much-needed peace and reconciliation after the eye-for-an-eye atrocities of the sectarian civil war.[6] Nouri Kamil al-Maliki was intent on punishing and disenfranchising the Iraqi Sunni populace for its hand in repressing the larger Shiite populace for centuries until Saddam Hussein's fall from power. Maliki's policies virtually guaranteed the next chapter in the Sunni-Shia blood fest. This time the firestorm arose first in Syria.

7.1   The Syrian Civil War Breeds Terrorism

Just as the toppling of repressive regimes in Iraq, Libya, and Yemen during the Arab Spring opened opportunities for Salafi-jihadi movements to infiltrate aggrieved local communities, the bloody revolt in Syria against the authoritarian government of Bashar al-Assad cleared the way for extremists to flourish. In fact, the Arab Spring met its match against the Assad dictatorship as it fought back ultimately to crush the rebels. The opposition to Assad began in March 2011 as small, peaceful demonstrations in the southern city of Deraa. But the Damascus regime overreacted to the protests with a heavy-handed crackdown.

By summer, the battle lines were drawn. They set the barbaric pattern for a take-no-prisoner war over the next eight years. To hang onto power, Assad relied on his natural allies, the Alawite sect, which make up some 12 percent of the approximately twenty million Syrian people, against the majority Sunnis with about 70 percent and the Kurds with 10 percent. Assad's Alawites benefited enormously from their decades-long hold on the security forces and commercial sector of the economy. Sharing some religious tenets with Iran's Shia faith, the Syrian Alawites also increasingly depended on the Iranian ayatollahs to fend off the anti-Assad insurrection. Tehran inserted fighters and advisers to beat back the rebels and save Assad's rule.

The Syrian Sunni and their Alawite adversaries both recruited other communities to their cause. Most Kurds, for example, sided with the rebels against Assad. Deadly encounters between Alawites and Sunnis transformed the struggle from a pro- and anti-government confrontation to an ethnic-sectarian Armageddon, with horrific atrocities committed by all sides but chiefly by the autocratic regime in Damascus. Assad's forces specialized in dropping barrel bombs out of helicopters on civilian populations. Cheaply made, crammed with nails and chunks of metal and high explosives, the deadly barrels killed and maimed tens of thousands on the ground.

The war killed over 400,000 Syrians. Some four million people moved within Syria or fled to Turkey, Lebanon, Jordan, or Iraq. A million of them went on to flood Europe, aggravating ethnic tensions on the Continent. Much of the country lay in ruins. Assad's pariah standing kept away international lenders with funds to rebuild the homes and factories necessary for a return to normalcy.

The Kurds made up the backbone of the Syrian Democratic Forces (SDF), the principal anti-Assad group. Both Iraqi and Syrian Kurds joined the SDF ranks. The SDF also included Sunni Arabs who opposed Assad's rule but likewise fought against the Salafist's ideology. By late

2013, the complex internecine war turned Syria into a checkerboard of militarized bailiwicks under the jurisdiction of various ethno-nationalist militias with distinct Islamic or secular orientations, all of which recalled the Balkanized country of Yugoslavia that fragmented in the mid-1990s.

The People's Protection Units or People's Defense Units (YPG) were a mainly Kurdish militia in Syria and the primary component of the Syrian Democratic Forces. Additionally, Kurdish women fought in an all-female brigade known as the Women's Protection Unit (or YPJ) within the larger YPG. The YPG mostly consisted of ethnic Kurds but also included Arabs and foreign volunteers; it allied with the Syriac Military Council, an Assyrian militia, against the Islamic extremist bands.

At the beginning, the United States stood aloof from the seething ethno-religious cauldron in Syria. President Obama made it abundantly clear that his administration would not preside over another large armed intervention in the Middle East. In addressing Australia's parliament in 2011, Obama propounded a "pivot" of America's diplomatic, economic, and, even, military attention to Asia. He announced his decision in unsparing language: "as president I have made a deliberate and strategic decision – as a Pacific nation, the United States will play a larger and long-term role in shaping this region."[7] Brushing aside the Syrian civil war ultimately proved impossible, but the White House made a strenuous effort.

Obama's America spurned calls for safe zones within Syria to protect the internally displaced people and curb the outflow of refugees to neighboring countries and Western Europe. When Damascus turned to chemical weapons, President Obama issued a distinct red line threat of retaliation to Assad. Yet nothing happened when the Syrian dictator crossed it with another gas attack, and Obama's credibility took a severe political hit at home and abroad.

A reevaluation of the White House's hands-off policy eventually sprang from the game-changing resurrection of America's former terrorist nemesis in Iraq. The resurgence of the Iraqi al Qaeda movement surprised Washington's foreign policy establishment. US political leaders, think tankers, and media pundits lacked the imagination to anticipate a reconstituted terrorist movement rising phoenix-like from the ashes of another. For its part, the Salafi-jihadi network exploited the chaos of the Syrian civil war.

Seeing an opportunity to regain its prominence, remnants of the battered Islamic State of Iraq moved west into the fierce civil war across the border in Syria and metamorphosed into a new terrorist group. In 2011, Abu Bakr al Baghdadi (who took over in April 2010 at the deaths of Abu Omar al Baghdadi and Abu Ayyub al Masri) sent militants into the Syrian fighting to found the al Qaeda affiliated Jabhat al-Nusra, which announced itself in 2012. This was followed by a falling out between the two groups during which the Islamic State of Iraq sought to dissolve Jabhat al-Nusra.

While it did not succeed in this effort, it did succeed in expanding in Syria, renaming itself the Islamic State of Iraq and al-Sham (ISIS). "Sham" means Levant or Greater Syria. But Obama officials stuck almost alone with calling it ISIL or the Islamic State of Iraq and the Levant. It was also known regionally by its Arabic acronym Daesh. Ayman al-Zawahiri (who took command after bin Laden's death) placed al Qaeda in opposition to IS for its grisly atrocities captured on video. He regarded IS's brutalities as counterproductive to the propagation of Sharia and the refounding of a legitimate caliphate.[8] The factionalism gave way to more intra-jihadi competition, while the Islamic State smashed its way into Iraq.

The Islamic State came down on the Iraqi defenders like Byron's "wolf on the fold." Yet the terrorist network's gruesome beheadings, in reality, initially placed it in a vanguard role to "penetrate the Sunni communities and build local relationships."[9] For Western observers, IS loomed large as the most brutal and effective Salafi-jihadi movement, eclipsing al Qaeda. President Obama's dismissive comment about the Islamic State being "the JV [i.e., junior varsity] team," turned out to be highly inaccurate.[10]

Under al Baghdadi, a Muslim preacher and former US prisoner in Iraq, the Islamic State developed an extremely effective quasi-conventional military force. At its peak, IS may have numbered 35,000–100,000 militants,[11] including some 20,000 foreign combatants, of which approximately 4,000 came from the Western world.[12] Using commandeered armored tanks, Humvees, and highly motivated fighters, the Islamic State's columns stormed into Iraq in early 2014. Its fighters overran Ramadi, Mosul, Tikrit, and Fallujah in a matter of weeks approximating a "blitzkrieg" invasion reminiscent of the Wehrmacht in 1940 France.

The Islamic State's pell-mell lunge southward, in fact, traversed rich soil for recruitment of fresh levies. Because of Shia exclusionary policies toward Sunni members in the Baghdad political hierarchy, many within the Sunni population looked to the invading Islamic State as liberators from the central government's oppression. Large numbers embraced the attackers and their jihad. In time, the Sunni populace regretted its collaboration because the Islamic State turned out to be brutal rulers, who barbarically enforced Sharia law on their charges. The new overlords adopted widespread extrajudicial killings, beheadings, and onerous piety, to boot. In short, IS wore out its earlier welcome, as it became viewed as an overbearing outsider. Jabhat al-Nusra, meanwhile, in its stronghold of northwest Syria, also found itself in a bitter conflict with al-Qaeda. In 2016, it rebranding itself Hayat Tahrir al-Sham, completing the break from its parent al Qaeda.[13] The two subsequently engaged in internecine skirmishes.

The heady victories marked the apogee of the Salafist-jihadi movement's conquest. Claiming the title of caliph for himself, Baghdadi declared in mid-2014 the establishment of a terrestrial caliphate from the marble pulpit in the historic al Nuri mosque, where Saladin rallied his followers in the twelfth century before expelling the Crusaders. At the Great Mosque in Mosul, the Islamist emir rebranded his movement the "Islamic State," while not so subtly identifying himself as a modern-day successor to the great medieval conqueror. Thus, he revived the Muslim theocracy that had ceased with the end of the Ottoman Empire. Such a civil and religious ruler was regarded as following in the footsteps of Muhammad, as had successive caliphs in Baghdad, Egypt, and finally the Ottoman sultans until the legendary Turkish leader Mustafa Kemal Ataturk abolished the office in 1924. Little wonder that Baghdadi's audacious claim rankled Ayman al-Zawahiri, the al Qaeda leader. The increasing rivalry between the two Salafi-jihadi networks resulted in occasional bloodshed amid their form of a cold war rivalry.

Fearful of the mortal danger posed by Islamic State invaders, Baghdad called in 2014 for the return of the American military to Iraq as the balance of the conflict turned decidedly against the anti-IS defenders. Before intervening, the Obama administration wisely pushed for the ouster of the al-Maliki government. Its stridently anti-Sunni policies paved the way for the minorities' receptiveness to the invading horde. Haider al-Abadi, a long-serving moderate Shiite politician, took up the governing reins in early September. Departing from his predecessor's exclusive pro-Shia policies, he appointed Sunni politicians, negotiated a revenue-sharing agreement with the Kurds for oil from Kurdish petroleum fields, and opened the army to limited Sunni enlistment.

7.2   America's Third Iraq War

In light of the Islamic State's fast-paced drive southward into Iraq, President Obama authorized a small American taskforce to return to the Persian Gulf country with a limited mission to assist Iraqi and Kurdish forces in safeguarding Baghdad and Erbil, the capital of Iraq's Kurdish Region. The air dimension of the counteroffensive was initially directed at stiffening Iraq's unprepared ground forces. Seeing IS as merely a renewed insurgency rather than a threatening proto-state, CENTCOM and the Air Force erred by not massively applying US and allied air assets against the network's vital installations in Syria from the outset. As the IS militants lunged forward, the Pentagon upped the first 300 Special Forces by additional Green Berets to steady the reeling Iraq army as it retreated into the country's midsection.

The Green Berets also trained up a high-performing Iraqi Counterterrorism Service, whose commandos struck the Salafi-jihadi militants. With the help of the United States and its allies, Baghdad also built up its regular forces, which initially underperformed, to halt the Islamic State onslaught. Yet Abadi relied on Shiite militias largely free of subordination to Baghdad's rule to fight the advancing IS attackers. They developed into effective frontline fighters. Numbering about 50 separate militia groupings with a total of 150,000 militiamen, they took orders, munitions, and subsidies from Tehran. Other Shiite factions were religiously aligned with theocratic Iran but with more autonomy from Tehran. Baghdad granted them legal status in Iraq under the banner of the Popular Mobilization Forces (PMF). The creation of PMF actually sowed dragon's teeth for the fractured Iraqi government, because the Iranian-backed militias deepened the mullahs' influence in Iraq, as subsequently noted.

Next, the US president authorized limited air attacks in August 2014 to protect the surrounded Yazidi people (an insular ethnic minority linked to the Kurds) stranded in Sinjar, a besieged northern town. The about-face from the hands-off approach moved Obama to assure his constituents that the United States wasn't embarking on another war: "As commander in chief, I will not allow the United States to be dragged into another war in Iraq."[14]

Six weeks after the president's reassurance, the US air strikes began against Islamic State targets within Syria. The Defense Department concentrated its air bombardment around Kobani, a town on the Syrian-Turkish border, to repulse IS's encirclement. The United States hastily organized a coalition of allies to coordinate the aerial defense against IS. But US airstrikes, according to airpower expert Benjamin Lambeth, was initially underutilized against the caliphate because of "the guidance of the man in the Oval Office."[15] Nevertheless, the American aerial coalition and Kurdish infantry broke the Kobani siege in 2015, four months after it began. It marked the first major defeat for the Islamic extremists.

The Kobani campaign gave birth to close American-Kurdish ties over the next years in the conflict against IS. Kobani held powerful symbolism for the Kurds and their struggle for self-rule. Thousands of SDF infantry and special forces received US instruction in reconnaissance, first aid, and close-in tactics to engage their common enemy on the battlefield. The American and Kurdish forces complemented one another. The US-led aerial coalition needed boots on the ground and the SDF needed air support. Coordination was tight and routine. Mutual trust ran deep. In fact, the two militaries bonded in soldiery camaraderie. The US command asked the SDF to enter a traditionally Arab region in Syria. There, the SDF recaptured major IS enclaves, such as Deir ez-Zour and Raqqa, the former Syrian capital of the Islamic State "caliphate." The seizure of Raqqa was one of the biggest victories of the Pentagon's counterattack, although the Kurds suffered sizeable casualties.

The veteran American diplomat Peter W. Galbraith, who had been US Ambassador to Croatia, summed up the realities of the US-Kurd alliance that "began with us helping them. But by the end, it was them helping us."[16] Still, the Kurds furthered their own cause as well by extending their grip in northeastern Syria, enabling them to carve out a semi-autonomous enclave (the Syrian Kurdistan is known as Rojava) to match the one in northern Iraq.

Because of its widening military engagement, America's chief executive assured his fellow citizens that the lengthening defense footprint was not a re-invasion of Iraq. He insisted that only Spec Ops forces were being dispatched and not "combat troops," making a distinction without a clear difference to most observers. Obama argued that he sent no "boots on the ground" to Iraq and Syria so as to keep his 2008 promise to end America's protracted wars. Instead, he turned to Special Operations Forces, whose spectral silhouette hid their combat operations in war zones. Two journalists called attention to how government appointees often used "linguistic contortions to mask the forces' combat role."[17] To Obama, the specialized forces offered an alternative to the large-scale occupation wars that he inherited from George W. Bush.

Baghdad also preferred a light US Armed Forces footprint. A large number of American troops on the ground would almost certainly replicate the 2003 intervention, which solidified a grassroots resistance to what Iraqis considered an army of occupation. Iraq's new leadership insisted on a low profile for foreign soldiers. Yet it wanted an effective counter to the Islamic State conquest. In sum, the solution encompassed heavy air strikes, Special Ops forces, and significant numbers of trained proxy fighters. Ashton Carter, Obama's defense secretary, announced the dispatch of more SOF at the end of 2015 to professionalize Iraqi and Kurdish forces and to conduct covert operations in Syria.[18] The strengthening anti-Assad rebellion knocked the regime back on its heels.

Amid the backdrop of a flagging Syrian regime, Russia entered the conflict in September 2015 to retrieve Assad's fortunes. Moscow joined Iran as an Assad ally to preserve his rule and to advance its own goals. The Kremlin pursued a Russian sphere in the eastern Mediterranean, which reflected a Soviet-era desideratum. It deployed warships, military aircraft, and troops to Syria. In time, the Wagner Group, headed by a Vladimir Putin crony, sent private contractors to fight in Assad's trenches. This support accomplished two feats. It circumscribed US options to shape the outcome in Syria and it rescued the Damascus regime. In the short term, Moscow's armed presence complicated the Pentagon's air and ground wars, for US forces had to coordinate flights and land actions with Russian officers to avoid trespassing in each other's space. Washington additionally protested the Russian air strikes on pro-Western Kurdish forces who fought the Syrian army

Russian warplanes also undertook bombing runs against Islamic State militias and other anti-Damascus foes. The Russian bombardment vainly tried to stop IS fighters from recapturing the ancient city of Palmyra from government troops in December 2016. When it came to the projection of airpower, the Kremlin's force was not in the same league as the US Air Force. In the longer run, the Russo-Iranian military cooperation contributed to salvaging Assad, whose army was earlier staggering from its adversaries' advances.

By mid-2016, US trained Kurdish and Iraqi units had begun taking the offensive against Islamic State strongholds. Toward the end of that year, DoD got on with its air campaign by hitting caliphate targets with repeated air bombardments. By the end of the active campaign in early 2019, coalition air strikes numbered around 50,000. The fledgling Iraqi air force received American F-16 aircraft, which required specialized training to convert them from piloting Soviet-made Su-23 ground-attack aircraft. In the interim, some Iraqi pilots flew the antiquated Su-23s to bombard IS targets.[19] They started hitting IS targets within Syria in early 2017, which required US "deconfliction" talks to avoid clashes with the Syrian or Russian warplanes.

The Islamic State adapted to the air attacks. Its militants traveled in civilian cars, and rarely more than three vehicles journeyed in a convoy. They hid cars indoors or camouflaged them with vegetation. They used "human shields" from the civilian population, knowing that the practice limited US attacks. When the caliphate's foot soldiers deviated from these defensive techniques, such as by traveling in military Humvees, they came in for punishing aerial assault. The war against the Islamic State observed much more intense fighting than the hit-and-run ambushes and fleeting shootouts in Somalia or Niger, where the militants held few fixed positions.

Beyond its enclaves in Syria and Iraq – about the territorial size of Britain and containing about twelve million people – the Islamic State caliphate went global. Either lone-wolf terrorists or murderous cells acted in its name with wanton killings of innocent people in a score of countries across the globe. IS pronouncements referred to the terrorists as "soldiers of the Islamic State" and cited affiliates or *wilayets* ("provinces") in Algeria, Tunisia, Libya, Niger, Nigeria, Mali, Yemen, and Egypt's Sinai Peninsula.[20] This international dimension of terrorism constituted another part of the sanguinary legacy attributable to Caliph Baghdadi's network.

As a practical matter, IS had to be destroyed because its very existence, plus its broadcasts and videos calling for death to crusaders and their kinsmen in the Western world, posed ever-present dangers outside of its Iraq-Syria strongholds. Self-radicalized or converted in Middle East training camps, young men, who became schooled in the deadly arts of maniacal murder, killed in the name of the Islamic State. As the world's deadliest terrorist network, despite losses of territory and the deaths of thousands of fighters, it carried out over 1,400 attacks and killed more than 7,000 people in 2016. These figures represented a 20 percent increase over the previous year.[21]

As the Iraqi army disintegrated ahead of the on-rushing Islamic State militiamen, the Maliki government fell back on the Popular Mobilization Forces, as previously noted. Overall, the PMF's quality varied, but they were much more effective than Iraq's regular army, which often fled the battlefield. Even Afghan Shiites joined their sectarian brothers from Iran and Iraq in the war to save the Assad regime. Some of these militias were trained and equipped by Tehran's elite and secretive Quds Force or its parent the Islamic Revolutionary Guards Corps, the Iranian theocracy's paramilitary vanguard.[22] Certain factions administered tiny parallel states, alarming the central government even though the PMF fighters played a prominent role in rescuing its fortunes and pushing back the IS offensive.

After the Islamic State lost its last territorial enclave, Adel Abdul-Mahdi, the new Iraqi prime minister, moved gingerly to limit the Popular Mobilization Forces' influence by tentatively placing them under the command of the Iraqi armed forces in July 2019.[23] But the marauders' rambunctiousness was not so easily reined in by the Parliament, which was often bitterly divided among Sunni, Shiite, and Kurdish factions that sometimes deadlocked the governing body. The tense duel between Baghdad and the PMFs (together with the larger issue of Iran's outsized influence in Iraq) sparked massive street riots in

Iraqi cities in late 2019, deepening political fissures between political and military figures in the Baghdad administration.

7.3   America's Endgame against the Islamic State

Coalitions are a vital part of the American way of war. Washington routinely looks for allies when embarking on military actions. The third Iraq war proved no exception to this standard operating procedure. The US Central Command organized the Combined Joint Task Force-Operation Inherent Resolve (OIR) in autumn 2014 to reverse the Islamic State's conquests. Composed originally of over thirty states, it eventually encompassed seventy-three partner nations, of which fifteen participated in air strikes against IS militias. OIR set out to "degrade and destroy" the Salafist-jihadi invaders and to supersede the original ad hoc multination defense framework thrown together in haste to blunt the fast-moving IS offensive in mid-2014. Operation Inherent Resolve delivered its main counterpunch via air strikes, not ground actions. Led by the United States, which flew more than 75 percent of the missions, many European states and Washington allies in the Middle East, such as Saudi Arabia, Jordan, Turkey and the United Arab Emirates, participated in the air campaign.

An unvarying negative side effect of the air war was the death or injury of civilians. US military personnel initially identified these victims as collateral damage, a term long since dropped for its callousness. The killing of innocents besmirched America's cause and prompted searches for discriminating weapons, such as small-warhead missiles with reduced lethality that eliminated just the targeted victim. None of the nongovernmental organizations, such as Amnesty International, succeeded in curtailing bombing. US air strikes, as noted, saved American lives on the battlefield so public opinion and the Pentagon rallied behind them.[24]

Operation Inherent Resolve also deployed Special Operations units for commando-style raids, partner training, consultancy, and intelligence gathering. Behind layers of classification, Delta Force and Navy SEAL missions only occasionally received news media coverage. The same secrecy enveloped CIA officials, who bribed and cajoled informants for information about the whereabouts of violent jihadis so as to target them with missiles or Special Ops raids.

A critical mission for the United States and its allies involved "building partner capacity." Some tens of thousands of Iraqis completed training made available by America and its partners within the multinational taskforce. NATO dispatched some 500 staff officers within Iraq, mostly for training-and-advisory missions above battalion level. NATO and other nations also deployed roughly 11,000 personnel in Iraq, Syria, and Kuwait mainly for troop training and mentoring.[25] Trainees filled the ranks of conventional infantry units while a small number went on to serve in the highly trained special forces to pursue terrorist elements, as in Afghanistan and Somalia.

Rolling back Daesh was an arduous and painful venture. Islamic State resistance was fierce, deadly, and without quarter. When IS militants fell back, they left a raft of booby-trapped explosives requiring painstaking disassembly or careful detonation. Most importantly, the United States decided that indigenous forces, not Americans or other foreigners, must retake their own land. This modus operandi spared American casualties. It also adhered to Lawrence of Arabia's oft-cited injunction about not trying to win the war for your partner forces.[26] On the other hand, Iraqi military casualties numbered approximately 26,000 since the war's start in 2014, whereas there were less than twenty US Army and Marine deaths by the end of 2017.[27]

US Special Ops teams and regular American military units managed to hold together a coalition of rival militias that stopped, turned, and then advanced the tide of battle against the violent extremists One by one, the IS-captured cities in Iraq and Syria fell to the counterattacking Iraqi forces, Iranian-backed militias, regular Syrian army, or the Syrian Democratic Forces. IS militants stubbornly defended their twin capitals – Raqqa in Syria and Mosul in Iraq. Intense resistance and air strikes left both cities in ruins. Amnesty International estimated 1,600 civilian deaths in Raqqa alone.[28]

The Islamic State fighters were not gracious losers. Retreating from a hideout in Mosul in June, 2017, they destroyed the Grand al Nuri Mosque and the famous al-Hadba minaret, just as Iraqi Security Forces overran their defenses after an eight-month siege. Prime Minister Haider al-Abadi greeted the news by asserting the end of the Islamic State's caliphate and declaring victory in July. That reality didn't actually take place until the next spring. To pressure the IS remnants, other forces joined the battle. In western Syria, Lebanon's army and Hezbollah fighters pushed Islamic State militants away from the Lebanese-Syrian border two months after Mosul's capture. Reflecting Iran's own strides in the use of drones, its Hezbollah proxy frequently lofted the unmanned aerial vehicles against IS units with growing effectiveness.

As the Islamic State's caliphate unraveled by early 2019, the PMFs raised anxiety in Washington, which believed that they tilted Baghdad too closely toward Tehran. Moreover, the Shiite militias ruled over much of Iraq's Sunni heartland, sometimes with "mafia-like practices" by extorting protection funds or shaking down motorists at checkpoints. They also denied the return of some of the 1.8 million displaced Sunnis to their own homes in Anbar province, contributing to instability and neglect of farmlands that grew wheat and produce. Obama appointees worried about Shiite militia gains but they were largely powerless to reverse them.[29]

The Islamic State's Syrian branch presented its own set of challenges for the United States. Washington could not turn to a semi-allied government in Damascus as it had turned to in Baghdad. The Obama administration had zero clout with the Syrian regime over the presence of Russian or Iranian forces. If anything, the Assad regime had been a thorn in the side of the United States since the Iraq War, when it allowed prospective terrorist recruits from abroad to cross its border into Iraqi territory to join up with al Qaeda insurgents fighting American forces. Once the Syrian civil war broke out with the Assad regime's horrific atrocities, the rift between the United States and the Syrian Arab Republic widened. Even though Washington and Damascus shared the dream of eradicating IS, they were anything but allies. Their expedient collusion lasted only so long as their common foe.

For a time, al-Baghdadi's Islamic State enlarged itself by incorporating competing networks under its black and white banner and by instilling a fierce fighting spirit among its frontline militants. When Obama left office, nevertheless, IS had been degraded but not destroyed through the heavy application of the president's strategy of air strikes. Bolstered by Special Operations Forces, allied ground forces, and US logistic and intelligence services, the air campaign decimated IS land-bound forces. But they fought on and inspired murderous attacks in Asia, Africa, and the West.

Upon assuming the presidency, Donald J. Trump increased the bombing and relaxed restraints on US attacks against IS. Just months in office, the new commander in chief approved a fifty-nine Tomahawk cruise missile strike on a Syrian airbase in response to Assad's use of chemical weapons on his own citizens in April 2017. Taken by surprise because Obama never followed up on threats for gassing civilians, Damascus lost 20 percent of its air force from the attack. A year later, the United States together with France and Britain bombed Syrian targets because Damascus resorted once more to chemical arms. Heavy US and coalition air strikes swung the pendulum toward defeat of the Islamic State. White House policy, nevertheless, undercut the gains.

Sensing complete victory as 2018 drew to a close, President Trump tweeted that the United States planned on withdrawing all 2,000

American military personnel from Syria. Since "we have defeated ISIS in Syria," there was no other reason to keep them in the country.[30] Defense Secretary James Mattis, who had not been briefed on this decision, differed with his commander in chief on this matter and others. So, the former Marine four-star officer wrote a letter of resignation early the next year. His departure from the Pentagon tossed the top civilian job in the Pentagon to his deputy, who lasted six months before resigning for personal reasons. When the dust settled, Army secretary and veteran Mark Esper ended up as the new Pentagon chief.

Trump's announced exit from northern Syria, and thus from the close alliance with the Kurds, threw a wrench into the Pentagon's partnering playbook. The Kurds, who lost a reputed 11,000 troops in the anti-Syrian war, were stung by Washington's unexpected torpedoing of their military bond. Not alone, Republican lawmakers aligned with Democrats to denounce the White House's untoward breach of faith with a close wartime ally. In February 2019, the Oval Office reversed the decision and asserted that several hundred US troops would remain in Syria after all to prevent the resurgence of the Islamic State. The actual number of military personnel was classified but numbered higher than the public figure of 200–400.[31]

The same month beheld the SDF's besieging of Baghouz, a village in eastern Syria's lower Euphrates River valley and the last territorial enclave of the rump Islamic State. Safe passage was granted to 20,000 civilians to leave Baghouz before the final SDF assault on the IS die-hards. Caught between hammer blows from American, coalition, and Russian air attacks and the anvil of Kurdish units, Sunni Arab fighters, and Iran-backed militia, the IS caliphate bit by bit folded with great loss of life and suffering. On March 23, 2019, Baghouz fell to the besiegers and the physical caliphate ceased to exist.

No one popped champagne corks. The Islamic State's millenarian ideology and its scattered fighters survived. So, while a page had been turned, virtually every observer – military officers, intelligence experts, political leaders – fully expected diffuse terrorist attacks from IS remnants and self-styled Salafi acolytes. Their predictions proved accurate. IS had the regenerative powers of a phoenix. US counterterrorism went from a war against a landholding enclave to a fight against an elusive insurgency with rampant jihadi bloodletting from Kabul to Casablanca to Cabo Delgado in northernmost Mozambique.

After expelling Islamic State gunmen from northeastern Syria, the SDF established a quasi-autonomous enclave, which included oil fields around the Deir ez-Zour province. Even their limited output of 0.5 percent of global production in 2010 declined further because of the outbreak of the civil war, international sanctions, and dilapidated extraction machinery. In October 2019, when the Kurds were compelled to vacate their territorial holdings along the Turkish border, because of the abrupt evacuation of most US forces from Syria, they managed to retain control parts of the province and its oil wells.[32] The SDF looked to restore oil production by signing a deal with a US company to develop and export crude from areas under its control. Beset with persistent attacks, the SDF accused the Assad regime and IS sleeper cells of interference and murdering military and civilian personnel in their territory to undermine their control and reclaim a hold in the disputed province.

The defeat of the Islamic State pocket did not immediately resurrect the Oval Office's talk about pulling out the remaining US troops from Syria. The White House, instead, committed to keeping 600 American troops to protect the oil facilities in Kurdish hands. Without giving a logical explanation, President Trump said: "When we commit American troops to battle we must do so only when a vital national interest is at stake." Continuing the acrobatic reversal, Operation Inherent Resolve officials laid out plans to double the size of some US proxy units and to complete training up a 2,200-personnel "oilfield guard" to ensure a revenue stream of between $1million to $3 million daily for SDF coffers.[33] Trump's about-face aligned the White House with the Pentagon's thinking to retain a presence in Syria to combat any resurgence of IS militants and to monitor other adversaries, such as Russia and Iran.[34] The Defense Department strove to stop another domino from falling to the ayatollahs after their gains in Lebanon and Yemen, along with Iraq. As it turned out, the SOF and CIA field officers continued to knock off senior terrorist planners, sometimes with the novel and secretive Ninja Hellfire missile that killed its victims with rotating blades rather than explosives to spare nearby noncombatants.

At the start of 2020, Iraq hosted approximately 5,300 US troops, who faced off against Kataib Hezbollah and scores of other Iranian-allied PMFs. Their presence in Baghdad's streets disconcerted Sunni leaders and populations to the west. The Iranians continually provoked the United States and its Sunni Arab regional associates with rocket attacks. Some armed groups within the Popular Mobilization Forces made no bones about their disdain for America's third intrusion into Iraq. The Pentagon maintained a counterterrorism footprint, military training capacity, and observation posts spanning the Persian Gulf arena, not just in Iraq. It was believed a US military presence "reassured friends and allies adjacent to Syria," in the words of one Middle East expert.[35]

The anti-IS campaign brought together a strange-bedfellows coalition made up of Kurds, Sunni Arabs, Iraqi Shiite militias (trained and resourced by Iran), Syrian regime soldiers, and Russian forces, along with US pilots and troops. Because they had a mutual enemy, the United States, Russia, Iran, and the Assad regime wound up as de facto allies on the same side against the Islamic State. The Salafi-jihadis acted as the "glue" holding them together. Even before the Islamic State folded, Iran and its PMFs engaged in repeated provocations against the United States as well as Israel. After one tit-for-tat exchange, the Pentagon fired a salvo of missiles at five Kataib Hezbollah bases in Iraq and Syria, killing a reported twenty-four militants. In retaliation, Iranian-affiliated PMF militias stormed the American Embassy in Baghdad.

Then, the United States escalated its retaliation with a drone missile attack that killed Major General Qassim Soleimani and other Iranian and Iraqi officials. As their convoy departed Baghdad's airport, a hovering MQ-9 Reaper drone shot off an air-to-surface Hellfire missile that obliterated the vehicles transporting Soleimani, the ruthless head of the Quds Force, which served as the Islamic Revolutionary Guard Corps' international special-forces outfit. Also killed was a leader of the Iraqi militias and eight of their confidants. Soleimani's death set off a furious political and rhetorical explosion in Shiite Iraq and Iran, where he was a revered figure. In protest, NATO also suspended its capacity-building mission in Iraq for a year.

His Iranian patron, the Supreme Leader Ali Khamenei, swore a devastating revenge for the martyred terrorist, who was blamed for the deaths of over 600 US troops during the sectarian civil war inside Iraq. General Soleimani saw to it that the Iran-backed Special Groups were armed with the infamous armor-piercing EFPs. The highly anticipated backlash from Iran never materialized. Tehran, instead, let loose sixteeen missiles that damaged two US outposts (in Erbil and Ayn al Asad in western Iraq) and injured some thirty troops with head concussions. The Iranian counter strike was labeled as a minimal face-saving attack that signaled a temporary de-escalation from the ayatollah regime.

The Pentagon temporarily doubled down on the US Embassy's defenses by stationing in Baghdad forces from the Marine Corps, 82nd Airborne paratroopers, and a Special Ops detachment, totaling almost 4,000 combat personnel. Meanwhile, the expenditure meter kept running as the Iraq War logged in a cost of $2 trillion.[36] There seemed to be no exit from Iraq, although in December 2020, Washington announced withdrawal of 2,500 troops from its over 5,000 Iraqi contingent by early the next year, a promise that was kept before Joseph Biden moved into the White House. Once in office, President Biden ordered a retaliatory air attack on an Iranian-backed proxy force in Syria for its rocket attack on US personnel in Iraq. The methodical decision-making leading up to the assault was intended to send a clear message to Tehran to cease its provocations. But Iran retaliated a week later with its own rocket barrage.

As an interim conclusion about America's involvement in Iraq since 2003, it is important to recognize the reality on the ground. Although the United States justified its invasion on a false premise, paradoxically, it fulfilled some of the initial objectives. Iraq is no longer a rogue nation pursuing nuclear arms. American and coalition partners destroyed a homicidal dictatorship, established a still-evolving and precarious democracy, gave a lifeline to the Kurds for a semi-autonomous entity, genuinely prevailed over a vicious insurgency, and returned in 2014 to stabilize an under-siege land from a terrorist movement bent on committing savagery for an earthly theocracy. Equally true is the unmistakable fact that the Islamic Republic of Iran benefited from the elimination of its chief rival, paving the way for Tehran's burgeoning political influence within Iraq and the Middle East. The saga is ongoing with Iraq, Iran, and, indeed, the entire Persian Gulf region hanging in the balance.

7.4   Barack Obama and the "Good War" in Afghanistan

By the time Barack Obama settled into the Oval Office in early 2009, security in the Afghan theater had badly deteriorated. Given the new president's campaign platform, his policies were sure to entail dramatic changes in Afghanistan as well as Iraq. In his acceptance speech at the Democratic Convention in mid-2008, the party's nominee staked out firm positions: "I will end this war in Iraq responsibly and finish the fight against al Qaeda and the Taliban in Afghanistan."[37]

Early on, America's forty-fourth commander in chief set in motion plans to disengage from the Afghan war in a surge-and-withdraw formula. As an Obama defense aide later reflected "the idea was to escalate in order to exit, enabling and empowering the governments of Afghanistan and Pakistan to take control overtime." This strategy, according to the Pentagon appointee, "would not lead to perfection" but the administration desired "an end state that ... was 'good enough.'"[38] The new president called for a buildup of the Afghan National Army (ANA) to 260,000 soldiers, with the ultimate goal of 400,000 security personnel. When he laid out his plans, the ANA stood at 100,000 troops and the Afghan National Police (as distinct from local police) comprised about 80,000 officers.[39] Arrayed against the US forces and their allies were the Taliban and the lesser known but deadly Haqqani group, a Sunni Islamist organization that emerged during the anti-Soviet war and conducted high-profile attacks against U.S and partner forces. Its leader, Sirajuddin Haqqai, was also deputy leader of the Taliban.

President Obama's promise to walk away from the shrinking insurgency in Iraq proved much easier to fulfill than his pledge to "finish the fight" in Afghanistan. Ironically, the calming Iraq front, due to his predecessor's surged forces, altered counterinsurgency strategy, and Sunni tribal uprising, in fact, switched the anxiety of the new foreign policy mandarins toward Afghanistan and its dimming prospects for a military solution. A Defense Department senior official urgently requested of the incoming government a "tourniquet of some kind" to staunch the bloodshed and the Taliban's territorial advances.[40]

So badly had battlefield conditions worsened in eastern Afghanistan that Obama announced in the weeks following his inauguration the intention to deploy immediately 17,000 more combat and support soldiers into the alpine nation.[41] Eleven thousand Marines streamed into Helmand Province, which the Taliban had nearly overrun completely. Since the revitalized Taliban infiltrated back into Afghanistan, they nearly transformed Helmand into a stronghold. Hearts and minds programs along with reconstruction projects failed to withstand the Taliban resurgence. They were the equivalent of casting pearls before swine. Even the US military in the provincial capital, Lashkar Gah, had only a tenuous hold on the city's outskirts.

A wave-top review of Helmand's history reveals the downward trajectory of the province since 2006, when the Taliban seeped back into the warlord-dominated province, which shared a border with Pakistan. As part of its expanding mandate beyond Kabul, the International Security Assistance Force (ISAF) had committed forces, mainly British paratroopers at first, to wrest back control. The insurgents fought back, for Helmand was a center of opium production and hence an essential source of funds. Over the years, the Pentagon and its ISAF partners mounted dozens of operational sweeps to dislodge the insurgents, attaining varying degrees of success to eke out a stalemate rather than a defeat. In short, Helmand was a microcosm of Afghanistan.

To address the brewing crisis in Afghanistan, devise a strategy, and recommend troop levels, Robert Gates, the Bush holdover defense secretary, ordered General Stanley McChrystal, the new commander of the separate US force and of the NATO-run International Security Assistance Force, to make a strategic assessment of the existing reality in the South Asian nation by September. Just before that deadline, the new president delivered a speech to the Veterans of Foreign Wars convention in Phoenix. He gingerly broached the subject of leaving Iraq because of his audience's keen sense of patriotism. He struck, by contrast, a hard-line stance about the war in Afghanistan. To Obama, "Afghanistan is not a war of choice. This is a war of necessity." Not defeating the Taliban insurgency "will mean an even larger safe haven from which al Qaeda would plot to kill more Americans."[42] This Afghan-centered policy from the start captured more attention from the White House than Iraq.

Despite a background in kinetic action units, McChrystal came down on the side of waging a population-centric counterinsurgency campaign. He embraced engaging the insurgents "in ways that respect the safety and well-being of the Afghan people." To win over the population, the four-star general instructed his soldiers: "Think of counterinsurgency as an argument to win the support of the people." His strategy set forth the priorities of protecting people, building a civil state, and making friends even with insurgents. McChrystal deprioritized killing the Taliban: "You can kill Taliban forever because they are not a finite number."[43] The Army officer's ambitious end game asked for a protracted commitment, as most counterinsurgencies took at least ten years to win, an estimate that ran counter to the White House's surge-and-exit strategy. Obama's inner-team dismissed the idea of an indefinite counterinsurgency war.

The White House closely reviewed McChrystal's sixty-six-page assessment of the Afghan war and a strategy for its conclusion.[44] His report contained no real surprises. It advocated classic counterinsurgency with a request for more boots on the ground and with a focus on protecting the Afghan population in order to isolate and defeat the insurgents. Prior to releasing his report at the end of August, McChrystal floated additional troop levels as high as 80,000 – figures that alarmed the president – before the four-star officer settled on a request for 40,000 service members.[45] For the Army general, a heavy US troop presence figured in his overall counterinsurgency strategy. Protection of the Afghan populace was COIN's main priority.

Barack Obama remained skeptical of his generals' forecasts of impending victory. As a student of history, he recalled reading predictions made by the military brass during the Vietnam War about an elusive light at the end of the tunnel.[46] He also often voiced the "admonition that there is 'no military solution' to the problems of Iraq and Afghanistan." The secretaries of state and defense, according to one journalistic account, exerted their influence on the troop-level question. "The Clinton-Gates combine helped to win over the president to sending more troops, despite the skepticism of senior" West Wing appointees.[47]

The American leader, as a result, cut down McChrystal's recommendation to 30,000 combatants in his long-anticipated speech at the US Military Academy on December 1st. But the president mandated that the troops begin coming home after eighteen months, even though the reinforcements did not completely reach Afghanistan until summer 2010. At his West Point speech, he also set the end of 2014 as the deadline for the cessation of US combat operations.[48] Thereafter, the Afghans were to take over the combat roles. And the American troops would switch gears to support roles for training and advising, except for air strikes, which stayed in US hands.

Not surprisingly, General McChrystal's strategic plan ignited a vigorous debate when the Obama White House insisted on its own strategic review of the Afghan war, which took months.[49] The Oval Office convened top brass from the US Armed Forces, cabinet secretaries, and a plethora of advisers in a lengthy deliberative process. The West Wing's cross-examination aided in forming other assumptions that would influence Obama's foreign policy outside of Afghanistan in future theaters such as Libya, Syria, Somalia, and Iraq.[50] But it delayed action, as one strategy session followed another. Troop strengths, deployment rates, and military formulations were analyzed and debated. The public's mood about casualties and financial costs were taken into account.[51]

An anatomy of America's international approach to terrorism pointed to three broad courses of action. The first adopted a minimalist tack incorporating drone and manned aircraft strikes against terrorist targets. Commando-type raids by Special Ops forces on terrorist agents formed another part of the circumscribed warfare to stay clear of more land wars, massive reconstruction projects, and nation-building commitments. These half-in elements of a classic counterterrorism strategy risked fewer military lives and averted large-scale financial expenditures. An early exponent of the counterterrorism model was Vice President Joe Biden, who aspired to dodge another Vietnam War, where the United States slid down a slippery slope from a lean military presence to a big land-war quagmire.[52]

A second strategy called for a bigger and better-trained Afghan military and police. Proponents of this middle way argued that expanded security forces offered the surest means to defeat or hold at bay the Taliban and al Qaeda jihadis. Keeping the Islamist terrorists off balance meant they would be too hard-pressed to mount attacks against the United States or Western Europe. So as to ratchet up the size and performance of Kabul's army and police, the Pentagon called upon its special warfare experiences from the Philippines, Somalia, and Iraq. This line of effort spared American fatalities and perhaps sinking into another protracted insurgent war à la Vietnam.[53]

The third approach urged a classical counterinsurgency. Such a course would enmesh the Pentagon in a lengthy, manpower-heavy, and financially costly commitment for what COIN hawks outlined as a "clear, hold, and build" formula. Enemy insurgents must first be cleared from territory. Then US combatants and their local partners would hold the terrain. Finally, American and allied troops backed up by skilled civilian technicians would supply civic amenities – medical clinics, schools, water wells, electricity, and micro-financing for a non-narcotics economy. In a decentralized, tribal society like Afghanistan, the fully resourced COIN envisaged nation-creation steps, to boot. Corruption and abuse were to be replaced by local and national governments displaying conspicuous integrity and fairness. To Obama and his close White House advisers, this vision struck them as utopian.[54]

Beyond the West Wing, the administration stood divided. The secretaries of state and defense, respectively, Hillary Clinton and Robert Gates, endorsed the broader military commitment, believing that Afghanistan hovered on the brink of being lost. Gates thought that multiplying the number of US troops on the ground enhanced the prospects for an independent Afghan army in "three to five years is reasonable."[55] Generals McChrystal and Petraeus, the COIN gurus, also bought into the fully resourced option with the ten-year commitment to see it through to victory. The primary opponent of huge troop deployments and of decade-long military investments in counterinsurgency was President Obama. He and his West Wing advisers opposed nation-building schemes and expenditures amounting to trillions of dollars.[56] Nothing emerged from marathon strategy sessions to change Barack Obama's mind about foreign wars.

Obama publically promised to bring home the US military in his presidential campaign. But once in office, his falling poll numbers also spurred his withdrawal pledges. Sixty-two percent Americans believed in July 2010 that the Afghan war was going badly, up from 49 percent two months earlier, according to a CBS poll. The same poll recorded an almost even split, 44–43 percent, disapproved versus approved of the president's handling of the war.[57] Ultimately, American troop strength reached nearly 100,000 soldiers before the Obama Pentagon began to reduce the number until slightly over 8,000 remained when he left office. As America's troop levels fell off, its co-belligerents precipitously cut their contributions also. The United States contributed the vast bulk of the manpower. So, its drawdowns were significant for the overall effort.

At its height, ISAF numbered roughly 132,000 personnel with contributions from all twenty-nine NATO Allies, plus twenty-two non-NATO partners. The United States furnished 90,000 troops with the balance coming from other states, with numbers ranging from 9,500 British military personnel to 3 from Austria. Additionally, the United States possessed a separate military command known as USFOR-A. It numbered 34,000 during its peak deployment at the end of 2013. USFOR-A shouldered much of the fighting burden until 2014, when it passed the combat baton to the Afghan armed forces.

In his strategic plan, General McChrystal advocated expanding the Afghan National Army, police, and border guards to top 400,000 members in the course of the next three years at a cost of $40 billion. The one-time commander of the hard-charging 75th Ranger Regiment applied the standard ratio of 20 security personnel (army, police, border guards) for every 1,000 inhabitants. Estimating that Afghanistan was home to some 25 million people at the time, he calculated that, because of the severity of the insurgency, a total of 400,000 security members were required to prevail in the Texas-sized territory. Afghans, he noted, were to make up the majority of this huge number before foreign forces left the country.[58]

In May, 2014, President Obama began implementing a sizeable drawdown of US military personnel and a curtailment of American combat operations, to be completed by year's end. Thereafter, the residual ground forces realigned their mission exclusively to training and advising the Afghan military. A major exception to the Obama diktat was the secretive involvement of Special Operations Forces in counterterrorism operations to capture or kill Taliban, Islamic State, or warlord chieftains. Saluting and carrying out their commander in chief's orders, Defense whittled down the US military presence. Its footprint shrank to 9,800 troops by the end of 2014. At the same time, DoD and ISAF turned over combat operations to the Afghan military. America's other allies followed suit.

By the end of 2015, the US troop numbers were scheduled to fall to 5,500 combatants. And by the time Obama was to vacate 1600 Pennsylvania Avenue, the American combat contingent was scheduled to have shrunk to zero. The only military presence on hand was to have been the usual Marine Corps embassy guards and a small extra security detachment of about 300 personnel to protect Americans living in Kabul.

Before these severe drawdowns took place, the Obama administration ratcheted up the number of boots on the ground to implement Stanley McChrystal's population-centric stabilization plan.[59] Under tutelage from General Petraeus, now CENTCOM chief, McChrystal espoused the people-centered warfare of his mentor. His blueprint prioritized protecting the population over killing insurgents.[60] Both generals believed that the sine qua non of their hearts-and-minds approach was noncombatant safety. Of the two, McChrystal favored the most restrictive Rules of Engagement (ROE), which defined the circumstances under which US troops could fire their weapons. Strict ROEs were designed to spare civilian casualties. Rank and file troops perceived restrictions on their firing as endangering them vis-à-vis enemy shooters.[61]

Subsequent ISAF and USFOR-A chiefs relaxed the restraints not only for tactical-level shooting but also in the Trump era for drone and piloted aircraft assaults. These new orders were another straw in the wind that a more narrowly focused counterterrorism strategy was replacing the population-centric counterinsurgency doctrine.

7.5   Government in a Box, Drug Wars, and Shake Ups

General McChrystal also introduced a "new war model" for winning over the locals' trust and goodwill by providing civilian services. When ISAF undertook a large-scale pacification offensive in 2010 to expel the Taliban from Marjah, a key city in central Helmand Province, the four-star commander promised a "government in a box ready to roll" forward to replace the long-standing Taliban shadow rule in their largest stronghold.[62]

Marshalled behind ISAF frontlines were more than 1,900 police officers, whose job it was to hold the recaptured Marjah in the application of the COIN doctrine of "clear, hold, and build" to impede a wholesale insurgent return. Next came the build phase of the operation. Experts and engineers stood ready to deliver public services, such as medical care, electricity, and water to the residents. The Marjah offensive was intended to roll out a prototype for future military actions.

Fate intervened to abort McChrystal's counterinsurgency plans. Soon after the start of the Marjah action, the general "retired" in June 2010 over disparaging comments about Joe Biden and administration appointees over their handling of the war attributed to him and his staff officers by a reporter with *Rolling Stone* magazine.[63] In his memoir, President Obama made it plain why he accepted his Afghan commander's offer of resignation. He sensed an "air of impunity ... among the military's top ranks ... that once war began, those who fought it shouldn't be questioned." Obama believed this attitude "eroded a bedrock principle of our representative democracy."[64] David Petraeus, then at four-star rank as Central Command head, stepped down a notch to take the Afghan post, which he held for a year before he became Director for Central Intelligence. He resigned from that post in November 2012, under a cloud for an extramarital affair. McChrystal's departure translated into more than just the end of a legendary career; it speeded up the turnover of the war to the Afghan security forces and, notably, diminished the emphasis on the canonical COIN strategy.

The war in Afghanistan exhibited another twist, which hindered American and allied forces in uprooting the Taliban. For decades, Afghan valleys, especially in Helmand Province, lay at the center of the world's illicit opium-poppy production. The Taliban superintended the growth to more than 90 percent of the illicit heron globally. They relied on the opium-poppy output as a means to finance the battle against international forces. The insurgents pocketed revenue from sales, taxes, and trafficking processed morphine, heroin, and opium. The centrality of heroin to the insurgency was recognized by President Ashraf Ghani, who argued: "Without drugs, this war would have been long over."[65] The illegal opium economy reached $3 billion in 2016, while during the past several years the United States futilely spent more than $8 billion to eradicate or replace poppies with corn, cotton, tobacco, or potatoes with no lasting success. Some Islamic militant bands turned to other illegal enterprises – weapons smuggling, sales of valuable antiquities, kidnapping, or extortion; none surpassed the Taliban's cash machine powered by drug money. The availability of narcotics also spelled trouble for US soldiers and Marines in the field, who distrusted their Afghan fellow combatants because they were often "high on hashish."[66]

Embedding Afghan and American fighting men together provided an opportunity for a particularly treacherous practice of "green-on-blue" attacks, whereby an Afghan infantryman gunned down his disarmed American mentors during a rest break or meal. The shooters were turncoats, Taliban infiltrators, or deranged individuals. Although this form of fratricide was never promiscuous, the insider shootings induced suspicion in US units that was partly mitigated by designating "guardian angles" – troops who stayed alert with their M-4 assault rifles cocked and ready when the two sides mixed. Enhanced vetting of recruits weeded out all but a few killers within joint US-Afghan ranks. Luckily, the insider attacks remained primarily an Afghan phenomenon. Other theaters escaped the menace of indigenous troops turning their rifles on their foreign allies.[67]

Despite screening precautions and posted guards, Afghan security forces turned their weapons on each other on average every four days during the closing months of 2019 according to the Special Inspector General for Afghanistan Reconstruction. Inside killers carried out attacks within the Afghan National Defense and Security Forces 33 times in the fourth quarter of 2019. ANDSF personnel participated in insider shootings in 82 instances and killed 172 comrades during all of 2019. In one particularly heinous case, an Afghan infiltrator shot to death 23 ANA soldiers in their sleep at a base in Ghazni Province in December 2019.[68]

7.6   Building Afghan Security Forces

Almost from the outset of the US invasion, the new occupiers moved to stand up a local force to take over from the outsiders and to secure territory from the fleeing Taliban. Afghan self-defense increasingly loomed as the crux of American military policy. Established in 2002, the Afghan National Army was ostensibly administered by the country's newly minted Ministry of Defense. In reality, specific units were sometimes dominated by local warlords, which contributed to a diffusion of effort. Often the Afghan private was officered by subcaliber leaders, some of whom were corrupt or marginal or both. At least 40 percent of army recruits were illiterate, placing a burden on their trainers to professionalize the military forces and to produce adequate cohorts of high-quality non-commissioned officers.[69] The Defense Department struggled to stand up an effective NCO corps, which served as the backbone of US ground forces.

Ethnicity played a major role in the ANA's makeup as non-Pashtun communities predominated to the point that that American instructors instituted affirmative action programs to recruit Pashtuns. This ethnic balancing was a foreign concept to the Afghans. But the United States insisted on ethnic and sectarian diversity. The ANA and ANP (Afghan National Police) attained numbers reflecting approximately the percentages of ethnic groups within society, according to one academic study.[70]

The ISAF did train some of the Afghan kandaks (battalions). Specific nations, such as the United States and Britain, groomed stand-alone Afghan units in combat skills. Some entered into Afghan commando units while others served as general-purpose soldiers, who staffed checkpoints or performed routine guard duties. Afghan officials claimed that their forces reached nearly 90,000 in 2009 and topped 178,000 ANA soldiers and 154,000 ANP officers by 2017.[71]

But there were problems with the actual headcounts in the ANA and ANP and as well as the forces themselves. High desertion rates of up to 30 percent plagued not a few Afghan military units. Such forces were hardly fit for high-action combat. There were also language difficulties since troops spoke just Pashto or Dari (a Persian dialect). In the early years, the Afghan soldiers accompanied American or NATO soldiers on patrols. The US troops usually gave the ANA all the credit for their joint actions: "put them forward in the eyes of the locals" as the "only way a real Afghan state will emerge," according to one astute observer.[72]

Still, the ANA expanded its ranks and assumed a larger role in fighting the Taliban insurgents. Foreign, especially American, mentorship over Afghan combat missions became the norm. By 2009, NATO-led operations fell off as better-trained and more motivated host-nation platoons maneuvered with a modicum of independence from their international sponsors. The Afghan elite forces, for example, established records for independent action and battlefield victories. Their effectiveness led to an enlargement of their ranks. A 2017 government plan called for the number of Afghan commandos to nearly double to 23,300 by 2020 as a way to contest Taliban control or dominance in nearly half of the country's 407 districts. The drawback to this expansion derived from its deleterious impact on the conventional army as the more motivated replacements went into elite teams rather than fill slots in the regular units.[73]

Many regular kandaks, on the other hand, needed international shoring up or they would often break and run from the battlezone at the first crack of gunfire. The non-Afghan soldiers could be counted on to steady their neophyte compatriots when skirmishes erupted or to correct logistical shortfalls in the delivery of ammunition, water, and food, in addition to maintaining vehicles and equipment. Unsteadily, the Afghan National Army moved from small independent operations to larger ones. The Defense Ministry also took control of the border police and some local policing units from the Interior Ministry to upgrade their effectiveness and to coordinate their deployments.

After the Obama administration kept its 2014 deadline to turnover combat operations to the host military, the ANA struggled to fight on its own without its American mentors at its side in firefights. They did so with appalling casualty rates among pro-government forces. Some 64,000 have died (in disputed figures) since 2001, with the bulk in the last half-dozen years, as noted by a university study.[74] Afghan casualties resonated less with Washington than American deaths.

In contrast, US military deaths from hostile fire came to 1,913 at the end of 2019, with a total of 2,445 dying when non-combat fatalities are tallied in the total.[75] US annual deaths peaked at 496 in 2010 as a result of a ferocious Taliban offensive, which resorted to a hefty step up in roadside bombs. The Taliban matched their NATO killings with atrocities against humanitarian workers, also murdering in cold blood ten members of an international medical mission in 2010.[76]

Even with peace talks underway, high casualties and attrition outpaced Afghan recruitment and retention. Deaths and desertions attrited the ANDSF. But the primary driver of this attrition sprang from soldiers going AWOL, or absent without leave, from their military formations.

The escalation in Taliban attacks also gave rise to this worrying metric in the Pentagon.[77] The Pentagon counted on Afghan soldiers and police to spare the United States from combat operations and casualties, all the while opening the gates for American withdrawals.

US warplanes delivered most of the air cover to embattled Afghan soldiers, while American service members struggled to stand up an independent Afghan air force. Without US aerial attacks on the Taliban, it is hard to see how the pro-Kabul forces could withstand the frequent ambushes, bombings, and shootings. Try as it might, the Pentagon faced daunting problems to create, train, and equip a modern-day air force from scratch. By early 2019, the United States had expended nearly $8 billion over the previous eleven years on an air force that still scrambled to achieve 60 percent self-sufficiency in helicopter and propeller aircraft nationwide. The American-led coalition airplanes still carried out fivefold as many air strike missions as the Afghan Air Force, with a total of 6,500 attacks in 2018 according to one report.[78] Improvement has been incremental with Afghan pilots slowly shouldering the mission to ferry troops, evacuate their wounded comrades, and deliver close air support to land forces in gun battles. In May 2014, Obama announced wholesale US military personnel departures by the end of 2016.[79] Two years later, as the frontline conditions deteriorated, Obama reversed course by stating 8,400 troops would stay as he left office.[80] Troop levels were not the only means used by the Obama administration to oversee the direction of its Afghan war policy.

7.7   Waging War with Aerial Drones

At the onset of his first term, Obama hesitantly assented to the COIN strategy that seemed to work so well for David Petraeus in Iraq. The general, in fact, garnered a near cult following in many Army circles for his role in salvaging American fortunes in that war. But of course, Afghanistan was not Iraq. Made up of towering peaks and craggy valleys, Afghanistan, physically larger, was more rural with a dispersed population. By contrast, Iraq (aside from Kurdistan) was flatter, with its somewhat smaller population concentrated in a collection of urban centers along the Tigris and Euphrates river valleys. Unlike Afghanistan, Iraq possessed an educated population, governing bureaucracy, and professional business sector.

Attitudes toward government institutions reflected night-and-day differences in the two countries. Iraq possessed a tradition of centralized authority and organization. In Afghanistan's semi-feudalism, the government was the enemy of the rural Taliban and warlords rather than a prize to be won, controlled, and utilized for the benefit of its rulers. Its physical and cultural variances rendered Afghanistan less than an ideal environment for the brand of COIN championed by Petraeus and McChrystal. Next door, Pakistan served as a thriving sanctuary for the closely linked Taliban, Haqqani network, and al Qaeda. Unlike Iraq, Afghanistan witnessed no repetition of an Awakening movement among US foes, who turned the balance of battle in America's favor.

The absence of a sudden turnaround on the Afghan battlefield did not go unnoticed at 1600 Pennsylvania Avenue. Already a Pentagon skeptic, Obama heeded his instincts and West Wing counsel. In mid-2011, he changed course toward counterterrorism operations that had taken down so many jihadi chiefs, not limited to Osama bin Laden. Besides, CT called for far fewer US boots on the ground than COIN and relied on aerial attacks, which spared US lives.

The Obama DoD greatly expanded its drone-bombing program within Afghanistan and, more critically, inside Pakistan, which kept open its borderlands to America's enemies. Afghanistan's insurgents crossed the frontier into the relative safety of the freewheeling Federally Administrated Tribal Areas. In these Pakistani sanctuaries, they rested, regrouped, and trained before stealing back across the poorly demarcated border. Sending ground forces into Pakistan in hot pursuit of the fleeing militants, which did happen a handful of times, kicked up a diplomatic furor in Islamabad for breaching Pakistani sovereignty.

The Pakistani authorities likewise protested US drones penetrating their airspace except with much less vigor, especially as the CIA reduced the number of errant missiles hitting innocent civilians. Some Pakistani officers secretly welcomed the US air strikes to check the growing power of the Taliban and their collaborators the Haqqani militias in the FATA. They wanted to reassert their control. Tribal *maliks* hated the Taliban for muzzling in on their businesses and for religiously indoctrinating young males, which loosened the chieftains' grip on them. So, some Pakistani authorities winked and nodded their approval of the bombings.[81]

President Obama got into the remote killing business in spades because of his aversion to sending more "boots on the ground" to the costly land wars in Afghanistan, Iraq, and elsewhere. Drone assassinations also permitted the United States to disrupt or destroy jihadis operating in the two declared warzones and outside them in Pakistan, Yemen, Somalia, and Syria. In sheer fact, Obama oversaw more strikes in his first year than Bush conducted during his entire presidency. One report stated that Obama presided over 563 air strikes (almost all by drones) during his two terms on targets in Pakistan, Somalia, and Yemen, "compared to 57 strikes under Bush."[82] Whereas George Bush ordered about 50 non-battlefield targeted killings, his successor upped the number to at least 375 such drone attacks.[83] The Bush strikes killed 296 terrorists and 195 noncombatants from their salvos in Yemen, Pakistan, and Somalia. Obama, according to the same source, took 3,040 terrorist lives and 391 civilians.[84]

Obama embraced the cloak-and-missile campaign as his preferred weapon against al Qaeda. As a matter of procedure, he personally reviewed the hit list, submitted by CIA and known as the "disposition matrix," with his closest advisers each Tuesday (called Terror Tuesdays) in the White House before issuing de facto death warrants.[85] One prominent missile attack, as noted in Chapter 6, killed Anwar al-Awlaki in Yemen in 2011.[86] There would be scores upon scores of deadly drone strikes in years to come.

The Department of Defense set out to pulverize insurgents from the air as a way to compensate for its thin ground-force presence. It hoped to push the Taliban into negotiations to end the conflict. The Taliban did establish an "embassy" in Doha in 2013 as a means to legitimize its international standing. It is unknowable how much the bombing motivated them, if at all. In 2016, it was reported that 1,337 weapons were dropped – "a 40 percent rise on 2015."[87] Yemen, another active hostility zone, recorded over 300 confirmed drone strikes up to early 2018.[88] Across the Red Sea in Somalia, the United States launched in excess of 100 drone missiles at al-Shabaab, an al Qaeda linked terrorist movement.[89]

The death of noncombatants stood out as the key shortcoming of the remote-killing technology. Critics cited various figures purporting to record civilian casualties. For example, Pakistan, which bore the brunt of CIA drone attacks that peaked at 128 in 2010 before leveling off.[90] That year the South Asian country reportedly suffered 89 nonmilitary fatalities.[91] The figures could be higher or lower, as counts heavily depended on outside monitoring groups, which experienced difficulties getting into hot zones. Thus, interviewers relied on unverifiable information from village respondents, long after the incidents.

A memorable departure in Obama's usual method of meting out justice to terrorists occurred with the takedown of Osama bin Laden, who masterminded the mass-death attack on America. The White House turned to a commando raid rather than a drone-killing operation to expunge bin Laden from the battlefield. Official Washington sought proof positive of the arch-terrorist's demise. Only a well-photographed intact corpse would suffice to silence skeptics and true believers that the West's most wanted man, in truth, got his just deserts.

The high-profile nature of the manhunt drew the Oval Office into a myriad of planning details. President Obama delayed the famed raiding mission a couple times out of concern about possible failure, reflecting "paralyzing indecision, political calculation, and a squandering of intelligence secrets" on his part. His caution stemmed, in part, from reflection on how the catastrophic 1980 hostage-rescue raid into Iran "hurt Jimmy Carter's reelection."[92] After more than two cancellations and multiple requests for more information, the hesitant commander in chief gave the green light for the operation in February 2001 after reportedly learning of bin Laden's secret hideaway the previous September.

Collaborating with the CIA, which had traced the whereabouts of bin Laden to his concrete compound in Pakistan's military town of Abbottabad, the secretive Joint Special Operations Command executed the killing operation. The roughly twenty-five-member kill team swooped down from the moonless sky in two Blackhawks (along with a quick reaction force in Chinook helicopters) next to bin Laden's secluded fortress in the after-midnight hours (local time) on May 2, 2011. The US Navy SEALs, who made up most of the super-secret unit, sprang into action. Racing upstairs to the second floor of the living quarters, one of the SEAL operators shot bin Laden in the doorway of his bedroom. Minutes after completing a thorough facial-recognition scan, a DNA test, and numerous pictures, the SEALs placed the corpse in a body bag for transportation to the USS *Carl Vinson* sailing in the Arabian Sea. The sea burial off the aircraft carrier was conducted according to Islamic law to fend off criticism from faithful Muslims.[93]

The tableau of Navy SEAL giant killers as warrior Jacks, who sawed down the terrorist beanstalk and chopped off the head of al Qaeda, was propagated by Obama loyalists as the 2012 election beckoned. Eliminating the arch-terrorist did bring a certain closure to the world manhunt for the mass murderer, which reflected favorably on the president's election prospects. There were street celebrations at Ground Zero in New York City, Washington, and other places. But the zero-dark-thirty operation brought no pause in the stepped-up fighting in Afghanistan with the Taliban insurgents. Bin Laden's longtime lieutenant, Ayman al Zawahiri, soon replaced him. Bin Laden's death and that of a spate of al Qaeda sub-leaders, bomb makers, financiers, and facilitators did render the network comparatively less effective than the Islamic State, which eclipsed al Qaeda in Syria in the mid-2010s.

Three months after the killing of the al Qaeda leader, a Taliban fighter fired a rocket-propelled grenade into a landing US Army CH-471 Chinook helicopter, killing all thirty-eight on board, including fifteen operators from the Naval Special Warfare Development Group, popularly known as SEAL Team 6. It was the single largest loss of American lives in the Afghan war. Known by its call sign, Extortion 17, the helicopter's downing just forty miles from Kabul in the Taliban-thick Tangi Valley generated a rash of conspiracy theories to explain the seemingly suspicious attack. One conspiratorial tale suggested complicity of high-level Afghan figures who relayed targeting information to the Taliban ahead of the helicopter's flight.[94] But just as bin Laden's death redoubled al Qaeda's rhetorical threats, the Extortion 17 incident resulted in no letup in U.S operations, as America prepared to leave Afghanistan.

7.8   Plans to Leave Afghanistan

Obama's decision to quit Iraq was widely regarded as a mistake, for it opened a vacuum filled in time by the cruelty and violence of the rampaging Islamic State.[95] So, the Pentagon chiefs warned the West Wing officials that a precipitous evacuation from Afghanistan would result in a similar outcome in the war-torn country, with an almost certain Taliban victory. They urged leaving 20,000 troops in place. The new Afghan president, Ashraf Ghani, also beseeched the White House to suspend its planned pullout because of escalating Taliban attacks and its political sway, if not outright control, in nearly half the country.[96] Their requests met limited success by ensuring the continuance of a rump US force. Six months before departing office, Obama, as noted earlier, agreed to leave 8,400 troops buttressing the Afghan security personnel for his successor to either augment or evacuate.

The war had settled into an unwinnable stalemate between the warring parties. To triumph, the United States would have to deploy over 100,000 troops for at least a decade and spend tens of billions of dollars more. That game was not worth the candle. What mattered more to Washington was preventing Afghanistan from becoming once again a terrorist base and launch pad for attacks on the American homeland.

For the insurgents, they could endlessly kill without scruple but could not win over the non-Pashtun peoples to their cause. Driven by their Pashtun nationalism, sense of dignity, and fierce desire for revenge, the Taliban reclaimed lost territory until their presence predominated among Pashtun lands in eastern and southeastern Afghanistan. They also struck northern districts. Their suicide bombers carried out spectacular blasts in major urban centers. The semiliterate, rural tribesmen stuck with the Taliban through thick and thin, even in the darkest days of 2002 when they had been ousted from rule. The Pashtun tribesmen clung to their historic code, the Pashtunwali, which called for a subordinate role for women in society and for vengeance when a clansman had been wronged or killed. These deeply held values made progress a hard sell for Americans delivering amenities with their "hearts and minds" programs. Put simply, the Afghan war was a civil war, as Vietnam had been.

Urban areas could be won over and held against insurgents, but the countryside became a hostile landscape to Kabul's security personnel. The rural Pashtun resented and distrusted the corrupt central government's administration and judiciary. The white sneaker–wearing Taliban struck highway traffic and police checkpoints while also bombing wedding parties and funerals. By fall 2019, that year's civilian deaths from terrorism exceeded those in the past decade.[97] Figures for US military deaths also jumped to twenty-four and the highest count since 2014.

Financial expenditures to reconstruct Afghanistan exceeded America's widely praised Marshall Plan (at $13 billion) from 1948 through 1951. By the end of September 2019, the United States had expended over $132 billion for Afghan recovery whereas the Marshall costs reached $103.4 billion (adjusted for inflation), according to the Special Inspector General for Afghanistan Recovery's Quarterly Report to the US Congress. Of that figure, some $70 billion had been expended to build up the Afghan security forces. Waste, fraud, and abuse of funds for shoddy construction, misappropriated projects, and cost overruns defined Afghan infrastructure endeavors. According to SIGAR, another $70 million went unaccounted for in the same time frame.[98]

Retrenchment and troop exits cut US expenditures to $45 billion by 2018 from a high of $120 billion in 2011, when military personnel peaked in Afghanistan. Some $5 billion went to the Afghan forces, nearly another billion for economic aid, and $13 billion to the American military ranks.[99] The fall off in American casualties and fiscal costs made the price sustainable at least in the short term.

7.9   Iraq's Islamic State Enters Afghanistan

Once again events in Iraq negatively impacted the Afghan insurgency. Earlier during the Bush administration, the diversion of resources toward the Iraq War applied a brake on the US Afghan campaign. Now, once more, Iraq's fate influenced the Afghanistan conflict. As the Islamic State swept from Syria into Iraq in the first part of 2014, conquering an area the size of Poland, the Persian Gulf country again attracted attention away from the Afghan battlefront. For several months, the IS hordes appeared unstoppable. Their militias threatened even Baghdad until US and allied air attacks, hastily thrown-together Iraqi units, along with Iranian militias stemmed the cresting momentum. Even with a somewhat stabilized Iraq front in time, the war there was not finished. The

Pentagon could not neglect Iraq while it dealt with mountainous land to its east.

The Islamic State announced its expansion into Afghanistan with the Islamic State-Khorasan (IS-K) in 2015. Historically, the Khorasan region vaguely lumped together parts of present-day Afghanistan, Pakistan, Iran, and Central Asia. In Afghanistan, IS-K staged a spate of vicious attacks mostly targeting civilians. One such suicide bombing killed at least sixty-three people at a Kabul wedding party in 2019. Neither the Taliban nor the United States viewed IS-K with any legitimacy. As a nationalistic Pashtun movement, the Taliban warred for control over Afghanistan. On the other hand, the Islamic State and its various "provinces," or branches, fought for the worldwide extension of radical Islam under the auspices of a temporal caliphate. Before destruction of the earthly caliphate and death of al-Baghdadi, IS-K was fleetingly seen as the strongest Islamic State front outside Iraq and Syria.

Numbering about 2,500 militants, IS-K (which drew fighters from Pakistan, Uzbekistan, and Southeast Asia) ran into ferocious resistance from the Taliban, who regarded them as non-Pashtun interlopers striving to displace them from their rightful inheritance. At this juncture, there is no clear winner, but it appears that IS-K has suffered severe setbacks.[100] The rise of IS-K prompted some wishful-thinking observers to consider it a plus for the United States, as the Taliban might be inclined to ally with their traditional adversaries against recent interlopers.[101] That said, it is an oversimplification to see terrorist groups always at sword's point. Their shared hatred of the United States and its partners transcended any short-term differences. For certain, the Taliban, al Qaeda, and other terrorist networks were interconnected within the mountainous Afghan-Pakistan border.

As the insurgency dragged on, the Obama administration stamped its unique way of war on Afghanistan and in other theaters. The president tightly restricted decisions on not only troop numbers but also military operations to the point that his detractors labeled the practice as micromanaging. Robert Gates, the Defense secretary, wrote in his memoir that "the controlling nature of the Obama White House and NSS (National Security Staff) took micromanagement and operational meddling to a new level."[102]

Obama's wariness about nation building made him averse to schemes that suggested societal reengineering to attain Western-style modernization in places like Afghanistan. Soldiers were not democracy missionaries. Nor could the US Defense Department impose a New Deal 2.0 on that tribal land. The president's deputy national security adviser, Benjamin J. Rhodes, summed up his boss' thinking about how the

American "military win wars and stabilize conflicts. But a military can't create a political culture or build a society."[103]

By the end of his first term, Obama's national security team regularly used the disparaging phrase "Afghan good enough," which conveyed their sense of frustration, even low expectations about America's supposed ally. Instead of carrying on the high hopes for the reconstruction of a Westernized society (cum affirmative action programs for excluded ethnic members in the security forces), they were willing to accept far less, as a measure of Afghan good enough. Under these ebbing aspirations, the Pentagon contented itself with eliminating terrorists, containing the Taliban, and drawing down US troops. The Obama DoD renewed its commitment to strengthening the Afghan National Defense and Security Forces. The subsequent years beheld improvements in the ANDSF but it continued to suffer high casualties and high rates of desertion, reaching 25–30 percent annually.[104] Rendered in less abstract terms, Afghan forces were being killed at a pace of about two dozen per day, a seemingly unsustainable rate.[105]

From its onset, the Obama administration underscored that its priorities differed from those of George W. Bush. At his announcement of 30,000 additional troops for Afghanistan in late 2009, Obama made it clear that he opposed an "open-ended escalation of our war effort – one that would commit us to a nation building project of up to a decade." Instead, the commander in chief envisioned "at reasonable cost" lesser efforts "to secure our interests.[106]

Thus, the Obama Pentagon now moved away from the McChrystal "population-centric" counterinsurgency paradigm. It doubled down on forming local defense units. The Afghan security forces were to protect villages and territory, thereby freeing the United States to hunt down al Qaeda and other terrorist bands. And in the longer run, the Afghanized armed forces would permit the United States and ISAF to withdraw all of their combat troops, perhaps leaving only a residual training and advising mission for some undetermined time.

Transitioning to an Afghan-led defense posture began in earnest in 2011 and was largely completed by December, 2014. Early in 2015, NATO unveiled its Resolute Support Mission; it numbered 16,500 soldiers, to train, advise, and enable the Afghan security forces and defense institutions.[107] Thus, the American-led ISAF put Afghanistan on the path toward full ownership of its own counter-militancy protection. From almost the start, the Obama White House's opposed a blank check to Karzai, the Afghan president, and insisted on reforms in the Kabul government to eliminate corruption and improve governing practices. Obama's message was often delivered without making any appreciable headway.[108] Thus, White House stressed its strategy for reducing the number of US forces and turning the war over to Kabul.

Obama's scaled-down strategy succeeded only in bequeathing a deteriorating war to the incoming White House occupant, not fundamentally different than he had inherited except longer in duration. The forty-fourth president's policy led to a stalemate. The Kabul government held the major urban centers, while the Taliban insurgents governed or contested nearly 50 percent of the countryside.[109] Additionally, the emphasis on getting out of the conflict likewise abdicated the fight against al Qaeda. In his 2009 Afghan War speech, Obama stated his objectives "to disrupt, dismantle, and defeat al Qaeda in Afghanistan and Pakistan, and to prevent its capacity to threaten America and our allies in the future."[110] There were scant provisions made for disrupting, dismantling, and destroying the al Qaeda as the White House edged toward the exits.

Over the years, some Washington lawmakers as well as members of the general public wearied of the protracted Afghan fighting without any foreseeable endpoint. President Obama's steady drawdown of military forces, matched by NATO and other partners, deepened the sense of futility and disenchantment with a war in a faraway land. Yet, more Americans gave the conflict little thought. One poll found that Afghanistan failed to make it into their top twenty-five concerns.[111]

7.10   The War Is Passed to Donald Trump

Like his predecessor, Donald J. Trump spoke out against forever wars while on the 2016 presidential trail. Candidate Trump campaigned on getting out of Afghanistan and other war zones such as Iraq and Syria. Once in the Oval Office, the former businessman listened to his generals and upped the number of US troops in Afghanistan, bringing the total to over 16,000 service members by the end of 2017. But unlike his predecessor, Trump refrained from micromanaging military operations. He lifted Obama's restraints placed on warfighters and commanders in the field to wage battle against adversaries. As a result, the pace of combat operations quickened.

The forty-fifth president laid out a strategy for Afghanistan and South Asia in a speech at Fort Myer in Virginia on August 21, 2017. He enumerated several pillars to include a "shift from a time-based approach to one based on conditions" and to calling out Pakistan for sheltering "organizations that try every single day to kill our people." He called for further developing a "strategic partnership with India" for its "important contributions to stability in Afghanistan." He envisioned a possible "political settlement that includes elements of the Taliban." He stressed: "We are not nation-building again."[112] Noticeably absent in Trump's remarks was an exit date for US forces.

Because the incoming commander in chief freed the Pentagon from many of the Obama-era restrictions on air strikes and the number of helicopters in Syria, the military brass could have unleashed a more muscular aerial bombardment of the Taliban, IS, and other militants. Its objective centered more on hardening the Afghan National Security Forces, which did most of the fighting and dying since Obama turned the ground war over to Kabul in 2014. The Trump Pentagon seemed uninterested in making a last stab at winning the war. Top military officers realized that the Oval Office wanted to close down the conflict.

If anything, with the fighting winding down in Syria, Afghanistan now replaced it as the most dangerous terrorist country worldwide.[113] The ANSF bore the brunt of the casualties from the roadside bombings and small-arms fire. Each day, the country suffered approximately eighty Taliban attacks on towns, highways, and security outposts, staffed mainly by police officers or marginally trained soldiers.

DoD's air strikes included the dropping of the "mother of all bombs" on an Islamic State cave complex in April 2017. In its first combat use, the GBU-43/B Massive Ordnance Air Blast flattened a tunnel system in Nangarhar Province. The estimate of IS militants killed topped a hundred but there was no way to independently confirm any numbers or specific damage from the 20,000-pound bomb.[114] Nor did the blast have any lasting impact on the insurgency's tempo. By the end of 2019, the Islamic State's stronghold in the eastern part of the country had caved in from repeated assaults by US and Afghan forces, who were joined by Taliban militias against their rival. Its fighting strength fell from 3,000 militants earlier in the year to about 300. American commanders warned that IS urban cells could still pack a deadly punch with suicide attacks in crowded spaces.[115]

While pleading for more troops and more resources, the Department of Defense settled out of necessity for a less ambitious policy of clipping the grass without eliminating the root causes. To be fair, millennial sectarianism, ethnic-chauvinism, and tribalism in ungoverned or under-served lands lacking jobs or hope for young men were not easily eradicated. In some ways, unfurling a counterterrorism strategy rather than engaging in state-building cum democracy-promoting counterinsurgencies was more practicable and much less financially expensive. Besides, installing or fostering democracy, according to more than one study, encountered reversals due to internal problems.[116] Iraq's deeply fractured parliament along sectarian lines, for example, presented no Westminster-style democratic showcase.

As a practical matter, the United States needed upright and effective central governments to govern countries, build infrastructure, adjudicate civil disputes, and reconcile internal enemies. In many developing nations, uncorrupted and modernizing regimes are in short supply. Afghan governance was marred by endemic corruption, official abuse, ministerial failures, politicized justice, and warlord turf battles that made up so much of its contemporary past.

7.11   The Taliban Come to the Table

As the war settled into a stalemate, the Taliban opened an office in Doha, Qatar, in 2013 to claim international recognition as representing the Islamic Emirate of Afghanistan. Hamid Karzai bristled at the symbolism of state sovereignty and refused to negotiate with the Doha-based representatives. The Afghan president even suspended for a time discussions with Washington on a strategic agreement for a post-2014 security relationship, when the United States temporarily ceased active combat operations to facilitate Taliban talks. In time, Karzai came around, acknowledging his weak hand and need for America's shoring up the Afghan military, economic, and diplomatic position. The Qatar talks led to no swift breakthrough in a settlement. In time, the Taliban diplomatic wing met with American diplomats while rejecting negotiations with representatives from President Ashraf Ghani (who won election in 2014), because they considered them just American lackeys. They wanted exclusive one-on-one talks with the power that truly mattered – the United States.

After Trump settled deeper into the White House, he showed growing impatience with the then seventeen-year-old insurgency. US diplomats kick-started negotiations including direct American talks with the Taliban starting in September 2018. The State Department appointed Zalmay Khalilzad, an Afghan-American diplomat, to serve as special representative for Afghanistan reconciliation. The former ambassador to Iraq and Afghanistan succeeded eventually in reaching an agreement, but not before months of continuous warfare and many ups and downs in the negotiations.

The United States mostly wanted security from terrorism hatched in a post-American Afghanistan. Senior military and civilian officials distrusted the Taliban leaders to keep their word to bar al Qaeda and other terrorist networks from basing themselves in the mountain-topped country. Another sticking point arose from Pentagon demands for continued use of two military bases within the country to strike al Qaeda cells planning attacks on the American homeland. The Taliban regarded US forces based at the country's largest installation in Bagram and at the vital Shorabak hub as a foreign occupation. Located forty miles from Kabul, Bagram's long runways accommodated the landing of any aircraft. Shorabak, situated in southern Helmand province, the world's foremost producer of opium, accounted for the most foreign casualties in the protracted conflict.

Negotiations also bogged down temporarily over the Taliban demands for the release of some 5,000 prisoners and implementation of Sharia, or Islamic law. President Ghani objected to concessions without his government's participation in the talks. The Trump White House abruptly pulled the plug on the diplomatic dialogue after a Taliban attack killed a civilian contractor in September 2019. Upon resurrecting the peace talks, special envoy Khalilzad hammered out a withdrawal agreement that the parties signed on February 29, 2020. It called for a US military departure by May 2021, although US interlocutors contended that decamping was based on the Taliban upholding the deal. Purposely, the negotiations excluded the elected government sitting in Kabul, because the Taliban opposed it.[117]

Other than Taliban chiefs and their sympathizers, no outsider had confidence that the terms would be lived up to by the insurgents. By this time, American public opinion overwhelmingly came down on the side of militarily leaving Afghanistan and Iraq. One poll recorded 76 percent of respondents "strongly supported" or "somewhat support" bringing home US troops.[118] The Washington administration keenly understood the domestic sentiments as it moved toward greater retrenchment from America's longest war after the presidential election in November 2020. Trump also wanted to make good on his pledge to end the forever wars in Afghanistan, Iraq, and elsewhere, something he failed to do.

Shortly after the Qatar peace talks resumed at the end of 2019, the recently retired Central Command chief, Joseph Votel, speculated that the Afghan conflict could have been ended on American terms in 2002, when "al Qaeda was dispersed and the Taliban shattered." That failure led to others. The four-star general summarized what went wrong in the intervening years. He noted American errors and the war's vicissitudes that contributed to a stalemate: "one failed strategy after another, each for identifiable reasons: diverted attention, lack of military resources, loss of political will, arbitrary timelines, a resurgent and externally supported Taliban, fatigue and severe internal problems within the Afghan government."[119] It will take a lengthy effort by military specialists to parse this catalog of missteps to arrive at a more complete understanding of why the conflict ended the way it did.

From his presidential candidacy to his first steps in the White House, Trump displayed at best an impatience with the Afghanistan war, if not a downright eagerness to leave the country. In one of his ubiquitous Tweets, the commander in chief expressed his frustration with the entire US enterprise, stating: "except at the beginning, we never really fought to win."[120] This misstatement neglected the early triumph in vanquishing and ousting the Taliban from power. It ignored the years of exertions. And finally, it trivializes the sacrifice of more than 2,500 US deaths and about 1,000 coalition soldiers killed in Operation Enduring Freedom. As a critique about the absence of a winning strategy on the ground, the presidential comment was more accurate.

Washington administrations never came up with a military or non-military game plan to neutralize the militants' sanctuaries in Pakistan or deny their militias outside aid. There is no gainsaying the unquestionable significance of the role played by Islamabad in allowing sanctuaries for the Taliban, al Qaeda, and the Haqqani group. In a comprehensive RAND study entitled *How Insurgencies End*, the authors concluded that "Mao, Giap, and most modern COIN theorists concur that insurgent sanctuary correlates with insurgent victory."[121] These cross-border havens minimized the odds of a US victory. Yet the sanctuary issue was never properly addressed by the United States.

Victory itself was never clearly articulated, either. Over the years, White Houses and Pentagons spoke of attacking US terrorist enemies, obliterating al Qaeda, and crushing the Taliban so they could not take over Afghanistan. One strategy expert concluded during the Trump era that the president and his top general in Afghanistan voiced a "mixture of ends, ways, and means, and not a clear picture of what victory in Afghanistan should look like."[122] Couple this factor with the frequent turnover of senior US officers in charge of the Afghan war and the deleterious consequences the rotations had on warfighting policies. Since the start of intervention until 2016, there have been eighteen commanding generals in charge of the overall campaign effort.[123] Social scientist Nadia Schadlow, writing about the revolving door among top military officers, underlined that "across the three lines of effort (political, security, and reconstruction) changes in leadership and individuals, command relationships, and organizations made the continuity necessary to address problems nearly impossible to achieve."[124]

Set aside the cavalcade of dismal reports, extended length, shortcomings, and Sisyphean calculus of COIN and instead concentrate on the crucial fact that the United States and its coalition partners denied

Afghan territory from being used to launch another 9/11-syle attack on American shores. The Pentagon's interventions into Afghanistan and other terrorist-infiltrated countries succeeded in blocking, dismantling, or keeping a lid on American-bound attacks. A retrenchment of US military units from Afghanistan and other battlefields cast doubts about America's homeland security. Qualms about America's strategy and endurance also swelled when General Mark Milley spoke in the closing weeks of 2020 that after twenty years in Afghanistan: "we've achieved a modicum of success." The Joint Chief of Staff chairman added: "We have been in a condition of strategic stalemate where the government of Afghanistan was never going to militarily defeat the Taliban, and the Taliban … is never going to defeat the regime."[125] The Army general's faint praise, in fact, damned the handling of the conflict and virtually justified Trump's call to end this forever war and Biden's order to do so.

Well before the Qatar agreement, concerns surfaced about the capability of Afghan forces to stand alone against the Taliban and IS-K insurgents. Afghanistan's premiere unit, the Afghan Special Security Forces (ASSF), still lacked total independence from reliance on their American partners during combat missions. The ASSF, according to a government watchdog report, conducted only 43 percent of their operations independently in 2019. The ASSF operators did hold their own by denying anti-government elements from achieving "significant territorial gains during the reporting period." But too many of the ground actions were "coalition enabled operations" rather than sole ASSF achievements.[126] The Afghan's continuing reliance on the Pentagon bred little confidence in the Kabul government's survivability, when the US military completely pulled up stakes and left. At the beginning of 2021, less than one-third of the country's 400 districts remained fully under the central government's control. Without prolonged outside military and financial resources, the Kabul government could soon fall prey to the Taliban, Haqqani, and al Qaeda, which could return Afghanistan to a terrorist haven for attacks on the West.

After the signing of the Doha agreement, the United States pulled out 7,500 troops, leaving some 5,000 at the tail end of 2020. Then the Trump White House cut this number to 2,500 troops in January, ahead of the newly elected Joe Biden administration taking office. Incoming President Biden lost little time before ordering all remaining US combat troops withdrawn from Afghanistan. He set the date for this retreat as September 11, 2021 – the twenty-year anniversary of the 9/11 terrorist attack, which initiated the Afghan intervention. Seven thousand NATO and allied forces will also have departed when the Pentagon airlifts out the last of the dwindling US contingent. When that happens, Afghanistan will stand denuded of foreign armies for the first time in four decades. Generals and civilian experts, such as David Petraeus and Marine General Frank McKenzie, the commander of the US Central Command, spoke up against the Biden withdrawal decision. They anticipated a return of Taliban rule and terrorist bases within the country.

Peace will probably not ensue, but the return of Taliban rule and terrorist bases are more likely outcomes from the American departure. Much depends on the kind and degree of support provided to embattled Kabul. It was often mentioned that without private contractors to service the fledgling Afghan air wing, the planes will not fly for close air support, transportation, or evacuation of wounded government troops. The eventual fall of Kabul to the Taliban and their auxiliaries cannot be ruled out. Therefore, widespread trepidation in the country and beyond greeted Biden's order to abandon Afghanistan. The Taliban's return to power would entail a deathblow to the foreign-funded progress in expanding the middle class, educational opportunities, health care, and women's rights in schooling and office-holding.

7.12 How This Ends for the United States

A resurgence of civil war involving warlords and militias seems all too likely to erupt, dragging the country back to its immediate post-Soviet era. Ethnic fragmentation is possibility. The Afghan Tajiks, for instance, have carved out a separate enclave in the country's north. To forestall a resuscitation of al Qaeda's terrorism-making activities, the United States might return to covert CIA operations. From the start of the Afghan war, CIA paramilitaries trained indigenous units to kill or capture Taliban insurgents. These Counterterrorism Pursuit Teams (CTPT) earned a reputation for effectiveness and ruthlessness. Critics referred to them as the "CIA's 3,000-man covert arm," as described by journalist Bob Woodward. Authorized by George W. Bush, these units "were a paid, trained and functioning tool of the CIA."[127]

Overseen by the Agency's SAD, some teams were known by local names, such as the Khost Pursuit Force (as named for the eastern province). The Pursuit Teams infiltrated across the border into Pakistan to carry out deadly raids against Taliban fighters, who took sanctuary there. Along the with Obama administration's narrowed focus on eliminating terrorists rather than nation-building endeavors, the CTPT honed their man-hunting skills to remove insurgents from the battlefield.[128] The transition to the Donald Trump presidency translated into no diminution in the paramilitaries' lethal actions, now concentrated in the disputed Khost and Nangarhar provinces.[129] Additionally, 20,000 well-trained Afghan army commandos are likely to carry on the war, either fighting in military units or joining up with warlords, who are certain to reemerge as violent powerbrokers.

When the US and coalition militaries pull out of Afghanistan, it is highly doubtful that the Central Intelligence Agency will follow suit, despite the demands by the Taliban for it to leave. Keeping watch on a resurgent al Qaeda is reason enough for lingering in the rugged terrain. Aside from jihadi plotters, CIA paramilitaries will have little choice but to keep an eye on their direct competitors. Together with the presence of other cloak-and-dagger agencies, such as the Pakistani and Russian spy services, the CIA could revert to its pre-9/11 role of collaborating with Afghan militias and their warlord masters as the country will slip back into a rekindled civil war.

Afghanistan quite possibly will return to a crossroads between ambitious outside powers that harkens back to Kipling's era of the great game. The rivalrous British and Russian empires contended for domination in Afghanistan and neighboring lands during the nineteenth century. In the Cold War struggle, Afghanistan again became a playground of intrigue between the CIA and its local assets against the Kremlin's interference. In an updated version of this geopolitical competition, the United States could be up against Russia, and possibly Iran, China, Pakistan, or India. Because Afghanistan has been a cockpit of warring parties for centuries, it is hard to see a sudden blossoming of peace. So, its conflicts will persist – nasty, brutish, and long.

8 A Conclusion
The New Era

> One sees that when princes have thought more of amenities than arms, they have lost their states.   Niccolò Machiavelli

> A wise man in time of peace prepares for war.   Horace, *Satires*

At the dawn of the twenty-first-century's second decade, America confronts a stark world. Engaged in a dozen mini-conflicts in the Middle East, Africa, and Asia to protect the homeland from terrorism, the United States is also beset with major-power threats for the first time since the Soviet Union disappeared. The surge of China and resurgence of Russia to global-power status is matched by their aggressive provocations that endanger US interests and values. Aligned with Beijing and Moscow are the adversarial states of Iran and North Korea, whose ongoing saber rattling adds to Washington's security burdens. Either of these two wild cards is capable of triggering a regional conflict consequential enough to drag the great powers into a major war.

The immediate post–Cold War years marking Washington's undisputed military dominance and its expansive and expensive Wilsonian-inspired policies belong to history. The passing of the East-West competition gave free rein to the White House occupants to undertake militarized humanitarianism in the Caribbean, Africa, Europe, and the Middle East, where their sense of moral obligation to improve the world was on full display. In the second half of the three decades after the Berlin Wall fell, the Pentagon waged high-cost wars in Afghanistan and Iraq (for phantom WMD) and joined in numerous brush-fire counterinsurgencies via partner forces to prevent the spread of Salafi terrorism. Today, America contemplates a greatly changed international environment.

Under earlier circumstances, America's far-flung war-fighting deployments may have been indefinitely sustainable in military resources, command oversight, and intelligence bandwidth. Now, two decades after the start of the global fight against terrorism, the cumulative costs in lives and dollars seem in some minds too prohibitive to continue, particularly with the growing Sino-Russian militarism. America's desire to retrench became evident in Obama's presidency and, more so, in Trump's tenure. In fact, Trump was the first president since Jimmy Carter not to initiate conflict with any nation.

Over the preceding three-decade span, America warred, regime-changed, and imposed peace with limited thought about peer competitors or the astronomical US national debt, which is often attributed solely to heavy defense spending. One study concluded that the war on terror cost $6.4 trillion through fiscal year 2020.[1] America's national debt currently stands at $29 trillion and constitutes over 100 percent of the gross domestic product, the highest percentage since the end of World War II. All indices point to accelerating debt levels, courting economics troubles ahead.

It is important to recognize that not all of America's national debt is a result of defense spending alone. John Cogan, an authority on federal expenditures, writes: "Incredible as it may seem, entitlements have accounted for all of the growth in federal spending as a percent of GDP during the post–World War II era." By 1972, entitlement spending soared higher than defense spending; by 1987, entitlement spending exceeded the expenditures on defense and all other federal programs combined. "Entitlements have also been the prime mover of the relentless post–World War II rise in the national debt."[2] In light of America's ballooning debt, the "guns-or-butter" dilemma will become agonizingly keen in the years ahead.

Politicians and average citizens will spar over the proper allocation of tax dollars, whether to defensive armaments or expanding civilian programs, as American governments struggle to come to grips with the shifting balance of international power. Worrisome great power competition and a depleted treasury almost ensures that Washington will find it difficult not to subordinate the causes of democracy and human rights to vital US strategic interests.

8.1   The Return to Superpower Politics

Nothing so shattered the status quo of the ex-Soviet world as the astounding economic ascent of the People's Republic of China (PRC), from a dirt-poor start in the late 1970s to its current ranking as the second largest economy worldwide. The PRC's abundant wealth fueled geopolitical ambitions to offer its brand of authoritarianism as a model for other nations. To expand and consolidate its political and commercial ascendancy, Chinese leader Xi Jinping announced the Belt and Road Initiative in 2013, which represented a global blueprint for the construction of roads, railways, and other transportation infrastructure to spur trade, development, and connectivity in seventy countries and international organizations.[3]

To advance its geostrategic agenda, China also embarked on a momentous weapons buildup by stealing secrets about US missiles, aircraft, and warships. It purchased arms from Russian manufacturers as its own industries raced ahead to turn out knock-off platforms.[4] The PRC's spanking-new aircraft carriers, recently constructed submarines, and state-of-the-art hypersonic missiles have been deployed to convert the South China Sea into a Chinese lake. The potential for excluding or limiting non-Chinese traffic through this waterway, which carries one third of the world's shipping (valued at $3 trillion annually), constitutes a grave risk to the well-being of America and other nations.[5]

The Chinese Communist Party's obsession with negating Taiwan's autonomy has become the world's most likely flashpoint for a war drawing in the United States and China. In addition, Beijing entered into a cooperative military relationship with Moscow, in spite of border incidents and a deadly clash as recently as 1969 between the two states. During the Cold War, the two Communist titans were rivals. In recent years, the two anti-American adversaries have staged joint military and naval training exercises. Additionally, they formed the Shanghai Cooperation Organization, a proto-alliance, that roped in several Central Asian nations, as a way to exclude the United States from this vital region, as it emerges from decades of Soviet Russian rule. The Sino-Russian rapprochement flashes ominous warnings for the United States. It holds the prospect of increasing America's enemies, complicating its relations with either, and heightening risks of conflict with both, especially should the Moscow-Beijing friendship recklessly embolden one or the other power to hazard war with their mutual bête noire.

Vladimir Putin's Russia, for its part, went all out to reclaim its international status after the USSR's disintegration. Lacking anything close to China's super-charged economy, the Kremlin has resorted to deceit, subversion, intimidation, and raw power to recapture its international standing by hook or by crook. It's military tanks and pugilistic tactics hived off two restive provinces from the Republic of Georgia, with no meaningful European or US response in 2008, other than sanctions from the Bush White House, already overtaxed with Iraq War. Next, the Russian military and spy services introduced "hybrid war" – the combination of stealth invasion, local proxy forces, and international propaganda – to take over Crimea and occupy eastern Ukraine in 2014, again with no appropriate Washington or European Union answer to its aggression, aside from economic sanctions. Obama's America knuckled under rather than embracing a forward policy.

By the start of Obama's second presidential term, it was not possible to ignore a world transformed. America was no longer an unchallenged superpower. Every year since then has witnessed accumulating evidence of Russian and Chinese muscular diplomacy backed with growing military power that has eroded America's unipolar moment. The Washington foreign policy establishment now considers carefully political or strategic sensibilities held in Moscow, Beijing, or even Tehran, when it advises or advocates policy for the executive branch.[6]

China's "peaceful rise" and Russia's bellicose resurgence (coupled with Iran's militant proxies, like Hezbollah, in the Middle East and North Korea's nuclear-arms breakthroughs) cast a dark cloud on America's continued underpinning of the world order. Throughout the past three decades, Washington could pretty much arbitrate global issues without fear of a threatening peer. That historical period has been transformed as great power competition intensified in the new century. The unipolar decade beheld US interventions in Panama, Iraq, Somalia, Haiti, and the Balkans twice, plus two medium-scale wars in Afghanistan and Iraq without fear of dissipating American military power, sapping its diplomatic clout, or presenting an opening for an expansionist rival. Those conditions pertain no more. Financial burdens and disengagement sentiments among the American public further a rethinking about our overseas role. Already the three world powers – the United States, China, and Russia – have shifted into a stepped-up competition as seen in public diplomacy, official tirades, and virulent cyberattacks, all of which show no sign of abating.

The greatly transformed geopolitical environment necessitated a reorientation in US foreign and defense policy. As the world moves toward multipolarity with the ascension of China and Russia to great power status, the United States can no longer pursue its liberal hegemony while disregarding the shift in the international balance of power, because, as professor John Mearsheimer writes, "there is sure to be security competition and maybe even war." He added that the Washington "will have little choice but to adopt a realist foreign policy."[7] America's paramount imperative must be to escape from some sort of Aesopian folly of fighting a war with both China and Russia at the same time.

8.2   Forging a New Strategy While Keeping the Old One

Top Pentagon and West Wing officials in the Trump administration recognized the realigned global security forces and drafted strategic reassessments to take into account the new international reality. Under the direction of Lieutenant General H. R. McMaster, the president's National Security Council released in late 2017 its National Security Strategy to Advance America's Interests, which singled out as the key challenge "the revisionist powers, such as, China and Russia, that use technology, propaganda, and coercion to shape a world antithetical to our interests and values."[8]

A month later, the Defense Department issued a similar assessment for its National Defense Strategy, under the supervision of Jim Mattis, the defense secretary. This DoD statement, subtitled "Sharpening the American Military's Competitive Edge," declared that America's Joint Forces faced "a security environment more complex and volatile than any we have experienced in recent memory." The Pentagon's 2018 strategy clarified its understanding of the "reemergence of long-term strategic competition."

Inter-state strategic competition, not terrorism, is now the primary concern in US national security. China is a strategic competitor using predatory economics to intimidate its neighbors while militarizing features in the South China Sea. Russia has violated the borders of nearby nations and pursues veto power over the economic, diplomatic, and security decisions of its neighbors.[9]

Given the new strategic marching orders, the Trump Pentagon began refocusing troop training, weapons purchases, and Joint Force deployments toward a deter-and-contain approach to the materializing great-power rivalry. DoD rotated US tanks, warships, and aircraft to the Black Sea, Eastern Europe, and the Baltic for military exercises with allied armies. It has also stepped up naval ship sailings in the South China Sea. Although President Trump sometimes mentioned drastic cuts, he carried out slow-paced downsizing of troops stationed in Afghanistan, Syria, Iraq, and Trans-Sahel Africa. So, the Pentagon remains involved in these places as well as others.

Mark T. Esper, who replaced Jim Mattis as defense secretary, was unable to achieve a thorough reorientation of the US Armed Forces in line with the West Wing's dramatic geopolitical thinking before he was forced out of his job in the last months of the Trump administration. The Pentagon itself has had some second thoughts about the wisdom of a complete retrenchment. Pulling out of Africa and the Middle East would attenuate the fight against Islamic terrorism while weakening US influence at the time when Russia, China, and Iran are rushing to fill any gaps. Congress is justifiably concerned about abandoning counterterrorism battles in remote spaces.[10]

Increasingly, there have been calls to close down the endless wars and bring home American military forces so that the United States can refocus entirely on its great-power rivals, in addition to boosted spending on domestic priorities. Reshuffling US troops to address new dangers promises to leave security voids that American partner forces alone might have difficulty filling. Ungoverned lands allow terrorists to set up launching pads for attacks on America or its allies. Staying put in counterterrorism fights, critics claim, diverts the DoD from countering China and Russia. Additionally, the two different threat scenarios require defense forces to train and equip for diverse missions and to prepare for multiple transportation or logistical requirements.

Aside from these operational-level issues, the main dilemma revolves around the risk to homeland security. No president wants to be accused of leaving the country unready for another 9/11-like catastrophe by permitting a Salafi jihadi group to take up residency in a nation beset by terrorist bands. Another Osama bin Laden could plot and carry out a sequel to the World Trade Center destruction. That distressing drama played out for George W. Bush. The 9/11 president came in for stinging criticism over a failure to heed warnings of imminent terrorism. One unsparing journalist concluded that "in the face of numerous warnings of an impending attack, Bush did nothing."[11]

In today's vitriolic news media climate, such a condemnatory comment from a member of the Fourth Estate can be shrugged off as an illustration of fairly typical press-hyped sensationalism. But the sober, official 9/11 Commission Report stopped just short of blaming George Bush for his inaction prior to the airline hijackings. It did characterize the milieu leading up to the terrorist attack as "The System Was Blinking Red."[12]

Therefore, the new commander in chief, Joseph R. Biden Jr., or future ones can be justified in hesitating to order a total retreat from the nation's counterterrorism operations, lest the pullout result in another nightmare on American soil. Leaving Afghanistan, the longest war, has proved to be a frustrating process, most recently because of the Taliban's reneging on its agreed terms to cease attacks. Whatever the outcome there, it is certain to serve as a test case for other withdrawals. One thing is certain – judging by the terrorism wars in Iraq, Afghanistan, Syria, and other places, these forever wars will unlikely see a "Missouri Moment" – like Japan's surrender on the deck of the USS *Missouri* battleship, bringing World War II to a conclusion and to a long peace in the former battleground states.

Moreover, contemporary counterterrorism points toward persistent "lawn mowing," since removing the socioeconomic roots of extremism is a herculean task and a stratospherically expensive course, even if it could be carried out in hostile nations. The hoped for intermediate end-state of forever conflicts is one in which the insurgent terrorists are unable to threaten the United States or its allies with attacks or to destabilize beleaguered nations or neighbors. Decades away, some insurgencies may burn themselves out, as happened in Northern Ireland and the Basque region of Spain.[13] But in the immediate time-span, no total pullout can be safely contemplated. Redeploying elsewhere the troops battling terrorist networks would also open the Middle East region to China's political influence and to Iran's aggressive tactics as well as its proxy militias in Lebanon, Iraq, Syria, and Yemen.

8.3   Counterterrorism in the New Era

Yet the United States cannot remain exclusively wedded to yesterday's defense policy in light of China's and Russia's militarized assertiveness. Weakness confronting 1930s-style machtpolitik invites aggression. The United States must prepare to deter or defeat peer-level threats. So, the Pentagon will need to reallocate more resources to fending off Sino-Russian truculence while protecting the nation's flank from distant terrorist havens, all the while coping with proposed cutbacks in funding for Special Operations Forces, which conduct the lion's share of counterterrorism missions.[14] A looming terrorist threat from desolate corners still haunts terrorism experts.[15]

Except for Afghanistan and Iraq, the US armed forces in the Philippines, Syria, Yemen, and the African Sahel nations are light-footprint deployments of highly trained military instructors, Special Ops teams, and aerial drone operators, mostly numbering in the mid-hundreds of personnel. Outgoing President Trump roughly halved the 5,000 troops each in Afghanistan and Iraq and transferred a "majority" of military personnel out of Somalia to Kenya, Djibouti, and offshore warships, where their air strikes continued to hit Salafi jihadis in the Horn country.

Their reduced presence and counterterrorist operations made for much less hazardous exposure. Casualties among Americans are few and annual financial costs low "at roughly 0.3 percent of DoD's personnel and budgetary resources."[16] One cost concerns the morale of the overtaxed SOF who are in danger of being worn out by frequent deployments with inadequate "dwell" periods for rest, recovery, and retraining. This issue is best handled by the US Special Operations Command (USSOCOM), which has addressed – and continues to address – it. Together with presiding over budgetary matters, technology development, and logistics, the USSOCOM was better suited to tackle morale and political issues than its subordinate Joint Special Operations

Command, which functioned as the sword arm of the secretive command.

The small-foot-print conflicts spanning the globe are not wars of choice, but many Americans see them that way. Preventing or disrupting terrorist bases is defense of the homeland at a distance. After 9/11, Americans saw the threat from abroad and backed the US intervention to snuff out al Qaeda in Afghanistan. Failing to unearth WMD after the Iraq incursion added to the disillusionment with foreign military deployments. As the number of interventions, albeit smaller than the Afghan invasion, expanded and their duration lengthened, popular disenchantment grew. Critics of the so-called forever wars with their tiny outposts, drones, and Special Operations Forces see a herd of white elephants, which the United States will have to feed at great expense for years.

Everyday Americans are not directly involved in the low-profile conflicts. Indeed, most citizens are emotionally detached from military engagements abroad. Those who do pay attention to foreign affairs also question the cost and value of the battles. Political leaders rarely make the case for the fight or what is at stake if the US military leaves terrorist hubs that are up and running in faraway lands. This failure of wartime leadership gave rise to bring-the-boys-home sentiments in spite of the risk of another massive terrorist attack on American territory. The United States "should invest in strategic competence," according to H. R. McMaster, a former national security adviser to President Trump. The retired Army lieutenant general added that "Educating the public about battlegrounds of today and tomorrow is an especially important task."[17]

Nor is it just the man or woman on the street who wants to reduce counterterrorism commitments. The Pentagon's upper echelons are weighing additional cuts in funds for counterterrorism operations in Africa.[18] Total funding for the Special Operations Command has hovered at $13 billion for the past three years, while new Salafi fronts have continued to open. An underreported jihadi outbreak in Mozambique heralds the proliferation of violent extremism up along the Swahili coast from that southeast African country. The seacoast town of Mocimboa da Praia temporarily fell to Islamist gunmen from an offshoot of the Islamic State.[19] The Biden Pentagon recognized the danger and dispatched a Green Beret squad to train local marines in counterinsurgency tactics. The insurgents, who have tapped into local grievances, will not be easy to eradicate. In a word, DoD will be unable to walk away from its "9/11 wars" in the near term.

Staying out of Iraq- or Afghan-sized wars is prudent given the new geostrategic landscape. Such wars consume resources and national attention now needed to deter America's two rivalrous competitors. Rather than a choice between disengaging and sapping American strength, the United States will have to wage economical conflicts. Washington cannot rely exclusively on homeland-based law enforcement, security teams, or the intelligence community for protection from international terrorism. The Pentagon needs to keep its strategy of a forward presence in order to project a forward defense "over there." At present, the White House must navigate carefully between the Scylla of too much counterterrorism and the Charybdis of too much Sino-Russian deterrence, lest unduly emphasizing one threat over the other could result in a catastrophe.

History is only modestly helpful as a guide to action. The American frontier wars are little more than a quasi-analogy for America's counterterrorism engagements today. Those conflicts lasted from the arrival of the first colonists to the early twentieth century, although they captured the popular imagination after the US Civil War. Settlers and Native Americans fought over the possession of land, not over Salafi ideology. The fighting took place close to army forts or settlements, not thousands of miles from the continental United States.

Still, the hit-and-run nature of today's warfare harkens back to something akin to the frontier era in America's past when the US Cavalry fought Native American tribes across the Great Plains. Company-sized troops of horse-riding soldiers tracked and struck back at an elusive enemy who was familiar, even comfortable, with forbidding natural environments. The horse-mounted troopers recruited scouts from the indigenous tribes. Then as now, they also had to navigate complex intra-tribal relations in efforts to divide and defeat native resistance. Fighting in the American West existed as a separate chapter in the nation's history. It holds some parallels to today's counterterrorism fight in distant and inaccessible terrain. The "War on Terror," as described by author Robert D. Kaplan in *Imperial Grunts*, "was really about taming the frontier."[20] These earlier frontier hostilities demonstrated that America fought long-running low-grade wars while getting on with the nation's business.

Yet US power is being extended today around the globe, not just west of the Mississippi as after the Civil War. Great Britain's imperial experience bears the closest resemblance to Washington's long-running, far-flung small wars in the earth's nooks and crannies. During Queen Victoria's long reign (1837–1901), British soldiers had not a single year of respite from what Rudyard Kipling, the poet of empire, called "savage wars of peace." These military expeditions started before Victoria came to the throne but "there were more of them during her sixty-four years of her reign than there had been in the previous two centuries." Their prevalence during the Victorian era "became an accepted way of life" – a normalcy with contemporary echoes.[21] Just as US troops fight nowadays, the British regiments battled in all-but-forgotten conflicts in Asia, Africa, and Arabia. For Britain, its militarism languished with imperial exhaustion, the shift in global power, and two world wars. The United States has yet to reach a similar denouement, but a reading of Edward Gibbon gives pause about a decline, if not fall, under defense burdens and internal political turmoil America confronts in this new chapter.

Notes

Introduction

1 Hannah Arendt, *On Revolution* (New York: Viking Press, 1965), page 1.

2 Franklin Foer, "The Last WASP President," *Atlantic*, December 2, 2018. www.theatlantic.com/ideas/archive/2018/12/george-hw-bush-last-wasp-president/577156. Accessed March 31, 2021.

3 Walter A. McDougall, *Promised Land, Crusader State: The American Encounter with the World since 1776* (Boston: Houghton Mifflin Company, 1997), pages 173 and 208.

4 Spencer R. Weart, *Never at War: Why Democracies Will Not Fight One Another* (New Haven: Yale University Press, 1998), pages 288–296.

5 Colin Dueck, *Age of Iron: On Conservative Nationalism* (New York: Oxford University Press, 2020), page 7.

6 A July 2019 Pew poll found that about 64 percent of US veterans think that the war in Iraq was not worth fighting, compared to 33 percent that did. For Afghanistan, 58 percent of veterans think the war was not worth fighting, and 38 percent think it was. These numbers are somewhat mirrored by the general population. See Ruth Igielnik and Kim Parker, "Majorities of U.S Veterans, Public Say Wars in Iraq and Afghanistan Were Not Worth Fighting," Fact Tank, Pew Research Center, July 10, 2019. www.pewresearch.org/fact-tank/2019/07/10/majorities-of-u-s-veterans-public-say-the-wars-in-iraq-and-afghanistan-were-not-worth-fighting/. Accessed March 31, 2021.

7 Rand Paul, "Why I Voted against the Latest Defense Budget," *American Conservative*, December 17, 2019. www.theamericanconservative.com/articles/rand-paul-why-i-voted-against-the-latest-defense-budget/. Accessed March 31, 2021.

8 "In the early 1970s, when the galloping entitlement spending roared past national defense, entitlements replaced defense as the federal budget's largest expenditure. From the early 1970s forward, the federal government's highest priority, as measured by its expenditures, would be on income transfer programs for elderly, disabled, and low-income people. National defense would stand second in line." John Cogan, *The High Cost of Good Intentions: A History of the U.S. Federal Entitlement Programs* (Stanford: Stanford University Press, 2017), page 265.

1 An End and a Beginning

1 "The Joint Operating Environment," US Joint Forces Command, February 18, 2010. https://fas.org/man/eprint/joe2010.pdf. Accessed March 31, 2021.
2 Thomas H. Henriksen, *America and the Rogue States* (New York: Palgrave, 2012), pages 19–22.
3 Charles Krauthammer, "The Unipolar Moment," *Foreign Affairs* 70, no. 1 (1991), pages 23–33.
4 John J. Mearsheimer, *The Great Delusion* (New Haven: Yale University Press, 2018), page 139.
5 Samuel Huntington, *The Clash of Civilizations and the Remaking of the World Order* (New York: Simon & Schuster Paperbacks, 2003), page 184.
6 Richard N. Haass, *The Reluctant Sheriff: The United States after the Cold War* (New York: Council of Foreign Relations, 1997), page 68.
7 Ivo H. Daalder and Michael E. O'Hanlon, *Winning Ugly: NATO's War to Save Kosovo* (New York: Brookings Institution, 2000), page 225.
8 Bernard-Henry Lévy, *The Empire and the Five Kings: America's Abdication and the Fate of the World* (New York: Henry Holt and Company, 2019), page 55.
9 Ronald Reagan, *An American Life* (New York: Simon & Schuster, 1990), page 569.
10 *Inaugural Addresses of the Presidents of the United States* (Washington, DC: US Government Publishing Office, 1989), page 347.
11 Stephen Sestanovich, *Maximalist: America in the World from Truman to Obama* (New York: Alfred A. Knopf, 2014), page 269.
12 Eric Schmitt, "The Push for Deeper Cuts in the U.S. Military," *New York Times*, January 6, 1992, page 1A.
13 "The Budget and Economic Outlook." Publication 54918, US Congressional Budget Office, 2019, Appendix F. www.cbo.gov/publication/54918. Accessed March 31, 2021.
14 George Tenet, *At the Center of the Storm: My Years at the CIA* (New York: HarperCollins, 2007), page 14.
15 Patrick E. Tyler, "U.S. Strategy Plan Calls for Insuring No Rivals Develop," *New York Times*, March 8, 1992, page A1.
16 Barton Gellman, "Keeping the U.S. First; Pentagon Would Preclude a Rival Superpower," *Washington Post*, March 11, 1992, page A1.
17 Stephan Halper and Jonathan Clarke, *America Alone: The Neo-Conservative and Global Order* (New York: Cambridge University Press, 2004), page 145; and George C. Herring, *From Colony to Superpower: U.S. Foreign Relations since 1776* (New York: Oxford University Press, 2008), page 922.
18 Alan McPherson, *A Short History of U.S. Interventions in Latin America and the Caribbean* (Chichester: Wiley Blackwell, 2016), pages 172–179.
19 Lindsey A. O'Rourke, *Covert Regime Change: America's Secret Cold War* (Ithaca: Cornell University Press, 2018), page 134.
20 See Tim Weiner, *Legacy of Ashes: The History of the CIA* (New York: Anchor Book, 2007).
21 O'Rourke, *Covert Regime Change*, pages 9–10 and 173–192.

22 Steven Hurst, *The Foreign Policy of the Bush Administration: In Search of a New World Order* (London: Cassell, 1999), page 22.

23 Bill McAllister, "Bush Vows to Press Noriega," *Washington Post*, December 23, 1988, page A8.

24 James A. Baker III, *The Politics of Diplomacy: Revolution, War, & Peace, 1989–1992* (New York: G. P. Putnam's Sons, 1995), page 177.

25 Colin Powell, *My American Journey* (New York: Random House, 1995), page 418.

26 Tom Kenworthy and Joe Pichirallo, "Bush Clears Plan to Topple Noriega," *Washington Post*, November 17, 1989, page A1.

27 Henriksen, *America and the Rogue States*, pages 19–25.

28 Abraham D. Sofaer, "The Legality of the United States Action in Panama," *Columbia Journal of Transnational Law* 29 (1991), pages 284–285.

29 Baker, *The Politics of Diplomacy*, page 189.

30 Powell, *My American Journey*, page 425.

31 Ibid.

32 National Military Strategy of the United States, January 1, 1992. https://history.defense.gov/Portals/70/Documents/nms/nms1992.pdf?ver=2014-06-25-123420-723. Accessed March 31, 2021.

33 Helmuth von Moltke, *Moltke on the Art of War: Selected Writings*, ed. Daniel J. Hughes (San Francisco: Presidio Press, 1995), page 92.

34 Lawrence A. Yates, "Operation JUST CAUSE in Panama City, December 1989," in *Urban Operations: An Historical Casebook* (Fort Leavenworth: Combat Studies Institute, Command & General Staff College, 2002), page 17.

35 Nadia Schadlow, *War and the Art of Governance: Consolidating Combat Success into Political Victory* (Washington, DC: George Washington University Press, 2017), page 203.

36 Margaret E. Scranton, *The Noriega Years: U.S.–Panamanian Relations, 1981–1990* (Boulder: Lynne Rienner, 1991), pages 207–208.

37 Kyle Rompfer, "Soldiers Recall Combat Jump Into Panama on 30th Anniversary," *Army Times*, December 20, 2019. www.armytimes.com/news/your-army/2019/12/20/soldiers-recall-combat-jumps-into-panama-on-30th-anniversary/. Accessed March 31, 2021.

38 John T. Carney and Benjamin F. Schemmer, *No Room for Error: The Covert Operations of America's Special Tactic Units from Iran to Afghanistan* (New York: Ballantine Books, 2002), page 110.

39 Yates, "Operation JUST CAUSE in Panama City, December 1989," page 17.

40 John Lindsay-Poland, *Emperors in the Jungle: The Hidden History of the U.S. in Panama* (Durham: Duke University Press, 2003), page 118.

41 D'Haeseleer, "Paving the Way for Baghdad," page 1210.

42 Baker, *The Politics Diplomacy*, page 184.

43 D'Haeseleer, "Paving the Way for Baghdad," page 1214.

44 Ted Galen Carpenter, "New War Order," *Cato Institute*. December 17, 2009. www.cato.org/publications/commentary/new-war-order. Accessed March 31, 2021.

2 The Persian Gulf War and Its Aftermath

1 Joel Brinkley, "Israel Puts a Satellite in Orbit a Day after Threat by Iraqis," *New York Times*, April 4, 1990, page A3.
2 James A. Baker III, *The Politics of Diplomacy: Revolution, War, and Peace* (New York: G. P. Putnam's Sons, 1995), page 263. Some mid-level Air Force officers anticipated a war against Iraq and prepared for it. See Matt Dietz, "Toward a More Nuanced View of Airpower and Operation Desert Storm," *War on the Rocks*, January 6, 2001. https://warontherocks.com/2021/01/toward-a-more-nuanced-view-of-airpower-and-operation-desert-storm/. Accessed April 3, 2021.
3 Michael R. Gordon, "U.S. Deploys Air and Sea Forces after Iraq Threatens 2 Neighbors," *New York Times*, July 25, 1990, page A1.
4 George H. W. Bush and Brent Scowcroft, *A World Transformed* (New York: Alfred A. Knopf, 1998), page 311.
5 Elaine Sciolino, "Envoy's Testimony Is Assailed," *New York Times*, July 13, 1991, page A1.
6 John F. Burns, "A Cadillac and Other Plunder," *New York Times*, December 30, 2002, page A1.
7 Bush and Scowcroft, *A World Transformed*, page 332.
8 Ibid., pages 346–347.
9 Rick Atkinson, *Crusade: The Untold Story of the Persian Gulf War* (Boston: Houghton Mifflin, 1993), pages 81–82.
10 Yevgeny Primakov, *Russia and the Arabs: Behind the Scenes in the Middle East from the Cold War to the Present* (New York: Basic Books, 2009), page 307.
11 Ibid., page 318.
12 Margaret Thatcher, *The Downing Street Years* (New York: HarperCollins, 1993), page 824.
13 Bush and Scowcroft, *A World Transformed*, page 429.
14 United Nations Security Council Resolution 687 (April 3, 1991), paragraphs 11–13.
15 Bush and Scowcroft, *A World Transformed*, page 484.
16 George J. Veith, *Black April: The Fall of South Vietnam, 1973–1975* (New York: Encounter Books, 2012), pages 493–499.
17 Collin Powell, *My American Journey* (New York: Random House, 1995), page 512.
18 Cited by George F. Will, "What to Ask the Nominee," *Washington Post*, November 17, 2004, page A27.
19 James Mann, *The Rise of the Vulcans: The History of the Bush War Cabinet* (New York: Viking, 2002), page 192.
20 Rick Fawn and Raymond Hinnebucsh, *The Iraq War: Causes and Consequences* (Boulder: Lynne Rienner, 2006), pages 153–160.
21 Stefan Halper and Jonathan Clarke, *America Alone: The Neo-Conservatives and the Global Order* (Cambridge: Cambridge University Press, 2004), pages 72–73.
22 Nicholas D. Kristof, "U.S. Cyclone Relief Forces Reach Bangladesh Port," *New York Times*, May 16, 1991, page A12.

23 Mark Sussman, "Celebrating the New World Order: Festival and War in New York," *The Drama Review* 39, no. 2 (Summer 1995), pages 147–195.

24 Ibid.

25 Geoffrey Parker, ed., "Epilogue: The Future of Western Warfare," in *The Cambridge History of* Warfare (Cambridge: Cambridge University Press, 2020), page 433.

26 Maureen Dowd, "War in the Gulf: The President; Bush, Scorning Offer, Suggests Iraqis Topple Hussein," *New York Times*, February 16, 1991, page 6.

27 "The Presidential News Conference on the Persian Gulf Conflict," Washington, DC, March 1, 1991, C-SPAN, "States of Events in the Persian Gulf." www.c-span.org/video/?16868-1/status-events-persian-gulf. Accessed March 31, 2021.

28 "Bush Statement: Excerpts From 2 Statements by Bush on Iraq's Proposal for Ending Conflict," *New York Times*, February 16, 1991, page 5A.

29 Tim Weiner, *Legacy of Ashes: The History of the CIA* (New York: Anchor Book, 2007), page 495.

30 David Ignatius, "The CIA And the Coup That Wasn't," *Washington Post*, May 16, 2003, page A20.

31 Michael R. Gordon and Bernard E. Trainor, *The Generals' War: The Inside Story of the Conflict in the Gulf* (Boston: Little, Brown, 1995), page 37.

32 George H. W. Bush, "Address before a Joint Session of Congress (September 11, 1990)," The Miller Center, University of Virginia. http://millercenter.org/president/bush/speeches/speech-3425. Accessed March 31, 2021.

33 Address to the United Nations General Assembly by George H. W. Bush, September 23, 1991, US Department of State. https://2009-2017.state.gov/p/io/potusunga/207269.htm. Accessed March 31, 2021.

34 Patrick Buchanan, *Suicide of a Superpower* (New York: Thomas Dunne Books, 2011), page 467.

3 Wars Other Than War

* Fred Kaplan, *The Insurgents: David Petraeus and the Plot to Change the American Way of War* (New York: Simon & Schuster, 2013), page 46. This is Kaplan's phrase.

1 Barbara Conry, "US 'Global Leadership': A Euphemism for World Policeman," CATO Institute, February 5, 1997. www.cato.org/publications/policy-analysis/us-global-leadership-euphemism-world-policeman. Accessed March 31, 2021.

2 "National Debt by Year Compared to GDP and Major Events," *The Balance*. www.thebalance.com/national-debt-by-year-compared-to-gdp-and-major-events-3306287. Accessed March 31, 2021.

3 Fred Kaplan, "The End of the Age of Petraeus," *Foreign Affairs* 92, no. 1 (January–February 2013), pages 75–90.

4 Bill Clinton, *My Life* (New York: Alfred A. Knopf, 2004), page 526.

5 Robert S. Litwak, *Rogue States and U.S. Foreign Policy: Containment after the Cold War* (Washington, DC: Woodrow Wilson Center Press, 2000), page 126.

6 For an insider's account of the failed rebellion, see Robert Baer, *See No Evil* (New York: Three Rivers Press, 2002), page 177–205.

7 A transcript of President William Jefferson Clinton's Inaugural Address was reprinted as "We Force the Spring," *New York Times*, January 21, 1993, page A11.

8 Richard W. Steward, *The United States Army in Somalia, 1992–1994* (United States Army Center of Military History). https://history.army.mil/brochures/Somalia/Somalia.htm. Accessed March 31, 2021.

9 Michael R. Gordon, "Christopher, in Unusual Cable, Defends State Dept." *New York Times*, June 16, 1993, page A13.

10 Colin L. Powell, *My American Journey* (New York, Random House, 1995), page 586.

11 Harlan K. Ullman, *Anatomy of Failure: Why America Loses Every War It Starts* (Annapolis: Naval Institute Press, 2017), page 130.

12 Mark Bowden, *Black Hawk Down: A Story of Modern War* (New York: New American Library, 1999), page 43.

13 Madeleine K. Albright, "Myths of Peace-Keeping," Statement before the Subcommittee on International Security, International Organizations, and Human Rights of the House Committee on Foreign Affairs, June 24, 1993, cited in US *Department of State Dispatch* 4, no. 26 (June 24, 1993), page 46.

14 Walter Clarke and Jeffrey Herbst, "Somalia and the Future of Humanitarian Intervention," in *Learning from Somalia*, ed. Walter Clarke and Jeffrey Herbst (Boulder: Westview Press, 1997), page 129.

15 Elizabeth Drew, *On the Edge: The Clinton Presidency* (New York: Simon & Schuster, 1994), page 138.

16 Robert G. Patman, "Disarming Somalia: The Contrasting Fortunes of United States and Australian Peacekeepers during United Nations Intervention, 1992–1993," *African Affairs* 96, no. 385 (October 1997), page 518.

17 Eric Schmitt, "Somalia's First Lesson for Military Is Caution," *New York Times* (March 5, 1995), page B15.

18 Kaplan, *The Insurgents*, page 45.

19 William G. Boykin, *Never Surrender: A Soldiers Journey to the Crossroads of Faith and Freedom* (New York: Hachette Books Group, 2008), pages 281–292.

20 Rowan Scarborough, "Mogadishu Lessons Help Foil Saddam's Strategy," *Washington Times*, April 8, 2003, page 1.

21 Marc Sageman, *Understanding Terror Networks* (Philadelphia: University of Pennsylvania Press, 2004), page 48.

22 Todd South, "The Battle of Mogadishu 25 Years Later: How the Fateful Fight Changed Combat Operations, *Army Times*, October 3, 2018. www.armytimes.com/news/your-army/2018/10/02/the-battle-of-mogadishu-25-years-later-how-the-fateful-fight-changed-combat-operations/. Accessed March 31, 2021.

23 Drew, *On the Edge*, page 139.

24 Douglas Jehl, "US Shifts Troops to Defensive Role in Somalia Mission," *New York Times*, October 20, 1993, page A1.

25 Donatella Lorch, "Last of the US Troops Leave Somalia; What Began as Mission of Mercy Closes with Little Ceremony," *New York Times*, March 26, 1994, page A1.

26 Susan Tomson, *Rwanda: From Genocide to Precarious Peace* (New Haven: Yale University Press, 2018), page 4.

27 L. R. Melvern, *A People Betrayed: The Role of the West in Rwanda's Genocide* (London: Zed Books, 2000), page 190.

28 John J. Mearsheimer, *The Great Delusion: Liberal Dreams and International Realities* (New Haven: Yale University Press, 2018), page 154.

29 George Bush Speech to the American Enterprise Institute, February 22, 2003, *The Guardian*. www.theguardian.com/world/2003/feb/27/usa.iraq2. Accessed March 31, 2021.

30 David Lauter, "Clinton Blasts Bush's Foreign Policy Record." *Los Angeles Times*, August 14, 1992, page A1.

31 Robert Fatton Jr., *Haiti's Predatory Republic: The Unending Transition to Democracy* (Boulder: Lynne Rienner, 2002), page 93.

32 Doyle McManus and Robin Wright, "U.S. Tried Covert Action to Rid Haiti of Rulers," *Los Angeles Times*, September 16, 1994, page A1.

33 Mearsheimer, *The Great Delusion*, pages 152–156.

34 Douglas Jehl, "From Haiti, Images of a Foreign Policy Success," *New York Times*, April 11, 1995, page A4.

35 Bill Clinton, 1996 State of the Union Address. https://clintonwhitehouse4 .archives.gov/WH/New/other/sotu.html. Accessed March 31, 2021.

36 Walter E. Kretchik, Robert F. Baumann, and John F. Fishel, *A Concise History of the US Army in Operation Uphold Democracy* (Fort Leavenworth: US Army Command and General Staff College Press, 1998), page 122. https://apps.dtic .mil/dtic/tr/fulltext/u2/a528265.pdf. Accessed March 31, 2021.

37 Noel Malcolm, *Bosnia: A Short History* (New York: New York University, 1994), page 20.

38 James A. Baker III, *The Politics of Diplomacy: Revolution, War, and Peace* (New York: G. P. Putnam's Sons, 1995), page 651.

39 Michael Kelly, "Surrender and Blame," *New Yorker*, December 19, 1994, page 45.

40 David Gardner, "EC Dashes into Its Own Backyard," *Financial Times*, July 1, 1991, page 2.

41 John Darnton, "Clinton's Offer of Troops Pleases Europe" *New York Times*, June 2, 1995. Page A11.

42 For an account of European diplomacy, see Stanley Hoffman, "Yugoslavia: Implications for Europe and European Institutions," in *The World and Yugoslavia's Wars*, ed. Richard H. Ullman (New York: Council on Foreign Relations, 1996), pages 97–121.

43 "U.S. Support for CSCE," *US Department of State Dispatch* 3, no. 28 (July 13, 1992), page 1.

44 Thomas L. Friedman, "Bosnia Reconsidered," *New York Times*, April 8, 1993, page A5.

45 Powell, *My American Journey*, pages 576–577.

46 Madeleine Albright, *Madame Secretary: A Memoir* (New York: Miramax Books, 2003), page 182.

47 Laura Silber and Allen Little, *Yugoslavia: Death of a Nation* (New York: Penguin Books, 1995), page 274.

48 Michael F. Gordon, "Modest Air Operation in Bosnia Crosses a Major Political Frontier," *New York Times*, April 11, 1995, page A1.

49 Gilles Kepel, *Jihad: The Trail of Political Islam* (Cambridge, MA: Harvard University Press, 2002), pages 247–253.

50 Tim Weiner, "Clinton Withholds Bosnia Data from Congress," *New York Times*, April 12, 1996, page A1.

51 Silber and Little, *Yugoslavia*, page 350.

52 P. W. Singer, *Corporate Warriors: The Rise of the Privatized Military Industry* (Ithaca: Cornell University, 2003), pages 127–129.

53 Ibid., pages 213–215.

54 Richard Holbrooke, *To End a War* (New York: Random House, 1998), page 106.

55 Strobe Talbott, *The Russia Hand: A Memoir of Presidential Diplomacy* (New York: Random House, 2002), page 186.

56 Richard Holbrooke, "America, a European Power," *Foreign Affairs* 74, no. 2 (March/April 1995), page 40.

57 Anonymous, "The Road to Ethnic Cleansing,'" *Wall Street Journal*, June 11, 1996, page 18.

58 Julian Borger, *The Butcher's Trail: How the Search for Balkan War Criminals Became the World's Most Successful Manhunt* (New York: Other Press, 2016), pages 78–80, 87–88, 93–94, 127–30, and 155–56.

59 Thomas L. Freidman, "U.S. Vision of Foreign Policy Reversed," *New York Times*, September 22, 1993), page A8.

60 The White House, A National Security Strategy of Engagement and Enlargement, February, 1996. https://fas.org/spp/military/docops/national/1996stra.htm. Accessed March 31, 2021.

61 Holbrooke, *To End a War*, page 359, italics is in the original.

62 David Binder, "Bush Warns Serbs Not to Widen War," *New York Times*, December 28, 1992, page A6.

63 Tim Judah, *War and Revenge* (New Haven: Yale University Press, 2002), pages 25–31 and 53–54.

64 Noel Malcolm, *Kosovo: A Short History* (New York: New York University Press, 1998), page 348.

65 Tim Judah, *Kosovo: War and Revenge* (New Haven: Yale University Press, 2002), page 127.

66 Michael Scheuer, *Marching toward Hell: America and Islam after Iraq* (New York: Free Press, 2008), page 125.

67 President William J. Clinton, Press Release, the White House on meeting with Russian President Boris Yeltsin, St. Catherine Hall, Kremlin, Moscow,

Russia on September 2, 1998. https://clintonwhitehouse5.archives.gov/WH/
New/Russia/19980902-3098.html. Accessed March 31, 2021.

68 United Nations Security Council Resolution 1199, September 23, 1998.
http://unscr.com/en/resolutions/1199. Accessed March 31, 2021.

69 Judah, *Kosovo*, page 183.

70 Talbott, *The Russia Hand*, page 302.

71 John Pilger, "What Really Happened at Rambouillet: And What Else Is Being Kept
under Wraps by Our Selective Media?" *New Statesman*, May 30, 1999, page 1.

72 Ian Bancroft, "Serbia's anniversary is a timely reminder," *The Guardian*,
March 24, 2009. www.theguardian.com/commentisfree/2009/mar/24/serbia-
kosovo. Accessed March 31, 2021.

73 Sidney Blumenthal, *The Clinton Wars* (New York: Farrar, Straus and Giroux,
2003), pages 632–633; Albright, *Madame Secretary*, page 406.

74 Clinton, *My Life*, pages 850–851.

75 Jane Perlez, "Step by Step: How the U.S. Decided to Attack, and Why So
Fast," *New York Times*, March 26, 1999, page A1.

76 J. L. Holzgrefe and Robert O. Keohane, eds., *Humanitarian Intervention:
Ethical, Legal, and Political Dilemmas* (New York: Cambridge University
Press, 2003, pages 76, 79, 209.

77 Mark Gillespie, "Crisis in Kosovo: Questions and Answers about American
Public Opinion," Gallup, April 16, 1999. https://news.gallup.com/poll/3925/
crisis-kosovo-questions-answers-about-american-public-opinion.aspx.
Accessed March 31, 2021.

78 A group of Serb economists estimated seven years after the bombing that
damages reached over $29 billion. "Seven Years since End NATO
Bombing." www.b92.net/eng/news/politics.php?yyyy=2006&mm=06&dd=
09&nav_id=35250. Accessed March 31, 2021.

79 Judah, *Kosovo*, pages 258 and 264.

80 Albright, *Madame Secretary*, page 408.

81 Benjamin S. Lambeth, *NATO's Air War for Kosovo: A Strategic and
Operational Assessment* (Santa Monica: RAND, 2001), page 1.

82 Benjamin S. Lambeth, *Transformation of American Air Power* (Ithaca: Cornell
University Press, 2000), pages 181–232.

83 Lambeth, *NATO's Air War for Kosovo*, page 33.

84 Ivo H. Daalder and Michael E. O'Hanlon, *Winning Ugly: NATO's War to
Save Kosovo* (Washington, DC: Brookings Institution, 2000), pages 122–124.

85 Judah, *Kosovo*, pages 259 and 264.

86 Daalder and O'Hanlon, *Winning Ugly*, page 138.

87 Talbott, *The Russia Hand*, page 297.

88 Ibid., page 314.

89 Stephen T. Hosmer, *The Conflict over Kosovo: Why Milošević Decided to Settle
When He Did* (Santa Monica: RAND, 2001), pages 91–120.

90 "In the President's Words: 'We Act to Prevent a Wider War,'" excerpts from
the *New York Times*, March 25, 1999, page A10.

91 Katherine Q. Seelye, "Clinton Resists Renewed Calls for Ground Troops,"
New York Times, May 19, 1991, page A10.

92 Jane Perlez, "Clinton and Joint Chiefs to Discuss Ground Invasion," *New York Times*, June 2, 1999, page A14.

93 The ground-war threat was *the* critical factor according to several experts. For example, see Wesley K. Clark, *Waging Modern War: Bosnia, Kosovo, and the Future of Combat* (New York: Public Affairs, 2001), page 425; Lambeth, *NATO's Air War for Kosovo*, page 76; and Daalder and O'Hanlon, *Winning Ugly*, pages 158–160, 214.

94 NATO & Kosovo: Military Technical Agreement, signed June 9, 1999. www.nato.int/kosovo/docu/a990609a.htm. Accessed March 31, 2021.

95 Mike Jackson, *Soldier: An Autobiography* (London: Bantam Books, 2006), pages 215–254.

96 Clark, *Waging Modern War*, page 394.

97 Tom Gallagher, *The Balkans in the New Millennium: In the Shadow of War and Peace* (New York: Routledge, 2005), page 112.

98 Jim Hoagland, "The Trouble with Playing Global Cop," *Washington Post*, September 2, 1999, page A39; Kay Bailey Hutchison, "The Case for Strategic Sense," *Washington Post*, September 13, 1999, page A27; and Michael Mandelbaum, "Foreign Policy as Social Work," *Foreign Affairs* 75, no. 1 (January/February 1996), pages 16–32.

99 William Hyland, *Clinton's World: Remaking American Foreign Policy* (Westport: Praeger, 1999), pages 64 and 202–204.

100 Rosemary Righter, *Utopia Lost: The United Nations and the World Order* (New York: Twentieth Century Press, 1995), page 81.

4 Afghanistan

1 Steve Cole, *Ghost Wars: The Secret History of the CIA, Afghanistan, and bin Laden, from the Soviet Invasion to September 10, 2001* (New York: Penguin Press, 2004), page 238.

2 Both sets of quotes in this paragraph are taken from Michael Scheuer, *Through Our Enemies' Eyes: Osama bin Laden, Radical Islam, and the Future of America* (Washington, DC: Brassy's, 2002), page 107.

3 For an explanation of Osama bin Laden's motives and his relationship with the Taliban government, see Daniel Benjamin and Steven Simon, *The Age of Sacred Terror* (New York, Random House, 2002), pages 124–28 and 137–50; and Lawrence Wright, *The Looming Tower: Al-Qaeda and the Road to 9/11* (New York: Vintage, 2007), pages 171–172, 213–214, 238–239, and 374–375.

4 Thomas Barfield, *Afghanistan: A Cultural and Political History* (Princeton: Princeton University Press, 2010), page 268.

5 George P. Shultz, *Turmoil and Triumph: My Years as Secretary of State* (New York: Charles Scribner's Sons, 1995), pages 896, 1086–1094.

6 Cole, *Ghost Wars*, pages 236–239.

7 *The 9/11 Commission Report: Final Report of the National Commission on Terrorist Attacks upon the United States*, authorized edition (New York: W. W. Norton & Company, 2004), pages 47–63 and 71–98.

8 Michael R. Gordon, "The 2000 Campaign: The Military; Bush Would Stop U.S. Peacekeeping in Balkan Fights," *New York Times*, October 21, 2000, page A1.

9 Public Law 107-40, 107th Congress, September 18, 2001. www.gpo.gov/fdsys/pkg/PLAW-107publ40/pdf/PLAW-107publ40.pdf. Accessed March 31, 2021.

10 George W. Bush, "Address to the Joint Sessions of Congress and the American People," September 30, 2001. www.gpo.gov/fdsys/pkg/WCPD-2001-09-24/pdf/WCPD-2001-09-24-Pg1347.pdf.   Accessed   March 31, 2021.

11 Bob Woodward, *Bush at War* (New York: Simon & Schuster, 2002), page 45.

12 Condoleezza Rice, *No Higher Honor: A Memoir of My Years in Washington* (New York: Crown Publishers, 2011), page 93.

13 George W. Bush, *Decision Points* (New York: Crown Publishers, 2010), page 187.

14 Steve Cole, *Directorate S: The CIA America's Secret Wars in Afghanistan and Pakistan* (New York: Penguin Press, 2018), pages 89–90, 95, 145–146, 397, 633, and 976.

15 James Mann, *The Rise of the Vulcans: The History of the Bush War Cabinet* (New York: Viking, 2002), page 342.

16 Suzanne Daley, "For First Time, NATO Invokes Pact with U.S," *New York Times*, October 13, 2001, page A1.

17 William Drozdiak and Rajiv Chandrasekaran, "NATO: U.S. Evidence on Bin Laden Compelling," *Washington Post*, October 3, 2001, page A11.

18 Suzanne Daley, "Alliance Says It Will Fight If It Is Asked," *New York Times*, October 3, 2001, page A1.

19 Joseph Fitchett, "U.S. Allies Chafe at 'Cleanup' Role," *International Herald Tribune*, November 26, 2001, page 1.

20 Patrick E. Tyler, "U.S. and Britain Strike Afghanistan, Aiming at Bases and Terrorist Camps," *New York Times*, October 8, 2001, page A1.

21 Marine Corps Institute, *Afghanistan: An Introduction to the Country and People* (Washington, DC: Marine Barracks, 2003), pages 12–17. https://permanent.access.gpo.gov/lps58082/ADA485637.pdf. Accessed March 31, 2021.

22 Mark P. Lagon, *The Reagan Doctrine: Sources of American Conduct in the Cold War's Last Chapter* (West Port: Praeger, 1994), pages xii, 55–59.

23 George Tenet, *At the Center of the Storm: My Years at the CIA* (New York: HarperCollins, 2007), pages 175–184; and Dick Cheney, *In My Time: A Personal and Political Memoir* (New York: Threshold Editions, 2011), pages 336–369.

24 Four-star Hugh Shelton held the CIA operatives in disdain and in his account of the meeting he only mentioned SOF. See Hugh Shelton, *Without Hesitation: The Odyssey of an American Warrior* (New York: St. Martin's Press, 2010), pages 355–356 and 445.

25 Richard A. Clarke, *Against All Enemies: Inside American's War on Terrorism* (New York: Free Press, 2004), page 190; and Eric Schmitt and Thom Shanker, *Counterstrike: The Untold Story of America's Secret Campaign against al Qaeda* (New York: Henry Holt and Company, 2011), page 25.

26 Stephen Tanner, *Afghanistan: A Military History from Alexander the Great to the Fall of the Taliban* (New York: Da Capo Press, 2002), page 293.

27 William Safire, "The Way We Live Now: 3-31-02: On Language: Pound Sand," *New York Times*, March 31, 2002, page 10A.

28 Gary C. Schroen, *First In: An Insider's Account of How the CIA Spearheaded the War on Terror in Afghanistan* (New York: Ballantine Books, 2007), pages 83–90.

29 Tenet, *At the Center of the Storm*, page 207.

30 For a critique of the operation for being handled in a conventional manner, see Hy S. Rothstein, *Afghanistan and the Troubled Future of Unconventional Warfare* (Annapolis: Naval Institute Press, 2006).

31 Will Irwin, *The Jedburghs: The Secret History of the Allied Special Forces, France 1944* (New York: Public Affairs, 2005).

32 Richard Harris Smith, *OSS: The Secret History of America's First Central Intelligence Agency* (Berkeley: University of California Press, 1972), pages 157–185.

33 Leigh Neville, *Special Forces in the War on Terror* (London: Osprey Publishing, 2015), page 25.

34 Donald Rumsfeld, *Known and Unknown: A Memoir* (New York: Sentinel, 2011), page 375.

35 For a study of the interaction between SOF and CIA, see Thomas H. Henriksen, *Eyes, Ears, and Daggers: Special Operations Forces and the Central Intelligence Agency in America's Evolving Struggle against Terrorism* (Stanford: Hoover Institution Press, 2017), pages 101–129.

36 *U.S. Army/Marine Corps Counterinsurgency Field Manual* (Chicago: University of Chicago Press, 2007), page 50.

37 For more on this curious misunderstanding, see Robert L. Bateman, "Lawrence and His Message," *Small Wars Journal*. https://smallwarsjournal .com/blog/lawrence-and-his-message. Accessed March 31, 2021.

38 Diana Stancy Correll, "How the 'Horse Soldiers' Helped Liberate Afghanistan from the Taliban 18 Years Ago," *Military Times*, October 19, 2019. www.militarytimes.com/news/your-military/2019/10/18/how-the-horse-soldiers-helped-liberate-afghanistan-from-the-taliban-18-years-ago/? utm_source=Sailthru&utm_medium=email&utm_campaign=EBB%2010 .21.19&utm_term=Editorial%20-%20Early%20Bird%20Brief.   Accessed March 31, 2021.

39 Elizabeth Collins, "First to Go: Green Berets Remember Earliest Mission in Afghanistan (Part 3)," *US Army Magazine*, January 19, 2018. www.army.mil/ article/199263. Accessed March 31, 2021.

40 Jackie Northam, "U.S., Pakistan At Impasse Over Afghan Supply Routes," *NPR*, March 15, 2012. www.npr.org/2012/03/15/148602953/u-s-pakistan-at-impasse-over-afghan-supply-routes. Accessed March 31, 2021.

41 Robert D. Kaplan, *Imperial Grunts* (New York: Vintage Books, 2006), page 199.

42 Stephen Tanner, *Afghanistan: A Military History from Alexander the Great to the Fall of the Taliban* (New York: Da Capo Press, 2002), pages 316–317.

43 Sean Naylor, *Not a Good Day to Die: The Untold Story of Operation Anaconda* (New York: Penguin Group, 2005), pages 97–115.

44 Tommy Franks, *American Soldier* (New York: HarperCollins, 2004), page 378.

45 Ibid., page 381.

46 Despite the rapidity, ease, and the seeming unconventionality of the American victory, one critic held that the United States employed its power in a conventional manner that hurt is post-invasion prospects after the opening months. Hy S. Rothstein, a former Special Forces colonel, who taught at the Naval Postgraduate School in Monterey, California, was commissioned to draft a report by the Pentagon and afterward he published a book on his views. See *Afghanistan and the Troubled Future of Unconventional Warfare*.

47 See Fred Kaplan, *The Insurgents: David Petraeus and the Plot to Change the American Way of War* (New York: Simon & Schuster, 2013), pages 344–345.

48 Woodward, *Bush at War*, page 241.

49 Dov S. Zakheim, *A Vulcan's Tale: How the Bush Administration Mismanaged the Reconstruction of Afghanistan* (New York: Brookings Institution Press, 2011), page 8.

50 Woodward, *Bush at War*, page 195.

51 Ibid., page 231.

52 Patrick E. Tyler, "U.S. Sees Limited Mission in Postwar Afghanistan," *New York Times*, November 28, 2001, page A1.

53 Kaplan, *The Insurgents*, page 322.

54 James Dobbin, John G. McGinn, Keith Crane, Seth G. Jones, Rollie Lal, Andrew Rathmell, Rachel Swanger, and Anga Timilsina, *America's Role in Nation-Building from Germany to Afghanistan* (Santa Monica: RAND, 2003), pages 132–134.

55 "Joint Statement by President George W. Bush and Chairman Hamid Karzai on January 28, 2002." www.govinfo.gov/content/pkg/WCPD-2002-02-04/pdf/WCPD-2002-02-04-Pg131.pdf. Accessed March 31, 2021.

56 Rice, *No Higher Honor*, page 91.

57 Bush, *Decision Points*, pages 205–206.

58 Douglas J. Feith, *War and Decision: Inside the Pentagon at the Dawn of the War on Terrorism* (New York: HarperCollins, 2008), page 140.

59 Neither President Bush nor other politicians gave much thought to the unique circumstances surrounding the Marshall Plan. For enlightening exposition, see Barry Machado, *In Search of a Unusable Past: The Marshall Plan and Postwar Reconstruction Today* (Lexington: George C. Marshall Foundation Press, 2007).

60 James Dao, "A Nation Challenged: The President; Bush Sets Role for U.S. in Afghan Rebuilding," *New York Times*, April 18, 2002, page A1.

61 Mohammed Ayoob, "The Taliban and the Changing Nature of Pashtun Nationalism," *The National Interest*, January 10, 2019. https://nationalinterest.org/feature/taliban-and-changing-nature-pashtun-nationalism-41182?utm_source=Sailthru&utm_medium=email&utm_campaign=

ebb%2014.01.19&utm_term=Editorial%20-%20Early%20Bird%20Brief.
Accessed March 31, 2021.

62 Barfield, *Afghanistan*, page 24.

63 While attending the 2011 Special Operations Command Central
Symposium, "Strengthening Regional Partnerships for the 21st Century,"
in Abu Dhabi, UAE, the author interviewed Special Operations officers and
non-commissioned officers on April 12 and 13, 2011.

64 Aron B. O'Connell, "Moving Mountains: Cultural Friction in the
Afghanistan War," in *Our Latest Longest War: Losing Hearts and Minds in
Afghanistan*, ed. Arron B. O'Connell (Chicago: University of Chicago Press,
2017), pages 26–28.

65 "ISAF's Mission in Afghanistan (2001–2014) (Archived)," North Atlantic
Treaty Organization. www.nato.int/cps/en/natohq/topics_69366.htm.
Accessed March 31, 2021.

66 Ian S. Livingston, Heather L. Messera, and Michael O'Hanlon, "Afghanistan
Index: Tracking Variables of Reconstruction & Security in Post-9/11
Afghanistan," *Brookings Institution*, June 30, 2011, page 5. www.brookings
.edu/wp-content/uploads/2016/07/index20110630-1.pdf. Accessed March
31, 2021.

67 Carl J. Schramm, " 'The Interagency' Isn't Supposed to Rule," *Wall Street
Journal*, December 5, 2019, page A17.

68 Brett Doyle, "Lessons on Collaboration from Recent Conflicts: The Whole-
of-Nation and Whole-of-Government Approaches in Action," *InterAgency
Journal* 10, no. 1 (2019), page 119. http://thesimonscenter.org/featured-art
icle-lessons-on-collaboration-from-recent-conflicts/. Accessed March
31, 2021.

69 Robert J. Bebber, "The Role of Provincial Reconstruction Teams (PRTs) in
Counterinsurgency Operations: Khost Province, Afghanistan," *Small Wars
Journal*. www.researchgate.net/profile/Robert_Bebber/publication/
237285971_The_Role_of_Provincial_Reconstruction_Teams_PRTs_in_
Counterinsurgency_Operations_Khost_Province_Afghanistan/links/
541ae1790cf203f155ae5b9e.pdf. Accessed March 31, 2021.

5 The Iraq War

1 Michael R. Gordon and General Bernard E. Trainor, *The Endgame: The
Inside Story of the Struggle for Iraq, from George W. Bush to Barack Obama*
(New York: Vintage Books, 2012), page 8.

2 For full Text, see "In Cheney's Words, Opening Session of the 103rd
National Convention of the Veterans of Foreign Wars," *New York Times*,
August 26, 2002. www.nytimes.com/2002/08/26/international/middleeast/
full-text-in-cheneys-words.html. Accessed March 31, 2021.

3 Thucydides, *The History of the Peloponnesian War*, trans. Richard Crawley
(Auckland: Floating Press, 2008), page 27.

4 Frank Newport, "Seventy-two Percent of Americans Support the Iraq War,"
Gallup News Service, March 24, 2003. https://news.gallup.com/poll/8038/

seventytwo-percent-americans-support-war-against-iraq.aspx.   Accessed
March 31, 2021.

5 Marc Sandalow, "Record Shows Bush Shifting on Iraq War/President's
   Rationale for the Invasion Continues to Evolve," *San Francisco Chronicle*,
   September 29, 2004. www.sfgate.com/politics/article/NEWS-ANALYSIS-
   Record-shows-Bush-shifting-on-2690938.php. Accessed March 31, 2021.

6 For Robert Byrd's comment, see *Congressional Record*, 148:S8966 (Daily
   Edition, September 20, 2002).

7 Top members of the Bush administration wrote of their deep apprehension
   about Saddam Hussein. See Dick Cheney, *In My Time: A Personal and
   Political Memoir* (New York: Threshold Editions, 2011), page 368; and
   Condoleezza Rice, *No Higher Honor: A Memoir of My Years in Washington*
   (New York: Crown Publishers, 2011), pages 148, 151, and 154.

8 George W. Bush, *Decision Points* (New York: Crown, 2010), page 228.

9 National Security Strategy Report, September 2002. www.globalsecurity.org/
   military/library/policy/national/nss-020920.htm. Accessed March 31, 2021.

10 Stefan Halper and Jonathan Clarke, *America Alone: The Neo-Conservatives and
   the Global Order* (New York: Cambridge University Press, 2004), pages 9–15
   and 141–145.

11 Thomas E. Ricks, *Fiasco: The American Military Adventure in Iraq* (New York:
   Penguin Press, 2006), pages 52–57; Bob Woodward, *Plan of Attack* (New
   York: Simon & Schuster, 2004), 295–296; and Todd S. Purdum, *Time of Our
   Choosing: America's War in Iraq* (New York: Henry Holt and Co., 2003),
   pages 261–263.

12 Michael J. Mazarr, *Leap of Faith: Hubris, Negligence, and America's Greatest
   Foreign Policy Tragedy* (New York: Hachette Book Group, 2019), page 396.

13 Len Colodny and Tom Shachtman, *The Forty Years War: The Rise and Fall of
   the Neocons* (New York: HarperCollins, 2016), pages 360, 363, 382–383.

14 Edward Chang, "Neocons Don't Deserve All the Blame for the Iraq War,"
   The Federalist, April 24, 2019. https://thefederalist.com/2019/04/24/neocons-
   dont-deserve-blame-iraq-war/. Accessed March 31, 2021.

15 Kenneth M. Pollack, "The Seven Deadly Sins of Failure in Iraq:
   A Retrospective Analysis of the Reconstruction," *Brookings Institution,
   Middle East Review of International Affairs*, December 1, 2006.

16 J. Baxter Oliphant, "The Iraq War Continues to Divide U.S. Public, 15 Years
   after It Began," FacTank, March 19, 2018. www.pewresearch.org/fact-tank/
   2018/03/19/iraq-war-continues-to-divide-u-s-public-15-years-after-it-began/.
   Accessed March 31, 2021.

17 Frederic M. Wehrey, "An Altered Landscape: The Shifting Regional Balance
   of Power," in *The Iraq Effect: The Middle East After the Iraq War* (Santa
   Monica: RAND, 2010), pages 17–47.

18 Richard Baum, "From 'Strategic Partners' to 'Strategic Competitors':
   George W. Bush and the Politics of the U.S. China Policy," *Journal of East
   Asian Studies* 1, no. 2 (August 2001), page 1. www.researchgate.net/publica
   tion/260142412_From_Strategic_Partners_to_Strategic_Competitors_
   George_W_Bush_and_the_Politics_of_US_China_Policy. Accessed March
   31, 2021.

19 Condoleezza Rice, "Campaign 2000: Promoting the National Interest," *Foreign Affairs* (January 2000). www.foreignaffairs.com/articles/2000-01-01/campaign-2000-promoting-national-interest. Accessed March 31, 2021.

20 Ibid.

21 The spate of challenges faced by UN nuclear inspectors is beyond the scope of this volume. Accounts of Saddam Hussein's noncooperation can be found in Richard Butler, *The Greatest Threat: Iraq, Weapons of Mass Destruction, and the Growing Crisis of Global Security* (New York: Public Affairs, 2000); and Hans Blix, *Disarming Iraq* (New York: Pantheon Books, 2004).

22 Joyce Battle (ed.), "Saddam Hussein Talks to the FBI: Twenty Interviews and Five Conversations with 'High Value Detainee #1' in 2004," *The National Security Archive*, July 1, 2009, Document 23: "Casual Conversation, May 13, 2004" and Document 24: "Casual Conversation, June 11, 2004." https://nsarchive2.gwu.edu//NSAEBB/NSAEBB279/index.htm. Accessed March 31, 2021.

23 Bush, *Decision Points*, pages 228–229 and 234–243; Rice, *No Higher Honor*, pages 196–199; Donald Rumsfeld, *Known and Unknown: A Memoir* (New York: Sentinel, 2011), pages 432–437.

24 George W. Bush, State of the Union Address, January 29, 2002. https://georgewbush-whitehouse.archives.gov/news/releases/2002/01/20020129-11.html. Accessed March 31, 2021.

25 George Tenet, *At the Center of the Storm: My Years at the CIA* (New York: HarperCollins, 2007), pages 341–358.

26 Jeffrey Smith, "Hussein's Prewar Ties To Al-Qaeda Discounted," *Washington Post*, April 6, 2007, page A12.

27 Joel Gehrke, "'It Wouldn't Have Worked': Colin Powel Balked at Telling George W. Bush Not to Invade Iraq," *Washington Times*, January 14, 2020. www.washingtonexaminer.com/policy/defense-national-security/it-wouldnt-have-worked-colin-powell-balked-at-telling-george-w-bush-not-to-invade-iraq. Accessed March 31, 2021.

28 James Mann, *Rise of the Vulcans: The History of Bush's War Cabinet* (New York: Viking, 2004), page 238.

29 Walter Pincus and Dana Priest, "Some Iraq Analysts Felt Pressure from Cheney Visits," *Washington Post*, June 5, 2003.

30 Hugh Shelton, *Without Hesitation: The Odyssey of an American Warrior* (New York: St. Martin's Press, 2010), pages 442, 444–445.

31 Amy Belasco, "Troop Levels in the Afghan and Iraq Wars, FY2001–FY2012: Cost and Other Potential Issues," *Congressional Research Service*, July 2, 2009. https://fas.org/sgp/crs/natsec/R40682.pdf. Accessed March 31, 2021.

32 Woodward, *Plan of Attack*, pages 30, 81–82, and 98; and Rumsfeld, *Known and Unknown*, pages 429–442.

33 Thom Shanker and David E. Sanger, "U.S. Envisions Blueprint On Iraq Including Big Invasion Next Year," *New York Times*, April 28, 2002, page A1; Eric Scmitt, "U.S. Plans for Iraq Is Said to Include Attack on 3 Sides," *New York Times*, July 5, 2002, page A1; and Thomas E. Ricks, "Timing, Tactics On Iraq War Disputed," *Washington Post*, August 1, 2002, page A1.

34 John Barry and Roy Gutman, "Rumors of War," *Newsweek*, August 12, 2002, page 36.

35 Rumsfeld, *Known and Unknown*, page 486.

36 David E. Sanger, "In the Reichstag: Bush Condemns Terror as New Despotism," *New York Times*, May 24, 2002, page A1.

37 Editorial, "The Need for One Voice on Iraq," *Financial Times*, July 30, 2002, page 14.

38 White House, President Bush Delivers Graduation Speech at West Point, June 1, 2002. http://georgewbush-whitehouse.archives.gov/news/releases/2002/06/20020601-3.html. Accessed March 31, 2021.

39 Julia Preston, "U.N. Spy Photo Shows New Building at Iraq Nuclear Site," *New York Times*, September 6, 2002, page A1.

40 President's Speech to the United Nations General Assembly, September 12, 2002. https://georgewbush-whitehouse.archives.gov/news/releases/2002/09/20020912-1.html. Accessed March 31, 2021.

41 Commission on Intelligence Capabilities of the United States Regarding Weapons of Mass Destruction, March 2005. http://govinfo.library.unt.edu/wmd/about.html. Accessed March 31, 2021.

42 National Security Strategy, September 17, 2002. https://georgewbush-whitehouse.archives.gov/nsc/nss/2002/. Accessed March 31, 2021.

43 Karen De Young, "Bush Cites Urgent Iraqi Threat," *Washington Post*, October 8, 2002, page A1.

44 Bob Graham, *Intelligence Matters* (New York: Radom House, 2004), page 181–184.

45 Richard Morin and Claudia Dean, "71% Of Americans Support War, Poll Shows," *Washington Post*, March 19, 2003, page A14.

46 Jim VandeHei and Juliet Eilperin, "Congress Passes Iraq Resolution," *Washington Post*, October 11, 2002, page A1.

47 George W. Bush, State of the Union Address, January 28, 2003, *Washington Post*. www.washingtonpost.com/wp-srv/onpolitics/transcripts/bushtext_012803.html?noredirect=on. Accessed March 31, 2021.

48 Steven R. Weisman, "Powell Calls His U.N. Speech a Lasting Blot on His Record," *New York Times*, September 9, 2005, A10.

49 Robert Kagan, *Of Paradise and Power: America and Europe in the New World Order* (New York: Alfred A. Knopf, 2003), page 3.

50 T. Michawl Moseley, "Operation Iraqi Freedom – by The Numbers," *U.S. Air Forces Central Command*, April 30, 2003. www.comw.org/pda/fulltext/oifcentaf.pdf. Accessed March 31, 2021.

51 "Text: Bush's Speech on Iraq," *New York Times*, March 18, 2003. www.nytimes.com/2003/03/18/politics/text-bushs-speech-on-iraq.html. Accessed March 31, 2021.

52 Ken Adelman, "Cakewalk in Iraq," *Washington Post*, February 13, 2002, page A27; and "'Cakewalk' Revisited,'" *Washington Post*, April 10, 2003, page A29.

53 Belasco, "Troop Levels in the Afghan and Iraq Wars, FY2001–FY2012," page 64–66.

54 Anthony H. Cordesman, *The Iraq War: Strategy, Tactics, and Military Lessons* (Washington, DC: CSIS Press, 2004), page 123.

55 Ibid., page 127.

56 The White House, "The President Announces the End of Major Combat Operations in Iraq," May 1, 2003. https://georgewbush-whitehouse.archives .gov/news/releases/2003/05/20030501-15.html. Accessed March 31, 2021.

57 Tommy Franks, *American Soldier* (New York: Regan Books, 2004), page 123.

58 Ibid., pages 418–419.

59 Philip H. Gordon and Michael E. O'Hanlon, "A Tougher Target: The Afghanistan Model of Warfare May Not Apply Very Well to Iraq," *Washington Post*, December 26, 2001, page A31.

60 Cordesman, *The Iraq War*, pages 228 and 247.

61 Niko Price, "AP Tallies 3,240 Civilian Deaths in Iraq," Associated Press, June 10, 2003.

62 Victor Davis Hanson, *The Second World War: How the First Global Conflict Was Fought and Won* (New York: Basic Books, 2017), page 287.

63 Rice, *No Higher Honor*, page 153.

64 David Petraeus and James Amos, *U.S. Army and Marine Corps, Counterinsurgency Field Manuel, No 3–24 and Marine Corps Warfighting Publication No. 3–33.5* (Chicago: University of Chicago, 2007), page 23.

65 John F. Burns, "Looting and a Suicide Attack in Baghdad," *New York Times*, April 11, 2003, page A1.

66 Michael R. Gordon and Bernard E. Trainor, *Cobra II: The Inside Story of the Invasion and Occupation of Iraq* (New York: Pantheon Books, 2006), page 46.

67 Hearing of the US Senate Armed Services Committee, 108th Congress, First Session, February 28, 2003; and Thom Shanker, "New Strategy Vindicates Ex-Army Chief Shinseki," *New York Times*, January 12, 2007, page A6.

68 Thom Shanker, "Rumsfeld Defends War Planning," *New York Times*, March 31, 2003, page A1.

69 James Fallows, "Blind into Iraq," *Atlantic*, January–February 2004. www .theatlantic.com/magazine/archive/2004/01/blind-into-baghdad/302860/. Accessed March 31, 2021.

70 Jeffrey Gold, "A Little Learning," *New Yorker*, May 9, 2005, page 12.

71 Both quotations are from Douglas J. Feith, *War and Decision: Inside the Pentagon at the Dawn of the War on Terrorism* (New York: HarperCollins, 2008), pages 189–190 and 239–240.

72 Rumsfeld, *Known and Unknown*, pages 489–490.

73 L. Paul Bremer, *My Year in Iraq: The Struggle to Build a Future of Hope* (New York: Simon & Schuster, 2006), page 1.

74 Larry Diamond, "What Went Wrong in Iraq," *Foreign Affairs* (September/ October 2004), page 45.

75 Press Release, Security Council Endorses Formation of Sovereign Interim Government in Iraq, Resolution 1546, June 5, 2004. www.un.org/press/en/ 2004/sc8117.doc.htm. Accessed March 31, 2021.

76 Malcolm W. Nance, *The Terrorists of Iraq: Inside the Strategy and Tactics of the Iraq Insurgency, 2003–2014* (Boca Raton: CRC Press, 2015), page 251.

77 Alexander Mikaberidze, *Conflict and Conquest in the Islamic World: A Historical Encyclopedia* (Santa Barbara: ABC-CLIO, 2011), page 304.

78 Mao Zedong, *On Guerrilla Warfare*, trans. Samuel B. Griffith (New York: Praeger, 1961), page 93.

79 Bob Scales, *Scales on War: The Future of America's Military at Risk* (Annapolis: Naval Institute Press, 2016), pages 39–40 and 42.

80 Michael E. O'Hanlon, "A Retrospective on the So-Called Revolution in Military Affairs, 2000–2020," Brookings Report, September 2018. www .brookings.edu/research/a-retrospective-on-the-so-called-revolution-in-mili tary-affairs-2000-2020/. Accessed March 31, 2021.

81 All the citations in this paragraph come from Fred Kaplan, *The Insurgents: David Petraeus and the Plot to Change the American Way of War* (New York: Simon & Schuster Press, 2013), pages 58 and 118.

82 Rumsfeld, *Known and Unknown*, pages 520–522.

83 Donald Rumsfeld, "Beyond Nation-Building," *Washington Post*, September 23, 2003.

84 Rumsfeld, *Known and Unknown*, pages 523–525. The quotation appears on page 524.

85 Rumsfeld, *Known and Unknown*, page 680.

86 Robert F. Worth, "Blast Destroys Shrine in Iraq, Setting Off Sectarian Fury," *New York Times*, February 22, 2006, page A1.

87 Kaplan, *Insurgents*, pages 174, 178, and 180.

88 Bob Woodward, *State of Denial: Bush at War, Part III* (New York: Simon & Schuster, 2006), page 470.

89 "Kaplan Replies to Fontenot's Review," *Military Review*, July–August, page 79. www.armyupress.army.mil/Portals/7/military-review/Archives/English/ MilitaryReview_20130831_art014.pdf. Accessed March 31, 2021.

90 T. E. Lawrence, *Seven Pillars of Wisdom* (London: Wordsworth Classic Edition, 1926.), page 183.

91 David Galula, *Counterinsurgency Warfare: Theory and Practice* (Westport: Praeger, 2006; first published, 1967), pages 61 and 64.

92 Peter R. Mansoor, *Surge: My Journey with General Petraeus and the Remaking of the Iraq War* (New Haven: Yale University Press, 2013), page 261.

93 Petraeus and Amos, *U.S. Army and Marine Corps, Counterinsurgency Field Manual*, page xlvi.

94 James N. Mattis, "Preparing for Counterinsurgency," in *Al-Anbar Awakening*, vol. 1, *American Perspectives, U.S. Marines and Counterinsurgency in Iraq, 2004–2009*, ed. Timothy S. McWilliams and Kurtis P. Wheeler (Quantico: Marine Corps Unversity Press, 2009), pages 21 and 24.

95 Michael Knights, "The Evolution of Iran's Special Groups in Iran," *Combating Terrorism Center's Sentinel* 3, nos. 11–12 (November 2010), pages 12–14. https://ctc.usma.edu/the-evolution-of-irans-special-groups-in-iraq/. Accessed March 31, 2021.

96 Kyle Rempfer, "Iran Killed More US Troops in Iraq than Previously Known, Pentagon Says," *Military Times*, April 4, 2019. www.militarytimes.com/news/ your-military/2019/04/04/iran-killed-more-us-troops-in-iraq-than-previ ously-known-pentagon-says/?utm_source=Sailthru&utm_

medium=email&utm_campaign=ebb%2004.05.19&utm_term=Editorial%
20-%20Early%20Bird%20Brief. Accessed March 31, 2021.

97 For background on the topic, see Joseph Felter and Brian Fishman, *Iranian Strategy in Iraq: Politics and "Other Means"* (West Point: Combating Terrorism Center, 2008). https://ctc.usma.edu/app/uploads/2010/06/Iranian-Strategy-in-Iraq.pdf. Accessed March 31, 2021.

98 James A. Baker III and Lee H. Hamilton, co-chairs, along with Lawrence S. Eagleburger, Vernon E. Jordan Jr., Edwin Meese III, Sandra Day O'Connor, Leon Panetta, William J. Perry, Charles S. Robb, Alan K. Simpson. *The Iraq Study Group Report: The Way Forward – a New Approach*, authorized edition (New York: Vintage Books, 2006), page 9. This report has also been referred to as the *ISG Report*, the *Baker Report*, the *Baker–Hamilton Report*, or the *Hamilton–Baker Report*.

99 Kimberly Kagan, *The Surge: A Military History* (New York: Encounter Books, 2009), page 28

100 Michael Abramowitz, "Second Life for Study Group," *Washington Post*, May 21, 2007, page A1.

101 Michael E. O'Hanlon and Ian Livingston, "Iraq Index: Tracking Variables of Reconstruction & Security in Iraq," Brookings Institution, July 23, 2013, page 3. www.brookings.edu/wp-content/uploads/2016/07/index20130726.pdf. Accessed March 31, 2021.

102 Casualty figures can be found at www.icasualties.org/. Accessed March 31, 2021.

103 The "build" in the much used "clear and hold" concept was incorporated to give us the "clear, hold, and build" phrase by Army General Ray Odierno working as an assistant to Condoleezza Rice, according to Kaplan, *The Insurgents*, page 195.

104 David E. Sanger and Michael R. Gordon, "Options Weighed for Surge in G.I.'s to Stabilize Iraq," *New York Times*, December 6, 2006, page A1; and David S. Cloud and Jeff Zeleny, "Bush Considers up to 20,000 More Troops for Iraq," *New York Times*, December 29, 2006, page A1.

105 David E. Sanger, "Bush Plan for Iraq Requests More Troops and More Jobs," *New York Times*, January 7, 2007, page A1.

106 Editorial Board, "Ten Years After," *New York Times*, March 19, 2013; and John J. Mearsheimer and Stephan M. Walt, "An Unnecessary War," *Foreign Policy*, March 3, 2019. https://foreignpolicy.com/2009/11/03/an-unnecessary-war-2/. Accessed March 31, 2021.

107 George W. Bush address to the nation on January 10, 2007. https://georgewbush-whitehouse.archives.gov/news/releases/2007/01/20070110-7.html. Accessed March 31, 2021.

108 Jim Michaels, *A Chance in Hell: The Men Who Triumphed in Iraq's Deadliest City and Turned the Tide of War* (New York: St. Martin's Press, 2010), pages 30, 50–55.

109 Michael Weiss and Hassan, *ISIS: Inside the Army of Terror* (New York: Regan Arts, 2015), pages 68–81.

110 Michaels, *A Chance in Hell*, pages 91–94.

111 William Knarr, "Al-Sahawa: An Awakening in Al Qaim," GlobalECCO. https://globalecco.org/al-sahawa-an-awakening-in-al-qaim/-/journal_con tent/56_INSTANCE_DsOuVYb6TvzU/10180/610133;jsessionid= C632088F858285261FE6DE903CA10F81?p_p_state=pop_up&_56_ INSTANCE_DsOuVYb6TvzU. Accessed March 27, 2019.

112 K. Kagan, *The Surge*, page 77.

113 Fatalities among British and other coalition partners drooped to zero in 2010. For death rates, see http://icasualties.org/. Accessed March 31, 2021.

114 For a sampling of this viewpoint, see K. Kagan, *The Surge*; Mansoor, *Surge*; James R. Crider, "A View from Inside the Surge," *Military Review* 89, no. 2 (March–April 2009), pages 81–88; and John McCain and Joe Lieberman, "The Surge Worked," *Wall Street Journal*, January 10, 2008, page A11.

115 For exponents of this view, see Michaels, *A Chance in Hell*; Dick Couch, *The Sheriff of Ramadi: Navy SEALs and the Winning of Anbar* (Annapolis: Naval Institute Press, 2008); and Austen Long, "The Anbar Awakening," *Survival* 50, no. 2 (April–May 2008), pages 67–94.

116 Patrick Cockburn, "Who Is Whose Enemy?" *London Review of Books* 30, no. 5 (March 6, 2008), page 14.

117 Linda Robinson, "Tell Me How This Ends: General Petraeus and the Search for a Way out of Iraq" (New York: PublicAffairs, 2008); and Bing West, *The Strongest Tribe: War, Politics, and the Endgame in Iraq* (New York: Random House, 2008).

118 Stephen Biddle, Jeffrey Friedman, and Jacob N. Shapiro, "Testing the Surge: Why Did Violence Decline in Iraq in 2007?" *International Security* 37, no. 1 (Summer 2012), pages 7–40.

119 K. Kagan, *The Surge*, page 28.

120 SIGIR reports are accessible at https://cybercemetery.unt.edu/archive/sigir/ 20131001084741/http://www.sigir.mil/publications/index.html. Accessed March 31, 2021.

121 Peter van Buren, *We Meant Well; How I Helped Lose the Battle for Hearts and Minds of the Iraqi People* (New York: Metropolitan, 2011), pages 117–121.

122 Joel Rayburn, Frank K. Sobchak, Jeanne F. Godfroy, Matthew D. Morton, James S. Powell, and Matthew M. Zais, *The U.S. Army in the Iraq War* (Carlisle: Strategic Studies Institute: US Army War College Press, 2019), pages 323–330, 448–454, 605–621.

123 Dexter Filkins, "U.S. Hands off Pacified Anbar, One Heart of the Iraq Insurgency," *New York Times*, September 1, 2008, page A1.

124 Bush, *Decision Points*, pages 389–390.

125 Jaime Walker, "How Obama Talked about Iraq from 2002 to 2014," *Washington Post*, June 19, 2014, page A1.

126 Barack Obama's Acceptance Speech at the Democratic Convention, August 28, 2008. http://elections.nytimes.com/2008/president/conventions/videos/ 20080828_OBAMA_SPEECH.html. Accessed March 31, 2021.

127 Peter Baker, "In Announcing Withdrawal Plan, Obama Marks Beginning of Iraq War's End," *New York Times*, February 28, 2009, page A6.

128 Barack Obama, *A Promised Land* (New York: Crown, 2020), page 319.

288 Notes to pages 174–184

129 Rowan Scarborough, "U.S. Exit from Iraq Leaves a Power Vacuum," *Washington Times*, December 23, 2011, page 1.
130 Jack Healy, "Arrest Order for Sunni Leader in Iraq Opens New Rift," *New York Times*, December 20, 2011, page A1.
131 Thom Shanker, Michael S. Schmidt, and Robert F. Worth, "In Baghdad, Panetta Leads Uneasy Moment of Closure to a Long Conflict," *New York Times*, December 16, 2011, page A19.

6 America's Small-Footprint Wars

1 Sean Naylor, *Relentless Strike: The Secret History of Joint Special Operations Command* (New York: St. Martin's Press, 2015), pages 40, 43, 45.
2 Thomas H. Henriksen, *Eyes, Ears, and Daggers: Special Operations Forces and the Central Intelligence Agency in America's Evolving Struggle against Terrorism* (Stanford: Hoover Institution Press, 2017), pages 104–105.
3 Jessica Stern, "Obama and Terrorism: Like It or Not, the War Goes On," *Foreign Affairs* 95, no. 5 (September/October 2015), page 17.
4 Ibid., page 18.
5 Stanley McChrystal, *My Share of the Task: A Memoir* (New York: Penguin Group, 2013), pages 23–36.
6 Mark Owen, *No Hero: The Evolution of a Navy SEAL* (New York: New American Library, 2014), pages 95 and 99.
7 McChrystal, *My Share of the Task*, pages 23–32.
8 Shawn Woodford, "Security on the Cheap: Whither Security Force Assistance (SFA)," *Mystics & Statistics*, The Dupuy Institute, July 17, 2018. www.dupuyinstitute.org/blog/2018/07/17/security-on-the-cheap-whither-security-force-assistance-sfa/. Accessed March 31, 2021.
9 Over the decades, British military and civilian institutions have made contributions to understanding counterinsurgency operations, particularly in Malaya and Northern Ireland. In regard to partnering, or to use the British term, remote warfare, see the Oxford Research Group. www.oxfordresearchgroup.org.uk/pages/category/remote-warfare. Accessed March 31, 2021.
10 Brian McAllister Lin, *The Philippine War, 1899–1902* (Lawrence: University Press of Kansas, 2000), page 328.
11 Robert Frank and James Hookway, "Manila Police Say Rebels Have Links to Bin Laden," *Wall Street Journal*, September 25, 2001, page A1.
12 Mark Bowden, "Jihadists in Paradise," *Atlantic* (March 2007), page 60.
13 Joseph Wheelan, *Jefferson's War: America's First War on Terror, 1801–1805* (New York: Carroll & Graf, 2003); and Richard B. Parker, *Uncle Sam in Barbary: A Diplomatic History* (Gainesville: University Press of Florida, 2004).
14 Bowden, "Jihadist in Paradise," page 60.
15 Ibid.
16 US Department of Defense, "Casualty Status," May 26, 2020. www.defense.gov/casualty.pdf. Accessed March 31, 2021.

17 Robert D. Kaplan, *Imperial Grunts: On the Ground with the American Military from Mongolia to the Philippines to Iraq and Beyond* (New York: Vantage Books, 2006), page 153.

18 All quotations in the paragraph are from Linda Robinson, Patrick B. Johnston, and Gillian S. Oak, "U.S. Special Operations Forces in the Philippines, 2001–2014," *Small Wars Journal*. https://smallwarsjournal.com/blog/us-special-operations-forces-in-the-philippines-2001%E2%80%932014. Accessed March 31, 2021.

19 Geoffrey Lambert, Larry Lewis, and Sarah Sewall, "Operation Enduring Freedom-Philippines: Civilian Harm and the Indirect Approach," *Prism: The Journal of Complex Operations* 3, no. 4. (2012), page 131. https://apps.dtic.mil/dtic/tr/fulltext/u2/a570399.pdf. Accessed March 31, 2021.

20 Felipe Villamor, "Key ISIS Operative in Philippines 'Taken' in Gunfight, President Says," *New York Times*, October 19, 2017, page A8.

21 Jake Maxwell Watts, "U.S. to Deploy Drone to Assist Philippine War on Militants," *Wall Street Journal*, September 11, 2017, page A8.

22 Jeoffrey Maitem and Mark Navales, "Philippines: Chief of Autonomous Muslim Region Says He Needs More Transition Time," *Bernar News*, December 2, 2020. www.benarnews.org/english/news/philippine/muslim-autonomy-southern-philippines-12042020152832.html. Accessed March 31, 2021.

23 Jake Maxwell Watts, "Islamic State Claims Responsibility for Philippine Attack That Killed at Least 20," *Wall Street Journal*, January 27, 2019, page A7.

24 Meghan Curran, "The Deadly Evolution of Abu Sayyaf and the Sea," Center for International Maritime Security (May 21, 2019). http://cimsec.org/the-deadly-evolution-of-abu-sayyaf-and-the-sea/40419. Accessed March 31, 2021.

25 Eric Schmitt and Thom Shanker, *Counterstrike: The Untold Story of America's Secret Campaign against Al Qaeda* (New York: Times Books, 2011), page 193–194.

26 Osama bin Laden, 1996 fatwa "Declaration of Jihad against the Americans occupying the Lands of the Two Holy Sites," from the Combating Terrorism Center, West Point. https://ctc.usma.edu/harmony-program/declaration-of-jihad-against-the-americans-occupying-the-land-of-the-two-holiest-sites-original-language-2/. Accessed March 31, 2021.

27 Daniel Benjamin and Steven Simon, *The Age of Sacred Terror* (New York: Random House, 2002), page 118–119.

28 Richard A. Clarke, *Against All Enemies: Inside America's War on Terror* (New York: Free Press, 2004), page 88.

29 Clint Watts, Jacob Shapiro, and Vahid Brown, "Al-Qa'ida's (Mis)Adventures in the Horn of Africa," *The Sentinel*, July 2, 2007, US Military Academy's Counterterrorism Center. https://ctc.usma.edu/al-qaidas-misadventures-in-the-horn-of-africa/. Accessed March 31, 2021.

30 Emily Wax and Karen DeYoung, "The U.S. Secretly Backing Warlords in Somalia," *Washington Post*, May 17, 2006, page 1.

31 Mark Mazzetti, "Efforts by CIA Fail in Somalia, Officials Charge," *New York Times*, August 8, 2006, page A1.

32 Naylor, *Relentless Strike*, page 63.

33 James Kitfield, *Twilight Warriors: The Soldiers, Spies, and Special Agents Who Are Revolutionizing the American Way of War* (New York: Basic Books, 2016), pages 82, 209, 281, and 297.

34 Karen DeYoung, "U.S. Strike in Somalia Targets Al-Qaeda Figure," *Washington Post*, January 9, 2007, page A1.

35 Jeffery Gettleman, "U.S. Military Official Offers a Bleak Assessment of Somalia," *New York Times*, November 11, 2006, page A6.

36 All quotations in this paragraph are from Mark Mazzetti, "Pentagon Sees Move in Somalia as Blueprint," *New York Times*, January 13, 2007, page A8.

37 Catie, Edmondson; "Move to Repeal Authorization of Military Force," *New York Times*, May 23, 2019, page A19.

38 Mark Mazzetti, *The Way of the Knife* (New York, Penguin Press, 2013), pages 149–150.

39 Craig Timberg, "Ethiopians Take over Somali Capital," *Washington Post*, December 29, 2006,) page A1.

40 Paul D. Williams, "Joining AMISOM: Why Six African States Contributed Troops to the African Union Mission in Somalia," *Journal of Eastern African Studies* 12 (2018), page 175.

41 Haviv Rettig Gur, "Israeli Aid Mission to Kenya Helps Somali Refugees," *The Jerusalem Post*, March 1, 2007. www.jpost.com/International/Israeli-aid-mission-to-Kenya-helps-Somali-refugees. Accessed March 31, 2021.

42 Chris Tomlinson, "U.S. Hires Firm for Somali Mission," *Boston Globe*, March 8, 2007, page 6.

43 Kyle Rempfer, "US airstrikes interrupt ISIS and al-Shabaab battleground," *Military Times*, May 29, 2019. www.militarytimes.com/news/your-army/2019/05/29/us-airstrikes-interrupt-isis-and-al-shabaab-battleground/. Accessed March 31, 2021.

44 For Delta's role in killing Pablo Escobar, see Mark Bowden, *Killing Pablo: The Hunt for the World's Greatest Outlaw* (New York: Grove Press, 2015), pages 141–142 and 147–154. For the part played by SEAL Team 6 in arresting Bosnian war criminals, see Julian Borger, *The Butcher's Trail: How the Search for Balkan Criminals Became the World's Most Successful Manhunt* (New York: Other Press, 2016), pages 81, 141, and 187–188.

45 McChrystal, *My Share of the Task*, page 200.

46 Michael Smith, *Killer Elite: The Inside Story of America's Most Secret Special Operations Team* (New York: St. Martin's Griffin Edition, 2008), pages 183–184.

47 Derek Chollet, *The Long Game: How Obama Defied Washington and Redefined America's Role in the World* (New York: PublicAffairs, 2016), pages 69, 100–101, and 141–145.

48 Eric Schmitt and Jeffery Gettleman, "Qaeda Leader Reported Killed in Somalia," *New York Times*, May 1, 2008, A7.

49 Jeffrey Gettleman and Eric Schmitt, "U.S. Kills Top Qaeda Leader in Southern Somalia," *New York Times*, September 14, 2009, page A3.

50 Ty McCormick, "Exclusive: U.S. Operates Drones from Secret Bases in Somalia," *Foreign Policy*, July 2, 2015. https://foreignpolicy.com/2015/07/02/exclusive-u-s-operates-drones-from-secret-bases-in-somalia-special-operations-jsoc-black-hawk-down/. Accessed March 31, 2021.

51 Catherine Besteman, "The Costs of War in Somalia," Watson Institute for International and Public Affairs, Brown University, September 5, 2019, page 1. https://watson.brown.edu/costsofwar/files/cow/imce/papers/2019/Costs%20of%20War%20in%20Somalia_Besteman.pdf. Accessed March 31, 2021.

52 Kyle Rempfer, "US Troops, Nonprofit Trainers, and a 'Lightning Brigade' Battle for Somalia," *Military Times*, May 21, 2019. www.militarytimes.com/news/your-army/2019/05/21/us-troops-nonprofit-trainers-and-a-lightning-brigade-battle-for-somalia/?utm_source=Sailthru&utm_medium=email&utm_campaign=ebb%205-22&utm_term=Editorial%20-%20Early%20Bird%20Brief. Accessed March 31, 2021.

53 For some of the considerations of targeting terrorist leadership, see Austin Long, "Assessing the Success of Leadership Targeting, *CTC Sentinel* 3, no. 11 (November 2010). https://ctc.usma.edu/assessing-the-success-of-leadership-targeting/. Accessed March 31, 2021. See also Jenna Jordan, "Attacking the Leader, Missing the Mark," *International Security* 38, no.4 (Spring 2014), pages 7–38.

54 Victor Davis Hanson, *The Second World Wars: How the First Global Conflict Was Fought and Won* (New York: Basic Books, 2017), page 287.

55 "America's Counterterrorism Wars: Drone Strikes Somalia," New America Foundation. www.newamerica.org/in-depth/americas-counterterrorism-wars/somalia/. Accessed March 31, 2021.

56 Shawn Snow, "US Launches Airstrikes on al-Shabaab in Response to Attack on US Commando Outpost in Somalia," *Military Times*, September 30, 2019. www.militarytimes.com/news/your-military/2019/09/30/extremists-launch-2-attacks-on-military-targets-in-somalia/. Accessed March 31, 2021.

57 Kevin J. Kelly and Aggrey Mutambo, "US Only Seeks to Weaken al-Shabaab to Reach Political Settlement," *The East African*, May 30, 2019. www.theeastafrican.co.ke/news/ea/US-only-seeks-to-weaken-Shabaab-to-reach-political-settlement-/4552908-5137870-r41g30/index.html. Accessed March 31, 2021.

58 General Thomas D. Waldhauser, Statement by US Commander of the United States Africa Command before the Senate Committee on Armed Services. February 7, 2010, page 21. http://www.armed-services.senate.gov/imo/media/doc/Waldhauser_02-07-19.pdf . Accessed March 31, 2021.

59 Ibid., page 36.

60 Spirit of America in Somalia. https://spiritofamerica.org/project/defeat-extremism-alongside-us-soldiers-somalia. Accessed March 31, 2021.

61 Bill Clinton, *My Life* (New York: Alfred A. Knopf, 2004), page 935.

62 Siobhan Gorman and Adam Entous, "CIA Plans Yemen Drone Strikes," *Wall Street Journal*, June 11, 2011, page A1.

63 Mark Mazzetti, Charlie Savage, and Scott Shane, "How a U.S. Citizen Came to Be in America's Cross Hairs," *New York Times*, March 9, 2013, page A1.

64 Maria Abi-Habib, "Yemen Exposes Difficulties in U.S. Strategy," *Wall Street Journal*, December 4, 2014, page A13.

65 For a review of the Yemen conflict, see Council of Foreign Relations. www.cfr .org/interactive/global-conflict-tracker/conflict/war-yemen?gclid=Cj0KCQjwov3n BRDFARIsANgsdoGAr4r88fBR1XagMrIWOvLoxAGw2fG9H9Tgp1M0gpl9d t9Ukf76JXoaAqhdEALw_wcB. Accessed March 31, 2021.

66 Declan Walsh, "U.S. Doesn't Pull the Triger in Yemen, but It Sent the Gun," *New York Times*, May 24, 2019, page A4.

67 Dion Nissenbaum, "Houthi Rebels Embrace Drones," *Wall Street Journal*, May 8, 2019, page A7.

68 Eric Schmitt, "Killing of Terrorists in Yemen Is Latest Blow to Qaeda Affiliate," *New York Times*, February 10, 2020, page A6.

69 Henriksen, *Eyes, Ears and Daggers*, page 138.

70 David Kirkpatrick, "Egypt and Israel Secretly Allied In Sinai Battle," *New York Times*, February 4, 2018, page A1.

71 Ben Hubbard, "Saudi Arabia Declares Cease-Fire in Yemen, Citing Fears of Coronavirus," *New York Times*, April 9, 2020, page A19.

72 Anonymous, "Islamist Terrorism in the Sahel: Fact or Fiction?" *Crisis Group Report*, March 31, 2005. www.crisisgroup.org/africa/central-africa/chad/islam ist-terrorism-sahel-fact-or-fiction. Accessed March 31, 2021.

73 Thomas P. M. Barnett, *The Pentagon's New Map: War and Peace in the Twenty-First Century* (New York: G. P. Putnam's Sons, 2004), page 150.

74 Malcolm Nance, *Defeating ISIS: Who They Are, How They Fight, What They Believe* (New York: Skyhorse, 2016), page 122.

75 Bernard-Henri Lévy, "The New War against Africa's Christians," *Wall Street Journal*, December 21, 2019, page A13.

76 Jared Malsin, "U.S. Pulls Some of Its Forces from Libya," *Wall Street Journal*, April 8, 2019, page A6.

77 Sean D. Naylor, "Libyan War Escalates amid Lack of U.S. Strategy for Secret Missions in Africa," *Yahoo News*, April 10, 2019. https://news.yahoo.com/ libyan-war-escalates-amid-lack-of-us-strategy-for-secret-missions-in-africa-090000507.html. Accessed March 31, 2021.

78 Vivian Salama, Jared Malsin, and Summer Said, "Saudis, Egypt Fueled U.S. Shift on Libya," *Wall Street Journal*, May 13, 2019, page A9.

79 Anonymous, "Mali Crisis: US Admits Mistakes in Training Local Troops," BBC News: Africa, January 25, 2013. www.bbc.com/news/world-africa-21195371. Accessed March 31, 2021.

80 Katherine Zimmerman, *Road to the Caliphate: The Salafist-Jihadi Movement's Strengths* (Washington, DC: American Enterprise Institute, 2019), page 15. www.aei.org/research-products/report/road-to-the-caliphate/.   Accessed March 31, 2021.

81 John Vinocur, "France Covers Obama's Middle East Retreat," *Wall Street Journal*, October 15, 2013, page A17.

82 Karen DeYoung, "U.S. Aid to France for Mali Operations Clears Legal Hurdles," *Washington Post*, January 26, 2013, page A7.

83 Adam Entous, David Gauthier-Villars, and Drew Hinshaw, "U.S. Boost War Role in Africa," *Wall Street Journal*, March 4, 2013, page A1.

84 James Blake, "Radical Islamist Have Opened a New Front in Mali," *Foreign Policy*, March 29, 2019. https://foreignpolicy.com/2019/03/29/radical-islam ists-have-opened-a-new-front-in-mali/. Accessed March 31, 2021.

85 Craig Whitlock, "Pentagon Setting up Drone Base in Africa to Track Boko Haram Fighters," *Washington Post*, October 14, 2015, page A20.

86 Eric Schmitt, "Pentagon Ends Review of Deadly Niger Ambush, Again Blaming Junior Officers," *New York Times*, June 6, 2019, page A1.

87 White House, National Strategy for Counterterrorism, October 2018. www .odni.gov/files/NCTC/documents/news_documents/NSCT.pdf.   Accessed March 31, 2021.

88 Joseph Trevithick, "SEAL Team Six Executes Long Distance Rescue Operation of Kidnapped American in Nigeria (Updated), *The War Zone*, October 31, 2020. www.thedrive.com/the-war-zone/37381/seal-team-six-exe cutes-long-distance-rescue-operation-of-kidnapped-american-in-nigeria. Accessed March 31, 2021. See also Eric Schmitt, "Navy Commandos Rescue American Kidnapped in Niger, *New York Times*, October 31, 2002, page A8.

89 Eric Schmitt and Thomas Gibbons-Neff, "Russian Exerts Growing Influence in Africa, Worrying Many in the West," *New York Times*, January 28, 2020, page A8.

7 America's Larger Forever Wars

1 Barack Obama, "My Plan for Iraq," *New York Times*, July 14, 2008, page A21.

2 Paul D. Miller, "Setting the Record Straight on Obama's Afghanistan Promises," *Foreign Policy*, March 29, 2016. https://foreignpolicy.com/2016/ 03/29/setting-the-record-straight-on-obamas-afghanistan-promises/#. Accessed March 31, 2021.

3 Rick Brennan, "Withdrawal Symptoms: The Bungling of the Iraq Exit," *Foreign Affairs* 93, no. 6 (November/December 2014), page 32.

4 William J. Bennett, "Obama Risks Iraq for Political Expediency," CNN, October 26, 2011. www.cnn.com/2011/10/26/opinion/bennett-losing-iraq-risk/index.html. Accessed March 31, 2021.

5 Liz Sly, "Iraqi Political Crisis Erupts as U.S. Leaves," *Washington Post*, December 18, 2011, page A10.

6 Jack Healy and Michael R. Gordon, "Large Bloc of Lawmakers Boycott Iraqi Parliament, Putting Coalition at Risk," *New York Times*, December 18, 2011, page A6.

7 Remarks by President Obama to the Australian Parliament, Parliament House, Canberra, Australia, November 17, 2011. www.whitehouse.gov/the-press-office/2011/11/17/remarks-president-obama-australian-parliament. Accessed March 31, 2021.

8 Daniel L. Byman, "Comparing Al Qaeda and ISIS: Different Goals, Different Targets," Brookings Institution, April 29, 2015. www.brookings .edu/testimonies/comparing-al-qaeda-and-isis-different-goals-different-targets/. Accessed March 31, 2021.

9 Katherine Zimmerman, *Road to the Caliphate: The Salafist-Jihadi Movement's Strengths* (Washington, DC: American Enterprise Institute, 2019), page 20.

10 David Remnick, "Going the Distance: On and Off the Road with Barack Obama," *New Yorker*, January 27, 2014, page 43.

11 "Briefing with Special Representative for Syria Engagement and Special Envoy for the Global Coalition to Defeat ISIS Ambassador James Jeffrey," US Department of State, March 25, 2019. https://ge.usembassy.gov/briefing-with-special-representative-for-syria-engagement-and-special-envoy-for-the-global-coalition-to-defeat-isis/. Accessed March 31, 2021.

12 Mary Anne Weaver, "Her Majesty's Jihadists," *New York Times*, April 14, 2015. www.nytimes.com/2015/04/19/magazine/her-majestys-jihadists.html. Accessed March 31, 2021.

13 Charles Lister, "The Syria Effect: Al-Qaeda Fractures," *Current Trends in Islamist Theology* 25 (February 2020), pages 54–55.

14 Helene Cooper, "Obama Allows Limited Airstrikes on ISIS," *New York Times*, August 7, 2014, page A1.

15 Benjamin Lambeth, *Airpower in the War against ISIS* (Annapolis: Naval Institute Press, 2021), page 94–96.

16 Eric Schmitt, Thomas Gibbons-Neff, Ben Hubbard, and Helene Cooper, "Pullback Leaves Green Berets Feeling 'Ashamed,' and Kurdish Allies Describing 'Betrayal,'" *New York Times*, October 14, 2019, page A1.

17 Mark Mazzetti and Eric Schmitt, "Obama's 'Boots on the Ground': U.S. Special Forces Are Sent to Tackle Global Threats," *New York Times*, December 27, 2015, page A1.

18 Helene Cooper, "Pentagon Officials Say They'll Bolster Special Operations Force in Iraq," *New York Times*, December 2, 2015, page A14.

19 Lambeth, *Airpower in the War against ISIS*, pages 130–131.

20 For a timeline and listing of terrorist attacks perpetrated by the Islamic State and its affiliates, see Woodrow Wilson International Center for Scholars, "Timeline: The Rise, Spread, and Fall of the Islamic State," April 30, 2019. www.wilsoncenter.org/article/timeline-the-rise-spread-and-fall-the-islamic-state. Accessed March 31, 2021.

21 For a listing of terrorist attacks conducted in the name of the Islamic State caliphate, see the report from the University of Maryland's Global Terrorism Database, August 2017. www.start.umd.edu/pubs/START_GTD_OverviewTerrorism2016_August2017.pdf. Accessed March 31, 2021.

22 Will Fulton, Joseph Holiday, and Sam Wyer, "Iranian Strategy in Syria," Institute for the Study of War, May 2013. www.understandingwar.org/report/iranian-strategy-syria. Accessed March 31, 2021.

23 Renad Mansour, "Reining in Iraq's Paramilitaries Will Just Make Them Stronger," *Foreign Policy*, July 9, 2019. https://foreignpolicy.com/2019/07/09/shiite-militias-are-taking-over-the-iraqi-state-from-the-inside/?utm_source=PostUp&utm_medium=email&utm_campaign=14003&utm_term=Flashpoints%20OC. Accessed March 31, 2021.

24 Mark Preston, "Poll: Americans Back Airstrikes, but Oppose Use of U.S. Troops in Iraq, Syria," CNN, September 29, 2014. www.cnn.com/2014/09/

29/politics/poll-americans-back-airstrikes/index.html.   Accessed   March 31, 2021.

25 James Marson, "NATO Aims to Add Personnel to Iraq Mission from Coalition Fighting ISIS," *Wall Street Journal*, January 27, 2020, page A1.

26 T. E. Lawrence, "Twenty-Seven Articles," *The Arab Bulletin*, August 20, 1917. (Reprint, New York: Simon & Schuster, 2017), page 39.

27 Leith Aboufadel, "Over 26,000 Iraqi Soldiers Killed in 4 Year War with ISIS," AMN News, December 13, 2017. www.almasdarnews.com/article/ 26000-iraqi-soldiers-killed-4-year-war-isis/. Accessed March 31, 2021.

28 Jack Detsch, "Top US General's Retirement Marks Turning Point in Mideast Operations," *Al-Monitor*, July 8, 2019. www.al-monitor.com/pulse/ originals/2019/07/top-general-votel-retirement-turning-point-mideast.html. Accessed March 31, 2021.

29 Tamer El-Ghobashy and Mustafa Salim, "As Iraq's Shiite Militias Expand Their Reach Concerns about ISIS Revival Grow," *Washington Post*, January 9, 2019, page A1.

30 Mark Landler, Helene Cooper, and Eric Schmitt, "Trump to Withdraw U.S. Forces from Syria, Declaring 'We Have Won against ISIS,'" *New York Times*, December 19, 2018. www.nytimes.com/2018/12/19/us/politics/trump-syria- turkey-troop-withdrawal.html. Accessed March 31, 2021.

31 Katie Bo Williams, "Outgoing Syria Envoy Admits Hiding US Troops Numbers; Praises Trump's Mideast Record," *Defense One*, November 12, 2020. www.defenseone.com/threats/2020/11/outgoing-syria-envoy-admits- hiding-us-troop-numbers-praises-trumps-mideast-record/170012/. Accessed March 31, 2021.

32 Jonathan Spyer, "The Fighting Continues in Northern Syria," *Wall Street Journal*, November 26, 2019, page A15.

33 Kyle Rempfer "Here's the Current U.S. Plans to Build up Syrian Proxies, Including an Oilfield Guard Force," *Army Times*, August 19, 2020. www .armytimes.com/news/your-army/2020/08/10/heres-the-current-us-plan-to- build-up-syrian-proxies-including-an-oilfield-guard-force/. Accessed March 31, 2021.

34 Vivian Salama, Michael R. Gordon, and Jared Malsin, "Trump Lifts Sanctions on Turkey as Moscow-Brokered Cease-Fire Takes Hold," *Wall Street Journal*, October 23, 2019, page A8.

35 Frederic C. Hof, "The United States in Syria: Why It Still Matters," Atlantic Council, September, 2019. https://atlanticcouncil.org/wp-content/uploads/ 2019/09/A-Long-Road-to-Syria-IB-FIN-web-092319.pdf. Accessed March 31, 2021.

36 Neta C. Crawford, "The Iraq War Has Cost the US Nearly $2 Trillion," *Military Times*, February 6, 2020. www.militarytimes.com/opinion/commen tary/2020/02/06/the-iraq-war-has-cost-the-us-nearly-2-trillion/?utm_source= Sailthru&utm_medium=email&utm_campaign=EBB%2002.06.20&utm_ term=Editorial%20-%20Early%20Bird%20Brief. Accessed March 31, 2021.

37 Barack Obama's Acceptance Speech at the Democratic Convention, August 28, 2008. http://elections.nytimes.com/2008/president/conventions/videos/ 20080828_OBAMA_SPEECH.html. Accessed March 31, 2021.

38 Derek Chollet, *The Long Game: How Obama Defied Washington and Redefined America's Role in the World* (New York: PublicAffairs, 2016), page 71.

39 Thom Shanker and Eric Schmitt, "U.S. Plans Vastly Expanded Afghan Security Forces," *New York Times*, March 19, 2009, page A1.

40 Julian F. Barnes, "Agencies Prep Obama for 'Tourniquet' Afghanistan," *Los Angeles Times*, December 23, 2008, page A1.

41 Helene Cooper, "Putting Stamp on the Afghan War, Obama Will Send 17,000 Troops," *New York Times*, February 17, 2009, page A1.

42 The White House, "Remarks by the President at the Veterans of Foreign Wars Convention," August 17, 2009, pages 3–4.

43 All quotations in this paragraph are from Dexter Filkins, "Stanley McChrystal's Long War," *New York Times Magazine*, October, 2009, page 38.

44 COMISAF, Initial Assessment (Unclassified) September 9, 2009. www .washingtonpost.com/wp-dyn/content/article/2009/09/21/AR2009092100110 .html. Accessed March 31, 2021.

45 Harlan K. Ullman, *Anatomy of Failure: Why America Loses Every War It Starts* (Annapolis: Naval Institute Press), page 182.

46 But he had not read widely enough to know how valid the assessments turned out to be. But by 1970, politicians no longer trusted the Nixon White House nor its Pentagon. For a reappraisal, see Lewis Sorely, *A Better War: The Unexamined Victories and Final Tragedy of America's Last Years in Vietnam* (New York: Houghton Mifflin Harcourt, 1999), page 217.

47 James Mann, *The Obamians: The Struggle Inside the White House How to Define American Power* (New York: Viking, 2012), pages 79 and 136.

48 Alessandra Stanley, "Before Audience of Cadets, a Sobering Message of War," *New York Times*, December 2, 2009, page A1.

49 Bob Woodward, "McChrystal: More Forces or 'Mission Failure,'" *Washington Post*, September 21, 2009, page A1.

50 Mark Landler, "The Afghan War and the Evolution of Obama," *New York Times*, January 1, 2017. www.nytimes.com/2017/01/01/world/asia/obama-afghanistan-war.html. Accessed March 31, 2021.

51 Trudy Rubin, "Obama Can't Delay Decision on Afghan Strategy Any Longer," *Philadelphia Inquirer*, September 20, 2009, page 15.

52 Peter Baker, "A Biden Challenge to Clinton Would Expose a Policy Split," *New York Times*, October 10, 2015, page A1.

53 Eric Schmitt and David E. Sanger, "Obama Is Facing Doubts in Party on Afghanistan," *New York Times*, September 11, 2009, page A1.

54 Ben Rhodes, *The World As It Is: A Memoir of the Obama White House* (New York: Random House, 2018), pages 72–78.

55 Bob Woodward, *Obama's Wars* (New York: Simon & Schuster, 2010), page 223.

56 Mann, *The Obamians*, pages 123–128.

57 Dalia Sussman, "Poll Finds Pessimism on the War," *New York Times*, July 14, 2010, page A9.

58 Stanley McChrystal, *My Share of the Task: A Memoir* (New York: Penguin Group, 2013), page 345.

59 Stanley McChrystal, COMISAF's Initial Assessment, August 30, 2009. www
    .washingtonpost.com/wp-dyn/content/article/2009/09/21/AR2009092100110
    .html. Accessed March 31, 2021.
60 "ISAF Commander Issues Updated Tactic Directive," International Security
    Assistance Force HQ Public Affairs, August 4, 2010. www.dvidshub.net/
    news/53927/isaf-commander-issues-updated-tactical-directive.   Accessed
    March 31, 2021.
61 Wesley Morgan, "Weighing Threats and Rules of Engagement in
    Afghanistan," New York Times, August 23, 2010, page A8.
62 Dexter Filkins, "Afghan Offensive Is New War Model," New York Times,
    February 12, 2010, page A1.
63 Michael Hastings, The Operators: The Wild and Terrifying Inside Story of
    America's War in Afghanistan (New York: Plume, 2012), pages 14 and 33–34.
64 Barack Obama, A Promised Land (New York: Crown, 2020), page 579.
65 Mujib Mashal, "Afghan Taliban Awash in Heroin Cash, a Troubling Turn
    for War," New York Times, October 29, 2017, page A1.
66 Thomas Gibbons-Neff, "A Marine Looks Back at His Battles in
    Afghanistan," New York Times, September 16, 2019, page A1.
67 Bill Roggio and Lisa Lundquist, "Green-on-Blue Attacks in Afghanistan: The
    Data," Long War Journal, June 12, 2017. www.longwarjournal.org/archives/
    2012/08/green-on-blue_attack.php. Accessed March 31, 2021.
68 Jared Keller, "Afghan Security Forces Averaged One Insider Attack Every
    4 Days in the Closing Months of 2019, New Data Shows," Task and Purpose,
    February 3, 2020. https://taskandpurpose.com/afghanistan-insider-attacks-
    2019-sigar?utm_source=Sailthru&utm_medium=email&utm_campaign=
    EBB%2002.04.20&utm_term=Editorial%20-%20Early%20Bird%20Brief.
    Accessed March 31, 2021.
69 GAO Report to Congress, "Afghan Army Growing, but Additional Trainers
    Needed, Long Term Costs Not Determined," January 2011. www.gao.gov/
    assets/gao-11-66.pdf. Accessed March 31, 2021.
70 Ian S. Livingston and Michael O'Hanlon, "Brookings: Afghanistan Index,"
    May 25, 2017, page 7.
71 Ibid., page 6.
72 Robert D. Kaplan, Imperial Grunts: On the Ground with the American Military
    from Mongolia to the Philippines to Iraq and Beyond (New York: Vintage Books,
    2006), page 209.
73 Dan Lamothe, "Afghanistan Is Building up Its Commando Force to Fight the
    Taliban. But at What Cost?" Washington Post, April 28, 2018, page A26.
74 Neta C. Crawford and Catherine Lutz, "Human Costs of Post-9/11 Wars:
    Direct War Deaths in Major War Zones," Brown University, Watson
    Institute for International and Public Affairs, November 2019. https://
    watson.brown.edu/costsofwar/costs/human/civilians/afghan. Accessed March
    31, 2021.
75 "Casualty Status," US Department of Defense, May 4, 2020. www.defense
    .gov/casualty.pdf. Accessed March 31, 2021.
76 Alissa J. Rubin, "2010 Is Deadliest Year for NATO in Afghan War," New
    York Times, September 21, 2010, page A8.

77 Shawn Snow, "Afghan Casualties and Attrition Are Outpacing Recruitment and Retention," *Military Times*, February 4, 2020. www.militarytimes.com/flashpoints/2020/02/03/afghan-casualties-and-attrition-are-outpacing-recruitment-and-retention/. Accessed March 31, 2021.

78 David Zucchino, "The U.S. Spent $8 Billion on an Independent Afghanistan's Air Force. It's Still Struggling," *New York Times*, January 10, 2019, page A1.

79 Mark Landler, "U.S. Troops to Leave Afghanistan, *New York Times*, May 27, 2014, page A1.

80 Mark Landler, "Obama Says He will Keep More Troops in Afghanistan Than Planned," *New York Times*, July 6, 2016, page A1.

81 Steve Cole, *Directorate S: The C.I.A. and America's Secret War in Afghanistan and Pakistan* (New York: Penguin, 2018), pages 358 and 532–535.

82 Jessica Purkiss and Jack Serle, "Obama's Covert Drone War in Numbers: Ten Times More Strikes Than Bush," Bureau of Investigative Journalism (January 17, 2017. www.thebureauinvestigates.com/stories/2017-01-17/obamas-covert-drone-war-in-numbers-ten-times-more-strikes-than-bush. Accessed March 31, 2021.

83 Micah Zenko, "How Barack Obama Has Tried to Open up the One-Sided Drone War," *Financial Times*, May 23, 2013, page 9.

84 Micah Zenko, "Obama's Embrace of Drone Strikes Will Be a Lasting Legacy," *New York Times*, January 12, 2016, page A1.

85 David E. Sanger, *Confront and Conceal: Obama's Secret Wars and Surprising Use of American Power* (New York: Crown, 2013), pages 128, 134–135, and 247–250; and Jo Becker and Scott Shane, "Secret 'Kill List' Proves a Test of Obama's Principles and Will," *New York Times*, May 29, 2012, page A1.

86 Charlie Savage, "Court Releases Parts of Memo Approving Killing of American in Yemen," *New York Times*, June 23, 2014, page A6.

87 In 2014, US aircraft released 2,365 weapons in Afghanistan. In 2019, they released 7,423. See "Combined Forces Air Component Commander 2013–2019 Airpower Statistics," United States Air Force Central Command, January 31, 2020. www.afcent.af.mil/Portals/82/Documents/Airpower%20summary/Jan%202020%20Airpower%20Summary.pdf?ver=2020-02-13-032911-670. Accessed March 31, 2021.

88 "Drone Strikes in Yemen," Bureau of Investigative Journalism, www.thebureauinvestigates.com/projects/drone-war/yemen. Accessed March 31, 2021.

89 "Drone Strikes in Somalia," New America Foundation, www.newamerica.org/in-depth/americas-counterterrorism-wars/somalia/. Accessed March 31, 2021.

90 Jessica Purkiss and Jack Serle, "Obama's Covert Drone War in Numbers: Ten Times More Strikes Than Bush," Bureau of Investigative Journalism, January 17, 2017. www.thebureauinvestigates.com/stories/2017-01-17/obamas-covert-drone-war-in-numbers-ten-times-more-strikes-than-bush. Accessed March 31, 2021.

91 Ibid.

92 Richard Miniter, *Leading from Behind: The Reluctant President and the Advisors Who Decide for Him* (New York: St. Martin's Griffin, 2013), page 116.

93 For an unauthorized account of the raid, see Mark Bissonette (pen name Mark Owen), *No Easy Day: The Autobiography of a Navy SEAL* (New York: Dutton, 2012), pages 213–256. For a newspaper account about the supposed killer of Osama bin Laden, see Joby Warrick, "Ex-SEAL Robert O'Neill Reveals Himself as Shooter Who Killed Osama bin Laden," *Washington Post*, November 6, 2014, page A1.

94 Billy Vaughn et al., *Betrayed: The Shocking Story of Extortion 17 as Told by a Navy SEAL's Father* (Stuart: Molon Labe Media, 2013); and Ed Darack, *The Final Mission of Extortion 17: Special Ops, Helicopter Support, Seal Team Six and the Deadliest Day of the U.S. War in Afghanistan* (Washington, DC: Smithsonian Books, 2017).

95 Ryan N. Mannina, "How the 2011 US Troop Withdrawal from Iraq Led to the Rise of ISIS," *Small Wars Journal*. https://smallwarsjournal.com/jrnl/art/how-2011-us-troop-withdrawal-iraq-led-rise-isis. Accessed March 31, 2021.

96 Mark Mazzetti and Eric Schmitt, "In Secret, Obama Extends U.S. Role in Afghan Combat," *New York Times*, November, 22, 2014, page A1.

97 Susannah George, "The Past Three Months in Afghanistan Have Been the Deadliest for Civilians in Decade," *Washington Post*, October 17, 2019, page A24.

98 Special Inspector General for Afghanistan Recovery, "Quarterly Report to the United States Congress," September 30, 2019, page 45. www.sigar.mil/pdf/quarterlyreports/2019-10-30qr.pdf. Accessed March 31, 2021.

99 Matthew Pennington, "Pentagon: Afghan War Costing US \$45 Billion a Year," *Military Times*, February 6, 2018. www.militarytimes.com/news/pentagon-congress/2018/02/07/pentagon-afghan-war-costing-us-45-billion-per-year. Accessed March 31, 2021.

100 Nancy A. Youssef and Warren P. Strobel, "U.S. Fights an Islamic State in Afghanistan," *Wall Street Journal*, December 26, 2019, page A1.

101 US CENTCOM Commander General Kenneth F. McKenzie Jr. stated that the US has provided "limited support" to the Taliban in the fight against the Islamic State forces in Nangarhar Province. See US House Armed Services Committee Hearing: "National Security Challenges and U.S. Military Activities in the Greater Middle East and Africa," March 10, 2020. https://armedservices.house.gov/2020/3/full-committee-hearing-national-security-challenges-and-u-s-military-activities-in-the-greater-middle-east-and-africa. Accessed March 31, 2021.

102 Robert M. Gates, *Duty: Memoirs of a Secretary at War* (New York: Alfred A. Knopf, 2014), page 587.

103 Mark Landler, "The Afghan War and the Evolution of Obama," *New York Times*, January 1, 2017, page A1.

104 Ali A. Jalaii, *Afghan National Defense and Security Forces: Mission, Challenges and Sustainability* (Washington, DC: Unite States Institute of Peace, 2016.

www.usip.org/publications/2016/05/afghanistan-national-defense-and-secur ity-forces. Accessed March 31, 2021.

105 Helene Cooper, "U.S. General Says Afghans Still Need Aid," *New York Times*, August 29, 2019, page A11.

106 Barack Obama, "Remarks by the President in Address to the Nation on the Way Forward in Afghanistan and Pakistan," US Military Academy at West Point, NY, December 1, 2009. https://obamawhitehouse.archives.gov/the-press-office/remarks-president-address-nation-way-forward-afghanistan-and-pakistan. Accessed March 31, 2021.

107 "Resolute Support Mission (RSM): Key Facts and Figures," NATO, February, 2020. www.nato.int/nato_static_fl2014/assets/pdf/2020/2/pdf/ 2020-02-RSM-Placemat.pdf. Accessed March 31, 2021.

108 Fred Kaplan, *The Insurgents: David Petraeus and the Plot to Change the American Way of War* (New York: Simon & Schuster, 2013), page 316.

109 Special Inspector General for Afghanistan Recovery, "Quarterly Report to the United States Congress,", January 30, 2017. www.sigar.mil/pdf/quarter lyreports/2017-01-30qr.pdf. Accessed March 31, 2021.

110 Barack Obama, "The New Way Forward – the President's Address," US Military Academy at West Point, December 1, 2009. https:// obamawhitehouse.archives.gov/blog/2009/12/01/new-way-forward-presi dents-address. Accessed March 31, 2021.

111 "What do you think is the most important problem facing the country today?" Gallup poll question, 2002–2020. For much of 2002, terrorism and war topped the list of most important non-economic problems. In 2010, Afghanistan was explicitly mentioned as number twelve. https://news .gallup.com/poll/1675/most-important-problem.aspx. Accessed March 31, 2021.

112 "Remarks by President Trump on the Strategy in Afghanistan and South Asia," Fort Myer, Arlington, Virginia. August 21, 2017. https://in .usembassy.gov/remarks-president-trump-strategy-afghanistan-south-asia/. Accessed March 31, 2021.

113 John Haltiwanger, "Afghanistan Is Officially the Most Dangerous Country in the World – More Proof the US War There Has Failed." *Business Insider*, June 12, 2019. www.businessinsider.com/afghanistan-is-officially-the-most-dangerous-country-in-the-world-2019-6. Accessed March 31, 2021.

114 Helene Cooper and Mujib Mashal, "U.S. Drops 'Mother of All Bombs' on ISIS Caves in Afghanistan," *New York Times*, April 13, 2017, page A1.

115 Thomas Gibbons-Neff and Mujib Mashal, "ISIS Is Losing Afghan Territory. That Means Little for Its Victims," *New York Times*, December 2, 2019, page A6.

116 Eathan Kapstein and Nathan Converse, *The Fate of Young Democracies* (New York: Cambridge University Press, 2008), pages 36–47; Larry Diamond, "Facing up to the Democratic Rescission," *Journal of Democracy* 26, no. 1 (January 2015), pages 141–155; and "Democracy in Retreat," *Freedom in the World 2019*, Freedom House. https://freedomhouse.org/report/freedom-world/freedom-world-2019/democracy-in-retreat. Accessed March 31, 2021.

117 Agreement to Bring Peace to Afghanistan. Department of State, February 29, 2020. www.state.gov/wp-content/uploads/2020/02/Agreement-For-Bringing-Peace-to-Afghanistan-02.29.20.pdf. Accessed March 31, 2021.

118 Rebecca Kheel, "Polls: About Three-Quarters Support Bringing Troops Home from Iraq, Afghanistan," *The Hill*, August 6, 2020. https://thehill .com/policy/defense/510851-poll-about-three-quarters-support-bringing-troops-home-from-iraq-afghanistan. Accessed March 31, 2021.

119 Joseph Votel, "Ending Our Endless War in Afghanistan," *Wall Street Journal*, December 12, 2019, page A13. Votel served as Central Command head from March 2016 to March 2019.

120 Missy Ryan, "For Most of the Afghanistan War, U.S. 'Never Really Fought to Win,' Trump Declares," *Washington Post*, May 18, 2020, page A1.

121 Ben Connable and Martin C. Libicki, *How Insurgences End* (Santa Monica: RAND, 2010), pages 34–35.

122 Donald Stoker, *Why America Loses Wars* (New York: Cambridge University Press, 2019), page 222.

123 Brett Boudreau, *We Have Met the Enemy and He Is Us: An Analysis of NATO Strategic Communications: The International Security Assistance Force in Afghanistan, 2003–2014* (Riga: NATO Strategic Communications Center of Excellence, 2016), pages 36–38; Mujib Mashal, "'Time for This War in Afghanistan to End,' Says Departing U.S. Commander," *New York Times*, September 2, 2018. www.nytimes.com/2018/09/02/world/asia/afghan-com mander-us-john-nicholson.html. Accessed March 31, 2021.

124 Nadia Schadlow, *War and the Art of Governance: Consolidating Combat Success into Political Victory* (Washington, DC: George Washington University Press, 2017), page 223–223.

125 Ellen Mitchell, "Joint Chief Chair: US Has 'Achieved a Modicum of Success' in Afghanistan," *The Hill*, December 2, 2020. https://thehill.com/policy/defense/528441-joint-chiefs-chair-us-has-achieved-a-modicum-of-success-in-afghanistan, Accessed March 31, 2021.

126 Shawn Snow, Leo Shane, and Joe Gould, "Afghan Special Operators Partnering with US forces More Often, Still Reliant on American Support," *Military Times*, February 6, 2020. www.militarytimes.com/flash points/2020/02/05/afghan-special-operators-partnering-with-us-forces-more-often-still-reliant-on-american-support/. Accessed March 31, 2021.

127 Woodward, *Obama's Wars*, page 355 and 366.

128 Greg Miller and Julie Tate, "CIA Shifts Focus to Killing Targets," *Washington Post*, September 1, 2011, page A1.

129 Mujib Mashal, "C.I.A.'s Afghan Forces Leave a Trail of Abuse and Anger," *New York Times*, December 31, 2018, page A1.

8 A Conclusion

1 Joseph Zeballos-Roig, "The US Has Blown Past $6 Trillion in 'War on Terror' Spending since 2001 – and Its Cost to Taxpayers Will Keep Climbing for Decades, Study Says," *Business Insider*, November 21, 2019.

www.businessinsider.com/us-spending-war-on-terror-stands-at-6-trillion-report-2019-11. Accessed March 31, 2021.

2 John Cogan, *The High Cost of Good Intentions: A History of the U.S. Federal Entitlement Programs* (Stanford: Stanford University Press, 2017), pages 370–380.

3 Jane Perlez and Yufan Huang, "Behind China's $1 Trillion Plan to Shake Up the Economic Order," *New York Times*, May 13, 2017. www.nytimes.com/2017/05/13/business/china-railway-one-belt-one-road-1-trillion-plan.html. Accessed March 31, 2021.

4 Dimitri Simes, "Russia up in Arms over Chinese Theft of Military Technology," *Nikkei Asian Review*, December 20, 2019. https://asia.nikkei.com/Politics/International-relations/Russia-up-in-arms-over-Chinese-theft-of-military-technology. Accessed March 31, 2021.

5 David Geaney, "China's Island Fortifications Are a Challenge to International Norms," *Defense News*, April 17, 2020. www.defensenews.com/opinion/commentary/2020/04/17/chinas-island-fortifications-are-a-challenge-to-international-norms/. Accessed March 31, 2021.

6 Kurt M. Campbell and Ely Ratner, "The China Reckoning: How Beijing Defied American Expectations," *Foreign Affairs*, February 13, 2018. www.foreignaffairs.com/articles/china/2018-02-13/china-reckoning#//www.foreignaffairs.com/. Accessed March 31, 2021. Another perfect example of this thinking is Graham Allison, *Destined for War: Can America and China Escape Thucydides's Trap?* (London: Scribe, 2017), pages 154–184.

7 John J. Mearsheimer, *The Great Delusion: Liberal Dreams and International Realities* (New Haven: Yale University Press, 2018), page 228.

8 The White House, National Security Strategy to Advance America's Interests, December 18, 2017. https://web.archive.org/web/20180108114553/www.whitehouse.gov/briefings-statements/president-donald-j-trump-announces-national-security-strategy-advance-americas-interests/. Accessed March 31, 2021.

9 Department of Defense, Summary of the 2018 National Defense Strategy of the United States of America, January 19, 2018. https://dod.defense.gov/Portals/1/Documents/pubs/2018-National-Defense-Strategy-Summary.pdf. Accessed March 31, 2021.

10 Rebecca Kheel, "House Defense Bill Targets Potential Troop Drawdowns in Africa, South Korea, *The Hill*, June 26, 2020. https://thehill.com/policy/defense/504629-house-defense-bill-targets-potential-troop-drawdowns-in-africa-south-korea. Accessed March 31, 2021.

11 Elizabeth Drew, "How Much Is George W. Bush Responsible for 9/11?," Huffpost, November 2, 2016. www.huffpost.com/entry/the-big-bush-question_b_8454434?guccounter=1&guce_referrer=aHR0cHM6Ly93d3cuZ29vZ2xlLmNvbS8&guce_referrer_sig=AQAAANkizcfs3cIrE_Sg6w7EvFPn5GV-wsw-W8DKVb_8a3iwhQ_LzXUdozxYymBfG8OSAsclwDZk7lTrCyWtiiWjzbbFi2oYqydfjuZCNidfvY5607_FlBL42pldk-vXrv5l1CPzib_A5oaqjWZo5Hx6MT3L-oo5pPBOj25gAcUbFEH. Accessed March 31, 2021.

12 *The 9/11 Commission Report*, authorized edition (New York: W. W. Norton Company, 2011), pages 254–277.

13 Audrey Kurth Cronin, *How Terrorism Ends: Understanding the Decline and Demise of Terrorist Campaigns* (Princeton: Princeton University Press, 2011), pages 94–110.

14 Jon Harper, "Special Ops Command Faces Funding Cuts," *National Defense*, April 23, 2020. www.nationaldefensemagazine.org/articles/2020/4/23/special-ops-command-faces-funding-cuts. Accessed March 31, 2021.

15 "Open Letter from National Security Professionals to Western Governments: Unless We Act Now, the Islamic State Will Rise Again," *The Soufan Center*, September 11, 2019. https://thesoufancenter.org/wp-content/uploads/2019/09/FTF-Open-Letter.pdf. Accessed March 31, 2021.

16 Herman J. Cohen, "Pulling Troops out of Africa Could Mean Endless War," War on the Rocks (March 13, 2020). Downloaded: https://warontherocks.com/2020/05/pulling-troops-out-of-africa-could-mean-another-endless-war/. Accessed March 31, 2021.

17 H. R. McMaster, *Battlegrounds: The Fight to Defend the Free World* (New York: Harper, 2020), page 440.

18 Eric Schmitt, "U.S. Military Cutting Medevac Flights for Troops in Africa," *New York Times*, April 18, 2020, page A8.

19 Deutsche Welle, "Dozens in Mozambique Killed for Refusing to Join Terrorists," April 22, 2020. www.dw.com/en/dozens-killed-in-mozambique-for-refusing-to-join-terrorists/a-53211140. Accessed March 31, 2021; and Danielle Paquette, Souad Mekhennet, and Joby Warrick, "ISIS Attacks Surge in Africa Even as Trump Boasts of a '100-Percent' Defeated Caliphate," *Washington Post*, October 18, 2020, page A1.

20 Robert D. Kaplan, *Imperial Grunts: On the Ground with the American Military from Mongolia to the Philippines to Iraq and Beyond* (New York: Vintage Books, 2006), pages 4 and 8–11.

21 Byron Farwell, *Queen Victoria's Little Wars* (London: Allen Lane, 1973), page 1.

Bibliography

Albright, Madeleine, *Madame Secretary: A Memoir* (New York: Miramax Books, 2003).

Allison, Graham, *Destined for War: Can America and China Escape Thucydides's Trap?* (London: Scribe, 2017).

Arendt, Hannah, *On Revolution* (New York: Viking Press, 1965).

Atkinson, Rick, *Crusade: The Untold Story of the Persian Gulf War* (Boston: Houghton Mifflin, 1993).

Baer, Robert, *See No Evil* (New York: Three Rivers Press, 2002).

Baker, James A. III, *The Politics of Diplomacy: Revolution, War, and Peace* (New York: G. P. Putnam's Sons, 1995).

et al., *The Iraq Study Group Report: The Way Forward – A New Approach*, Authorized Edition (New York: Vintage Books, 2006).

Barfield, Thomas, *Afghanistan: A Cultural and Political History* (Princeton: Princeton University Press, 2010).

Barnett, Thomas P. M., *The Pentagon's New Map: War and Peace in the Twenty-First Century* (New York: G. P. Putnam's Sons, 2004).

Benjamin, Daniel, and Steven Simon, *The Age of Sacred Terror* (New York: Random House, 2002).

Blix, Hans, *Disarming Iraq* (New York: Pantheon Books, 2004).

Blumenthal, Sidney, *The Clinton Wars* (New York: Farrar, Straus and Giroux, 2003).

Borger, Julian, *The Butcher's Trail: How the Search for Balkan Criminals Became the World's Most Successful Manhunt* (New York: Other Press, 2016).

Boudreau, Brett, *We Have Met the Enemy and He Is Us: An Analysis of NATO Strategic Communications: The International Security Assistance Force in Afghanistan, 2003–2014* (Riga: NATO Strategic Communications Center of Excellence, 2016).

Bowden, Mark, *Black Hawk Down: A Story of Modern War* (New York: New American Library, 1999).

Killing Pablo: The Hunt for the World's Greatest Outlaw (New York: Grove Press, 2015).

Boykin, William G., *Never Surrender: A Soldiers Journey to the Crossroads of Faith and Freedom* (New York: Hachette Books Group, 2008).

Bremer, L. Paul, *My Year in Iraq: The Struggle to Build a Future of Hope* (New York: Simon & Schuster, 2006).

Buchanan, Patrick, *Suicide of a Superpower* (New York: Thomas Dunne Books, 2011).

Bush, George H. W., and Brent Scowcroft, *A World Transformed* (New York: Alfred A. Knopf, 1998).

Bush, George W., *Decision Points* (New York: Crown, 2010).

Butler, Richard, *The Greatest Threat: Iraq, Weapons of Mass Destruction, and the Growing Crisis of Global Security* (New York: Public Affairs, 2000).

Carney, John T., and Benjamin F. Schemmer, *No Room For Error: The Covert Operations of America's Special Tactic Units from Iran to Afghanistan* (New York: Ballantine Books, 2002).

Cheney, Dick, *In My Time: A Personal and Political Memoir* (New York: Threshold Editions, 2011).

Cholett, Derek, *The Long Game: How Obama Defied Washington and Redefined America's Role in the World* (New York: PublicAffairs, 2016).

Clark, Wesley K., *Waging Modern War: Bosnia, Kosovo, and the Future of Combat* (New York: Public Affairs, 2001).

Clarke, Richard A., *Against All Enemies: Inside American's War on Terrorism* (New York: Free Press, 2004).

Clarke, Walter, and Jeffrey Herbst (eds.), *Learning from Somalia* (Boulder: Westview Press, 1997).

Clinton, Bill, *My Life* (New York: Alfred A. Knopf, 2004).

Cogan, John, *The High Cost of Good Intentions: A History of the U.S. Federal Entitlement Programs* (Stanford: Stanford University Press, 2017).

Cole, Steve, *Directorate S: The C.I.A. and America's Secret War in Afghanistan and Pakistan* (New York: Penguin, 2018).

   Ghost Wars: The Secret History of the CIA, Afghanistan, and bin Laden from the Soviet Invasion to September 10, 2001 (New York: Penguin Press, 2004).

Colodny, Len, and Tom Shachtman, *The Forty Years War: The Rise and Fall of the Neocons* (New York: HarperCollins, 2016).

Connable, Ben, and Martin C. Libikci, *How Insurgences End* (Santa Monica: RAND, 2010).

Cordesman, Anthony H., *The Iraq War: Strategy, Tactics, and Military Lessons* (Washington, DC: CSIS Press, 2004).

Couch, Dick, *The Sheriff of Ramadi: Navy SEALs and the Winning of Anbar* (Annapolis: Naval Institute Press, 2008).

Cronin, Audrey Kurth, *How Terrorism Ends: Understanding the Decline and Demise of Terrorist Campaigns* (Princeton: Princeton University Press, 2011).

Daalder, Ivo H., and Michael E. O'Hanlon, *Winning Ugly: NATO's War to Save Kosovo* (New York: Brookings Institution, 2000).

Darack, Ed, *The Final Mission of Extortion 17: Special Ops, Helicopter Support, Seal Team Six and the Deadliest Day of the U.S. War in Afghanistan* (Washington, DC: Smithsonian Books, 2017).

Dobbin, James et al., *America's Role in Nation-Building from Germany to Afghanistan* (Santa Monica: RAND, 2003).

Drew, Elizabeth, *On the Edge: The Clinton Presidency* (New York: Simon & Schuster, 1994).

Dueck, Colin, *Age of Iron: On Conservative Nationalism* (New York: Oxford University Press, 2020).

Farwell, Byron, *Queen Victoria's Little Wars* (London: Allen Lane, 1973).

Fatton, Robert Jr., *Haiti's Predatory Republic: The Unending Transition to Democracy* (Boulder: Lynne Rienner, 2002).

Fawn, Rick, and Raymond Hinnebucsh, *The Iraq War: Causes and Consequences* (Boulder: Lynne Rienner, 2006).

Feith, Douglas J., *War and Decision: Inside the Pentagon at the Dawn of the War on Terrorism* (New York: HarperCollins, 2008).

Felter, Joseph, and Brian Fishman, *Iranian Strategy in Iraq: Politics and "Other Means"* (West Point: Combating Terrorism Center, 2008).

Franks, Tommy, *American Soldier* (New York: Regan Books, 2004).

Gallagher, Tom, *The Balkans in the New Millennium: In the Shadow of War and Peace* (New York: Routledge, 2005).

Galula, David, *Counterinsurgency Warfare: Theory and Practice* (Westport: Praeger, 2006, originally published in 1927).

Gates, Robert M., *Duty: Memoirs of a Secretary at War* (New York: Alfred A. Knopf, 2014).

Gordon, Michael R., and Bernard E. Trainor, *Cobra II: The Inside Story of the Invasion and Occupation of Iraq* (New York: Pantheon Books, 2006).

The Endgame: The Inside Story of the Struggle for Iraq, from George W. Bush to Barack Obama (New York: Vintage Books, 2012).

The Generals' War: The Inside Story of the Conflict in the Gulf (Boston: Little, Brown, 1995).

Graham, Bob, *Intelligence Matters* (New York: Radom House, 2004).

Haass, Richard N., *The Reluctant Sheriff: The United States after the Cold War* (New York: Council of Foreign Relations, 1997).

Halper, Stefan, and Jonathan Clarke, *America Alone: The Neo-Conservatives and the Global Order* (Cambridge: Cambridge University Press, 2004).

Hanson, Victor Davis, *The Second World War: How the First Global Conflict Was Fought and Won* (New York: Basic Books, 2017).

Hastings, Michael, *The Operators: The Wild and Terrifying Inside Story of America's War in Afghanistan* (New York: Plume, 2012).

Henriksen, Thomas H., *America and the Rogue States* (New York: Palgrave, 2012).

Eyes, Ears, and Daggers: Special Operations Forces and the Central Intelligence Agency in America's Evolving Struggle against Terrorism (Stanford: Hoover Institution Press, 2017).

Herring, George C., *From Colony to Superpower: U.S. Foreign Relations since 1776* (New York: Oxford University Press, 2008).

Hoffman, Stanley, "Yugoslavia: Implications for Europe and European Institutions," in *The World and Yugoslavia's Wars*, edited by Richard H. Ullman (New York: Council on Foreign Relations, 1996), 97–121.

Holbrooke, Richard, *To End a War* (New York: Random House, 1998).

Holzgrefe, J. L., and Robert O. Keohane (eds.), *Humanitarian Intervention: Ethical, Legal, and Political Dilemmas* (New York: Cambridge University Press, 2003).

Hosmer, Stephen T., *The Conflict over Kosovo: Why Milošević Decided to Settle When He Did* (Santa Monica: RAND, 2001).

Huntington, Samuel, *The Clash of Civilizations and the Remaking of the World Order* (New York: Simon & Schuster Paperbacks, 2003).

Hurst, Steven, *The Foreign Policy of the Bush Administration: In Search of a New World Order* (London: Cassell, 1999).

Hyland, William, *Clinton's World: Remaking American Foreign Policy* (Westport: Praeger, 1999).

Inaugural Addresses of the Presidents of the United States (Washington, DC: US Government Publishing Office, 1989).

Irwin, Will, *The Jedburghs: The Secret History of the Allied Special Forces, France 1944* (New York: Public Affairs, 2005).

Jackson, Mike, *Soldier: An Autobiography* (London: Bantam Books, 2006).

Jalaii, Ali A., *Afghan National Defense and Security Forces: Mission, Challenges and Sustainability* (Washington, DC: United States Institute of Peace, 2016).

Judah, Tim, *War and Revenge* (New Haven: Yale University Press, 2002).

Kagan, Kimberly, *The Surge: A Military History* (New York: Encounter Books, 2009).

Kagan, Robert, *Of Paradise and Power: America and Europe in the New World Order* (New York: Alfred A. Knopf, 2003).

Kaplan, Fred, *The Insurgents: David Petraeus and the Plot to Change the American Way of War* (New York: Simon & Schuster, 2013).

Kaplan, Robert D., *Imperial Grunts: On the Ground with the American Military from Mongolia to the Philippines to Iraq and Beyond* (New York: Vintage Books, 2006).

Kepel, Gilles, *Jihad: The Trail of Political Islam* (Cambridge, MA: Harvard University Press, 2002).

Kitfield, James, *Twilight Warriors: The Soldiers, Spies, and Special Agents Who Are Revolutionizing the American Way of War* (New York: Basic Books, 2016).

Kretchik, Walter E., Robert F. Baumann, and John F. Fishel, *A Concise History of the U.S. Army in Operation Uphold Democracy* (Fort Leavenworth: US Army Command and General Staff College Press, 1998).

Lagon, Mark P., *The Reagan Doctrine: Sources of American Conduct in the Cold War's Last Chapter* (West Port: Praeger, 1994).

Lambeth, Benjamin S., *Airpower in the War against ISIS* (Annapolis: Naval Institute Press, 2021).

NATO's Air War for Kosovo: A Strategic and Operational Assessment (Santa Monica: RAND, 2001).

Transformation of American Air Power (Ithaca: Cornell University Press, 2000).

Lawrence, T. E., *Seven Pillars of Wisdom* (London: Wordsworth Classic Edition, 1926).

Lévy, Bernard-Henry, *The Empire and the Five Kings: America's Abdication and the Fate of the World* (New York: Henry Holt and Company, 2019).

Lindsay-Poland, John, *Emperors in the Jungle: The Hidden History of the U.S. in Panama* (Durham: Duke University Press, 2003).

Linn, Brian McAllister, *The Philippine War, 1899–1902* (Lawrence: University Press of Kansas, 2000).

Litwak, Robert S., *Rogue States and U.S. Foreign Policy: Containment after the Cold War* (Washington, DC: Woodrow Wilson Center Press, 2000).

Machado, Barry, *In Search of a Unusable Past: The Marshall Plan and Postwar Reconstruction Today* (Lexington: George C. Marshall Foundation Press, 2007).

Malcolm, Noel, *Bosnia: A Short History* (New York: New York University, 1994). *Kosovo: A Short History* (New York: New York University Press, 1998).

Mann, James, *The Obamians: The Struggle Inside the White House How to Define American Power* (New York: Viking, 2012). *The Rise of the Vulcans: The History of the Bush War Cabinet* (New York: Viking, 2002).

Mansoor, Peter R., *Surge: My Journey with General David Petraeus and the Remaking of the Iraq War* (New Haven: Yale University Press, 2013).

Marine Corps Institute, *Afghanistan: An Introduction to the Country and People* (Washington, DC: Marine Barracks, 2003).

Mattis, James N., "Preparing for Counterinsurgency," in *Al-Anbar Awakening, Volume 1, American Perspectives, U.S. Marines and Counterinsurgency in Iraq, 2004–2009*, edited by Timothy S. McWilliams and Kurtis P. Wheeler (Quantico: Marine Corps University Press, 2009).

Mazarr, Michael J., *Leap of Faith: Hubris, Negligence, and America's Greatest Foreign Policy Tragedy* (New York: Hachette Book Group, 2019).

Mazzetti, Mark, *The Way of the Knife* (New York, Penguin Press, 2013).

McChrystal, Stanley, *My Share of the Task: A Memoir* (New York: Penguin Group, 2013).

McDougall, Walter A., *Promised Land, Crusader State: The American Encounter with the World Since 1776* (Boston: Houghton Mifflin Company, 1997).

McMaster, H. R., *Battlegrounds: The Fight to Defend the Free World* (New York: Harper, 2020).

McPherson, Alan, *A Short History of U.S. Interventions in Latin America and the Caribbean* (Chichester: Wiley Blackwell, 2016).

Mearsheimer, John J., *The Great Delusion: Liberal Dreams and International Realities* (New Haven: Yale University Press, 2018).

Melvern, L. R., *A People Betrayed: The Role of the West in Rwanda's Genocide* (London: Zed Books, 2000).

Michaels, Jim, *A Chance in Hell: The Men Who Triumphed Over Iraq's Deadliest City and Turned the Tide of War* (New York: St. Martin's Press, 2010).

Mikaberidze, Alexander, *Conflict and Conquest in the Islamic World: A Historical Encyclopedia* (Santa Barbara: ABC-CLIO, 2011).

Miniter, Richard, *Leading From Behind: The Reluctant President and the Advisors Who Decide for Him* (New York: St. Martin's Griffin, 2013).

Nance, Malcolm, *Defeating ISIS: Who They Are, How They Fight, What They Believe* (New York: Skyhorse, 2016). *The Terrorists of Iraq: Inside the Strategy and Tactics of the Iraq Insurgency, 2003–2014* (Boca Raton: CRC Press, 2015).

Naylor, Sean, *Not a Good Day to Die: The Untold Story of Operation Anaconda* (New York: Penguin Group, 2005).

Relentless Strike: The Secret History of the Joint Special Operations Command (New York: St. Martin's Press, 2015).

Neville, Leigh, *Special Forces in the War on Terror* (London: Osprey, 2015).

Obama, Barack, *A Promised Land* (New York: Crown, 2020).

O'Connell, Arron B. (ed.), *Our Latest Longest War: Losing Hearts and Minds in Afghanistan* (Chicago: University of Chicago Press, 2017).

O'Rourke, Lindsey A., *Covert Regime Change: America's Secret Cold War* (Ithaca: Cornell University Press, 2018).

Owen, Mark, *No Easy Day: The Autobiography of a Navy SEAL* (New York: Dutton, 2012).

No Hero: The Evolution of a Navy SEAL (New York: New American Library, 2014).

Parker, Geoffrey (ed.), *The Cambridge History of Warfare* (New York: Cambridge University Press, 2005).

Parker, Richard B., *Uncle Sam in Barbary: A Diplomatic History* (Gainesville: University Press of Florida, 2004).

Petraeus, David, and James Amos, *U.S. Army and Marine Corps, Counterinsurgency Field Manual, No 3–24 and Marine Corps Warfighting Publication No. 3–33.5* (Chicago: University of Chicago, 2007).

Powell, Colin, *My American Journey* (New York: Random House, 1995).

Primakov, Yevgeny, *Russia and the Arabs: Behind the Scenes in the Middle East from the Cold War to the Present* (New York: Basic Books, 2009).

Purdum, Todd S., *Time of Our Choosing: America's War in Iraq* (New York: Henry Holt and Co., 2003).

Rayburn, Joel et al., *The U.S. Army in the Iraq War* (Carlisle: Strategic Studies Institute: US Army War College Press, 2019).

Reagan, Ronald, *An American Life* (New York: Simon & Schuster, 1990).

Rhodes, Ben, *The World As It Is: A Memoir of the Obama White House* (New York: Random House, 2018).

Rice, Condoleezza, *No Higher Honor: A Memoir of My Years in Washington* (New York: Crown, 2011).

Ricks, Thomas E., *Fiasco: The American Military Adventure in Iraq* (New York: Penguin Press, 2006).

Righter, Rosemary, *Utopia Lost: The United Nations and the World Order* (New York: Twentieth Century Press, 1995).

Robinson, Linda, *Tell Me How This Ends: General Petraeus and the Search for a Way Out of Iraq* (New York: PublicAffairs, 2008).

Rothstein, Hy S., *Afghanistan and the Troubled Future of Unconventional Warfare* (Annapolis: Naval Institute Press, 2006).

Rumsfeld, Donald, *Known and Unknown: A Memoir* (New York: Sentinel, 2011).

Sageman, Marc, *Understanding Terror Networks* (Philadelphia: University of Pennsylvania Press, 2004).

Sanger, David E., *Confront and Conceal: Obama's Secret Wars and Surprising Use of American Power* (New York: Crown, 2013).

Scales, Bob, *Scales on War: The Future of America's Military at Risk* (Annapolis: Naval Institute Press, 2016).

Schadlow, Nadia, *War and the Art of Governance: Consolidating Combat Success into Political Victory* (Washington, DC: George Washington University Press, 2017).

Scheuer, Michael, *Marching Toward Hell: America and Islam After Iraq* (New York: Free Press, 2008).

Through Our Enemies' Eyes: Osama bin Laden, Radical Islam, and the Future of America (Washington, DC: Brassy's, 2002).

Schmitt, Eric, and Thom Shanker, *Counterstrike: The Untold Story of America's Secret Campaign against al Qaeda* (New York: Henry Holt and Company, 2011).

Schroen, Gary C., *First In: An Insider's Account of How the CIA Spearheaded the War on Terror in Afghanistan* (New York: Ballantine Books, 2007).

Scranton, Margaret E., *The Noriega Years: U.S.-Panamanian Relations, 1981–1990* (Boulder: Lynne Rienner, 1991).

Sestanovich, Stephen, *Maximalist: America in the World from Truman to Obama* (New York: Alfred A. Knopf, 2014).

Shelton, Hugh, *Without Hesitation: The Odyssey of an American Warrior* (New York: St. Marin's Press, 2010).

Shultz, George P., *Turmoil and Triumph: My Years as Secretary of State* (New York: Charles Scribner's Sons, 1995).

Silber, Laura, and Allen Little, *Yugoslavia: Death of a Nation* (New York: Penguin Books, 1995).

Singer, P. W., *Corporate Warriors: The Rise of the Privatized Military Industry* (Ithaca: Cornell University, 2003).

Smith, Michael, *Killer Elite: The Inside Story of America's Most Secret Special Operations Team* (New York: St. Martin's Griffin Edition, 2008).

Smith, Richard Harris, *OSS: The Secret History of America's First Central Intelligence Agency* (Berkeley: University of California Press, 1972).

Sorely, Lewis, *A Better War: The Unexamined Victories and Final Tragedy of America's Last Years in Vietnam* (New York: Houghton Mifflin Harcourt, 1999).

Steward, Richard W., *The United States Army in Somalia, 1992–1994* (Washington, DC: United States Army Center of Military History, 2002).

Stoker, Donald, *Why America Loses Wars* (New York: Cambridge University Press, 2019).

Talbott, Strobe, *The Russia Hand: A Memoir of Presidential Diplomacy* (New York: Random House, 2002).

Tanner, Stephen, *Afghanistan: A Military History from Alexander the Great to the Fall of the Taliban* (New York: Da Capo Press, 2002).

Tenet, George, *At the Center of the Storm: My Years at the CIA* (New York: HarperCollins, 2007).

Thatcher, Margaret, *The Downing Street Years* (New York: HarperCollins, 1993).

The 9/11 Commission Report: Final Report of the National Commission on Terrorist Attacks Upon the United States, authorized edition (New York: W. W. Norton & Company, 2004).

Thucydides, *The History of the Peloponnesian War*, translated by Richard Crawley (Auckland: Floating Press, 2008).

Tomson, Susan, *Rwanda: From Genocide to Precarious Peace* (New Haven: Yale University Press, 2018).

Ullman, Harlan K., *Anatomy of Failure: Why America Loses Every War It Starts* (Annapolis: Naval Institute Press, 2017).

van Buren, Peter, *We Meant Well: How I Helped Lose the Battle for Hearts and Minds of the Iraqi People* (New York: Metropolitan, 2011).

Vaughn, Billy et al., *Betrayed: The Shocking Story of Extortion 17 as Told by a Navy SEAL's Father* (Stuart: Molon Labe Media, 2013).

Veith, George J., *Black April: The Fall of South Vietnam, 1973–1975* (New York: Encounter Books, 2012).

von Moltke, Helmuth, *Moltke on the Art of War: Selected Writings*, edited by Daniel J. Hughes (San Francisco: Presidio Press, 1995).

Weart, Spencer R., *Never at War: Why Democracies Will Not Fight One Another* (New Haven: Yale University Press, 1998).

Wehrey, Frederic M. et al., "An Altered Landscape: The Shifting Regional Balance of Power," in *The Iraq Effect: The Middle East after the Iraq War* (Santa Monica: RAND, 2010).

Weiner, Tim, *Legacy of Ashes: The History of the CIA* (New York: Anchor Book, 2007).

Weiss, Michael, and Hassan, *ISIS: Inside the Army of Terror* (New York: Regan Arts, 2015).

West, Bing, *The Strongest Tribe: War, Politics, and the Endgame in Iraq* (New York: Random House, 2008).

Wheelan, Joseph, *Jefferson's War: America's First War on Terror, 1801–1805* (New York: Carroll & Graf, 2003).

Woodward, Bob, *Bush at War* (New York: Simon & Schuster, 2002).

Obama's Wars (New York: Simon & Schuster, 2010).

Plan of Attack (New York: Simon & Schuster, 2004).

State of Denial: Bush At War, Part III (New York: Simon &Schuster, 2006).

Wright, Lawrence, *The Looming Tower: Al-Qaeda and the Road to 9/11* (New York: Vintage, 2007).

Yates, Lawrence A., "Operation JUST CAUSE in Panama City, December 1989," in *Urban Operations: An Historical Casebook* (Fort Leavenworth: Combat Studies Institute, Command & General Staff College, 2002).

Zakheim, Dov S., *A Vulcan's Tale: How the Bush Administration Mismanaged the Reconstruction of Afghanistan* (New York: Brookings Institution Press, 2011).

Zedong, Mao, *On Guerrilla Warfare*, translated by Samuel B. Griffith (New York: Praeger, 1961).

Zimmerman, Katherine, *Road to the Caliphate: The Salafist-Jihadi Movement's Strengths* (Washington, DC: American Enterprise Institute, 2019).

Index